AMERICAN BAR ASSOCIATION
Forum on Construction Law

Design Professional's Guide to Construction Law

Matthew J. Ninneman, Buck S. Beltzer,
and Mark W. Mercante, Editors

Cover design by Cory Ottenwess / ABA Design

Printed in the United States of America.

25 24 23 22 21   5 4 3 2 1

A catalog record for this book is available from the Library of Congress.

CONTENTS

CHAPTER 4

INTRODUCTION

The Burj Khalifa, the Blue Planet, the Gardens by the Bay, the Olympic Bird Nest, the Seattle Public Library, and the Shard all represent architectural and engineering feats of the twenty-first century. Before them, the Taj Mahal, the Eiffel Tower, the Colosseum. All of these projects began with an idea, a concept, a design. The ability to bring these artful projects to reality through construction is based on the foundation of design services of architects and engineers.

With each of these projects, however, comes incredible risk and the fundamental duty to protect the lives, safety, and welfare of those that build and occupy these structures. Every construction project carries these fundamental duties and risks regardless of its size and complexity.

Two of the primary tools to navigate these risks, beyond application of science, are the law and the legal counselors employed to explore, foresee, and transfer these risks among the project participants.

As with the advancement of the architecture, engineering, and construction industries, the legal industry too must adapt, learn, and employ new methods and theories in application of construction law to these projects and disputes.

This book is intended to serve as an essential tool to educate design and construction professionals, and the legal professionals who consult with them, to understand the fundamental issues that the field of construction law brings to any project and to understand those new legal issues that emerge from advancements in the design and construction industry. This is particularly true with constant advancement in technology, automation, and robotics.

This is the second edition of the American Bar Association's Forum on Construction Law's *Design Professional* textbook. The first edition was titled *Design Professional and Construction Manager Law.* As prophesized by the authors and editors of the first edition, the body of law impacting construction managers grew, requiring the Forum to break this book in two for the second edition. This second edition updates and expands those previous design chapters focusing entirely on the fundamental and emerging laws applicable to design professionals. A standalone second edition of the *Construction Manager* textbook is also in the works.

Chapters 1 and 2 focus on state regulations of professionals, followed by an in-depth explanation in Chapter 3 of the contractual responsibilities of engineers and architects through the pre-design, design, and construction phases of a project. Chapter 4 delves into the responsibilities existing in the construction and post-construction phases. Chapter 5 advances on the exploration of the separate roles and responsibilities existing in the ever-increasing use of design-build methodology; it is followed by Chapter 6, which is an update on the design professional's liability in tort. A design professional's guide to the law would be incomplete without in-depth analysis of the design professional's intellectual property rights in his or her work product, as outlined in Chapter 7. The indemnity obligations and professional liability insurance components common in almost all projects are summarized in Chapter 8. Chapter 9 explores the rights and obligations of the prime designer's subconsultants and risk-shifting provisions of the subconsultant agreement. Unfortunately, risk equates to damages when disputes arise. Accordingly, Chapter 10 educates practitioners on the damages and remedies available to the designer and the other project participants who rely on those design services. Finally, Chapter 11 walks us through various special topics in litigation and dispute resolution, including statutory limitations and protections; litigation/arbitration management tools, including discovery; evidence, and teaming agreements between the parties.

As with the first edition, one of the goals was to update the chapters with an eye toward making them stand alone. While there is some dovetailing and minor duplication of issues throughout the book, each chapter is intended to take a deep dive into its specific focus.

Finally, it must be recognized that this book would not have been possible without the efforts of the ABA Forum's Governing and Publication Committees, including in particular David Scotti, in driving the need for this updated edition and keeping us all on task. A special thank-you to ABA Publishing, including specifically Sarah (Sam) Orwig, who has been instrumental in bringing this project to life.

Of course, fundamental to the existence of this book are the contributions of the individual authors and editors. While many of the original authors from the first edition continued to participate in the updating of their respective chapters, new blood has been infused into the author and editor contributions. We have endeavored to recognize those authors who passed the baton to others in the field within each chapter, which is one of the principal goals of the Forum—opportunity. We also wish to recognize here the prior editors of the book, Stephen Hess, Jerome Bales, P. Douglas Folk, and L. Tyrone Holt, for their continued contributions and guidance through this process. As with the prior list of authors and editors, this second edition is littered with former and current Forum Division Chairs, many of whom served the Forum's Division 3—Design. Finally, a special thanks to my co-editors and former Division 3 Chairs, Buck Beltzer and Mark Mercante, for working with me to edit the chapter contents, assisting the authors in structuring the updated information, and, of course, "herding the cats."

We all hope this book serves its purpose and helps to educate design professionals and legal practitioners on the legal issues impacting the design industry. From here, we look forward to what advancements are on the horizon for this field. Thanks again.

Matthew J. Ninneman, Executive Editor
November 2020

ABOUT THE AUTHORS AND EDITORS

Buck S. Beltzer (Co-Editor) is a founding partner in the Denver, Colorado, law firm of Beltzer Bangert & Gunnell, LLP, a law firm that concentrates in both the transactional and litigation aspects of construction law. In addition to serving in several industry associations, including the Colorado Contractors Association (CCA), the Associated General Contractors of Colorado (AGC), and Design-Build Institute of America (DBIA), Mr. Beltzer has been recognized by various legal publications as a top lawyer. Most recently, *Best Lawyers* named him "Lawyer of the Year" for Construction Law, Denver (2020) and Litigation—Construction, Denver (2020). He was also recognized in *The Best Lawyers in America* for work in Construction Law and Litigation—Construction. Mr. Beltzer holds a Bachelor of Civil Engineering from Auburn University and a Juris Doctorate from the University of Denver, where he graduated Order of the Coif, was awarded several American Jurisprudence awards, co-founded the Construction Law Society, and was an Associate Editor of the Law Review.

Jessica Clouse (Chapter 11) is an associate in the Construction practice group in the firm of Gordon & Rees Scully Mansukhani's San Francisco office. Her practice focuses on construction litigation in the defense of design professionals, architects, engineers, general contractors, and developers in a variety of construction-related matters, including residential, commercial, and public projects. She has experience litigating claims related to complex disputes involving delay and loss of efficiency claims, payment claims, breaches of contract, and construction and design defects (among others) in state court, federal court, and judicial reference proceedings throughout Northern California. Mrs. Clouse received her B.A. in Political Science from Chapman University in 2010 and her J.D. from the University of San Francisco School of Law in 2013, where she graduated cum laude.

Anna Covert (Chapter 5) is an associate in the Construction and Real Estate Litigation group of Faegre Drinker Biddle & Reath LLP's Chicago office. She represents public entities in design-build and public infrastructure projects. She also represents clients in complex commercial and construction matters in state and federal court, including matters involving construction defects and delay, mechanic's liens, fraud, breach of contract, breach of warranty, differing site conditions, public-private partnerships, and surety and insurance issues. Ms. Covert also advises clients regarding contract drafting on construction and real estate projects. Her design-build experience includes acting as procurement counsel on behalf of public owners for design-build projects involving local, state, and federal funding. These projects include railway infrastructure, correctional and rehabilitation facilities, and judicial buildings. She has also drafted and advised clients regarding DBOFM project developments and represented private clients in disputes involving energy savings agreements. Ms. Covert obtained her B.A. and B.S. from the University of Missouri–Columbia in 2011 and her J.D. from Loyola University Chicago School of Law in 2014.

Karen Erger (Chapter 8) is Senior Vice President, Director of Practice Risk Management for Lockton, the world's largest privately owned, independent insurance brokerage. Ms. Erger consults with Lockton's architecture, engineering, and construction clients on practice management issues, including complex claims and contracts, and provides risk management training and resources. She is an active participant in the American Council of Engineering Companies (ACEC) Risk Management Committee, the Immediate Past Chair of Division 3 (Design) of the American Bar Association Forum on Construction Law, a former Professional Affiliate Director of the American Institute of Architects of Chicago, and a former volunteer docent for the Chicago Architecture Foundation. Since 2001, Ms. Erger has authored a bimonthly column in the *Illinois Bar Journal*. She was elected to the Society of Illinois Construction Attorneys in 2015 and was awarded the ABA Forum on the Construction Industry's Women and Minority Fellowship in 2012. She graduated Phi Beta Kappa from the University of Chicago at 20 years of age with a degree in politics, economics, rhetoric and law, and earned her law degree at the University of Chicago Law School.

Mehrdad Farivar (Chapter 3), is a member of Clark Hill. His practice is focused exclusively on the construction industry, and his clients include design professionals, owners, developers, contractors, subcontractors, and material suppliers. He is a former practicing architect and is licensed as an architect in California and the UK; he is also a fellow of the American Institute of Architects and a former member of the Royal Institute of British Architects (RIBA). As an architect, Mr. Farivar has many years of experience in the design and construction of institutional, commercial, and residential projects, including hospitals and medical office buildings, university buildings, office buildings, retail stores, and single and multi-family housing, as well as large civic urban design projects. He worked with Jaquelin T. Robertson, FAIA, on a master plan for a major urban design project in Iran, and with John Weeks, RIBA, on the design of major hospitals and health facilities in the UK and in Europe. He had his own architecture firm in Santa Monica, California, from 1982 until approximately 1994. Projects he has designed or contributed to have been built in California, the UK, Belgium, and Iran. As a lawyer, Mr. Farivar counsels and advises his clients on contract formation and negotiation, business, and risk management issues including international contracts and disputes; copyright; design-build contracts; construction and related claims; mechanics liens and design professionals liens; land use and zoning matters, and ownership transitions; he also advises in the litigation, arbitration, and mediation of disputes involving design, construction, real estate, land use, and related matters.

Patricia A. Harris (Chapter 1) is special counsel at Zetlin & De Chiara LLP and provides legal and business counsel to architects and engineers across the country. A serial entrepreneur, Ms. Harris is the founder and CEO of LicenseSure LLC, which provides business and licensing compliance services to design professional firms. From 2000 to 2013, Ms. Harris served as the Managing Partner of Zetlin and De Chiara. She is very active in design industry organizations and is a member of the Board of Directors and President-Elect of the Global Design Alliance. She is also a member of the Board of Directors of the Beverly Willis Architecture Foundation, having served as Board Chair in 2015. In 2012, she served on the Mayor's Task Force for Rebuilding New York City. She speaks and writes about business organization and professional licensing to industry organizations including the AIA and ACEC. Ms. Harris received her B.A. from Pomona College and her J.D. and M.B.A. *with distinction* from New York University.

David J. Hatem (Chapter 4) is a partner in the Boston-based law firm Donovan Hatem LLP. Nationally recognized for his expertise in representing engineers, architects, and construction management professionals, Mr. Hatem leads the firm's Professional Practices Group, which serves design professionals. He has been practicing law for approximately 40 years and has served as ACEC/MA Counsel since 1988. In recognition of his extraordinary career dedicated to the engineering sector, Mr. Hatem received the Engineering Center Education Trust 2016 "Leadership in Professional Practice Legal Services" award and the 2008 ACEC Distinguished Service Award. Mr. Hatem teaches Legal Aspects of Engineering at Tufts University and Legal Aspects of Civil Engineering at Northeastern University Graduate School of Engineering. He has authored and edited numerous articles and publications in his field of expertise, including the third edition of *Public-Private Partnerships and Design-Build: Opportunities and Risks for Consulting Engineers*, *Subsurface Conditions: Risk Management for Design and Construction Management Professionals*, *Design-Build Subsurface Projects*, and *Megaprojects: Challenges and Recommended Practices.*

Troy Hatfield (Chapter 6) is an associate at Cairncross & Hempelmann in Seattle, Washington. His practice focuses on construction law and complex commercial litigation, and he assists clients of all sizes and in all phases of case development. Mr. Hatfield earned his B.A. from Boise State University and his J.D. and his M.B.A. simultaneously from Seattle University. This background gives him a unique perspective on the challenges facing businesses and the corporate legal landscape. Mr. Hatfield also externed for Judge Robert J. Bryan in the U.S. District Court and has experience with regulatory compliance, public records law, and employment law.

Stephen A. Hess (Chapter 10) practices Construction Law and Sports Law through the Denver and Colorado Springs offices of Sherman & Howard LLC. He is the former Editor of *The Construction Lawyer* and served as Editor-in-Chief of the first edition of this title. Mr. Hess is a Fellow of the American College of Construction Lawyers and is the author of many law review articles, book chapters, and educational programs related to construction law. He also serves as an Adjunct Professor at the Sturm College of Law at University of Denver, where he created and teaches the school's Construction Law Seminar.

L. Tyrone Holt (Chapter 9) is the managing principal of the law firm The Holt Group, LLC. He serves as a client advocate in a large number of design and/or construction disputes in courts and before arbitration tribunals in various jurisdictions throughout the United States. He is actively engaged in the structuring, negotiating, and documenting of design, construction, and design-build contract relationships in the construction industry throughout the United States. Mr. Holt has a B.A., 1971 (summa cum laude), from Morehouse College; J.D., 1974, from Stanford University; and M. Theology, 1997, from the Peace Theological Seminary and College of Philosophy. He is a Member of Phi Beta Kappa National Honor Society, Delta of Georgia Chapter (1971). Mr. Holt is a member of the Colorado Bar; the U.S. Supreme Court; the Eight, Ninth, and Tenth Circuit Courts of Appeal; and a number of federal district courts. He is admitted Pro Hac Vice in a number of state courts of record.

Mr. Holt is a member of the American Arbitration Association's Construction Arbitration Master Panel, CPR Arbitrator and Construction Panel, AAA/ICDR Commercial Panel and Resolute Systems, and LLC Insurance Mediation Panel. He served as the President of the College of Commercial Arbitrators from 2013 to 2014 and on the Governing Committee of the American Bar Association Forum on the Construction Industry from 2007 to 2010. Mr. Holt is a member of the Dean's Advisory Council of Stanford Law School. In 2009, he attended The Diploma Course in International Commercial Arbitration of the Chartered Institute of Arbitrators, Keble College, Oxford University, Oxford, England, UK.

Mohammad (Mo) Iqbal (Chapter 2) received his B.Sc. in Civil Engineering from UET, Pakistan; M.S. from Middle East Technical University, Ankara, Turkey; Doctorate in structural engineering from Washington University in St. Louis; MBA from the University of Chicago; J.D. from NIU, College of Law; and L.L.M. from UIC, John Marshall Law School, Chicago. He is a licensed P.E. and S.E. in several states and is admitted to practice law in Illinois, the U.S. Court of Appeals, and the U.S. Supreme Court.

Ernest Isola (Chapter 11) is a partner at Gordon & Rees Scully Mansukhani, co-chair of the firm's National Construction Practice Group, and the Group Leader for the Construction Practice Group in the San Francisco office. Mr. Isola's practice is focused on complex construction litigation, environmental litigation, and transactional matters. He has represented design professionals and construction managers, among others, in every type of construction claim, including claims for project delay, loss of productivity, inefficiency, acceleration, compensation and payment claims, cost overruns, change orders, design/construction deficiencies, design professional copyright claims, differing site conditions, and worksite injuries. In addition to his litigation practice, Mr. Isola specializes in transactional work for his construction and environmental clients, including advising his clients on ongoing construction projects and formulating contracts utilizing myriad project deliveries such as design/bid/build, design/build, public private partnership, CM at risk, and integrated project delivery.

Theodore D. Levin (Chapter 3) is a member of Clark Hill. The primary focuses of his practice are design professional liability, construction law, and general liability litigation. Mr. Levin is both a practicing lawyer and a registered civil engineer, and he specializes in the representation of architects, engineers, contractors, owners, and insurers in all aspects of construction law, including contract and defect claims, risk management, contract analysis and advice, and mechanic's lien/design professional law. He also represents numerous private and public entities in tort liability claims. In addition, Mr. Levin previously served as practice group leader for the design and construction team of attorneys at Morris Polich & Purdy LLP.

Kevin Major (Chapter 5) is an associate in the Construction and Real Estate Litigation group of Faegre Drinker Biddle & Reath LLP's Chicago office. His practice includes representing clients in design-build and public infrastructure projects as well as construction and real estate litigation. Mr. Major's design-build and public infrastructure experience includes acting as procurement counsel and representing public entities in drafting requests for qualifications and design-build contracts. His litigation experience focuses on construction defects, mechanic's liens, and commercial foreclosure. Mr. Major is a member of the Chicago Building Congress's Future Leaders group. He received his B.A. from DePaul University in 2014 and his J.D. from Loyola University Chicago School of Law in 2018.

Mark W. Mercante (Co-Editor) is based in New Orleans, Louisiana, and is Co-Chair of Baker, Donelson, Bearman, Caldwell & Berkowitz's thirty-plus-member Construction Department. He represents owners, developers, contractors, subcontractors, and design professionals in all aspects of construction, including construction contract negotiation and drafting, pre-claim counseling during the construction process, and disputes before courts and arbitration panels. Mr. Mercante received a B.B.A. from Southern Methodist University (1992) and a J.D. from Loyola Law School, New Orleans (1995). He is a Band 1 rated Construction Attorney by Chambers and Partners. Active in the ABA Forum on Construction Law, Mr. Mercante has served as Chair of an Annual Meeting (2008) and Chair of Division 3: Design (2016–2018), and as author and contributor on numerous publications and papers.

Stephen R. Miller (Chapter 10) is the founding member of Miller Schirger, LLC. He has practiced construction law since 1983, representing contractors, subcontractors, fabricators, suppliers, architects, engineers, and owners. Mr. Miller has tried construction cases throughout the United States and has appeared before tribunals in more than 25 different states as well as numerous arbitrations and administrative proceedings. He also serves as a mediator and arbitrator. In addition, Mr. Miller counsels clients on transactions, construction contracting, sound business practices, and risk avoidance relating to procurement, contract formation, contract performance, and dispute resolution. He is a frequent speaker for construction and commercial groups and has lectured and written articles for several industry groups and professional organizations in the construction industry. Mr. Miller received his B.A., M.A., and J.D. from the University of Notre Dame. He is rated an AV® lawyer by Martindale-Hubbell and has been recognized annually by his peers as "Best of the Bar" in the *Kansas City Business Journal* and as a SuperLawyer in *SuperLawyer Magazine.*

Paul T. Muniz (Chapter 4) is a partner in the Boston-based law firm Donovan Hatem LLP, which is nationally recognized for its expertise in representing engineers, architects, and construction management professionals. Mr. Muniz leads the firm's litigation practice, which primarily serves design professionals. He has been practicing law for approximately 30 years and has been a member of ACEC/MA since 2016.

Jaimee L. Nardiello (Chapter 1) is a partner at Zetlin & De Chiara LLP in New York, New York. Her practice is focused on litigating complex construction disputes on behalf of architects, engineers, owners, developers, and contractors in court and arbitration throughout the United States and abroad. Ms. Nardiello is a member of the Governing Committee of the American Bar Association Forum on Construction Law and is a former Chair of the Forum's Design Division. She writes and speaks frequently. Some of her publications include "Architect-Engineer Contracting" in the ABA's *Federal Government Contracts*, Third Edition; *AAA Construction Arbitration: A Step-by-Step Guide, Annotated Construction Glossary*; *Civil Liability for False Claims in Public Construction*; and *The Bar Exam Survival Guide: The Insider's Handbook to Passing the Bar Exam.*

Matthew J. Ninneman (Executive Editor) is an equity member of Hall & Evans, LLC, a regional law firm based in Denver, Colorado. He practices in its Construction and Design practice group. Mr. Ninneman has been recognized by various legal publications as a top lawyer, including *The Best Lawyers in America* for work in Construction Law and Litigation—Construction. Mr. Ninneman litigates complex commercial and construction disputes in state and federal courts and arbitration, representing owner/developers, general contractors, design-builders, subcontractors, architects, engineers, and suppliers on private, public, and hybrid projects, including heavy civil infrastructure, sports arenas, schools, hotels, hospitals, mass transit, roadways, industrial warehousing, and renovation and development of apartments, multi-family, mixed-use, and single-family residences. In addition to litigating, he advises design and construction professionals on day-to-day risk management issues; drafting and negotiation of custom and form contracts, including AIA, DBIA, EJCDC, and ConsensusDOCS; licensing; payment and delay disputes; and pre-litigation dispute resolution/mediation. Mr. Ninneman is a frequent author and lecturer on issues concerning construction claims, contract drafting, design licensure, liability mitigation, and current issues impacting the construction industry, including co-authoring several books published by the ABA Forum on Construction Law.

Bernard (B.J.) Nodzon (Chapter 5) is a partner in the Construction and Real Estate Litigation group of Faegre Drinker Biddle & Reath LLP's Minneapolis office. Mr. Nodzon has drafted and negotiated billions of dollars' worth of design-build contracts. He represents owners, developers, contractors, engineers, and designers in connection with significant projects throughout the country, including energy projects, sports facilities, apartment complexes, food and agricultural facilities, airports, and office towers. Mr. Nodzon is a frequent speaker on construction issues.

Carrie Lynn H. Okizaki (Chapter 9) is the co-founder and president of Modus Strategic Solutions, Inc., a consulting firm that helps organizations manage and successfully deliver multibillion-dollar capital projects through thorough and objective project oversight, assessment, project management, data and systems integration, and project controls services. She has broad experience in providing consulting and legal services for project owners and other stakeholders for the successful execution of all stages of the construction project lifecycle, including supporting project planning, contracting strategies, contract negotiation, contractor management, project controls, and dispute avoidance and resolution. Ms. Okizaki received a B.S. degree in Foreign Service from Georgetown University in 1996 and her J.D. from the University of Colorado School of Law in 2000, where she was a casenote and comment editor for the *University of Colorado Law Review*. She is licensed to practice law in Colorado and Illinois. Ms. Okizaki has contributed to several other ABA Forum on the Construction Industry publications including as editor of *THE Construction Contracts Book: Annotated Analysis and Comparison of the AIA, ConsensusDocs, and EJCDC Contract Forms*, Third Edition (2020) and *Construction Checklists* (2008).

J. Benjamin Patrick (Chapter 7) is a partner with Gordon & Rees Scully Mansukhani and represents companies in the construction industry, including general contractors, engineers, architects, and sureties. He has represented companies varying in size from small contractors and design firms to ENR Top 50 Firms in mediations, litigations, and arbitrations with claims ranging from under $100,000 to over $300,000,000. Mr. Patrick has represented clients on projects in every sector of the construction industry. He is also recognized as a leading author on intellectual property rights in the construction industry. In 2004, Mr. Patrick was counsel for the defendant architect in the largest construction copyright infringement lawsuit ever brought in the United States. Following three years of litigation and six weeks of trial, the jury returned a verdict finding no liability on the part of his client.

Lindsey M. Pflugrath (Chapter 6) is a partner at Cairncross & Hempelmann in Seattle, Washington. Her clients include owners, owner's representatives, contractors, international multidisciplinary design firms, and local engineering and architecture firms. Ms. Pflugrath takes great pride in offering an integrated suite of services to her clients, providing advice on risk management, contract negotiation, and conflict resolution, as well as defending her clients from claims. She has earned several distinguished titles and roles in notable organizations such as the Urban Land Institute, American Institute of Architects, and Seattle Architecture Foundation, where she has spent many years as a volunteer and board member. Ms. Pflugrath earned her B.A. from the University of Iowa in 2002 and her J.D. from the University of Iowa College of Law in 2005. She has been recognized as a leader by a number of legal ranking organizations including Chambers USA and Super Lawyers, and she is also a recent recipient of the American Institute of Architects Seattle Honorary Membership.

Terence J. Scanlan (Chapter 6) is a partner at Cairncross & Hempelmann in Seattle, Washington. For more than 20 years, he has represented commercial entities with an emphasis on engineering and architectural firms in complex civil litigation in state and federal courts. His practice includes contract disputes, risk management, and professional negligence, as well as wrongful death claims and catastrophic torts. Construction and commercial industry groups regularly ask Mr. Scanlan to present and write articles on a range of topics relevant to design professionals and construction companies. He serves as Chair of the Legal Affairs Committee of the Geoprofessional Business

Association, is a member of the American Council of Engineering Companies (Legal Counsel Forum), and is on the Board of the Architecture Construction Engineering (ACE) Mentor Program of America. Mr. Scanlan attended Seattle University and received his B.A. in Economics in 1983 and his J.D. in 1986. He has been recognized as a leader in his field by a number of legal ranking organizations including Chambers USA, Super Lawyers, and Martindale-Hubbell.

Nicole R. Springstroh (Chapter 6) is an associate at Cairncross & Hempelmann in Seattle, Washington. She works across practice groups at the firm and supports the business, construction, real estate, and litigation teams. Ms. Springstroh is highly skilled at legal research and drafts agreements, contracts, and litigation documents. Prior to her legal career, she worked with several agencies involved in social services and was a volunteer at the Washington Innocence Project Clinic. Ms. Springstroh earned her B.A. from the University of Wisconsin in 2009 and her J.D. from the University of Washington School of Law in 2019.

CHAPTER 1

State Regulation of the Design Professional

PATRICIA A. HARRIS, JAIMEE L. NARDIELLO[1]

I. Introduction

This chapter discusses the regulation of the professions principally involved in the design of improvements to real estate—architecture and engineering. These same general legal concepts and regulatory requirements also apply to the closely allied professions of landscape architecture, interior design, geology, and land surveying, which may be similarly regulated by particular jurisdictions.

The practice of engineering or architecture as a professional requires a state-issued license or registration in all jurisdictions of the United States. The requirements for an individual to obtain and maintain professional licensure as an architect or engineer is found in the applicable statutes, regulations issued by licensing boards, and case law interpreting the statutes and regulations on a state-by-state basis. In addition to a requirement for individual licensure, any design professional who practices in the form of a corporation, limited liability company, professional corporation, professional association, or other similar limited liability fictitious business entity ("Fictitious Business Entity") may be required to obtain appropriate separate qualification, registration, or

1. The authors of this second edition wish to acknowledge and thank G. William Meyers for his contributions to this chapter as the author of the first edition.

authorization for the Fictitious Business Entity. As a general rule, state jurisdictions do not license Fictitious Business Entities as design professionals—only individuals.

The registration or licensing of individual design professionals is almost always handled by a professional board or registration agency that handles examination, disciplinary proceedings, and other professional matters for the affected professional. The registration or authorization of Fictitious Business Entities that provide design professional services typically happens at the professional board or registration agency but may be processed through that governmental department or agency responsible for the formation and qualification of all business entities.

Most states have legislation and supporting regulations that address the issue of firm practice for architecture as a separate and distinct matter from the firm practice of engineering. However, a few states, such as Illinois,[2] Virginia,[3] and Wisconsin,[4] issue one certificate or license to practice both architecture and engineering. These jurisdictions have a single board regulating both architecture and engineering; granting a single certificate of authorization or license to practice both architecture and engineering is a result of only one board regulating both professions.

II. Individual Licensure

To practice architecture or engineering in the United States, an individual has to be licensed by the state in which the professional services are to be delivered. The practice of architecture and engineering is defined by state law and can vary greatly from state to state. Some state definitions of "practice" include the offering of services, meaning an individual and/or firm must be licensed in advance of solicitation within the state.[5]

In some cases, the distinction between architecture and engineering can be elusive. For example, Pennsylvania defines the practice of architecture as follows:

---

2. 225 Ill. Comp. Stat. Ann. §§ 305/21, 325/23 (2019). Note as well that Illinois distinguishes the practice of professional engineering from the practice of structural engineering, 225 Ill. Comp. Stat. Ann. §§ 325, 340.

3. Va. Code Ann. § 54.1-411.

4. Wis. Stat. Ann. § 443.08 (2014).

5. Ark. Code § 17-15-102(4)(A)(i) (2017); S.C. Code Ann. § 40-3-30(c); NY Education Law §§ 7391, 7210.

> The rendering or offering to render certain services, hereinafter described, in connection with the design and construction of a structure or group of structures which have as their principal purpose human habitation or use, and the utilization of space within and surrounding such structures. The services referred to in the previous sentence include planning, providing preliminary studies, designs, drawings, specifications, and other design documents, construction management and administration of construction contracts. The foregoing shall not be deemed to include the practice of engineering as such, for which separate registration is required . . . , excepting only engineering work incidental to the practice of architecture.[6]

> Pennsylvania defines the practice of engineering as follows:

> (a)(1) "Practice of Engineering" shall mean the application of mathematical and physical sciences for the design of public and private buildings, structures, machines, equipment, processes, works or engineering systems, and the consultation, evaluation, engineering surveys, construction management planning and inspection in connection therewith, the performance of the foregoing acts and services being prohibited to persons who are not licensed under this act as professional engineers unless exempt under other provisions of this act.
>
> (2) The term "Practice of Engineering" shall also mean and include related acts and services that may be performed by other qualified persons, including but not limited to, municipal planning, incidental landscape architecture, teaching, construction, maintenance and research but licensure under this act to engage in or perform any such related services shall not be required.
>
> (3) The foregoing shall not be deemed to include the practice of architecture as such, for which separate registration is required . . . , excepting only architectural work incidental to the "practice of engineering."
>
> (4) The "Practice of Engineering" shall not preclude the practice of the sciences which shall include but not be limited to: soil science, geology, physics and chemistry.[7]

Because of the ambiguous and broad language of both definitions, which is similar to the statutory language in other states, issues arise as to what

---

6. 63 Pa. Cons. Stat. Ann. § 34.3 (2019).
7. 63 Pa. Cons. Stat. Ann. § 149(a) (2019).

is included in the practice of architecture or engineering and what may be included in both. Where there are two separate boards regulating these professions, this problem seems to be exacerbated.

Rosen v. Bureau of Professional and Occupational Affairs, State Architects Licensure Board[8] is one example of this tension. In this case, the Architects Licensure Board imposed a civil penalty on an engineer, Rosen, for having signed and sealed plans to convert a four-story building in Philadelphia from a private club into law offices for the first three floors and an apartment for the fourth floor. The court noted that the most substantial aspects of the renovation project were the addition of an elevator shaft to the rear of the building and reinforcement of the first floor to accommodate a law library.

The Pennsylvania intermediate appellate court first noted that the matter appeared to be part of an ongoing turf war between the two learned professions over the design of buildings. The court then concluded that both statutes have to be read *in pari materia* and that there is an overlap between the two statutes, with neither statute establishing a clear, mutually exclusive delineation between the two professions.

The court examined the architecture and engineering statutes recounted above and reasoned that both addressed the design of buildings, there was no bright line between the two professions, and the engineering statute was broader than the architecture statute because the latter limited the practice of architecture to structures of human habitation and use.

The court also looked at three similar cases from Alabama,[9] Florida,[10] and Georgia[11] where architect licensure boards had cited engineers for the unlawful practice of architecture. Ultimately, the court concluded that the practice of engineering includes the design of buildings and structures; thus, Rosen was within the practice of engineering when he designed the renovations. Instead of interpreting the architects' law as limiting the practice of engineering, the court read it as limiting the practice of architecture to habitable structures.[12]

---

8. 763 A.2d 962 (Pa. Commw. Ct. 2000), *appeal denied*, 781 A.2d 150 (Pa. Super. Ct. 2001).

9. State v. Jones, 267 So. 2d 427 (Ala. 1972).

10. Verich v. Florida State Bd. of Architecture, 239 So. 2d 29 (Fla. Dist. Ct. App. 1970).

11. Georgia State Bd. for Examination, Qualification and Registration of Architects v. Arnold, 249 Ga. 593, 292 S.E.2d 830 (1982).

12. *Rosen*, 763 A.2d at 970.

An individual's initial license is obtained by education, examination, and experience.[13] For engineers, this means: (1) graduating from an ABET[14] accredited engineering program at a college or university; (2) passing the fundamentals in engineering (FE) examination; (3) gaining the requisite years of experience in engineering under the supervision of professional engineers; and (4) passing the principles and practice of engineering (PE) examination. Those who pass the FE examination are usually referred to as an engineering intern (EI) or an engineer in training (EIT).[15]

Obtaining an architect's license requires: (1) graduating from an NAAB[16] accredited architecture program at a college or university;[17] (2) gaining the required number of years of architectural experience under the supervision of registered architects; and (3) passing the ARE.

An experienced architect or engineer who wants to become licensed in another state can often do so without taking an additional examination.[18] This can be accomplished by comity, endorsement, or reciprocity. For example, one may obtain registration as an architect or an engineer in Michigan if the requirements of the other state for that person's registration are equivalent to the requirements of the Michigan board.[19]

Professional licenses are maintained by updating the applicable board on the registrant's current address, other contact information, the payment of periodic fees, and fulfillment of continuing education requirements. For example, in Florida, each biennial renewal of an engineering license requires the completion of eighteen hours of continuing education, including four professional development hours in the licensee's area of practice, one hour in professional

13. Before modern licensure statutes, licensure could be obtained merely by graduating from an accredited college and gaining the requisite experience. These licenses typically date back to before the 1960s.

14. ABET stands for Accreditation Board of Engineering and Technology.

15. *See* the National Council of Examiners for Engineering and Surveying website, https://ncees.org/.

16. NAAB stands for National Architectural Accrediting Board.

17. New York does not require an individual to graduate from college or university but evaluates an individual's education and experience in order to determine when an individual is permitted to sit for the architect registration exam (ARE).

18. The hours of architectural experience required to sit for the ARE vary from state to state. *See* http://www.ncarb.org/get-licensed/licensing-requirements-tool. Even if an individual earns a license in one state, he or she may be unable to obtain a reciprocal license in a state with greater experience requirements until he or she has fulfilled the additional experience hours required.

19. MICH. COMP LAWS ANN. § 339.2013 (2018).

ethics, and one hour specific to Florida laws and rules.[20] Similarly, Florida architects have to show they have completed twenty-four hours of continuing education at each biennial renewal.[21]

While multistate licensure for design professionals is relatively common, a word to the wise about disciplinary matters is imperative. Should a licensed architect or engineer be subject to discipline, including a settlement or consent order from any regulatory board by which he or she is licensed, it is often required that the licensee report the disciplinary actions to all other jurisdictions in which he or she is licensed. Some state boards, such as the North Carolina Board of Engineers and Land Surveyors, require such actions to be reported within 30 days of the disciplinary action,[22] although most boards ask for disclosure of such actions upon license renewal.

III. Firm Licensure

A. Overview

Once an individual architect or engineer is granted a license to practice in a jurisdiction, there may be additional requirements to be satisfied in order for that person to practice through a Fictitious Business Entity. Just as individual licensing requirements and procedures vary from state to state, there are separate, but equally important requirements that apply to groups of professionals who wish to provide services through a Fictitious Business Entity. Generally, the Fictitious Business Entities will be required to proffer in-state individual licensees, who may be required to hold particular ownership or management positions within the entity. The entity-level authorization or registration requirements can vary depending on the specific profession.

Pennsylvania demonstrates this dichotomy. Under the Engineer, Land Surveyor and Geologist Registration Law,[23] Pennsylvania does not require

20. Fla. Stat. Ann. § 471.017 (2019). Since 2000, Florida engineers participating in the design of structures covered by the Florida Building Code also must prove they have completed any advanced or specialized courses on any portion of the Florida Building Code applicable to the licensee's area of practice. Fla. Stat. Ann. § 471.0195 (2019).

21. Fla. Stat. Ann. § 481.215(3) (2019). Pursuant to the rulemaking authority granted in Fla. Stat. Ann. § 481.215(5) (2019), the Florida Board of Architecture requires a licensee take two hours in Florida Building Code advanced courses during each biennial renewal cycle.

22. Title 21, Chapter 56 PN NCAC 56.0505 (2019).

23. 63 Pa. Cons. Stat. Ann. § 148.

separate licensing of firms to practice engineering because it considers the practices of engineering, land surveying, and geology to be the function of individuals or individuals working in concert.

The only requirement for a firm to practice engineering is as follows:

> [T]he directing heads and employees of such firm or corporation in responsible charge of its activities in the practice of such profession be licensed and registered in conformity with the requirements of this act, and whose name, seal, and signature, along with the date of signature, shall be stamped on all plans, specifications, plats, and reports issued by such firm or corporation.[24]

However, under the Pennsylvania Architects Licensure Law,[25] an individual architect or group of architects may only practice architecture as a sole proprietorship, partnership, professional association, business corporation, limited liability company, or limited liability partnership. Such entities are, in turn, subject to certain partnership, membership, directorship, and ownership restrictions.[26] For example, a business corporation may only practice architecture in Pennsylvania if it meets the following requirements:

> (1) At least two-thirds of the directors are licensed under the laws of any state to practice architecture, engineering, or landscape architecture.
>
> (2) At least one-third of its directors are licensed under the laws of any state to practice architecture.
>
> (3) At least two-thirds of all classes of voting stock issued and outstanding at any one time shall be owned by an individual or individuals licensed under the laws of any state to practice architecture, engineering, or landscape architecture.
>
> (4) At least one-third of all classes of voting stock issued and outstanding at any one time shall be owned by an individual or individuals licensed under the laws of any state to practice architecture.[27]

When considering practice in a new state, one must determine whether licensure is required at the firm level. If licensing is required at the firm level, the next inquiry is what requirements the firm has to meet to become

---

24. 63 Pa. Cons. Stat. Ann. § 153.
25. 63 Pa. Cons. Stat. Ann. § 34.1.
26. 63 Pa. Cons. Stat. Ann. § 34.13.
27. 63 Pa. Cons. Stat. Ann. § 34.13(e).

licensed, which begins with an examination of the permissible legal forms for the business.

In New York, a firm may not be a general business corporation unless the corporation was formed before April 15, 1935, and lawfully practiced engineering in New York continuously thereafter.[28] Thus, if a firm is a general business corporation, a separate entity, wholly owned by individuals, will have to be formed to gain firm licensure in New York. This entity will have to be a professional service corporation, a design professional service corporation, a professional service limited liability company, a registered limited liability partnership, a partnership, or a specific type of joint enterprise.[29]

After determining the legal form the firm must take in a particular jurisdiction, the next step is to evaluate what other requirements, if any, are placed on the firm to gain licensure. As discussed earlier with respect to an architectural firm in Pennsylvania, there may be minimum ownership, directorship, or officership requirements for registrants in that state.

Also, there may be limitations on the firm name in a particular state,[30] or the name presently used by the firm may not be available in that jurisdiction because it is already in use by another firm. The firm, in turn, will have to adopt an assumed or fictitious name for use in that state. For example, an architectural firm in Oregon may not include the surname of an individual who is not presently or was not previously associated in the practice of architecture or engineering in Oregon or in any jurisdiction recognized by the State Board of Architect Examiners or the State Board of Examiners for Engineering or Land Surveying.[31]

In most jurisdictions, a design firm is required to qualify with the secretary of state in that jurisdiction to conduct intrastate business.[32] An argument

---

28. N.Y. EDUCATION LAW § 7209 subd. 6. For architecture, such general business corporations must have been formed prior to April 12, 1929, and continuously engaged in the provision of architectural services thereafter. N.Y. EDUCATION LAW § 7307 subd. 4.

29. N.Y. EDUCATION LAW § 7210 subd. 1.

30. In New York, a firm may not use a name or initials that imply a relationship with another business entity. RULES OF THE BOARD OF REGENTS, § 29.1 (2020); *see also* http://www.op.nysed.gov/corp/pcorptips.html.

31. OR. REV. STAT. § 671.041(2)(d) (2020).

32. There is a lack of clarity about the meaning of the term "doing business." It means doing intrastate business in that state versus providing services in interstate commerce. *See* CT CORPORATION, WHAT CONSTITUTES DOING BUSINESS (2016), *available at* https://ct.wolterskluwer.com/sites/default/files/CT_What-Constitutes-Doing-Business-2016.pdf, for an excellent discussion of this issue.

can be made that the Commerce Clause[33] of the U.S. Constitution should shield firms from having to do this if no office has been established in that state;[34] others have suggested that registration with the secretary of state should be undertaken.[35]

The application form and related instructions that are to be submitted for firm authorization or registration are a helpful guide to the statutory and regulatory framework for any particular state. These documents should be acquired early in the process of evaluation and are available from the licensure boards in each state. In some cases, the practice of the state may be more onerous or more liberal than suggested by the statutes under which it operates.

B. Noncompliance Has Its Price

The consequences can be severe if a firm provides design professional services without properly registering the firm with the state's professional licensure board(s). This problem often arises in the context of a lawsuit to collect fees due to the firm. The Tennessee professional corporation of Ellers, Oakley, Chester & Rike, Inc. (Ellers Oakley) learned this the hard way when it tried to collect $275,000 in unpaid fees for engineering design and construction-related services for air cargo facilities constructed at two airports in Missouri. Ellers Oakley first served a demand for arbitration pursuant to the arbitration clause in its contracts with its Missouri clients. Ellers Oakley's clients, however, filed suit in the Missouri court to stay the arbitration proceedings, contending that the contracts with Ellers Oakley and their arbitration clauses were invalid because engineering service contracts are unenforceable if the engineering firm was not authorized to provide engineering services in Missouri.[36] Although the Ellers Oakley engineers who actually provided the design services held Missouri licenses, Ellers Oakley was not registered to offer engineering services in Missouri.[37]

---

33. U.S. Const. art. I, § 8, cl. 3. Congress is to regulate commerce with foreign nations and among the several states.

34. Cement Asbestos Prods. Co. v. Hartford Accident and Indem. Co., 592 F.2d 1144, 1146–48 (10th Cir. 1979).

35. Robert F. Cushman & James C. Dobbs, Design Professionals Handbook of Business and Law § 2.2 (John Wiley & Sons, Inc. 1991).

36. Haith & Co. v. Ellers, Oakley, Chester & Rike, Inc., 778 S.W.2d 417 (Mo. Ct. App. 1989).

37. Mo. Rev. Stat. §§ 327.011(6), 327.191, 327.401 (2016). These statutory provisions have remained virtually unchanged since the *Ellers Oakley* decision.

The trial court issued the injunction and the Missouri Court of Appeals affirmed this decision.[38] The appellate court highlighted the statutory provision, which read as follows:

> [e]very contract for . . . engineering . . . services entered into by any person who is not a . . . registered or authorized professional engineer . . . shall be unenforceable by the unregistered or unauthorized professional engineer.[39]

When Ellers Oakley entered into its first contract, it instructed its Tennessee counsel to "take the steps necessary to comply with Missouri law." Consequently, Ellers Oakley obtained a certificate of authority to do business in Missouri.[40] However, it did not obtain a certificate of authority to practice engineering from the Missouri Board of Architects, Professional Engineers and Land Surveyors until after Ellers Oakley's client filed the action to stay the arbitration proceedings.[41] That was too late.

Ellers Oakley argued that it had substantially complied with the statutory requirements; therefore its contracts should be enforced despite the Missouri statute cited above. The court rejected this argument based on the statutory mandate that contracts cannot be enforced when entered into by engineering firms that were not registered at the time the contract is formed.[42]

Of further interest, registering to do business with the Missouri Secretary of State, which Ellers Oakley did shortly after it entered into the first contract, was not actually necessary at that time in order to later enforce its contracts. This registration would have been required only before suit was filed. The Missouri appellate court compared the statute requiring registration with the secretary of state with the statute requiring registration with the Missouri Board of Architects, Professional Engineers and Land Surveyors and noted that registration with the secretary of state can be accomplished later, but registration with the board is required in advance of entering into a contract for

---

38. *Ellers Oakley*, 778 S.W.2d at 419.

39. *Id.* at 420 (citing Mo. Rev. Stat. § 327.461 (1986)). This statute remains substantially the same today, except the language has been broadened to provide that such a contract "shall be unenforceable by the unlicensed or unauthorized person, whether in contract, quantum meruit or other legal theory, regardless of whether a benefit has been conferred." Mo. Rev. Stat. § 327.461 (2012).

40. *Ellers Oakley*, 778 S.W.2d at 418–19. This case serves as a good warning to attorneys counseling professionals who work in other jurisdictions.

41. *Id.* at 419.

42. *Id.* at 421.

engineering services. The court found that failure to register with the secretary of state can be cured, whereas failure to register with the Missouri Board of Architects, Professional Engineers and Land Surveyors cannot.[43]

Undaunted, Ellers Oakley filed a breach of contract and *quantum meruit* cause of action in the United States District Court for the District of Kansas to obtain its fees in the case of *Ellers, Oakley, Chester & Rike, Inc. v. St. Louis Air Cargo Services, Inc.*[44] The district court granted defendants' motion for summary judgment on the breach of contract claim based on the earlier state court decision discussed above, but allowed the *quantum meruit* claim to survive summary judgment.

The parties stipulated to the entry of final judgment in favor of Ellers Oakley and against the two defendants in the amount of $275,000, so the defendants could appeal the issue of Ellers Oakley's right to a *quantum meruit* recovery to the United States Court of Appeals for the Tenth Circuit. In making its decision, the federal appellate court first noted that the Missouri statute does not by its express terms preclude *a quantum meruit recovery* by an unregistered engineer. Nonetheless, the Tenth Circuit court rejected Ellers Oakley's *quantum meruit* cause of action and reversed the lower court, reasoning that to do otherwise would frustrate the Missouri statutory scheme requiring engineering firms to obtain a certificate of authority before entering into contracts for engineering services.[45]

IV. Firm Practice

Once the firm's application has been approved and the firm is authorized, or registered to practice architecture or engineering, the real work begins—ascertaining all the nuances of practice in that jurisdiction and meeting the challenge of complying with these requirements that are subtly different from what is required in other jurisdictions. The following discussion will focus on some of these differences, but there are many more than are discussed here and they can only be found in the statutes and regulations of the fifty states.

At first blush, the act of sealing architectural and engineering work product would seem to be a reasonably straightforward undertaking. Nevertheless, this practice area can be problematic. The use of the professional seal is almost

43. *Id.*

44. 984 F.2d 1108 (10th Cir. 1993) (applying Missouri law).

45. *Id.* at 1111–12.

always addressed in the applicable licensing regulations. For this reason, one must always check regulations carefully.

A. Who Is to Seal?

The general answer is that the registered professional or professionals in responsible charge of the work reflected in the document should seal the architectural and engineering work product. Thus, it is important to consider the concept of who is "in responsible charge of the work." This term or similar terms are often defined in a state's statutes or regulations and may also be defined as or referred to as the architect or engineer of record.

The concept of the architect or engineer being in responsible charge or in supervisory control is one side of the coin and the architect or engineer of record is the other. One side of the coin focuses on the execution of professional services and the other focuses on the deliverable or work product resulting from the provision of professional services.

In New Jersey, "responsible charge" is defined as the "rendering of regular and effective supervision by a competent professional engineer . . . to those individuals performing services which directly and materially affect the quality and competence of the professional services rendered by the licensee."[46] The statute goes on to specify what is not considered responsible charge as follows:

> A licensee engaged in any of the following acts or practices shall be deemed not to have rendered regular and effective supervision:
>
> (1) The regular and continuous absence from principal office premises from which professional services are rendered, except for performance of field work or presence in the field office maintained exclusively for a specific project;
>
> (2) The failure to personally inspect or review the work of subordinates where necessary and appropriate;
>
> (3) The rendering of a limited, cursory or perfunctory review of plans or projects in lieu of appropriate detailed review;
>
> (4) The failure to personally be available on a reasonable basis or with adequate advance notice for consultation and inspection where circumstances require personal availability.[47]

---

46. N.J. STAT. ANN. § 45:8–28(g) (2018). *See* N.J. STAT. ANN. § 45:3–1.1.1(2018) (nearly identical statutory language with respect to the practice of architecture in New Jersey).

47. N.J. STAT. ANN. § 45:8–28(g) (2018).

The term architect or engineer of record is not typically used in the licensing statutes and regulations, but is more often contained in statutes and regulations comprising building codes where the concept of architect or engineer of record is used to denote the architect or engineer who has in fact signed and sealed the construction documents under consideration. In Connecticut, prior to the issuance of a certificate of occupancy for certain structures, the local building official must require a statement signed by the architect or engineer of record responsible for the design of the structure affirming the professional opinion that the completed structure is in substantial compliance with the approved plans and specifications on file with the building official.[48]

Under the International Building Code (IBC), the registered design professional in responsible charge is the person designated by the building owner on the building permit application as such.[49] The IBC also states that the registered design professional in responsible charge is accountable for reviewing submittal documents prepared by others for compatibility with the design of the building,[50] as well as the preparation of the statement of required special inspections.[51]

In summary, architects and engineers may only seal documents prepared under their personal supervision. Once these documents are sealed, the sealing architect or engineer becomes the architect or engineer of record for that project, or at least for that portion of the project represented by the sealed documents.

However, there may be some exceptions to the direct supervision requirement. One such exception is sealing of documents produced by others, such as a subconsultant. Under Illinois law, an architect may seal documents prepared by or under the responsible control of others who hold a license and have sealed the documents if the architect has reviewed in whole or in part such portions and has coordinated their preparation or integrated them into his or her own work.[52] Also in Illinois, a partner or a corporate officer of a professional design firm who has professional knowledge of the content of the technical submissions and intends to be responsible for the adequacy of the technical submission may sign and seal technical submissions that are prepared by or

48. Conn. Gen. Stat. Ann. § 29-276c(b) (2012).

49. International Building Code § 106.3.4.1 (2006).

50. *Id.*

51. *Id.* at § 1704.1.1.

52. 225 Ill. Comp. Stat. Ann. 305/14 (2019).

under the responsible control of architects who are licensed in Illinois and are in the regular employ of the professional design firm.[53]

The recommended practice is to have the architect or engineer in the most direct operational or supervisory role sign and seal the documents created, regardless of his or her corporate status in the firm and the exceptions discussed earlier. The identification of the licensed professional, who will apply a seal and signature to the design documents, at the appropriate time, must be addressed prior to the commencement of the creation of the design documents. This person supervises the development of the documents throughout the design process and normally would interface with the code compliance and building department officials when the design documents are submitted for plan check and permitting. Under the laws of most jurisdictions, there is potential for personal or individual liability to the professional licensing authorities for failure to properly discharge the duties associated with service as the responsible design professional. These duties are extremely important and must be taken seriously by properly qualified personnel.

Some states may require that multiple signatures and seals be placed on documents to comply with the applicable statutes and regulations. Pennsylvania law effectively requires multiple signatures and seals on architectural documents prepared by larger firms because, in addition to the signature and seal of the architect who prepared or personally supervised the creation of the documents,[54] the signature and seal of the corporate director under whose personal supervision the document was prepared are also required.[55]

In some jurisdictions, the firm also must obtain a seal and place it on documents it issues. South Carolina requires architectural firms to obtain a seal containing the firm's name, place of business, and the words "Registered Architect, State of South Carolina." Further, both the seal of the architect in responsible charge and the seal of the firm must be used.[56] A similar requirement exists for architectural firms in North Carolina.[57]

---

53. *Id.* The statute further specifies that the architect exercising responsible control shall be identified on the documents or portions of documents by name and Illinois license number.

54. 49 PA. CODE § 9.141(b)(2).

55. 63 PA. CONS. STAT. ANN. § 34.13(i).

56. S.C. CODE ANN. § 40-3-280 (2016).

57. N.C. GEN. STAT. § 83A-10; N.C. ADMIN. CODE tit. 21, r. 2.206 (2017).

B. What Is to Be Sealed and When?

Florida law provides the generally accepted practice as to what and when a document is to be sealed:

> All final construction documents and instruments of service which include drawings, plans, specifications, and reports prepared or issued by the registered architect and being filed of public record shall bear the signature and seal of the registered architect who prepared or approved the document and date on which they were sealed.[58]

As a matter of general practice, plans and specifications, usually referred to as construction documents, are sealed when they are issued for permitting, public bid, or construction. South Carolina law provides that original seals shall appear on each print of the drawings, the index sheets of each set of specifications offered to secure a building permit, and one record set for use on the construction site.[59]

Under Michigan law, architects are to seal plans, plats, drawings, maps, and the title sheet of specifications, addenda, bulletins, and reports. If a bound document is submitted, the index sheet of plans, specifications, and reports shall be stamped or sealed.[60]

Although it seems rather obvious that schematic, design development, partially complete construction documents, and other draft or incomplete documents should not be sealed, there appears to be little treatment of this issue in state statutes or regulations. Perhaps that is because the answer is obvious. Only documents intended for some significant purpose such as permitting, bidding, or construction should be sealed and then only when they are considered complete by the design professional. New Jersey, however, does address this issue in its regulation of engineers stating that incomplete or draft documents may be signed but shall not be sealed, providing the licensee inserts the words "This is not a sealed document" in the place of the seal in the title block.[61]

C. How Are Documents to Be Sealed?

As noted above, the procedure for sealing and signing documents is generally addressed by the applicable regulations. Although there are variations,

---

58. Fla. Stat. Ann. § 481.221(2) (2019).
59. S.C. Code Ann. § 40-3-280(B) (2013).
60. Mich. Comp. Laws Ann. § 339.2008(1) (2014).
61. N.J. Admin. Code tit. 13, § 40-8.1(f) (2015).

documents generally are sealed by the registrant applying a rubber stamp of the seal or impressing the document with an embossed metal seal followed by registrant's signature near or over the stamped or impressed seal. Also, the document is dated with the date of the stamping or sealing. In Pennsylvania, when a document is signed, the signature must be applied near or over the seal and without obliterating the registration number.[62]

Some states may require additional certifications or statements. In addition to the date, seal, and signature, Iowa requires a certification that the work was done by the licensee or under the licensee's direct personal supervision.[63] New York law regulating the provision of engineering services requires a warning that it is illegal to alter the document in any way unless under the direction of a licensed engineer.[64]

The size and scale of today's larger and more sophisticated projects, as well as the advent of electronic documents, have raised the issue of facsimile seals and signatures. Not all states have addressed this issue. Engineers in New Jersey may only use impression or digital seals but not rubber stamps.[65] Illinois allows a computer-generated seal and signature.[66]

Oregon regulations pertaining to the practice of architecture state that the registrant's stamp and manual or digital signature must appear on the original title page of specifications and on every sheet of drawings intended for permit or construction. However, the regulations then provide that originals may be reproduced for permit and construction purposes.[67] This statute appears to allow reproduction of additional copies for permitting and construction purposes without having to individually seal and sign each page of the drawings.

Pennsylvania allows the use of facsimile seals on all but the first page of drawing sets prepared by its architects and engineers.[68] However, Florida has more directly addressed the electronic documents issue in its architectural statutes and the Electronic Signature Act of 1996.[69] Final plans, specifications, or reports prepared by Florida architects may be dated, sealed, signed, and transmitted electronically.[70]

---

62. 49 Pa. Code § 37.59 (2019).
63. Iowa Code Ann. § 542B.16 (2019).
64. N.Y. Education Law § 7209(2).
65. N.J. Admin. Code tit. 13, § 40-8.1(a) (2015).
66. 225 Ill. Comp. Stat. Ann. 325/14 (2019).
67. Or. Admin. R. 806-010-0045 (2019).
68. 49 Pa. Code §§ 9.141, 37.59 (2019).
69. Fla. Stat. Ann. §§ 668.001–006 (2019).
70. Fla. Stat. Ann. § 481.221 (2019).

D. Other Requirements Imposed by Some States

Placing the firm's registration number on any documents prepared by the firm is another potential requirement. Illinois imposes such a responsibility on its architectural firms[71] and New Jersey imposes it on engineering firms.[72]

Another aspect of firm practice, particularly for larger firms with several offices, is the requirement to have licensed staff in responsible charge at each office offering or providing professional services. There are many states, particularly in the southern United States, imposing this requirement for the practice of architecture, engineering, or both, such as Alabama,[73] Florida,[74] Kentucky,[75] Michigan,[76] North Carolina,[77] South Carolina,[78] and Virginia.[79]

Out-of-state firms offering or providing services in Georgia must indicate their name and license number as registered in Georgia on all firm letterhead, publicity, and instruments of service.[80] Contracts for architectural services to be provided in Massachusetts have to be signed by the officers who are Massachusetts licensees and who will exercise professional and supervisory control over the contracted services.[81]

V. Conclusion

There is no quick and easy answer or solution to the many laws regulating the practice of architecture and engineering in the fifty states. It takes a concerted and dedicated effort to identify the licensure requirements for individuals and firms in each state, and to practice legally under the granted licenses.

---

71. 225 Ill. Comp. Stat. Ann. 305/14 (2019).
72. N.J. Admin. Code tit. 13, § 40-8.3(a)6 (2015).
73. Ala. Code § 34-11-9(e).
74. Fla. La. Stat. Ann. § 481.225(1)(g) (2020).
75. Ky. Rev. Stat. Ann. § 322.060(1)(c) (2014).
76. Mich. Comp. Laws Ann. § 339.2010(4) (2020).
77. N.C. Admin. Code tit. 21, r. 56.901(a) (2019).
78. S.C. Code Ann. § 40-22-250(F) (2016).
79. Va. Regs. § 10-20-780 (2016).
80. Ga. Comp. R. & Regs. r. 50-3-.03(g) (2020).
81. Mass. Gen. Laws ch. 112, § 60L.8.

VI. Practice Aids

A. Checklist for Practice in a New Jurisdiction

Firm Professional Licensure and Practice Checklist and Analysis

State: _______	Area of Professional Practice: ❑ Architecture ❑ Engineering ❑ Land Surveying ❑ Geology ❑ Landscape

Question	**Answer**	**Comment**
1. Does firm have owners, directors, officers, or employees currently licensed in state to provide this service?		
2. Who will have to become licensed in state to be in responsible charge of services to be provided?		
3. Must firm be registered to provide this service? If no, do not complete balance of form.		
4. Is firm's current legal form or that of one of its affiliates acceptable for firm registration?		
5. What ownership, directorship, officership, or employee requirements must be met to register firm?		

Question	Answer	Comment
6. Which owners, directors, officers, or employees who are not already registered will have to become registered so firm can be become registered?		
7. Are there any restrictions on firm name?		
8. Does board require firm to register with secretary of state?		
9. Will firm have branch office in state? If yes, must an in-state licensee be in that office full-time and what position must that licensee hold?		
10. Does firm have to obtain its own seal, and does it have to be applied along with licensee's seal on documents?		
11. Is there requirement for licensee to be resident in each office providing professional services to state?		
12. Who, what, and when are professionals to seal professional work products?		

Question	Answer	Comment
13. Is there a requirement for certifications, warnings, or any other unusual insertions when sealing documents?		
14. Are there any unusual requirements for drawing title blocks?		
15. Are there any requirements for how professional contracts are to be entered?		
16. Are there any requirements imposed on how correspondence is issued to clients in state?		
17. Are there any requirements imposed to content of marketing materials issued to clients in state?		

B. NCARB Certificates and NCEES Records

The National Council of Architectural Registration Boards (NCARB) and the National Council of Examiners for Engineering and Surveying (NCEES) provide valuable assistance to firms involved in the multistate practice of architecture and engineering.

The NCARB Web site, at www.ncarb.com, provides a reference of registration requirements at both the individual and firm level for the fifty states based on information gathered by the NCARB from state architectural registration boards. NCARB also offers a certification program that expedites reciprocal registration of individual architects among the 55 member boards in the United States and Canada. However, certification is not the same as registration and does not automatically qualify an individual to practice architecture in any particular jurisdiction. For firms with multistate practices, the NCARB certification program greatly facilitates the licensure process for those stockholders, directors, officers, and employees that have to be registered in various jurisdictions.

Similar registration information for engineers and engineering firms is available from the NCEES Web site, at www.ncees.org, based on a 2005 NCEES survey of engineering and land surveying licensing boards. The NCEES program to facilitate comity registrations is called its records program, but it works in the same way as the NCARB certification program. The NCEES records program is also essential for stockholders, directors, officers, and employees of engineering firms with a large multistate practice, and for its key engineers who will have to become licensed in many states.

CHAPTER 2

Ethics and Rules of Conduct Governing Design Professionals

MOHAMMAD IQBAL

I. Introduction

Design professionals,[1] like lawyers, physicians, and accountants, are members of learned professions. The very essence of a profession is that its members cannot undertake their duties on behalf of a client without awareness of and responsibility for the public welfare.[2]

In the execution of professional services, it is well accepted that a design professional's legal duty is to conform to the reasonable standard of care prevalent in the industry and regulations applicable to that profession.[3] Design professionals operate under the jurisdiction of state licensure laws and are subject to discipline for a violation thereof. Design professionals are also subject to discipline by their respective professional societies for a violation of the public

---

1. In general, the phrase "design professional" refers to licensed engineers and architects; however, some authors also include surveyors, landscape architects, and interior designers as design professionals. *See* ROBERT F. CUSHMAN & G. CHRISTIAN HEDERMANN, ARCHITECT AND ENGINEER LIABILITY: CLAIMS AGAINST DESIGN PROFESSIONALS (2d ed. 1995).

2. A. E. Investment Corp. v. Link Builders, Inc., 214 N.W.2d 764, 769 (Wis. 1974).

3. RESTATEMENT (SECOND) OF TORTS, § 288C (1963–1964); *see also* R. F. CUSHMAN & G. C. HEDERMANN, *supra* note 1, at 136.

trust.[4] The professional codes of ethics detail the aim, guidelines, duties, and obligations in serving the public good, and are deemed so fundamental that failure to fulfill them warrants reproach or formal sanctions.

A. Ethical Issues in the Design Process

The collapse of the Hyatt Regency sky walkways in 1981 (discussed in Section IX *infra),* which killed 114 people and injured 216, and the aftermath of destruction caused by hurricanes in recent years, brought to light that the practices of design professionals contributed to the loss of life, personal injuries, and property damage.[5] Although no court found a design professional guilty of any criminal act, these events serve as classic examples of the potential consequences of design professionals ignoring their ethical obligations—thus creating greater pressure on design professionals to strictly abide by their responsibilities to serve the public good.

Generally, "ethics" is synonymous with ordinary morality.[6] In broad terms, ethics is concerned with how to go about life, what it means to "live well," to accomplish "good" in the world, and be "just" or "fair" in one's personal and professional life.[7] Ethics are considered precatory and not mandatory; however, ethical commitments are of no less importance than legal obligations. As the late Chief Justice of the United States, Earl Warren, declared:

> Society would come to grief without ethics, which is unenforceable in the courts and cannot be made part of law. . . . Not only does law in a civilized society presuppose ethical commitment, it presupposes the existence of a broad area of human conduct controlled only by ethical norms and not subject to law at all. . . .

---

4. *See, e.g.*, AIA 2018 Code of Ethics and Professional Conduct, *at* http://content.aia.org/sites/default/files/2019-10/181018_Code_of_Ethics.pdf.

5. U.S. Department of Commerce, National Bureau of Standards Report on the Investigation of the Kansas City Hyatt Regency Walkways Collapse (Feb. 1982). In terms of loss of life and injuries, the collapse was the most devastating structural collapse in this country. For reference to Hurricane Katrina, *see* Byron Newberry, Katrina: Macro-Ethical Issues for Engineers (2009).

6. Personal ethics is the set of one's own ethical commitments, which are usually acquired in early home or religious training and often modified by later reflection. Common morality or common sense is the set of moral ideals shared by most members of a culture or society. Barry Wasserman, Patrick Sullivan & Gregory Palermo, Ethics and the Practice of Architecture (2000).

7. Wasserman, Sullivan & Palermo, *supra* note 6.

> The individual citizen may engage in practices which, on the advice of counsel, he believes strictly within the letter of the law but which he also knows from his own conscience are outside the bounds of propriety and the right. Thus, when he engages in such practices, he does so not at his own peril—as when he violates the law—but at peril to the structure of civilization, involving greater stakes than any possible peril to himself. . . . This law beyond law, as distinct from law, is the creation of civilization and is indispensable to it. . . .[8]

Though ethical concerns pertain to all of us in our everyday lives, the design professional's ethics stem from the relationships and obligations with others and become paramount in the design and construction of the landscape in which we live.

The design professional's obligations arise in response to two sets of needs: individuals and other members of society require design professionals to design facilities to meet their needs; and, the public at large requires protection from potentially devastating effects of poor and insensitive building practices. In assuming these diverging obligations, society charges the design professional with dichotomous demands. This balancing process justifies the special status and distinguishes the design professional from an artist or a technician.[9]

Ethical issues arise as the design process moves from schematic, to design development, and on to the construction phase. The design professional encounters both moral and technical problems in dealing with clients; building codes; quality of work performed by coworkers, subconsultants and contractors; pressure imposed by time and superiors; and whims of the marketplace. The iterative nature of the design process presents ethical dilemmas. Changes made during one stage not only will affect subsequent stages but also may require assessment of prior decisions. The design professional must handle requests for changes during the construction phase with particular care or tragic consequences, such as the Hyatt Regency walkway failure, may result.[10]

Ethical responsibility means accountability or blameworthiness (or praiseworthiness) and is distinguishable from contractual or legal responsibility,

---

8. Unidentified opinion cited in Milton F. Lynch, *Can the Professions Survive without Ethics?* Professional Eng'r 38, 39 (Oct. 1976).

9. Tom Spector, The Ethical Architect: The Dilemma of Contemporary Practice (2001).

10. M. Levy & M. Salvadori, Why Buildings Fall Down (1992). *See also* http://ethics.tamu.edu/wp-content/uploads/sites/7/2017/04/HyattRegency.pdf.

although they overlap to some extent. Contractual or job responsibility consists of one's assigned tasks at his or her place of employment or under contract with the client. A particular law could be morally unjustified or inapplicable due to a contractually limited scope of the assignment undertaken.[11] Therefore, the study of ethics is integral to the design professional's ability to balance morality, law, and contractual obligations to the client.

The public requires professionals to meet certain ethical standards as a part of the social contract.[12] The media has published public opinion surveys on the image or perception of the ethical conduct of various professions.[13] In that respect, the code of ethics is an implicit contract between professionals and the public defining what professional conduct the public expects of design professionals. Design professionals agree among themselves to abide by uniform standards and with the public that these uniform standards will ensure competence and promote the well-being of the public as it relates to the professional's expertise.[14] It also enables a potential client to anticipate certain professional conduct.

Although codes of ethics may commend ideals that go beyond the legal standard of care, these commendations are abstract and vague, leaving it unclear how they apply to individual circumstances encountered by members of the profession.[15] The ever-present pressure and professional risk involved in the practice of architecture and engineering may cause design professionals to inadvertently overlook professional and ethical obligations. Further, the day-to-day pressure associated with the practice of architecture and engineering in the marketplace is such that it is easy to lose sight of professional and ethical obligations. "Architects live and work today in a functioning but weakened profession that lacks a dominant design ethics."[16] Unfortunately, a design professional who is a member of a professional society may not be aware of the

---

11. Charles B. Fleddermann, Engineering Ethics (2004).

12. For a discussion on social contract theory and other ethical concepts and theories justifying a moral system, *see* Herman T. Tavani, Ethics and Technology (2016).

13. *See Survey Says Engineers Image Nearly Divine*, Engineering Inc. (May–June 2002) (reporting Gallop honesty and ethics polls of various professions).

14. U.S. Department of Commerce Report, *supra* note 5, at 12.

15. For example, the American Institute of Architects (AIA) 2018 Code of Ethics and Professional Conduct, Ethical Standard No. 1.3, requires that "[m]embers should respect and help conserve their natural and cultural heritage while striving to improve the environment and the quality of life within it," *available at* http://www.aia.org.

16. Spector, *supra* note 9.

existence of that society's code, or may not have read it. Quite often, design professionals learn ethical lessons only after something goes wrong. Responsible design professionals need to know what circumstances in practice call for ethical sensitivity and reflection.

B. Rules of Professional Conduct

Ethics and professional rules of conduct are the hallmark of all professions. While adherence to ethical standards is voluntary, abiding by the rules of professional conduct is mandatory for professionals and violation of a rule is grounds for disciplinary action by the professional society of which the professional is a member. In other words, ethics are goals to which the organization asks its members to aspire, but rules represent the minimum acceptable level of conduct below which the professional should not fall or face discipline from the professional society.

Additionally, pursuant to their police powers, states have created agencies, promulgated licensure laws, and appointed regulatory boards to oversee professionals such as architects, engineers, land surveyors, and landscape architects. State laws govern both individuals and entities offering design services. Every state has adopted its own rules and regulations, which may vary widely from one jurisdiction to the next for each profession or specialty. For lawyers representing design professionals, it is necessary to understand the interplay and hierarchy of ethics, rules of professional conduct, and the licensure laws.

This chapter reviews codes of ethics and rules of professional conduct for design professionals. It includes a list of available resources,[17] followed by a discussion on the state licensure laws that govern the practice of engineering and architecture and state-imposed disciplinary actions to which design professionals may be exposed.

II. Code of Ethics

A. Basic Concepts and Fundamental Principles

A professional code of ethics is the standard adopted by professionals to govern their own professional conduct. It provides a framework for the professional's ethical judgment. The code simply reiterates principles and standards that constitute accepted and responsible practices, which define the roles and

---

17. The list is an update of an earlier paper by this author, Mohammad Iqbal, *Researching the Internet: Ethics and Rules of Conduct Governing Professionals*, Constr. Law. (Winter 2001), at 37.

obligations of design professionals.[18] The code articulates the ways in which moral and ethical principles apply to unique situations encountered in professional practice. It indicates to others that the profession is seriously concerned about responsible and professional conduct.[19] For example, the American Council of Engineering Companies' (ACEC) guidelines on ethics and professional conduct state:

> Consulting engineering is an important and learned profession. The members of the profession recognize that their work has a direct and vital impact on the quality of life for all people. Accordingly, the services provided by consulting engineers require honesty, impartiality, fairness, and equity and must be dedicated to the protection of public health, safety, and welfare. In the practice of their profession, consulting engineers must perform under a standard of professional behavior which requires adherence to the highest principles of ethical conduct on behalf of the public, clients, employees and the profession.[20]

Although there is considerable overlap in the codes of various professional organizations, there is no unified code of ethics for design professionals.[21] There are many organizations devoted to the numerous specialties within the design profession. Virtually every occupational or specialty group claiming to have professional status has a code of ethics. For example, the practice of engineering comprises many disciplines and each has a professional society, such as the American Society of Civil Engineers (ASCE) for civil engineers, the Institute of Electrical and Electronics Engineers (IEEE) for electrical engineers, and the American Society of Mechanical Engineers (ASME) for mechanical engineers. There is no engineering society applicable to all engineers. The National Society of Professional Engineers (NSPE) attempts, like the American Bar Association (ABA) and the American Medical Association (AMA), to function as the umbrella professional society for engineers. Architects, though they may offer specialty services, identify with the American Institute of Architects (AIA) as their architectural society.

---

18. Charles E. Harris Jr., Michael S. Pitchard & Michael J. Rabin, Engineering Ethics—Concepts and Cases (2004).

19. *Id.*

20. *ACEC Professional and Ethical Conduct Guidelines*, Engineering Inc. (Sept.–Oct. 2003), *also available at* https://www.acec.org/about/ethics/.

21. Levy & Salvadori, *supra* note 10.

B. Historical Development

Design professionals began organizing their professional societies in the United States in the nineteenth century. In 1877, the board of the ASCE addressed the issue of whether it should have a code of ethics for its members. Initially, the ASCE resolved not to adopt a code of ethics, explaining "[t]hat it is inexpedient for the Society to instruct its members as to their duties in private professional matters."[22] However, in 1914 the ASCE membership approved the first version of its code of ethics.[23] The original code, like other professional codes in early part of the twentieth century, focused largely on issues related to conducting business. For example, it forbade advertising and price competition for design services among the ASCE members. The code gave less emphasis to issues of service and responsibilities to the public, including safety.[24]

One of the common provisions in the early codes was that members would not underbid other members of the same professional organization—a provision that triggered antitrust action against principal professional organizations. In particular, before 1971 the ASCE *Code of Ethics* contained a provision that made it unethical for an ASCE member "to invite or submit priced proposals under conditions that constitute price competition for professional services."[25] The ASCE enforced the anti-competition provision against its members. This triggered an action by the Department of Justice (DOJ) wherein the DOJ alleged that the ASCE *Code of Ethics* unreasonably restricted interstate trade and commerce by limiting price competition among its members and depriving customers of the benefits of free and open competition in the sale of services.[26] In order to resolve the controversy, ASCE voluntarily removed the anticompetitive provision from its code, annotated the code to state that the submission of fee quotations was permissible, and entered into a consent decree.[27]

---

22. Matthew Tilley, *Evolution of Engineering Ethics during the Last 150 Years*, ASCE J. Professional Issues in Engineering Education and Practice (June 2013), *available at* https://ascelibrary.org/doi/pdf/10.1061/%28ASCE%291052-3928%282003%29129%3A3%28131%29. *See also* National Institute of Engineering Ethics, Engineering Ethics—Concepts, Viewpoints, Cases, and Codes (2008).

23. American Society of Civil Engineers, *Development of the First ASCE Code of Ethics* (2007), https://www.asce.org/question-of-ethics-articles/dec-2007/.

24. *Id. See also* https://www.asce.org/about/ethics/.

25. *Supra* note 22.

26. United States v. American Soc'y of Civil Eng'rs, 1972 WL 551, No. 72-1776 (S.D.N.Y. May 1, 1972).

27. *Id. See also Profit or Public Good, available at* https://www.architects.org/stories/just-practice-1.

Like the ASCE *Code of Ethics,* the AIA code also contained an anti-competitive provision. The provision, known as Standard No. 9 of the AIA *Code of Ethics,* came into focus in *Mardirosian v. American Institute of Architects.*[28] In deciding whether the AIA violated antitrust laws, the court held that although the activities of professional societies have long been thought as "deserving of special treatment under the antitrust laws, it is now clear that an anti-competitive practice cannot be justified if it is unreasonable."[29]

The NSPE also had an anticompetitive provision in its rules of professional conduct. The DOJ challenged the provision as improper, and the Supreme Court agreed.[30] The Court held that the NSPE provision was unlawful. It reasoned that although professional services may differ significantly from other business services and the nature of the competition may vary, this difference does not create a broad exemption under the Rule of Reason for learned professions.[31]

Most contemporary codes emphasize commitments to safety, public health, and even environmental protection as the most important duties of a design professional. The rules of the free marketplace now govern design professionals' fees.

C. Discussion of Professional Codes of Ethics

Though the professional codes of ethics and rules of conduct have different origins, they overlap not only with themselves but also with moral ideals such as honesty and fairness. The Boston Society of Architects analyzed the 1997 AIA *Code of Ethics and Professional Conduct* and determined that the rules primarily require the members to follow the law and not lie. Specifically:

- Laws—29% of rules require members to obey the law;
- Lies—33% of rules require members not to lie; and
- Other—38% of the rules refer to some other admonition or standard of conduct.[32]

---

28. 474 F. Supp. 628 (D.D.C. 1979).
29. *Id.* at 648.
30. National Soc'y of Prof'l Eng'rs v. United States, 435 U.S. 679 (1978).
31. *Id.* at 696.
32. Boston Society of Architects, *AIA Code of Ethics and Professional Conduct—Content Analysis*, ETHICS FORUM (2002).

Although the ethical standards and rules profess conformity with laws and societal values, professional standards occasionally may differ from personal or common morality. For example, an engineer may refuse to design a military project believing that war is immoral based on personal conviction, and not on professional or common morality. An architect may refuse to undertake a project that is contrary to his or her individual professional ethics. An engineer, believing that certain design decisions might jeopardize public safety, may "whistle-blow" and violate the employer's obligation to maintain confidentiality.[33] The design professional may not anticipate many questions regarding project purposes, client and personal values, kickbacks, corner-cutting, and diverse and multicultural perspectives, but the codes of ethics and rules of professional conduct of the professional societies generally address these issues.

A code of ethics can be brief, dealing with generalities, or detailed. For example, the IEEE code is short, but the codes of ethics of the NSPE, ASCE, and AIA are more explicit. Some argue that a short code lacking in specificity is more understandable and that members of a professional society are more likely to read it.

The Illinois Institute of Technology's Center for Study of Ethics in Professions (CSEP) has the largest collection of codes of ethics and related material on its Web site, including a search engine and an index organized by professional area.[34] The CSEP site also provides links to other ethics centers, organizations, and directories on the Web. Additional organizations that provide links to Web sites with ethics postings are the National Institute of Engineering Ethics (NIEE) (www.niee.org) and the Online Ethics Center for Engineering & Sciences (www.onlineethic.org). In addition to posting its code of ethics, the NSPE (www.nspe.org), makes available the cases and advance opinions of its Board of Ethical Review (BER). These cases provide an insight into NSPE's interpretation of its code of ethics. Similarly, several other professional organizations have their respective codes of ethics and related cases posted on their Web sites (see Appendix A).

The following is a brief discussion on selected codes of ethics.

33. FLEDDERMANN, *supra* note 11. (A good case study of political or institutional pressure affecting engineering performance is NASA's Challenger disaster.)

34. http://ethics.iit.edu.

III. AIA Ethical Standards and Rules of Professional Conduct

A. Overview

Founded in 1857, the AIA is the principal professional organization of architects. To persons engaged in the business and profession of architecture, membership in the AIA is a valuable asset that enhances their ability to compete for and obtain architectural business. AIA members normally use the insignia "AIA" following their names to denote membership.

Ethical issues arising in architecture develop during the design and construction processes as an architect deals with the motives and values of clients and society.[35]

The preamble to the AIA's *Code of Ethics and Professional Conduct* describes the principles on which the code is based. It states AIA members "are dedicated to the highest standards of professionalism, integrity, and competence," and that the code provides "guidelines for the conduct of Members in fulfilling those obligations."[36] The AIA has arranged its code of ethics in three tiers: Canons, Ethical Standards, and Rules of Conduct. Canons are broad principles of conduct. The Ethical Standards are specific goals to which AIA members aspire in their performance and behavior. The Rules of Conduct are mandatory, and their violation is grounds for disciplinary action by the AIA.[37] To guide its members in using its code, the AIA has provided a commentary to its code and rules.

One of the most important issues facing the architectural profession is the attribution of credit to other architects in connection with work on a project. The AIA Web site provides guidelines on how to structure and provide that credit.[38]

---

35. Wasserman, Sullivan & Palermo, *supra* note 6 ("Architecture is an ethical discipline before it is an aesthetic one. When we build, we have not just the responsibility to our client, but to those who came before and those who will come after.").

36. AIA 2004 Code of Ethics and Professional Conduct, Rules of Application, Enforcement, and Amendment, *available at* http://www.aia.org/about_ethic.

37. *Id.*

38. *Id. See also* designers' reaction to AIA Code language, *available at* https://www.architects.org/stories/coded-langage.

B. Enforcement

The AIA administers its code of ethics through the National Ethics Council (NEC), which is appointed by the AIA Board of Directors.[39] An aggrieved party files formal charges with the NEC.[40] The NEC processes and disposes of complaints in accordance with "Rules of Procedure," which are intended to provide a fair and expeditious procedure for the disposition of cases. The Rules of Procedure include penalties ranging from admonition, suspension of membership, and expulsion from the AIA.[41] The NEC makes its decisions available with the names of the parties redacted. In addition, NEC publishes advisory opinions that illustrate its interpretations of the code. The AIA posts both types of decisions on its Web site.[42] The appeal procedures are confidential, as is the imposition of an admonishment; however, the AIA publicizes all other penalties.[43]

IV. ASCE Code of Ethics and Rules of Professional Conduct

The American Society of Civil Engineers (ASCE) adopted its original code of ethics in 1914. Since then, other professional organizations have used the ASCE code as a primer in the development of their codes. The ASCE *Code of Ethics* has seven fundamental canons.[44] The code does not give equal weight to all canons—it considers the ethical duty to safety, health, and public welfare to be paramount.[45] Recognizing the ethical duty to the public as the highest level of responsibility, the ASCE's Board of Directors defined the civil engineering profession as a calling where an engineer in the service of humanity uses special knowledge and skill in a distinctly intellectual plane.[46]

In order to preserve the high ethical standards of the civil engineering profession and to govern ethics practices in the profession, the ASCE has

---

39. AIA 2004 Code of Ethics and Professional Conduct, Rules of Application, Enforcement, and Amendment, *available at* http://www.aia.org/about_ethic.

40. *Id.*

41. *Id.*

42. *Id.*

43. *Id.*

44. *ACEC Professional and Ethical Conduct Guidelines*, Engineering Inc. (Sept.–Oct. 2003), *available at* https://www.acec.org/about/ethics/.

45. *Id.*

46. *Id.*

developed its "Standards of Professional Conduct" which encompasses issues such as:

- conflicts of interest;
- ensuring legal compliance;
- employees and public safety;
- workplace quality;
- use and protection of employer assets;
- maintaining accurate and complete records;
- gifts, meals, services, and entertainment;
- confidential or proprietary information;
- outside employment/activities;
- purchases of goods and services;
- bribes and kickbacks;
- relationships with competitors;
- relationships with clients, outside contractors, and consultants;
- environmental protection; and
- whistle-blowing.[47]

An ASCE member who violates the ASCE's Standards of Professional Conduct is subject to a disciplinary action up to and including removal or suspension from the ASCE.[48] The ASCE maintains and enforces its code of ethics and allows anyone to bring charges of unethical conduct against a member.[49] It refers complaints to ASCE's Committee on Professional Conduct (CPC) for investigation. During the investigation, the CPC acts like a grand jury; if it finds sufficient evidence to warrant disciplinary action, it refers the case for hearing before the Executive Committee.[50]

The Executive Committee holds proceedings to discipline an ASCE member upon the CPC's recommendation or by written request of ten or more ASCE members. The Executive Committee acts as an unbiased trier of fact and a CPC member acts as a prosecutor.[51] The Executive Committee conducts hearings in accordance with the procedure for professional conduct in cases. The organization affords additional due process to the accused member by serving a reasonable notice of the charges and the hearing, and by providing

---

47. www.asce.org/code-of-ethics/
48. https://www.asce.org/question-of-ethics-articles/dec-2014/.
49. *Id.*
50. *Id.*
51. *Id.*

a fair opportunity to hear the evidence, question witnesses, and refute the evidence.[52] Upon finding a violation of the code, the Executive Committee may take disciplinary action such as a letter of admonition or suspension from membership. The Executive Committee cannot expel a member from the ASCE, but can make that recommendation to the Board of Direction.[53] If the Executive Committee votes to recommend expulsion, it refers the case to the Board of Direction, which maintains the same due process protection as afforded at the Executive Committee hearing. A decision to expel a member requires a 75 percent vote by the Board of Direction. Both the Executive Committee and the Board of Direction have authority to publish the action and to notify other professional organizations or registration boards of their decision.[54] The ASCE's legal staff publishes its opinions on ethical issues reviewed by the CPC in a monthly newsletter sent free to its members. The ASCE also posts opinions on its Web site.[55]

The most notable action taken by the ASCE for violation of its ethics was against Jack Gillum, the engineer of record for the Hyatt Regency Hotel in Kansas City where the sky walkways collapsed. The ASCE evaluated the evidence supplied by the Missouri licensing board and announced a policy of holding structural engineers responsible for all elements of structural safety in the buildings they design.[56] However, it decided that Gillum—the only ASCE member whose license was revoked by the Missouri licensing board—was not guilty of gross negligence or unprofessional conduct, and the ASCE merely suspended his membership for three years. Later, Gillum voluntarily relinquished his membership altogether.[57] Section IX of this chapter further discusses the Hyatt walkways collapse case.

---

52. *Id.*

53. *Id.*

54. *Id.*

55. http://www.asce.org. *See also* Steven K. Starrett, Amy L. Lara & Carlos Bertha, Engineering Ethics: Real World Case Studies (2017).

56. Sarah K. A. Pfatteicher, *The Hyatt Horror: Failure and Responsibility in American Engineering*, ASCE Journal of Performance of Constructed Facilities (May 2000), 62–66.

57. *Id.*

V. NSPE Code of Ethics

A. Overview

In 1946, the NSPE adopted a *Code of Ethics for Engineers,* the canons of which provide that its members should:

1. hold paramount the safety, health, and welfare of the public;
2. perform services only in areas of their competence;
3. issue public statements only in an objective and truthful manner;
4. act for each employer or client as faithful agent or trustee;
5. avoid deceptive acts;
6. conduct themselves honorably, responsibly, ethically, and lawfully so as to enhance the honor, reputation, and usefulness of the profession.

The NSPE posts its code of ethics, rules of professional conduct, and enforcement procedures on its Web site.[58] The NSPE has formulated numerous hypothetical cases on ethics in order to stimulate the moral imagination and challenge design professionals to anticipate possible alternatives in resolving complex ethical issues. Although these case studies assist in understanding the code, they do not provide ready-made answers to all ethical questions that a design practice generates, and reasonable design professionals may disagree about the correct course of action.

B. Indemnification, Limitation of Liability, and Ethics

Design professionals often attempt to negotiate a limitation of liability (LOL) clause in their contracts with clients as a risk management technique. However, parties have challenged the LOL clause in numerous cases on public policy grounds.[59] One method of attacking a LOL clause is to allege that it violates the NSPE's *Code of Ethics for Engineers,* Section III.8, which requires professional engineers to "accept personal responsibility for their professional activities, provided, however, that engineers may seek indemnification for services arising out of their practice for other than gross negligence, where the engineer's interests cannot otherwise be protected."

---

58. http://www.nspe.org.

59. CUSHMAN & HEDERMANN, *supra* note 1 at § 17.8; *see also* Howard W. Ashcroft, *Enforceability of Limitation of Liability*, 14 CONSTR. LAW. 12 (1994).

The NSPE's Board of Ethical Review (BER) examined the issue of whether it is ethical to require clients to indemnify and hold an engineer harmless from and against any damages or legal expenses arising from negligence in the performance of pollution-related services.[60] The BER interpreted Section III.8 to mean that an engineer has an obligation to accept responsibility for professional activities and, where appropriate, obtain professional liability insurance or other protection available either in the market or in other spheres.[61] The BER opined that where such protection is commercially available at an affordable cost to the engineer and it protects the interests of both the client and the engineer, barring special or additional circumstances, the engineer has an ethical obligation to obtain such protection and not seek indemnification from the client for ordinary negligence. However, it reserved its right to modify its view as circumstances within the professional practice warrant due to the cyclical and fluid nature of the professional liability insurance environment.[62]

Three years later, the BER carved an exception to its earlier opinion on the indemnification clause.[63] The BER considered whether an engineer could include such a provision in an agreement with clients after "carefully surveying and analyzing the hazardous waste insurance market and determining that the hazardous waste liability insurance coverage currently available (was) inadequate to protect himself and his firm during the performance of hazardous waste remediation services for his clients."[64]

In distinguishing its earlier decision, the BER noted that "unlike traditional and customary engineering services, hazardous waste remediation services require engineers to perform actual physical work (sampling, testing) on the remediation site and such activities could easily expose professional engineers to significant third-party liability exposures."[65] Further, the BER noted that "the risk incurred in performing hazardous waste work may be quite significant, not necessarily based on fault and may significantly increase due to strict joint and several liability standards. . . . Because of these factors,

60. *Case No.* 93-8, Board of Review, National Soc'y of Prof'l Eng'rs, *available at* https://www.nspe.org/resources/ethics/ethics-resources/board-ethical-review-cases/use-broad-indemnification-clause.

61. *Id.*

62. *Id.*

63. *Case No. 96-12*, Board of Review, National Soc'y of Prof'l Eng'rs, *available at* https://www.nspe.org/sites/default/files/Ber96-12-app.pdf.

64. *Id.*

65. *Id.*

engineers practicing in this challenging field should be allowed a degree of flexibility to explore a variety of risk management techniques which include insurance, contractual provisions (e.g., indemnification, limitation of liability) and other professional practice considerations."[66]

VI. Law, Ethics, and Professional Conduct

Legal requirements may establish minimum standards of performance; however, ethics provide a richer guide for conduct. Trying to determine the right thing to do is a value-driven quest. How does a design professional assist a community in evaluating alternate designs? How does the design professional account for a project's impact on the environment? Beyond technical and scientific knowledge and design talent, many of the design professional's activities require judgment, respect, and trust among the community of people participating in and affected by a project. When such issues arise, they are ethical ones defined in neither contract nor tort doctrines.[67]

A code of ethics is not a legal document. It applies only to the members of the professional society. For example, the AIA rules apply only to its members and violating its provisions may result in expulsion from that professional society. With the current state of professional societies, expulsion from a professional society generally will not necessarily result in an inability to practice engineering or architecture. Unless the state licensing board takes action, there may be no real consequence for violating professional ethical principles. However, the loss of credibility and lowered personal reputation could be significant for a design professional.

Very few courts have addressed the issue of how an ethical violation impacts a civil action for damages filed against a professional. Some courts have held that while the violation of a professional ethical rule may subject a design professional or a firm to disciplinary sanctions by the profession, a code of ethics does not create a civil cause of action.[68] Drawing on cases dealing with the legal profession, courts have also held that the violation of profession rule does not create a presumption that an attorney has breached a legal duty

66. *Id.*

67. WASSERMAN, SULLIVAN & PALERMO, *supra* note 6, at 5.

68. Woodbridge Care LLC v. Englebrecht & Griffin Architects, 1997 WL 162808, 19 Conn. L. Rptr. 130 (Conn. Super. Ct. 1997).

to the client.[69] However, the trier of fact may consider the construction of a relevant rule of professional conduct as evidence of the standard of care and a breach thereof.[70] Finally, some courts have held that an attorney's ethical violation creates a rebuttable presumption of actionable malpractice.[71] Thus, the design professional should anticipate that an ethics violation might have some effect in a suit brought by the injured client or third party.

In order for a professional society to subject a design professional to its code of ethics, he or she must be a member of that society. However, many states have incorporated ethical codes into their licensing statutes, meaning that a violation of a provision of an ethical code would also constitute a violation of state licensing statute.[72] In addition, a client might incorporate the ethical code into its contract with a design professional. Two sample contractual provisions are:

> § 1.1 ETHICAL STANDARDS
>
> The Owner has informed the Design Professional and the Design Professional hereby acknowledges that the Owner is an entity operated under the highest level of ethical standards. To ensure that the Project will be designed in a manner consistent with the Owner's high level of ethical standards, the Owner has requested that the Design Professional agree, and the Design Professional does hereby agree, to

---

69. Two Thirty-Nine Joint Venture v. Joe, 60 S.W.3d 896, 905 (Tx. Ct. App. 2001).

70. *Id.*; Lipton v. Boesky, 110 Mich. App. 589, 313 N.W.2d 163 (1981).

71. 110 Mich. App. at 598; *Lipton*, 313 N.W.2d at 167.

72. The Illinois Structural Engineering Practice Act has incorporated unethical or unprofessional conduct as cause for discipline. For example, the Structural Engineering Act states:

> Sec. 20. (a) The Department may, singularly or in combination, refuse to issue, renew, or restore, or may suspend or revoke any license or certificate of registration, or may place on probation, reprimand, or fine, with a civil penalty not to exceed $10,000 for each violation, any person, corporation, partnership, or professional design firm registered or licensed under this Act for any of the following reasons:
>
> (2) Negligence, incompetence or misconduct in the practice of structural engineering;
>
> . . .
>
> (9) Engaging in dishonorable, unethical or unprofessional conduct of a character likely to deceive, defraud or harm the public.
>
> 225 ILCS 340.

immediately disclose to the Owner in writing any financial connection, business relationship, contractual relationship, or other potential or actual conflict of interest between the Design Professional (including the owners, principals, directors, officers, and employees of the Design Professional) and any entity or individual (including the owners, principals, directors, officers, and employees of such party) which is under consideration for the award of a contract to perform work or provide services or materials which relate to the Project. The Design Professional further agrees that, at the Owner's option, the Design Professional and any entity affiliated or related to the Design Professional may be disqualified from providing materials, work, or services (other than the performance of the services by the Design Professional to be provided hereunder) for the Project during the term of this Agreement.

§ 1.2 NO BENEFIT

Neither the Design Professional nor any owner, principal, director, officer, shareholder, or employee of the Design Professional will accept for its or their own benefit any quantity discount, promotional discount, trade commission, rebate, discount or similar payment, or any personal or business benefit ("Benefit") in connection with activities pursuant to this Agreement or in the discharge of its obligations hereunder. Any such Benefit shall be provided to the Owner. In the event that the Design Professional has any agreement in existence prior to or after the effective date of this Agreement, with any entity or individual that provides for any Benefit of any kind to the Design Professional or to any owner, principal, director, officer, shareholder, or employee of the Design Professional if a client of the Design Professional, such as the Owner, purchases materials, equipment, or services from such entity or individual, the Design Professional shall identify such entity or individual, as well as the nature of such agreement to the Owner in writing, within five (5) days after the execution of this Agreement, as well as within five (5) days after executing any such agreement after the effective date of this Agreement.

If the parties incorporate professional ethics into their contract, a court would undoubtedly hold that a violation thereof would constitute actionable breach of contract. In addition, to the extent that these contract provisions increase the applicable standard of care, the obligation may not be insurable under the design professional's errors and omissions coverage.

VII. Ethical Dilemma

Ethical dilemmas arise when morals come into conflict or the application of moral values is unclear. As each project is unique, so are the ethical challenges that the design professional must face and resolve. The design professional's seal on a set of drawings is evidence that he or she has addressed and resolved all ethical considerations and dilemmas.[73]

There are two broad categories of ethical dilemmas: first, dilemmas that are traditionally resolved with a well-settled solution that codes of ethics clearly address, such as to tell the truth, obey the law, heed the standard of care, not offer or accept bribes, maintain confidentiality, etc.; and second, dilemmas that have several solutions or considerations. These include "gray areas" where it is often hard to differentiate right from wrong. The NIEE, AIA, NSPE, ASCE, and other professional organizations provide numerous case histories and hypothetical scenarios to illustrate the interplay of different moral values in the design process.[74] Case studies illustrating ethical dilemmas serve a critical role in understanding professional ethics.[75]

Several case studies illustrate embedded ethical issues and a framework to solve ethical problems.[76] The first step in solving an ethical problem is to completely understand all the issues involved and divide them into three categories: factual, conceptual, and moral. After delineating the issues, frequently a solution or a range of solutions to the problem will become apparent.[77] Some may be better and others may be clearly wrong. This analytical approach aids the organization of solutions and is largely analogous to solving legal issues; however, the selected solution may rest with personal ethics.

The ASCE advises its members to follow the "PLUS" method to determine whether their acts in professional dealings conform to ethical standards. PLUS is an acronym that stands for Policies, Legal, Universal, and Self. The PLUS method requires the professional to answer the following questions about the act:

---

73. Spector, *supra* note 9.

74. *See, e.g.*, National Institute of Engineering Ethics, Engineering Ethics—Concepts, Viewpoint, Case, and Codes (Jimmy H. Smith & Patricia M. Harper eds., 2008); Harris et al., *supra* note 18.

75. Fleddermann, *supra* note 11.

76. *Id.*

77. *Id.*

Policies	Is it consistent with your employer's policies, procedures, and guidelines and ASCE's code of ethics?
Legal	Is it acceptable under applicable laws and regulations?
Universal	Does it conform to the universal principles/values that your employer and the profession have adopted?
Self	Does it satisfy your own personal definition of right, good and fair?[78]

The ASCE also suggests that a member facing an ethical dilemma should discuss it with his or her supervisor or the CPC through ASCE's legal counsel.[79]

VIII. Licensing Boards Governing Design Professionals

A. Licensure Laws

A regulatory framework or state "licensure laws" governs professionals and restricts the practice of a profession to individuals who have demonstrated professional competency traditionally acquired through education, experience, and examination.

State licensure laws have been in effect for a very long time,[80] predicated upon the states' police power and justified as a mean to protect the public health, safety, and welfare.[81] The purpose of licensing statutes is to protect the public rather than to punish the licensed professional.[82]

State statutes use licensing and registration, often interchangeably, to establish licensing requirements. Individuals who satisfy specific criteria may receive a "license" to practice that profession. Registrations are distinguishable from licenses. A registration is a regulatory framework with substantially less or no criteria for competency. Registration may simply require an individual to enroll or register with the state in order to provide a regulated service.

---

78. American Society of Civil Engineers, Ethics—Standards of Professional Conduct for Civil Engineers (2000), *available at* http://www.asce.org.

79. *Id.*

80. For example, the Illinois Architecture Act, enacted in 1897, was the first architectural licensing law in the nation.

81. *See, e.g.*, 225 Ill. Comp. Stat. Ann. 340 (2000).

82. State *ex rel.* Lentine v. State Board of Health, 334 Mo. 220, 65 S.W.2d 943 (1933).

Many jurisdictions call the framework for regulating professional engineers' "registration" instead of "licensure."[83]

Typically, a business entity or firm that desires to practice architecture, engineering, or surveying must obtain a license in its own name from the appropriate licensing board. In such jurisdictions, there are two levels of licensing requirements—one at the individual or professional level and the other at firm or business level.[84] The boards' Web sites are an excellent source of licensure laws. Summaries of state licensure laws governing design professionals are also available.[85]

B. Licensing Board Powers

Licensing (or licensure) boards derive their authority from the various state statutes creating them and empowering them to act.[86] Fifty-five jurisdictions govern design professionals in the United States.[87] Every jurisdiction has a licensing board to administer laws and to regulate design professionals.[88] The licensure boards are executive branch entities and have investigative, disciplinary, and operational responsibilities as required by or authorized by the statute.[89] As a part of a regulatory scheme, boards have enforcement and disciplinary power. The board uses the former against non-licensees and the latter against licensee violators.

The licensure laws, and thus the power of the boards, vary from one jurisdiction to the other. Some boards serve purely disciplinary and licensing functions, while others provide intervention and mechanisms for rehabilitation or correction of professionals rather than mere punishment. Licensure boards regulate professional engineers (PEs), PEs and land surveyors, or multiple

---

83. National Soc'y of Prof'l Eng'rs, Engineering Licensing Laws (2004) (the terms "license" and "certificate of registration" are used interchangeably).

84. *Id.*

85. State-by-State Guide to Architects, Engineers, and Contractor Licensing (Stephan G. Walker 2012).

86. 5 Bruner & O'Connor Construction Law § 16:25 (2002).

87. *Id.* The 55 jurisdictions include the 50 states, the District of Columbia, Guam, North Mariana Islands, Puerto Rico, and Virgin Islands.

88. The addresses and phone numbers of the licensing boards are published at many Web sites. For example, visit the NSPE and AIA Web sites.

89. 5 Bruner & O'Connor Construction Law § 16:25 (2002).

professions; however, the joint boards are predominant.[90] The licensing system may divide the engineering profession into different categories for effective administration. For example, California licenses and regulates fifteen categories of engineers.[91]

Typically, a board makes decisions on policy, operational, investigative, and disciplinary issues at public meetings, subject to applicable state administrative and procedural laws. Additionally, a board may guide the building code officials on the building design requirements of the licensure act. Some boards have the authority to waive licensure requirements for case-specific purposes, while others play a role in reinforcing state laws governing the procurement of regulated services.[92]

In the interest of achieving uniformity in the licensure laws among all jurisdictions, the National Council of Examiners for Engineering and Surveying (NCEES) was formed. It is the umbrella organization of state and territorial engineering licensure authorities, and promulgates "Model Laws" and "Model Rules" as guides for engineering licensure boards and legislatures.[93] The NSPE endorses enactment of uniform licensure laws in all jurisdictions; however, it is unlikely that will ever occur. The National Council of Architectural Boards (NCARB), similar to NCEES, is the umbrella organization of architectural boards.[94]

To deal with the maze of state licensure laws, a compliance checklist can serve as a good starting point for evaluating licensure law issues.[95]

C. Enforcement Powers

State laws authorize their attorneys general to seek punishment of unlicensed individuals when they violate the law by engaging in the practice of engineering or architecture without a license. Normally, actionable conduct includes the unauthorized use of words such as "engineer," "engineering," "architect," or derivations thereof (except as authorized by the act); using the seal

---

90. *Id.* According to the NSPE analysis, there are 41 joint boards and 13 PE-only boards.

91. Board for Professional Engineers and Land Surveyors, 17-WTR CAL. REG. REP. 154 (Winter 2001).

92. NSPE, *supra* note 83.

93. http://www.ncees.org.

94. http://www.ncarb.org.

95. Paul W. Berning & John W. Rails, *Complying with Licensing and Registration Laws: A Compliance Checklist, available at* http://paulberninglaw.com/tools/contractor-license-checklist.

of another individual; providing false information to the licensing authority; falsely impersonating a licensee; using an expired, suspended, or revoked license; practicing engineering when not qualified; and falsely claiming a licensed status.[96] The engineering and architectural licensure laws generally consider these violations to be criminal offenses for which the state attorney general is responsible for prosecuting, and individuals found guilty are subject to criminal penalties, such as fines or prison terms.[97] Some states empower the licensure boards to issue letters of warning and to levy fines, including the costs of investigation, on unlicensed violators.[98]

Nearly all jurisdictions have empowered their respective licensing boards to subpoena witnesses and to require licensees and others to submit documents in connection with an investigation of an alleged violation.[99] The licensing boards petition the courts to enforce compliance with subpoenas and for injunctions against violators to compel them to cease the illegal practice.

Some boards are empowered to include the professional rules of conduct in their rules.[100] Licensure boards generally publish their decisions in their newsletters to licensees and on their Web sites. A published decision usually identifies the violator and briefly describes the complaint and the board's decision.[101]

D. Investigative and Disciplinary Powers

Because design professionals operate under the jurisdiction of state licensure laws, they are subject to discipline for violation of these laws. Discipline is not necessarily concerned with harm to the client, but with professional conduct and ethics in dealing with client.[102] Licensing boards open investigations for violations of licensure rules based on complaints filed with the board, personal knowledge of the board members or both. In many jurisdictions, a design professional has an ethical and/or legal obligation to report violations of rules to the board, including claims resolved through settlement or trial.[103]

---

96. 5 Bruner & O'Connor Construction Law § 16:25.

97. *Id.*

98. *Id.*

99. *Id.*

100. *Id. See also supra* note 5.

101. *See, e.g.*, California Board's Web site for enforcement actions against licensed architects *at* https://www.cab.ca.gov/consumers/enforcement_actions/.

102. *Lipton*, 313 N.W.2d at 596.

103. *See, e.g.*, Colo. Rev. Stat. § 12-25-108(1)(h) (2006).

A licensing board's statutory ability to investigate and prosecute violations of the rules varies considerably from one jurisdiction to another. For example, in some jurisdictions, boards can directly regulate violations, while in others the boards must act through the state attorney general's office. The NSPE has published an analysis of the engineering licensure laws in the fifty-five jurisdictions comprising the United States.[104] That analysis reveals that the grounds for disciplinary action include engaging in behavior or conduct deemed dishonorable, unethical, or unprofessional such as negligence, gross negligence,[105] incompetence, misconduct, conviction, or pleas of no contest to any felony crimes, practice-related misdemeanor crime, action taken by another jurisdiction that led to disciplinary action there,[106] failure to provide information requested by the licensing authority, making false statements, attempting to mislead,[107] aiding others in violating the licensure laws, violating terms of probation or suspension, sealing or signing documents not prepared by the licensee or under the licensee's direct supervision, providing false testimony to the board, conviction of a drug offense, habitual intoxication or addiction to drugs or alcohol, failure to pay child support, delinquent student loans or taxes, and failure to comply with licensure laws.[108]

---

104. 5 Bruner & O'Connor Construction Law § 16:25 (2002).

105. The Missouri Supreme Court has stated that plaintiff gains nothing by branding negligence "gross" and has consistently refused to recognize differing categories of negligence. Boyer v. Tilzer, 831 S.W.2d 695 (Mo. Ct. App. 1992). However, the term "gross negligence" in a statute authorizing disciplinary action against architects and professional engineers did not render the statute unconstitutional because of vagueness. Duncan v. Missouri Bd. for Prof'l Eng'rs, Architects and Land Surveyors, 744 S.W.2d 524, 533 (Mo. Ct. App. 1988) (noting that the term "gross negligence" has been defined in various manners in different states and the court defined it as an act or course of conduct that demonstrates conscious indifference to a professional duty).

106. 5 Bruner & O'Connor Construction Law § 16:25 (2002) (37 jurisdictions consider a disciplinary action taken by one jurisdiction as a cause for disciplinary action in another).

107. Sheils v. Florida Eng'rs Mgmt. Corp., 886 So. 2d 426 (Fla. Dist. Ct. App. 2004) (under Florida Administrative Code, a mere attempt to mislead the client, employer, or public constitutes misconduct in engineering, and success in misleading was not a required finding of professional misconduct against a professional engineer).

108. 5 Bruner & O'Connor Construction Law § 16:25 (2002).

E. Revocation and Suspension of Licenses

If the state law authorizes a board to grant a professional license, it may also empower it to revoke or suspend a license for cause.[109] Boards have disciplined design professionals primarily under the rubric of gross negligence, incompetence, and misconduct for such activities as:

1. relying upon the judgment of untrained individuals;
2. certifying work as completed and knowing that it was not;
3. performing welding operations without being properly certified;
4. preparing misleading plans;
5. permitting the licensee's seal to be affixed to plans neither prepared by the licensee nor under the licensee's revising control;
6. appropriating another's plans, removing that professional's seal, replacing the seal with one's own and then submitting the plans as one's own;
7. representing land surveys as one's own without performing an actual survey; and
8. offering a bribe to certain public officials in order to obtain a contract.[110]

Generally, the misconduct must relate to the profession to justify a disciplinary action, unless the conduct calls into question the professional's integrity.[111]

F. Disciplinary Reciprocity

Thirty-seven of fifty-five jurisdictions in the United States consider a disciplinary action taken by one jurisdiction as grounds for disciplinary action in another state.[112] For example, after the Hyatt walkway collapse, all twenty-eight states involved revoked Jack Gillum's PE license.[113]

Another issue is whether the law authorizes a licensure board to discipline a licensee for misconduct that occurred before the board granted a license to the accused. The California Supreme Court considered this issue in

109. 5 Am. Jur. 2d. *Architects* § 6 (2006).

110. 5 Bruner & O'Connor Construction Law § 16:25 (2002).

111. *Id.*

112. *Id.*

113. https://en.wikibooks.org/wiki/Professionalism/Jack_Gillum_and_the_Hyatt_Regency_Skywalks; https://en.wikipedia.org/wiki/Hyatt_Regency_walkway_collapse.

Hughes v. Board of Architectural Examiners.[114] There, the California Board of Architectural Examiners revoked Hughes's architectural license, accusing him of wrongful conduct that took place outside California and before he obtained a California license.[115] The Superior Court of Sacramento denied Hughes's petition for a writ of administrative mandamus seeking to overturn the board's decision, and the court of appeals reversed the lower court's decision.[116] The California Supreme Court reversed, holding that the California Architect's Practice Act did not limit discipline to post-licensure misconduct and no constitutional violation arises from the consideration of pre-licensure conduct.[117] After remand, the court of appeals upheld the board's decision to revoke Hughes's license, and reasoned that as a preventive response the board could revoke his license based upon pre-licensure professional dishonesty and without a showing of actual harm to a California client.[118]

G. Judicial Review

It is well-accepted that the right of an individual to engage in any of the common occupations of life is among the fundamental liberties protected by the due process and equal protection clauses of the Fourteenth Amendment.[119] The courts have also recognized that an individual, having obtained a license to engage in a particular profession or vocation, has a "fundamental vested right" to continue in that activity.[120] A licensee is entitled to greater procedural protections than accorded to an applicant, requiring a licensure board to prove the allegations filed against a licensee by clear and convincing evidence rather than the preponderance of the evidence.[121]

Procedural due process demands a fair trial before a neutral or unbiased decision maker, but it does not require perfect error-free governmental decision making.[122] It also demands an appearance of fairness and absence of the

---

114. 952 P.2d 641 (Cal. 1998).

115. *Id.*

116. *Id.*

117. *Id.* at 763.

118. Hughes v. Board of Architectural Exam'rs, 68 Cal. Ct. App. 4th 685, 80 Cal. Rptr. 2d 317 (Cal. Ct. App. 1998).

119. *Hughes*, 952 P.2d 641, *citing* Schware v. Board of Bar Exam'rs, 353 U.S. 232, 238–39 (1957).

120. *Hughes*, 952 P.2d at 788–89.

121. *Id.* at 789.

122. Bracy v. Gamley, 520 U.S. 890, 904 (1997).

probability of outside influence on the adjudication.[123] To avoid the appearance of unfairness in the licensing board's execution of its roles as police, prosecutor, jury, judge, and executioner, some state legislators have interposed a hearing commission into the process to hold hearings and issue finding of facts and conclusion.[124]

Design professionals have attacked the board's power to revoke or suspend a license on numerous grounds. However, most attempts to avoid disciplinary sanctions on the basis that the board lacked authority to take a particular action have met with little success. Another common challenge is to claim that statutory grant is unconstitutionally vague. However, the courts have upheld statutes containing undefined terms such as "unprofessional and dishonorable conduct," "bad moral character," "misconduct or dishonesty," "gross negligence," and other general terms.[125]

Moreover, the courts have ruled that it is indeed impossible to define or categorize all the acts of impropriety.[126]

Based upon the specificity of charges in the board pleadings filed against that licensee, design professionals may also challenge an action taken by the board. One court held that "simply a statement that the accused has violated one or more of the statutory grounds for discipline without further elaboration, i.e., he has been grossly negligent" is insufficient to allow preparation of a viable defense and therefore does not comply with due process requirement.[127] Specificity is required in pleadings to set the course of conduct deemed to establish statutory ground for proposed disciplinary action.[128] Further, the board cannot find a violation if that charge does not appear in the board's complaint against the accused licensee.[129]

---

123. Utica Packing Co. v. Block, 781 F.2d 71, 77 (6th Cir. 1986).

124. Daniel R. E. Jordan, *Licensing Issues at the Administrative Hearing Commission*, 50 J. Mo. B. 23 (1994).

125. Holmes v. Missouri Dental Bd., 703 S.W.2d 11 (Mo. Ct. App. 1985); Duncan v. Missouri Bd. for Prof'l Eng'rs, Architects and Land Surveyors, 744 S.W.2d 524 (Mo. Ct. App. 1988).

126. Ray v. Dept. of Registration, 419 N.E.2d 413 (Ill. Ct. App. 1981); *Duncan*, 744 S.W.2d at 532.

127. *Duncan*, 744 S.W.2d 524.

128. *Id.* at 539.

129. *Id.*

H. Standard of Review

A professional can challenge the licensing board decision exercising its disciplinary or enforcement power by appealing to a court.[130] After the trial court's independent review of the facts, an appellate court determines whether the trial court's findings are supported by substantial evidence.[131] The appellate court independently may exercise its ability to decide issues of law.[132] The function of a court in reviewing a challenge to a regulation is limited—the challenger of a regulation must establish that the regulation is arbitrary and capricious.[133] The courts presume that a board's decision is valid and the adversarial party has the burden of overcoming that presumption.[134] In *Moheet v. State Board of Registration for the Healing Arts,* a physician appealed the Missouri State Board of Registration for the Healing Arts' decision to publicly reprimand him. The Missouri Supreme Court held that it would affirm the board's decision unless it:

1. is in violation of constitutional provisions;
2. is in excess of the statutory authority or jurisdiction of the agency;
3. is unsupported by competent and substantial evidence;
4. is, for any other reason, unauthorized by law;
5. is made upon unlawful procedure or without a fair trial;
6. is arbitrary, capricious or unreasonable; or
7. involves an abuse of discretion.[135]

IX. Hyatt Regency Sky Walkway Collapse

On July 17, 1981, the second and fourth floor walkways of the Hyatt Regency Hotel in Kansas City collapsed and fell to the floor of the main lobby, killing 114 people and injuring 216. In terms of loss of life and injuries, it was the

---

130. *Id.*

131. Taylor, Thon, Thompson & Peterson v. Cannadays, 749 P.2d 63 (Mt. 1988).

132. Kelly v. Board of Registered Nurses, 2005 WL605459 (Cal. Ct. App. March 16, 2005).

133. General Bldg. Contractors of New York State, Inc. v. New York State Education Department, 670 N.Y.S.2d 697 (Sup. Ct. 1997); *see also* Adams v. North Carolina State Bd. of Registration for Prof'l Eng'rs and Land Surveyors, 501 S.E.2d 660, 663 (N.C. Ct. App. 1998).

134. Moheet v. State Bd. of Registration for the Healing Arts, 154 S.W.3d 393 (Mo. Ct. App. 2005).

135. *Id.* at 397.

most devastating structural collapse ever to take place in this country at that time.[136] The improper design of connections was the cause of collapse.[137] Due to a mammoth failure of communication, no one ever designed the rod hanger connections.[138]

In February 1984, the Missouri Board for Architects, Professional Engineers and Land Surveyors filed its complaint seeking a determination that the engineering certificates of registration of Daniel Duncan and Jack Gillum and the engineering certificate of authority of G.C.E. International were subject to discipline pursuant to Missouri licensing statute.[139] G.C.E. was a Missouri corporation holding a certificate of authority to perform professional engineering services in Missouri and had assumed contractual responsibility for performing all of such engineering services for the Hyatt. Gillum was a licensed PE in Missouri and president of G.C.E. Duncan was a licensed PE in Missouri and an employee of G.C.E. Gillum was the engineer of record for the Hyatt and supervisor of all professional engineering activities of G.C.E. in Missouri. Duncan was the project engineer for the Hyatt in direct charge of the actual structural engineering work on the project, under the direct supervision of Gillum.[140]

Judge Deutsch, Administrative Law Judge for the hearing commission, found Duncan guilty of gross negligence in the preparation and completion of a structural drawing and in failing to review shop drawings for the Hyatt

136. U.S. Department of Commerce, National Bureau of Standards Report on the Investigation of the Kansas City Hyatt Regency Walkways Collapse (Feb. 1982).

137. Engineer Jack Gillum's first words when he saw the wreckage were, "[W]here are the stiffeners?" (G. William Quatman, *The Hyatt Skywalk Revisited: What Happened? Could It Happen Again?* Schinnerer's 42nd Annual Meeting of Invited Attorneys, *available at* https://www.victorinsuranceus.com/Content/Risk_Management/Risk_Management/News_and_Events/Proceedings_-_Public/PastPapers/Quatman-hyatt_pdf.aspx).

138. *Id. see also* Administrative Law Judge Opinion of James B. Deutsch, Nov. 15, 1985, Case No. AR 84-0239; Duncan v. Missouri Bd. for Prof'l Eng'rs, Architects and Land Surveyors, 744 S.W.2d 524 (Mo. Ct. App. 1988). Numerous articles have been written on the causes of collapse. The ASCE devoted its entire May 2000 issue of the Journal of Performance of Constructed Facilities to the articles addressing the Hyatt collapse. Jack Gillum contributed *The Engineer of Record and Design Responsibility*.

139. Administrative Law Judge Opinion of James B. Deutsch, Nov. 15, 1985, Case No. AR 84-0239.

140. *Duncan*, 744 S.W.2d 524.

project.[141] He also found Duncan guilty of misconduct in misrepresenting to the architects the safety of a connection (the double hanger rod-box beam connection), when in fact he had failed to perform engineering tests and calculations. The judge found that Gillum:

- was vicariously liable and responsible for the acts and omissions of Duncan because he had affixed his professional engineering seal on the structural drawings;
- was grossly negligent in failing to himself review or assure that someone had reviewed the connection drawing before affixing his seal thereto;
- had engaged in unprofessional conduct in failing and refusing to take responsibility for the entire engineering project; and
- was guilty of misconduct for his failure to perform a review of the Hyatt atrium design following a specific request by the architect for such review, and for continuing misrepresentations to the owner and architect concerning the atrium design review.

Judge Deutsch recommended that the Missouri Board for Architects, Engineers and Land Surveyors discipline Gillum, Duncan, and G.C.E. (which he found was vicariously responsible for the acts and omissions of Duncan and Gillum).[142] Upon this recommendation, the board revoked all three licenses. Gillum and Duncan petitioned the trial court challenging the board's decision, but that court affirmed the outcome. Duncan and Gillum appealed that decision to the Missouri appellate court.[143] The appellants challenged, in part, the validity of the engineering statute based on the definition of gross negligence and the fact that engineers customarily rely upon fabricators to design certain structural steel connections.[144] Affirming the revocation, the court held that the engineer was responsible for the design, reasoning that custom, practice, or "bottom line" necessity cannot alter that responsibility.[145]

The court held the statutory definition of gross negligence was not sufficiently vague to present a substantial constitutional challenge and affirmed the commission's definition of gross negligence as "an act or course of conduct which demonstrates a conscious indifference to a professional duty."[146] The

---

141. *Id.*

142. *Id.*

143. *Id.*

144. *Id.* at 536.

145. *Id*

146. *Id.* at 541.

court also noted that the structural engineer's duty was to determine whether the structural plans it designed and approved provided structural safety in order to prevent a strong probability of harm. The court said that indifference to the duty is indifference to the harm.[147] Reasoning that the purpose of disciplinary action against licensed professionals is the protection of the public, not the infliction of punishment, the court affirmed the revocation of all three licenses.[148] When the appellate court delivered its decision in 1988, the victims and their families had settled their lawsuits arising from the collapse, so the court's decision did not affect them.[149]

Although Gillum denied responsibility during the disciplinary hearing and appeal, he made three operational changes in G.C.E.:

1. A P.E. should prepare all steel shop drawings provided by fabricators; the fabricator's P.E. must seal the shop drawings before the engineer of record will approve them;
2. All project engineers within G.C.E. should personally seal and sign and take responsibility for all aspects of the project performed under their direction; and
3. All engineers, technicians, and draftsmen should follow the quality control/quality analysis manual.[150]

Gillum's first operational change aimed to shift design responsibility during the shop drawing phase from the design professional to the steel fabricator and erector did not meet full acceptance by the American Institute of Steel Construction (AISC). The AISC codified:

> 4.2. . . . When the Owner's Designated Representative for Design provides the design, design drawings, and specifications, the Fabricator and Erector are not responsible for the suitability, adequacy, or building code conformance of the design. . . .
> 1.5.1. When the Fabricator submits a request to change Connection details that are described in the Contract Documents, the Fabricator shall notify the Owner's Designated Representatives for Design and

147. *Id.*

148. *Id.*

149. Mathew A. Victor, *The Hyatt Collapse—A Post Mortem*, CONSTR. LAW. (NOV. 1990).

150. Jack D. Gillum, *The Engineer of Record and Design Responsibility*, THE AMERICAN SOC'Y OF CIVIL ENG'RS J. OF PERFORMANCE OF CONSTRUCTED FACILITIES (May 2000), at 67–70.

> Construction *in writing in advance* of the submission of the Shop and Erection Drawings.
> The Owner's Designated Representative for Design shall review and approve or reject the request in a timely manner.[151]

Gillum's second change implied that a design professional sealing and signing the design had a nondelegable responsibility for the project.[152] In general, it presented a narrow view of the design process. Since then, it has been well-accepted that a design professional sealing and signing the design does not hold a monopoly on all design knowledge necessary to complete a successful, modern construction project, and it is often prudent for him or her to rely upon the expertise of experienced contractors or suppliers to design certain components of required work.[153] However, design delegation does not imply design abdication. The licensure statutes permitting design delegation regulate the process by which a licensee may delegate design tasks.[154]

Gillum's third operational change to have staff follow a quality control process has been an excellent risk management tool and a challenge for the design profession.

X. Conclusion

Professional ethics and rules of conduct is an expansive and complex discipline. It provides a basis for considering personal, professional, and communal values with respect to business practices and moral questions. Normally, codes of ethics do not have the force of law, but they can be binding on design professionals when incorporated into the licensure law. The violation of code may

---

151. American Institute of Steel Construction, Code of Standard Practice for Steel Buildings and Bridges, at http://www.aisc.org (emphasis added).

152. Coincidently, *Duncan* reached the same conclusion. *Duncan*, 744 S.W.2d at 535.

153. Nancy A. Potter, *Design Delegation Provisions of AIA Document A201—1997 Edition*, 18-Jul Construction Law 27.

154. *See, e.g.*, N.Y. Comp. Codes R. & Regs. tit. 8, § 29.3(b)(2)(vi), requiring that delegator determine in writing that the design prepared by delegatee conforms to the overall project design and can be integrated into it. *See* The Design/Build Process (ABA 1997) for licensing and procurement requirements. *See also* 5 Bruner & O'Connor Construction Law § 16:25 (2002), for a summary of licensure laws on sealing and signing of design documents and definitions of "responsible charge" of design.

be admissible into evidence in a civil action brought by the client or an injured third party. To further the profession and protect the interests of the client and public safety, it is incumbent upon design professionals to be familiar with and abide by the rules of conduct adopted by applicable professional organizations and those embodied in the state's regulatory scheme.

XI. Appendices

A. Professional Organizations

Profession	Organization
Agricultural engineer	American Society of Agricultural & Biological Engineers
Architect	American Institute of Architects
Building designer	American Institute of Building Design
Certified public accountant	American Institute of Certified Public Accountants
Chemical engineer	American Institute of Chemical Engineers
Civil engineer	American Society of Civil Engineers
Computer engineer	Association of Computing Machinery
Consulting engineer	American Consulting Engineers Council
Cost engineer	Association for the Advancement of Cost Engineers
Electrical engineer	American Institute of Electrical Engineers

Profession	**Organization**
Engineering and technology	Accreditation Board of Engineering and Technology
Environmental engineer	American Academy of Environmental Engineers
Fire protection engineer	American Society of Fire Protection Engineers

CHAPTER 3

Design Professional Contract Responsibilities—Pre-Design, Design, and Pre-Construction Phases

THEODORE D. LEVIN, MEHRDAD FARIVAR*

I. Introduction

This chapter is the first of several dealing with contractual and legal issues affecting design professionals. It focuses on the design professional's involvement with the process up to the time of actual construction and covers a broad range of topics, as the pre-design, design, and pre-construction phases of a project involve an array of activities and obligations. The authors provide a general overview of the key issues and concerns in this chapter to provide the groundwork for understanding the import and impact of key contract clauses and allow further investigation and consideration by the design professional and his or her counsel. The specific provisions of the design professional's contract are treated in greater depth in other chapters.

The contract is the lifeblood of any construction project. The parties in most commercial transactions rely on written contracts to document and validate their intentions and rights, but in the typically fragmented design and construction process, there are a multitude of contracts governing complex relationships among several tiers of parties. Typically the contract between the owner and the

*The authors wish to thank Christopher J. Menjou for his assistance in the preparation of this chapter.

prime design professional is the first in the sequence of many such contracts, although recently other models of project delivery have emerged wherein the owner contracts with someone other than a design professional, such as a project manager, design-builder, or construction manager, who will then retain the prime design professional either directly or as an agent of the owner.

Still, the contract between the owner and the prime design professional—usually the architect—remains, predominantly, the first step in the design and construction process. The owner-architect contract is uniquely challenging as it aims at the creation of a precise design for a large and complex object that is only an idea in the mind of the owner and perhaps a vision in the mind of the architect. Inevitably, in the course of the design, the owner's idea and the architect's vision evolve and sometimes change fundamentally. The challenge of an effective owner-architect agreement, or an agreement between the owner and a prime design professional other than an architect, is to permit, not stifle, the evolution of the idea/vision of the project and yet remain within a framework that is consistent with the expectation of the parties and protective of their respective legal and business interests. Such a framework requires the recognition and acceptance of the key project parameters and variables and a fair and equitable allocation of risk between the parties, commensurate with their roles and interests.

Library References

C.J.S. *Contracts* §§ 2–3, 9, 12.
West's Key No. Digests, Contracts <KEY>1.

II. Conceptual/Pre-Design Phase: Contractual and Extra-Contractual Roles of the Design Professional

The conceptual and "pre-design" phase of a design-bid-build project[1] typically starts when the owner forms the initial idea or intent to build. Depending on the

---

1. A design-bid-build project is considered the traditional form of "project delivery system" and is characterized by defined participants, roles, budget, and most importantly, design. Project delivery systems are methods by which construction projects are designed, financed, and built; organizing participants; marshalling resources; and giving direction for management. As the name suggests, under design-bid-build, once the design has gone through distinct stages of development, a complete set of bid documents (the "bid set" of plans and specifications) then is released for competitive bidding and a construction contract is awarded. Phillip G. Bernstein, FAIA, Chapter 10, *Delivery Methods and Compensation*,§ 10.1, *Project Delivery Options*, *in*

project, the owner may know "what" he or she intends to build, but not necessarily the scope or scale of the project or the complexities involved, including the process of design and construction, the project budget and schedule, and the owner's responsibilities. Even if the owner is experienced and has previously been through the process, the reality of modern construction projects (particularly in metropolitan areas) is that each project different and presents its own unique set of challenges. Within this framework, there are contractual responsibilities, as well as roles of the design professional that fall outside those that might be expressed in contract (i.e., extra-contractual obligations).

A. The Process and the Product Unique Aspects of the Design and Construction Process

Although construction is conceptually similar to fabrication or manufacturing in the sense that a building or a construction project is ultimately a physical object, the process of design and construction remains fundamentally different from the manufacturing process because construction remains a highly fragmented mixture of manufacturing and craft.[2]

THE ARCHITECT'S HANDBOOK OF PROFESSIONAL PRACTICE, AMERICAN INSTITUTE OF ARCHITECTS (Joseph A. Demkin, AIA, ed., 13th ed., John Wiley & Sons, Inc. 2001). The publication may be considered the official handbook of the American Institute of Architects (AIA) for architects and other persons interested in the construction industry. Section 10.1, in part, quotes from Gordon H. Chong, FAIA, Editorial Task Group, HANDBOOK ON PROJECT DELIVERY, AMERICAN INSTITUTE OF ARCHITECTS (California Council 1996).

2. In fact, since the first edition of this book was published, significant trends have emerged, led by procurement-driven methodologies of large private and public institutional owners to integrate and streamline the design and construction processes toward greater collaboration aimed at increasing speed and efficiency and reducing claims and friction. Such efforts have manifested themselves in the increasing use of "Lean" project delivery method, "Integrated Project Delivery" or IPD, and various advanced forms of design-build, extending the application of that delivery method to nearly every type of project. The Lean project delivery method is closely modeled after advanced manufacturing processes—in particular the "Toyota" quality control model. In parallel, the use of multi-prime, fast track, CM at risk, CM as agent, and lately "supply chain" approaches to project delivery has been growing. These trends are slowly but steadily changing the landscape of project delivery methods. Yet, the traditional design-bid-build method of project delivery remains widely in use, particularly with ordinary residential and commercial projects not involving sophisticated institutional owners.

After formulation of the initial concept, a manufacturer first develops a prototype, extensively tests it in an experimental mode, and then modifies and refines it. The manufacturer then streamlines the production sequence and mass produces the item in a controlled factory environment. The finished product can be sold and transported anywhere. In the design-bid-build method of project delivery, each project is unique. It is the prototype *and* the end product. The opportunity for experimentation is limited or nonexistent. Each project is "manufactured" one at a time, on location. This distinction is not just factual. It also has legal significance that has been recognized and given particular treatment by legislatures throughout the United States in determining the underlying liabilities of design professionals and builders of new "for sale" housing.[3] Courts have also recognized a narrow segment of the construction industry (tract homes or other mass-produced housing units) as "manufactured products" as concerns liability analysis.

Outside this narrow segment, in most cases in the design-bid-build method of project delivery, the design process is where "conceptual" prototype(s) must be developed, tested, debugged, and streamlined (on paper) by design professionals for "manufacturing" on location. Once construction (manufacturing) begins, the result cannot be discarded, as it can be in a factory. It must be finished and "delivered" for use and occupancy. Also, the physical construction does not occur in a controlled setting. Hence, there is a much greater reliance on the building plans as a means of controlling in detail what is built. Therefor the consequences of faulty design can be drastic for the owner, the contractor, and of course, the design professional.

The design professional is typically the first in the line of many professionals, consultants, and contractors retained by the owner. The design professional participates in giving vision to and the realization of the owner's idea or intent through the design process and customarily in the "delivery" of the completed project to the owner and/or users. Therefore, the design professional has the opportunity to win the owner's trust and confidence at the inception of the project and become his advisor for the duration of the project. In the design-bid-build method of project delivery, the design professional's unique role as owner's advisor is at times assumed by the contractor at the start of construction because once construction begins, the contractor has more opportunities for interacting with the owner as compared to the architect or other design professional—out of sight, out of mind. Construction managers, who

---

3. *See, e.g.*, CAL. CIV. CODE § 900.

are a relatively new breed, may also assume this initial role, particularly with certain public and institutional clients, or with projects involving multiple bid packages. See Chapters 10 and 11.

I. *The Design Professional as Advisor: Assumption of Fiduciary Duties*

When an owner approaches a design professional at the conceptual stage of a project, the design professional must be mindful of knowingly or unknowingly assuming the position of "advisor" to the owner, rather than the more arm's-length technical and professional role of a design professional. This consideration must be carefully weighed by the design professional, based on the circumstances surrounding the project and the design professional's willingness and ability to assume the role of the owner's "trusted advisor." If the design professional finds him or herself being relied upon by the owner for general guidance and advice, the design professional and the owner should enter into a written contract setting forth the nature and scope of this initial relationship, so that there is no confusion as to the role of the design professional. Absent the contractual articulation of his or her role, the design professional may unknowingly place him or herself in the position of the owner's fiduciary and agent, which implies broader duties and obligations than the design professional may be willing to assume.[4]

Typically, at this stage of the project, the design professional is either operating under an oral "hourly" contract or is providing services gratuitously without a contract in anticipation of a formal written contract, pending greater definition of the scope of the project.

---

4. *E.g.*, B. Gurney, D. Curtis, and R. Murphy, *Fiduciary Duty Claims Against Construction and Design Professionals*, New York Law Journal (ALM 2014) (discussing the case of *City of Victorville v. Carter & Burgess/Jacob's Engineering*, wherein a jury awarded $52 million in damages to the City of Victorville, California, based in part on alleged breach of fiduciary duties in providing project financial projections by the designer of a cogeneration power plant).

Practice Tip

It is advisable that the design professional operate under a written contract with the owner even when acting in an initial advisory capacity. The hourly contract is suitable for this purpose due to its inherent flexibility. The advantage of operating under a written contract at this stage is to apply specific terms and disclaimers to the relationship that may otherwise not be clear, such as not assuming the role of the owner's agent or fiduciary (with it being advisable that these specific terms and disclaimers as to any fiduciary duty of the design professional being carried through to the design contract with the owner). The purpose of these terms would be to diminish and control risks assumed by the design professional, and to prevent unfulfilled expectations on both sides. This chapter will discuss some of these terms.

The design professional who assumes the role of owner's trusted advisor must act in a prudent manner. He should have the ability to educate the owner as to the complexities of the design and construction process, without making this complex process seem too overwhelming, and must also have the knowledge, time, and resources to research particular issues presented by the project or the owner and recommend appropriate courses of action. For example, if the project is contingent on a particular event such as a governmental permit or approval, or a particular function (e.g., a particular type of machinery or process around which a building must be designed), the design professional must devise and recommend a sequence of actions (such as securing entitlements, discussed *infra)* to meet those needs. The danger is that when the design professional serves as an advisor, he may inadvertently assume responsibilities beyond the terms of his contract with the owner.[5]

5. *See* Sweet v. Gribaldo, Jones & Assoc., 40 Cal. App. 3d 573, 567, 115 Cal. Rptr. 99 (1974) (where a soils engineering firm, employed solely in an advisory capacity and paid by the hour with no interest in the property being improved, nor its sale, nevertheless faced allegations of express warranty and strict liability for damages from cracks in the constructed home, resulting from an instability of the improved lot. It was undisputed that the firm was at no time consulted as to final grading or excavation of the finished lot, never had the opportunity to approve the foundations for the house thereon, and never was even shown the plans for the final grading or foundation. The court thus rejected the allegations and held that the engineering firm would be responsible only for its advisory services that were not shown to have breached applicable professional standards or provided with guaranteed results).

2. Understanding the Owner's Initial Concept

The design professional involved in a project during the conceptual stage should be aware that the owner might have difficulty clearly communicating goals and objectives for the project, because the owner may not have formulated many of these details yet. The design professional can assist the owner in formulating and refining key concepts by asking the right questions and focusing the owner's attention in the right direction. Through this process, the missing details should emerge.

a. Project Use

Perhaps the most fundamental aspect of the owner's concept is the intended use of the facility or project. If the design professional has prior experience in designing for that particular use, he would be able to ask the right questions of the owner. On the other hand, if the design professional is unfamiliar with the particular use, he might study the use to become familiar with it, or associate with another design professional with the requisite experience. The design professional will design the project either to meet the specific needs of a known user group or to address a general need in the marketplace. In either case, the "use" drives the project and sets the initial parameter. If the use is complex, and the design professional is inexperienced in the particular use, the design professional may want to consider associating with another design professional experienced in that use. In fact, the use or function of the project determines the discipline of the prime design professional. For example, while an architect is the prime design professional in most instances involving a building for human occupancy, if the project is a power plant or energy center, the prime design professional may appropriately be a mechanical engineer, and for a bridge the prime design professional may be a structural engineer or bridge designer.

b. Size of the Project

The next parameter is the size of the project, which is as significant as the use or function of the project. Even if the design professional is qualified with respect to a use or function, he should also be certain he has the requisite experience and qualifications with respect to the size of the project. Designing a single house is vastly different than designing a sub-division of hundreds of houses, although the use is identical. Similarly, designing a single retail store is very different from designing a large retail center, although the use is the same. It would not be prudent for a design professional to assume the role of the owner's trusted advisor with respect to a project for which the design professional is not qualified. Lack of experience with the type, size and scale of the project may cause the design professional to mislead his client by misquoting a fee for design services, incorrectly estimate the schedule for the performance of the design services, or worse fail to perform properly. In short, the design professional must either be fully competent or qualified to undertake a project or associate with another professional who is. This initial self-appraisal, which must be honest and realistic, is the first and a fundamental step in risk avoidance. Accepting an assignment for which the design professional is not qualified would be reckless, in addition to constituting misrepresentation or possibly gross negligence.

3. *Initial Formation of the Project Team*

The project team usually consists of multiple design professionals and other non-design consultants. For ease of reference, we will refer to these as "design consultants" and "project consultants," respectively.

a. Design Consultants

Design consultants closely integrate their work product with that of the prime design professional. The most frequently retained design professionals at the inception of a project involving a building are the structural, mechanical, and electrical engineer; code and elevator consultants; and as others who work closely with the design professional to prepare design documents, such as a lighting consultant, an acoustical consultant, or a landscape designer or architect. Design consultants are typically retained by the design professional, providing the design professional with an opportunity to select his preferred consultants. In addition, a direct contractual relationship between the design professional and design consultants facilitates design coordination. The design professional can also recommend that the owner retain the design consultants, but most owners are reluctant to get involved in such details and prefer to only contract with the prime design professional.[6]

---

6. It should be noted that the architect is typically at the center of the design team, but other design professionals such as civil engineers have assumed that central role, providing similar services. *See* Ponderosa Ctr. Partners v. McClellan/Cruz/Gaylord & Assocs., 45 Cal.App.4th 913, 91, 53 Cal. Rptr. 2d 64 ("Architectural services and engineering services frequently overlap and may be rendered by a licensed architect or a registered engineer:") *See also* Wynner v. Buxton, 97 Cal. Ct. App. 3d 166, 158 Cal. Rptr. 587 (1979) (equating the functional role of engineers and architects on a construction project in terms of their contractual undertakings).

Practice Tip

If the design professional recommends that the design consultants be retained by the owner, he or she may want to consider pre-qualifying the consultants, providing the owner with more than one name in each discipline, and informing the owner that, because of absence of contractual privity between the design professional and the design consultants, the design professional will not have control or oversight responsibilities for such consultants. However, the design professional would endeavor to coordinate his own work toward the overall design of the project with the work of such consultants.

b. Project Consultants

The owner usually hires other consultants who provide services concerning the project but do not necessarily serve a design role. These include the land surveyor, the geotechnical consultant, environmental consultant, and the land use consultant or attorney. Such consultants do not have a direct role in the design of the structures for the project, and thus are not required to closely coordinate and integrate their work product with that of the design professional.

Ordinarily, the design professional may rely on the accuracy and completeness of the information provided by or through owner's consultants. For example, a design professional would not generally be responsible for losses arising from an erroneous survey prepared by the land surveyor under contract with the owner. When the design professional is in contractual privity with a consultant, he may assume vicarious liability for the errors and omissions of these consultants. (See Section III, A, *infra.)*

Practice Tip

The provision of initial information about the project site is ordinarily the owner's responsibility. This is because the owner may have superior knowledge as to the history of the project site and its prior uses (such as possible contamination). Therefore, as a matter of risk management, it is not prudent for the design professional to take on the responsibility of hiring and coordinating consultants whose responsibility it is to provide information about the site, such as the land surveyor, geotechnical engineer, and/or environmental consultant. The design professional's written contract should confirm this division of responsibility.

4. *Issues and Obligations in Dealing with Governmental Agencies/Approvals*

Prior to the issuance of a building permit, projects may be subject to other governmental permits and approvals at various stages of their planning and design ("Land Use Entitlements" or "Entitlements"). Projects may also be subject to "private" as opposed to public restrictions or approvals, such as easements, covenants, or covenants, conditions, and restrictions (CC&Rs). "Plan check" and inspections are typically required in connection with, respectively, the issuance of the building permit and its enforcement at various stages of construction, to verify compliance with the building codes and health and safety codes. Therefore, entitlements regulate "what" is built, and health and safety and building codes regulate functional and quality standards.

a. Entitlements

Entitlements regulate and secure the owner's right to develop or improve real property as to size and permitted use(s) of the improvements, traffic and environmental impacts, and sometimes aesthetic or architectural controls. In urban areas, entitlements involve obtaining multiple approvals from governmental agencies and political bodies, many of which are discretionary and subject to public comment and public hearings. These range from the ever-proliferating federal environmental statutes, such as the National Environmental Policy Act of 1969 (NEPA)[7] and the Clean Air Act of 1970,[8] and various state regulatory controls and procedures, such as Environmental Impact Reports under the California Environmental Quality Act of 1970[9] to local regulatory reviews and land use controls.[10] The latter includes zoning and land use permits, conditional use permits, planning approvals and permits, subdivision map approvals, traffic approvals, and planning commission and architectural review approvals.

Due to the political environment in most urban jurisdictions, particularly in coastal areas, metropolitan areas, and historic cities and communities, the entitlement process is fraught with risk and uncertainty. Complex urban projects can take years. In fact, in some projects the entitlement phase is far longer and perhaps riskier than the detailed design and construction phases that follow.

---

7. 42 U.S.C. § 4321 (1970).

8. 42 U.S.C. § 7401 (1990).

9. Cal. Pub. Res. Code § 21000 (1979).

10. For an analytical review of state and federal land use laws, *see* Peter W. Salsich, Jr. and Timothy J. Tryniecki, Land Use Regulation: A Legal Analysis & Practical Application (American Bar Association, Section of Real Property, Probate and Trust Law 1998).

b. Building Permits and Approvals/Inspections

Governmental agencies exercise comparatively less discretion in reviewing plans for issuance of a building permit. Here, the law (often the model building code that has been adopted in whole or in part by the local governing body for application in its jurisdiction) is more prescriptive and is not dependent on the political judgment of elected officials.

c. Private Restrictions

Separate and apart from entitlements, building permits and approvals are private encumbrances on the use and improvement of real property such as easements and CC&Rs that are not enforced by governmental agencies and yet can be crucial in permitting a project to proceed. These private restrictions are imposed and enforced through deed restrictions and similar mechanisms as contractual obligations. In many instances owners of projects may be unaware of the existence of such private restrictions and, if confronted with them after the start of construction of their projects, may seek recourse from their design professionals for designing improvements that are in violation of such restrictions.

5. *Implied Obligations of the Design Professional in the Conceptual/Pre-Design Phase: Dealing with Governmental Agencies and Approvals and Private Restrictions on the Improvement and Use of Real Property*

The design professional should be familiar with the model codes and laws governing his or her discipline. Typically, issues relating to compliance with locally adopted model codes and the issuance of building permits and approvals do not arise during the conceptual phase of the project. In some states, failure to comply with a building code or standard is deemed "negligence per se" and, depending on the jurisdiction and the project, represents either conclusive proof of negligence or enough evidence of negligence to justify submitting the question to the jury.[11] In either application, the question is

---

11. Justin Sweet & Marc M. Schneier, Legal Aspects of Architecture, Engineering and the Construction Process 59–60 (7th ed. 2004), generally applying the tort concept of *negligence per se* when based on violation of code to the construction industry. Section 14.03 of this treatise provides multiple illustrations taken from judicial opinions of types of claims that have been made against design professionals during the design phase, including *inter alia*, specifying material that did not comply with building codes; positioning a building in violation of setback requirements; failing to know local building codes and safety laws; and, during the construction phase, allowing material not approved by code to be installed and failing to make changes needed to comply with codes (citations omitted). *Id.* at 232–34.

whether the legislature intended to protect the person injured and prevent the type of harm that occurred.[12]

During the entitlement phase, the design professional should work closely with the expediter or land use lawyer in securing discretionary permits. When a subdivision of land is involved, the law in some states, such as California, requires that other design professionals such as civil engineers review and verify the adequacy of the infrastructure for a proposed project.[13]

During the pre-design phase, the architect's role is to guide the owner to assemble the proper team to test the overall feasibility of the project. If a design professional practices extensively in a certain jurisdiction, he may become a "local" expert in the entitlement process. In that situation, the design professional takes on the role of the entitlement consultant or land use advisor. The design professional must properly allocate and control the risks and rewards associated with the assumption of this role, although it is generally the owner's responsibility to notify the design professional of the existence of a private restriction or encumbrance on the use or improvement of the owner's property. Also, the design professional must be careful not to give legal advice, and should recommend that a lawyer represent the client during public hearings as procedural missteps could result in the loss to the owner of valuable entitlement or appeal rights.

Practice Tip

It is not prudent for a design professional to advise an owner during the entitlement phase of the project without a written contract delineating the role of the design professional in relationship to other project participants, including limitations and disclaimers applicable to the design professional's services. Counsel for the design professional should carefully negotiate these services and draft the professional services agreement so that a court can enforce these limitations and disclaimers. Given that in most jurisdictions' entitlements "run with the land," design professional's counsel must pay close attention to the assignment clause and the intellectual property clause in the design professional's contract to address the scenario of the owner selling the "entitled" land, thereby assigning the design professional's work

---

12. *Id.* at 59–60; *see also* Alber v. Owens, 66 Cal. 2d 790, 59 Cal. Rptr. 117 (1967) (safety regulations imposed on a prime contractor were for the benefit of a subcontractor).

13. *See generally* The Subdivision Map Act, CAL. GOVT CODE § 66410 (1975).

product to a subsequent owner, without the design professional's knowledge. If the project is subject to private restrictions on the use or improvement of land, the design professional's agreement with the owner should address the issue and allocate responsibility to the appropriate party for compliance with such private restrictions or obtaining the required approvals.

B. Potential Liabilities of the Design Professional in the Pre-Design Phase

There are competing needs in the pre-design relationship between the design professional and the owner. The owner needs to gather information and evaluate the project, the design professional, the design process, costs, time involved, and the overall feasibility of the project. From the design professional's point of view, the pre-design phase involves the need to evaluate the project and the client and, if the result of this evaluation is favorable, secure a professional services contract that may include services beyond design, such as contract administration which is performed during construction of the project (discussed in Chapter 4).

1. Liability Arising from Initial Proposals

During the initial contact with the design professional, the owner will likely ask for a multitude of information and rough cost estimates. The design professional can only answer such questions based on prior experience with similar projects. The opinions of the design professional in the early stages of the project may later prove erroneous due to an aspect of the project that he may not have known at the time. Equally, certain project parameters may change in the course of the design and construction of the project, which may render early opinions of the design professional inapplicable.

Usually, the parties at this early stage are rather optimistic in their assumptions concerning the project but for different reasons. The design professional may be trying to impress the owner with his capabilities, while being careful not to intimidate or overwhelm the owner with his initial conceptualizations for the project.

The owner, on the other hand, may be overly optimistic in hearing the design concepts from the design professional. Ultimately, the owner may be disappointed with the project because the design professional failed to achieve certain results due to a change in the key parameters of the project. The owner will typically focus on the unattained result and will ignore the change in the project parameters.

On some projects, if the owner becomes disappointed with the project or the design professional, he or she may assert a claim against the design professional based on what was an avoidable miscommunication. A common practice among design professionals is to attach to their written contract the initial proposal that was presented to the client. Sometimes the owner or the owner's attorney wants to incorporate the proposal into the contract by attaching it to the contract as an exhibit. However, this could create internal inconsistencies in the contract, particularly if there is a large time lag between the initial proposal and the contract. Certain project parameters may have changed since the preparation of the proposal, and that may create inconsistencies between the contract and the attached proposal.

Practice Tip

It is generally inadvisable to attach to the final written design contract the initial proposal or similar document, prepared at the inception of the parties' relationship, as the project parameters may have changed in the intervening period. In addition, the tone of the proposal as a sales tool may be inappropriate as contract language.

---

2. *Setting the Project Parameters*

a. Generally

Before a contract can be negotiated and finalized between an owner and a design professional, the parties must agree on certain project parameters that form the basis of the contract, including the design professional's compensation. These parameters include, but may not limited to, project scope, size, the owner's budget, and schedule for the project.

Therefore, project parameters must be ascertained as carefully as possible by the design professional in the exercise of all due diligence and confirmed by the owner. Although the owner has an obligation to accurately represent the project parameters to the design professional, this is not necessarily a linear process. For the sake of the owner, the design professional, and the integrity of the project, the design professional may have to take the lead in ascertaining and articulating the project parameters by conducting some preliminary investigation and asking the right questions of the owner. Although the owner may not necessarily know what information the design professional may need, in order to formulate the essential contract terms, the design professional should be familiar with possible areas for foundational information.

Ultimately, it is not the finality of the project parameters that is critical to the negotiation and finalization of a successful contract between the owner and the design professional. Instead, the clarity and ability of the contract to deal with the uncertain, dynamic nature of such parameters, and their effect on the nature and progress of the design, determine the quality of the contract.[14] One should expect, and provide in the contract, that the project parameters will continue to change after the parties sign the contract.[15] The important issues are: (1) reaching a consensus of the parties as to what potential project parameters exist at the time they enter into the contract; and (2) identifying which parameters they will address and incorporate into the contract. Equally important is the recognition by the owner that changes in project parameters can lead to changes in the essential terms of the contract, such as the design professional's compensation and the project schedule.

b. The Initial Program

The initial program is the "script" for the project and the first indication of its scope. Design professionals approach the program in different ways based upon the type of project. For example, with single-family dwellings, the design professional is more likely to incorporate the initial program into a conceptual plan or layout, rather than reducing it to writing. However, with hospitals, courts, and criminal justice facilities, and other complex projects some design professionals primarily devote their careers to preparation of the program.

The challenge for the design professional is rather unique. It is to document changes in the program and the project clearly and over time, and have a mechanism in his contract with the owner to adjust the design professional's compensation and schedule of performance because of these program changes. Not every change in the program warrants a change in the compensation and schedule of performance of the design professional. Only those changes that impact the design professional's scope of work are significant. However, recognizing which changes are significant is easier said than done because changes in the program and the project often occur incrementally. These incremental changes may not appear to be significant to the owner or to the design

---

14. American Institute of Architects, Document B141-1997, Article 1.2, Responsibilities of the Parties, § 1.2.3 at 1 1.2.3.2 (recognizing the need for and providing for flexibility in the project schedule).

15. *Id.* at Article 1.3, Terms and Conditions, § 1.3.3 at ¶¶ 1.3.3.1 and 1.3.3.2 (recognizing the possible impact of and making provision for changes in project parameters, and their effect on the services of the architect).

professional. However, taken as a whole and over a significant period of time, these incremental changes can be significant.

The term "scope creep" that has entered the design professional's vocabulary refers to this type of slow incremental change that over time can significantly erode the design professional's fee to the point that the design professional may have to work without compensation to complete his contractual obligations. In addition, scope creep can also lead to liabilities and legal exposure to the design professional, typically from unexpected consequences of the change in scope.

Working with the owner, the design professional must document the project program and attempt to identify all major contingencies that can affect the scope of the project. Ultimately, the parties to a design agreement must agree to a "snap-shot" of the scope of the project at the time they sign the contract. In addition, the parties must understand that changes in project parameters, such as the program, may impact the project scope and possibly alter the design professional's fee and schedule of performance. The parties must clearly express this understanding in the contract.

It is the responsibility of the design professional to timely notify the owner of the need for an adjustment to the design professional's fee and schedule of performance as a result of a change in the project parameters or the scope of the project. If this is done timely by seeking an authorization to perform "Additional Services," the design professional has a much better chance of obtaining an equitable adjustment to his fee, as compared to raising the issue for the first time after the Additional Services at issue have already been performed without notice to the owner. Unlike construction contracts, there is rarely a mechanism for a "claim" by the design professional against the owner arising from unforeseen changes in the design professional's scope of services. Most design professional agreements require advanced written authorization by the owner as a prerequisite for any fee increase beyond the contractual limit. Absence of such advance written authorization is a fundamental barrier against seeking an equitable adjustment in the fee to account for changes in scope.

3. *Initial Budget Estimates*

Many lawsuits and claims against a design professional arise from the owner's unmet expectation that the project would be completed within a specific budget or unit cost established at the onset of the project. There are a couple of possible scenarios.

Scenario 1: The owner asks the design professional for a preliminary unit cost or budget at the inception of the project. The design professional (sometimes against his better judgment) yields to the pressure and supplies a number based on unverified assumptions, and usually a past project. Subsequently, the owner claims that he proceeded with the project in reliance upon the erroneous budget. The owner makes a claim against the design professional for misrepresentation, negligence, or even fraud, seeking damages the owner allegedly incurred by relying upon the information provided by the design professional and proceeding based on it.

Scenario 2: At the inception of the project, the owner provides the budget to the design professional. The design professional either makes no representation as to the adequacy of the budget or expresses a guarded opinion as to the adequacy of the budget given the project scope. The budget proves to be incorrect, either because it was inadequate from the beginning or because of intervening changes in the project parameters. The owner makes a claim against the design professional for not informing the owner at the onset that his budget was insufficient or failing to notify the owner that his budget became inadequate due to specific changes in the project. The owner claims that had he been timely advised as to the true cost of the project, he would not have proceeded with the project and would not have incurred design costs for a project that exceeded the owner's budget.

In Scenario 1, the claim against the design professional is for an erroneous estimate. In Scenario 2, the claim against the design professional is for failure to notify the owner that his budget was inadequate or became so in the course of the design of the project. Both scenarios can occur during the pre-contract phase of the project.

Practice Tip

If the owner unilaterally announces his budget for the project during the pre-contract phase, the design professional should not remain silent for fear of offending the owner or losing a potential project. The owner may interpret silence as acquiescence. The design professional must inform the owner that he is in no position to endorse or reject the owner's proposed budget; and by agreeing to becoming further involved in the project, he is not endorsing the owner's budget. The design professional cannot guarantee the adequacy of the owner's budget, and it is the contractor that can best objectively test the owner's budget after the parties identify and adequately document the specifics of the project scope.

---

4. *Initial Schedule Estimates*

Similar to cost estimates, a forecast of the construction schedule is problematic for the design professional. Again, the design professional must not remain silent in the face of a major schedule contingency unilaterally set or announced by the owner. Additionally, the design professional must resist pressures to provide a preliminary schedule to the owner in the conceptual phase of the project.[16] Any proposed schedule agreed to by the design professional must be carefully qualified. If possible, the design professional should not agree to or warrant any fixed completion deadline in the initial stages of the project.

Library References

C.J.S. *Agency* §§ 12–13, 15–16, 18–19, 21–22; C.J.S. *Architects* §§ 19, 21–23; C.J.S. *Contracts* §§ 2–3, 9, 12, 271, 333, 346–347, 407–420, 434–435, 450–455, 507–508, 531–532, 534–544, 557–576, 584, 592–593, 596; C.J.S. *Health and Environment* §§ 106, 116, 131, 163–165, 173; C.J.S. *Negligence* §§ 162–164, 399, 595–596, 600; C.J.S. *Zoning and Land Planning* §§ 70, 191, 193–203.

West's Key No. Digests, Alternative Dispute Resolution <KEY>111, 441; Contracts <KEY>1, 114, 168, 236–246, 283, 312–321; Damages <KEY>118; Environmental Law <KEY>129, 265, 531, 580; Indemnity <KEY>26–31, 33(5); Negligence <KEY>321, 322, 1205(4); Principal and Agent <KEY>3(1); Zoning and Planning <KEY>371–394.

III. Contract Negotiation and Formation

As discussed previously, the design professional typically provides initial design services during the conceptual/pre-design phase on an hourly basis and based on an initial proposal to the owner.[17] Once the client and design professional have sufficiently defined the project in this phase and established a working relationship, they can consider a contract for the design of the project.[18]

A series of judicial decisions have explained the nature of the contractual undertaking of design professionals and the duty of care expected when rendering professional services. The cases are instructive for understanding the nuances of the various roles of the design professional in the construction project.

---

16. However, the B101-1997 does, in § 3.2.2 have a requirement that the architect is to prepare a preliminary evaluation of the owner's schedule.

17. James R. Franklin, Architect's Professional Practice Manual, § 1.72 (McGraw-Hill 2000).

18. *Id.*

For example, *Huber, Hunt and Nichols v. Moore*[19] explained that, under the AIA Document B141, Standard Owner/Architect Agreement, an architect has three possible roles to perform in the overall construction project.[20] An architect serves as an *independent contractor* to the owner in preparation of plans and specifications for the project. Then, during the course of construction, the architect serves as the *owner's representative* performing a number of administrative duties under the contract (the Contract Administration or "CA" phase under AIA Document B141). Lastly, during the course of construction, the architect may also serve as *a quasi-judicial officer* resolving disputes between owner and contractor. One or more of these roles could change depending on the project and the participants therein. Accordingly, the liability exposure of the architect can vary greatly when performing services in these various and distinct roles.

Courts evaluate the services of an architect in the role of independent contractor in terms of compliance with the professional standard of care for architects in that locale. The Maine Supreme Court first applied the standard of care to design professionals over a hundred years ago in *Coombs v. Beede.*[21] The holding in *Coombs* echoed across the country with *Paxton v. County of Alameda.*[22] It is interesting to note that while the design professional's compliance with the standard of care may vary by local practices within any given jurisdiction, the courts across the nation have consistently applied the standard since *Coombs*.

Wynner v. Buxton[23] examined the variations in the scope of work undertaken by a design professional on a construction project. The court explained that the contract controls the design professional's scope of work on a project, not the general notions of what a design professional does or ought to do. It stated that an engineer who prepared civil engineering plans required for three steel structures was not absolutely responsible for the plans covering all aspects of the project.[24] The fact that the civil engineering plans did not include all details governing every aspect of the three steel structures did not

---

19. 67 Cal. Ct. App. 3d 278, 136 Cal. Rptr. 603 (1977).

20. *Huber, Hunt and Nichols v. Moore* was decided with reference to the prior AIA B141 owner-architect contract. As discussed herein, this form of agreement has generally been replaced with the B101-2017 form.

21. 89 Me. 187, 36 A. 104 (1896).

22. 119 Cal. Ct. App. 2d 393, 259 P.2d 934 (1953).

23. 97 Cal. Ct. App. 3d 166, 158 Cal. Rptr. 587 (1979).

24. *Id.* at 174.

render them defective, based on a California statute allowing non-engineers to design certain building components.[25]

The *Wynner* rationale may also apply to projects involving a sharing of design responsibility by construction professionals (such as trade contractors providing design services for their portion of the project). For this type of project, the drawings and specifications prepared by the design professional are not considered to be a complete "bid set" since negotiated agreements fill in various design details, and ultimately the scope of the design professional's duties is determined by the project contract responsibilities, and not necessarily by the standard of care. In this type of project, design responsibility is *shared* rather than delegated, since the owner does not retain the architect to furnish the entire design.[26] It is also notable in the context of shared project responsibilities that since the year 2000, the use of design-build and other a project delivery methods has increased greatly, such that many of the projects in the United States are now delivered using a project delivery method other than the traditional design-bid-build. Design-build and its impact on changing the role and contractual relationships of the design professional are discussed in Chapter 5 of this book.

A. The Roles, Responsibilities, and Obligations of the Parties in Entering into the Contract

The negotiation and preparation of the contract may be the most important aspects of the design professional/client relationship. Some states have enacted legislation requiring written contracts between the design professional and the client.[27] The owner, design professional, and the rest of the design team should commit to paper their exact intentions, responsibilities, and expectations for a project.

It is at this time that the design professional should be most aware of liabilities, real and potential. Normally, the type of project will govern, at least in part, the nature and form of the contract the parties will use for a specific project. If the project is residential, then usually the architect will propose the contract, since homeowners (unless they are very sophisticated and/or have atypical legal resources) usually lack the experience to suggest the form of

25. *Id.*

26. *See* Arthur F. O'Leary, *Third Party Legal Claims against Architects: Pitfalls for the Architect Who Prepares Plans and Specifications for Owner-Builder-Developers*, Design & Cost Data (Jan.–Feb. 1980) (discussion on this type of project by noted forensic architect).

27. Cal. Bus. & Prof. Code § 5536.22 (1995).

agreement.[28] On the other hand, on commercial projects the owner proposes the form of contract as often as the design professional. Finally, in the public works arena, the contact form is usually, if not exclusively, that of the public entity, and often not subject to significant negotiation.

In the traditional "design-bid-build" project delivery system, the owner will contract separately with the project contractor and the design professional. The design professional's contract will typically provide that he is to include in his services some range of consultants' design services, which may include those such as structural engineering, mechanical engineering, and other similar services. Although, as discussed in *Wynner*,[29] the design professional does not always retain each consultant, but often does this in a typical design-bid-build project. The reason is that the owner wants the design professional to provide a complete design for the project and be the head of the "design team." The owner does not want to be responsible for and may not even be aware of all of the consultants that may be involved in the design process.

However, the responsibility of the design professional to assemble the entire design team does not come without risk. Several legal concepts affect the design professional's potential liability with respect to the actions (or inactions) of his consultants. The first is the doctrine of vicarious liability. Under this principle, one who delegates contractual responsibility to another is generally liable for the actions of their subcontractor. Therefore, if the consultant makes an error, irrespective of whether the prime design professional incorporates that error into his design or merely fails to timely detect and correct it, the prime design professional will generally be liable to the owner for the damage that results.[30] For this reason it is prudent for the prime design professional to

---

28. As for the liability of the design professional to third parties, see the California Supreme Court's decision in *Beacon Residential Community Association v. Skidmore, Owings & Merrill LLP, et al.*, 59 Cal. 4th 568, 327 P3d 850 (2014), holding that design professionals may owe a duty of care to third-party residential property purchasers with whom they may not be in privity of contract. The court distinguished earlier case law that had restricted liability in cases where the design professionals had only prepared plans or made design recommendations, holding that design professionals may be liable to a purchaser for negligence even if they do not actually construct the project or exercise control over construction. However, a California case limiting the potential liability of design professionals to parties in privity of contract is *State Ready Mix, Inc. v. Moffatt & Nichol*, 232 Cal.App.4th 1227 (2015), wherein the court held for the first time in California that the "economic loss rule" applies to design professionals.

29. *See supra* text accompanying note 3.

30. *See generally* Johnson v. Salem Title Co., 246 Or. 409, 425 P.2d 519 (1967) (architect was held liable for the negligence of his consulting engineer; this concept

require that the key terms of his contract with the owner prevail over conflicting provisions in his contract with his consultants.

Practice Tip

If the owner will agree, it may be preferable for the design professional to have the owner contract directly with the project consultants. This may relieve the design professional of certain risks and obligations, including the obligation of payments directly to the consultants and the potential vicarious liability for the consultants' acts or omissions. At the same time, the design professional who contracts directly with consultants should always make certain that the consultant(s) have adequate professional liability insurance.

In addition, the design professional might be liable for the negligent hiring of a consultant if the owner could show that he hired, recommended, or referred a consultant who was not qualified to do the work.[31] Although this may be difficult to prove in many situations, some courts have allowed this type of claim against design professionals.[32]

applies equally to a consultant that might hire a subconsultant); Duncan v. Missouri Bd. For Archs, Prof., Engineers & Land Surveyors, 744 S.W. 2d 524 (Mo. 1988) (same). However, *see also* Hansell v. Santos Robinson Mortuary, 64 Cal. App. 4th 608, 614–15 (1998), wherein a California court held that a mortuary was entitled to delegate its professional duty for the handling of decedent remains to a licensed crematorium and therefore was not liable for the negligence of the delegated licensed professional (citing to Dow v. Holly Manufacturing Co., 49 Cal. 2d 720, 725, 321 P.2d 736 (1958), for the counter-proposition that a general contractor is liable for any defects in construction even though the work was actually done by a subcontractor).

31. *See, e.g.*, Gonzalzles v. American Exp. Credit Corp., 315 Ill. Ct. App. 3d 199, 733 N.E.2d 345 (2000) (claim was brought against an Illinois attorney for the "tort of negligent referral" of a client to another attorney); Burlington Ins. Co. v. Oceanic Design & Const., Inc., 383 F.3d 940 (9th Cir. 2004) (claim was brought against a contractor for negligently recommending an unqualified mason to do excavation work); Capel v. Allstate Ins. Co., 78 Ark. Ct. App. 27, 77 S.W.3d 533 (2002) (property insurer was charged with making a negligent recommendation of a roof repair contractor); Sapp v. State Farm Fire & Cas. Co., 226 Ga. Ct. App. 200, 486 S.E.2d 71 (1997) (claim based on contractor's negligent recommendation and installation of hardwood flooring).

32. *See, e.g.*, Hubert v. Aiken, 15 Daly 237, 2 N.Y.S. 711 (1888) (Architect was found liable for negligently recommending use of a product or material, rather than a consultant or sub-contractor. The architect had specified a particular chimney design

B. The Contract

Considerations for the scope and terms of the contract for professional services, particularly the terms that will most affect the design professional, are viewed against the backdrop of his relationship to the project (discussed above). Although a detailed analysis of all possible contract clauses and their ultimate effect is beyond the scope of this chapter, some provisions that the design professional must consider are discussed below.

1. Standard Form Contracts—the Test of Time?

Several organizations promulgate standard form contracts for the construction industry. The better known are the American Institute of Architects (AIA), the Associated General Contractors of America (AGC), the Engineering Joint Contracts Design Committee (EJCDC), the Design-Build Institute of America (DBIA), and ConsensusDocs. Certainly, each of these organizations has its own view and perceived bias in the contracts it creates. However, these groups have generally attempted to create their "family" of documents to be as fair as possible, so the widest audience within the construction industry would use them. This chapter will primarily focus on the provisions and risks contained

---

based exclusively upon the representations of the installing contractor without his own independent investigation as to its performance characteristics. The court explained that "[r]esponsibility could not be shifted in that way." Interestingly, with implications for the specification of solar power and other "green technologies," the 1888 court also said that "when, in the progress of civilization, new conveniences are introduced into our homes, and become, not curious novelties, but the customary means of securing the comfort of the unpretentious citizen, why should not the architect be expected to possess the technical learning respecting them that is exacted of him with respect to other and older branches of his professional studies?" [meaning, an exercise of due diligence and compliance with professional standards].). *Id.* at 712–13; *see also* Scott v. Potomac Ins. Co., 217 Or. 323, 341 P.2d 1083 (1959) (citing *Hubert* and explaining in dicta that an architect would have been found liable for violation of professional standards when he negligently recommended use of an alternative imbedded piping system for heating a hospital without appropriate changes in the flooring to allow for expansion of the piping. The argument of the architect had been that he had the right to rely without independent investigation on the representation of the manufacturer and of the approval of its use by the heating engineer employed by the architect to design the heating system. Although not specifically at issue in the appeal, the *Scott* court let it be known that the architect would have been found liable for professional negligence for such blind reliance, citing the *Hubert* decision.).

in the AIA family of documents,[33] with a secondary reference to the EJCDC and AGC contract forms.[34]

---

33. As a brief background, the AIA was founded in 1857 when a group of American architects met together and formed what would become the American Institute of Architects. The stated purposes for the professional organization were to "promote the scientific and practical perfection of its members" and to "elevate the standing of the profession." Up to this point, no American schools of architecture or architectural licensing laws, standards, regulations, or formal organization had existed in any state of the union. Anyone up to this point could call him- or herself an architect, including masons, bricklayers, and various other members of the building trades. *See History of the American Institute of Architects*, on the AIA Web site, *at* http://www.aia.org; and DANA CUFF, ARCHITECTURE: THE STORY OF PRACTICE (1991).

As part of this effort, it was believed that standard construction documents could assist by providing guidance and regularity to the system of building. In fact, one of three standing committees formed by the AIA in its founding year was the Committee on Papers, dealing with construction documents. The first ever construction document promulgated by the AIA focused on the contractual needs of its client community in the building process, indicating an early sensitivity to its clientele and a professional response to the realities of the construction industry. The history of the AIA Contract Documents dates to 1888, when the AIA first published its *Uniform Contract* for use between an owner and a contractor. *See History of Contract Documents at* http://www.aia.org. In keeping with this broad, industry-wide vision, the organization in 1911 published its first standardized general conditions for construction. *Id.* However, it was not until 1917 that the AIA first published its B141 owner/architect agreement. AIA Documents B141, Standard Form of Agreement Between Owner and Architect (now in its 2017 edition), along with A201, General Conditions of the Contract for Construction, have since become documentary workhorses of the construction industry, providing common documentary references for design and construction practice if not (off-the-shelf) useable, model agreements. *See* Howard G. Goldberg, Esq., Hon. AIA, *Commentary on AIA Document B141-1997*, at 12, on the AIA Web site, *at* http://www.aia.org. Since the inception of standard forms, the AIA has adhered to a document *Revision Policy*, revising its standard documents every ten years, generally. The current 2017 edition of AIA Document A201 is the seventeenth edition, while 2017 is also the 130-year anniversary of the Documents Committee, which drafts the AIA contract documents. The stated purpose of the AIA's document revision policy is to maintain a high level of accuracy and timeliness in AIA contract documents, given ever-changing social and construction industry conditions, and to ensure that AIA contract documents are current and fair to all participating parties.

34. The ConsensusDocs are the most recent entry into the collection of form construction and design contracts, and they result from input of several industry associations including owners, contractors, subcontractors, designers, and sureties.

What are the current benefits and risks of the use of industry form agreements, including AIA form contracts? From their inception, the use of the AIA form contracts, as well as form documents by any number of other publishers, has been the subject of debate. Some have criticized the documents, not because of the appropriateness or sufficiency of a form document for a given project, but on the perceived bias or favoritism to one or more project participants, especially the architect. A number of publications with suggested revisions to these forms have been offered to the construction industry, often with alternative revisions (additional and/or substitute language) tailored to the interests of each party.[35] Even form documents related to design-build have been the subject of debate and suggested revisions.[36]

2. *The Use of Custom Contracts*

In addition to form contracts, design professionals and other project participants use custom contracts specifically prepared by or for the users. Business or public agencies often draft custom contracts, either with or without legal counsel.

Custom contracts are advisable or essential when the requirements of a project, or the nature or the number of the project participants (such as multiple primes for project construction or project design), cannot fit into the standard terms of the form contract. The drafter can modify a form contract from any publisher to fit a given project only to a point; beyond that, he will need a custom contract.

Justin Sweet, law professor and noted author, states this caution with regard to the modification of form contracts, "[w]e cannot emphasize sufficiently the need for *careful* modification of any AIA document. [emphasis added.] If this cannot be done, it is better to use the document unchanged or to use a custom-made contract."[37] Overall, the use of a form contract properly modified to fit the project's particular characteristics is the best alternative.

---

35. Most notably, *see* JUSTIN SWEET & JONATHAN J. SWEET, SWEET ON CONSTRUCTION INDUSTRY DOCUMENTS: MAJOR AIA DOCUMENTS (4th ed. 1999); GOWER W. JONES, ALTERNATIVE CLAUSES TO STANDARD CONSTRUCTION CONTRACTS (1998); WERNER SABO, LEGAL GUIDE TO AIA DOCUMENTS (4th ed. 1998); and JAMES ACRET, CONSTRUCTION INDUSTRY FORMBOOK (2d ed. 1979).

36. G. WILLIAM QUATMAN, DESIGN-BUILD FOR THE DESIGN PROFESSIONAL (2001), including Appendixes with Supplementary Conditions to current design-build documents by various publishers.

37. SWEET & SWEET, *supra* note 35, at 17 (emphasis added); *Relevance: Source of Pertinent Information*, AIA CALIFORNIA COUNCIL NEWSLETTER (April 2004) (the AIACC reports that the most common complaint it receives from consumers of archi-

Another difficulty in modifying form contracts is that they are often *inter-related* to other form documents. Thus, modifying one form without changing other related forms can create conflicts. Similarly, it may be problematic to use both form and custom agreements on a project without appropriate modification. For example, AIA Document B101-1997 (Owner-Architect Agreement) references AIA Document A201-2017 (General Conditions for construction of the project). The blind use of such a form contract for design services "off the shelf' may create legal inconsistencies and operational problems with custom-made construction contracts not utilizing A201 for the same project.[38]

It is also dangerous to mix different editions of AIA documents on the same project, as AIA forms are revised every 10 years and different editions of AIA forms may contain inconsistent terms.

Sweet has observed, "AIA documents [as well as form documents by other publishers] are most useful for small and middle-priced projects as well as large-scale residential and commercial projects in which design and construction are separated, and in which the architect [rather than a construction manager or multiple primes] plays a central administrative role."[39]

3. *Specific Contract Provisions—the Risks Defined*

Contracts of any length and complexity may contain hundreds of provisions, terms, and conditions. It would exceed the scope of this chapter to delve into all of these provisions, let alone provide counsel with sufficient information as to the interpretation of and liabilities involved with all of this contract language. However, there are several key provisions in design professional contracts that frequently arise and which the parties often heavily negotiate. It is no surprise that these contract provisions are almost exclusively "business terms" (as opposed to project "scope terms" that delineate what work the design professional is or is not going to perform). In addition, "business terms" typically involve greater risk considerations for the design professional; e.g., indemnity provisions, discussed *infra*.

The authors do not intend this discussion to be exhaustive, but to provide a general background discussion on these topics, including practice tips to handle these issues and increase the reader's awareness of liability traps. The professional and legal practitioner who requires a more detailed discussion

---

tectural services [the client] regarding owner/architect agreements is not that there was no agreement, but rather, that the agreement was silent on important issues).

38. ANDREW M. CIVITELLO, CONSTRUCTION OPERATIONS MANUAL OF POLICIES AND PROCEDURES, at § 3.2 (3d ed. 2000).

39. SWEET & SWEET, *supra* note 35, at 18.

and analysis should consult the many treatises and sources cited herein for additional consideration. However, one excellent source for discussion of many of these topics is *The Construction Contracts Book: How to Find Common Ground in Negotiating Design and Construction Contract Clauses*, published by the ABA's Forum Committee on the Construction Industry.[40]

Practice Tip

Whether a form or custom contract is used, the architect or other prime design professional should make certain that there is consistency between their prime contract with the owner and the subconsultant contract with its consultants (if the owner contracts directly with the consultants; see discussion, ***supra***). This is necessary to avoid any inconsistent contractual terms between the contracts (including those terms that may increase the possible legal exposure of the architect/prime design professional), for example, those involving indemnity, limitations of liability, governing law, dispute resolution, copyright issues, and termination.

---

4. *Indemnity*

The indemnity provision could be argued to be the most important "business term" of any design professional's contract (or for that matter, any commercial contract). Negotiated indemnity rights can ultimately have the greatest impact on the handling and resolution of claims arising after completion of the construction project.

First, what is "indemnity"? One court defines an indemnity contract as one in which "one engages to save another party from a legal consequence of the conduct of one of the parties, or of some other person."[41] The court in *Myers Building Industry, Ltd. v. Interface Tech., Inc.* further explained that "an indemnity agreement is to be interpreted according to the language and contents of the contract as well as the intention of the parties as indicated

---

40. THE CONSTRUCTION CONTRACTS BOOK: HOW TO FIND COMMON GROUND IN NEGOTIATING DESIGN AND CONSTRUCTION CONTRACT CLAUSES (Daniel S. Brennan et al. eds. 2004). There are also other valuable guides available on the market to practitioners to assist with the revision of design contracts, including THE CONSTRUCTION CONTRACTS BOOK on negotiating industry form contract documents, published by the American Bar Association.

41. Long Beach Un. Sch. Dist. V. Margaret Williams, LLC, 43 Cal.App.5th 87, 91 n.1 (2019), quoting CAL. Civ. CODE § 2772. .

by the contract."[42] However, this is overly complicated wording. Simply put, indemnity is the allocation of loss.[43] It can arise in many ways, including by statute, operation of law, or contract.

It is noteworthy that the "B" series of the AIA form contracts (owner-architect agreements) do not include an indemnity provision, as contrasted with the "A" series (owner-contractor agreements).[44] Of course, in the absence of contractual indemnification the design professional will nevertheless be liable for *negligent* errors and omissions, which violate the standard of care.[45]

The owner and architect are always free to enter into an agreement to allocate loss between them without resort to standardized language. However, indemnity provisions contain many dangers for the design professional. For example, professional liability insurance policies may not provide coverage for a contractual undertaking beyond the liability imposed by law, such as indemnity for losses caused by others.[46] Thus, by indemnifying an owner against "any and all losses," the design professional might become liable for injuries and losses that were not his fault (usually including the cost of defense incurred by the owner)[47] and caused by the mistakes of others, such as the contrac-

42. *Id.*

43. For a more complete discussion of the different types of indemnity that might be considered or applied (such as noncontractual, equitable indemnity) in the construction context, *see generally* SWEET & SCHNEIER, *supra* note 11, Chapter 31.

44. However, AIA "C" series agreements, such as the C401-2017, do contain contractual indemnity provisions. (See cross-indemnity provision in §§ 8.1.2 and 8.1.3 of the C401.)

45. John R. Clark, *Indemnification by Design Professionals*, THE CONSTRUCTION SPECIFIER, 23–24 (Sept. 1989), offers an excellent discussion of these issues. Mr. Clark was serving at the time of this article as special counsel to the Engineers Joint Contract Documents Committee.

46. *Id.*; AVA J. ABRAMOWITZ, ARCHITECT'S ESSENTIALS OF CONTRACT NEGOTIATION 215–21 (2002).

47. Since publication of the first edition of this treatise, there have been court decisions and legislative efforts in several states affecting the obligation of an indemnitor (such as a design professional contractually agreeing to indemnify an owner) to pay for the defense attorney's fees and costs of the indemnitee. However, two significant California cases have changed the duty to defend landscape: *Crawford v. Weather Shield*, 44 Cal. 4th 541 (2008), and *UDC v. CH2M-HILL* 181 Cal. App. 4th 10 (2010), generally held that the duty to defend commences at the inception of a lawsuit, if there is an implication of liability for the indemnitor. (For a comprehensive discussion of the subject, see *An Overview of Indemnification and the Duty to Defend* published by the ACEC Risk Management Committee, *at* https://docs.acec.org/pub/DA77E02A-C742-9915-1727-73DF2CCC23B9.) At the same time, legislation in jurisdictions such

tor and subcontractors, over whose activities he had no authority or control.[48] This language may also be sufficient to subject the architect to liability for economic loss resulting from design or construction defects, contrary to the economic loss rule applied in many jurisdictions (providing there is no cause of action in tort to recover solely economic loss).[49]

The owner often asks the design professional to indemnify it from "errors, omissions, or negligent acts" (in that particular sequence). However, this proposed language could extend the liability of the design professional beyond negligent acts, and include errors and omissions where there was no violation of the standard of care. Thus, this provision might not be insurable since it would increase the liability of the design professional beyond the duty imposed by law.[50]

The purpose of indemnity is to create a duty by contract where none may have existed. However, a design professional has always had a common law duty to meet the professional standard of care. Therefore, as seen in the foregoing paragraphs, *depending on the language used,* an indemnity clause may simply be a redundant recitation of that preexisting duty or an uninsurable provision creating through contract an additional *basis* of liability on the part of the design professional.[51]

---

as California have worked to address the effects (sometime onerous) of such "upfront and immediate" defense obligations. *See* CAL. CIV. CODE § 2782.8

48. John R. Clark, *Indemnification by Design Professionals*, THE CONSTRUCTION SPECIFIER (Sept. 1989).

49. *See, e.g.*, Moorman Mfg. Co. v. National Tank Co., 91 111.2d 69, 435 N.E.2d 443 (1982); Seely v. White Motor Co., 63 Cal. 2d 9, 403 P.2d 145 (1965); Aas v. Superior Court, 24 Cal. 4th 627, 101 Cal. Rptr. 2d 718 (2000). However, see note 28, *supra*, regarding *State Ready Mix, Inc. v. Moffatt & Nichol*, 232 Cal. App. 4th 1227 (2015), wherein the court held for the first time in California that the "economic loss rule" applies to design professionals.

50. ABRAMOWITZ, *supra* note 46, at 217–18.

51. *See* Paxton v. County of Alameda, 119 Cal. Ct. App. 2d 393, 399, 259 P.2d 934 (1953) (the professional standard of care and whether it has been violated can be established only through professionals from that discipline); *see also* SWEET & SCHNEIER, *supra* note 11, § 14.05 B. and § 14.06, citing, *inter alia*, Eugene J. Farrug, *The Necessity of Expert Testimony in Establishing the Standard of Care for Design Professionals*, 38 DEPAUL L. REV. 873 (1989) (attacking Illinois law, which does not require expert testimony in cases of professional malpractice). Contractual indemnity would be more immediate and readily available, especially when containing indemnification from any "claims" since only mere allegations could trigger it.

5. Basic vs. Additional Services

A dichotomy between "Basic" and "Additional" services has been prevalent in design practice from the earliest editions of the AIA documents. This concept of Basic and Additional services is derived from the nucleus of traditional services provided by the design professional versus those additional services he might provide to the owner. The present edition of the AIA Document B101-2017 draws a distinction between Basic and Additional services, while other versions of the AIA form contracts do not.[52] Article 3 of the B101-2017 contains five Basic Services: the Schematic Design Phase, the Design Development Phase, the Construction Documents Phase, the Procurement Phase (including competitive bidding), and the Construction Phase (also typically known as the contract administration phase).[53]

At the same time, Article 4 of the B101-2017 addresses Additional Services. As opposed to prior iterations of the Owner-Architect agreement, the Additional Services article now contains a new section titled Supplemental Services (which are services that are "not included in Basic Services but may be required for the project," with this section providing a detailed list of possible such supplemental services the architect can potentially provide). In addition to Supplemental Services, Article 4 now provides another section titled Architects Additional Services. This dichotomy is a somewhat simplified method to allow the owner to contact for the additional services, as opposed to the scheme in the prior B151-1997 and B151-2007 agreements, which separated the additional services into three different categories: Project Representation Beyond Basic Services, Contingent Additional Services, and Optional Additional Services.

What are the risks involved with the distinctions between basic and additional (as well as "supplemental") services? They generally arise from the fact that the Basic Services are those that are included in the general compensation that the design professional is to receive for their work (regardless of the manner in which that is determined, such as on a flat fee, a percentage of construction, or other method).[54] However, the Additional Services are those that are within the control of the owner, in that the owner must specifically order or request them for them to be paid. (*See* B101, § 4.2.1, providing that the owner

---

52. *See, e.g.*, AIA Document B105-2017, Standard Short Form of Agreement Between Owner and Architect.

53. The details of the architect's obligations under the contract administration phase (during construction of the project) are discussed elsewhere in this text; *see* Chapter 4.

54. *See* AIA B101-2017, at §§ 11.1–11.3.

must make a written request for the Additional Services.) Still, disputes may arise as to what services the owner requested, and whether the services are truly Additional Services or part of the Basic Services agreement. Moreover, even if the owner did not specifically request any Additional Services, many claims arise when there are changes to the scope of the work that the design professional performs and for which he wants to be paid. At the same time, the owner may dispute that the design work is an Additional Service, believing that it is part of what the owner should receive as part of Basic Services. Complications may also arise when there is a contractual requirement of *a written* authorization before the design professional may perform such Additional Services. The owner can explicitly or implicitly waive this requirement, especially under the pressure of completing a project (e.g., the owner's verbal promise to the design professional to "go ahead, we will take care of payment for that when the project is done").

What can the design professional do to reduce these risks and the potential for claims? The key is better business practices through such techniques as appropriate contract terms, confirming letters throughout the life of the project, and structuring interactions of project participants through methods such as periodic "partnering" meetings, as poor communication precipitates most claims. The use of the Supplemental Services/Additional Services dichotomy should serve both the owner and the architect well, as it allows them to provide for certain additional services when the contract is entered into (i.e., the "menu" of Supplemental Services in B101 § 4.1.1), or to allow additional services to be added to the project as necessary, as it proceeds.[55]

6. Payments to the Design Professional

Architects are usually paid for their services in various ways (at least with respect to Basic Services), including on a fixed fee (called the "Stipulated Sum" in § 11.1.1 of the B101), an hourly fee, or a percentage of the construction cost (called the "Percentage Basis" in § 11.1 of the B101). The project consultants are often paid on an hourly basis, but depending on the project size and complexity, as well as the basis for the architect's compensation, can be paid on a fixed fee basis.[56] In this sense, the concept of Basic versus Additional

---

55. See AIA Document Commentary, B101-2007 Standard Form of Agreement Between Owner and Architect, published by the American Institute of Architects.

56. Complaints by design professionals based on fee disputes and misunderstandings with owners have a way of leading to retaliatory cross-complaints for professional negligence. THE ARCHITECT'S HANDBOOK OF PROFESSIONAL PRACTICE, *supra* note 1, § 14.3.

Services, as reflected in the B101-2017 owner architect agreement discussed above, is really a subpart of the larger issue of the appropriate compensation the owner should pay to the design professional.

7. Termination Issues

The importance of a termination provision in the design professional contract cannot be underestimated. At the beginning of the project, the prospect of disputes that might require contract termination seems distant. Disputes certainly arise, however, and it is important that there be some mechanism for the contractual relationship to end if necessary.[57]

Termination provisions usually fall into two categories: termination for convenience, and for cause. Termination for convenience is often thought of as an owner's remedy, and in fact, the AIA B101-2017 allows the owner to terminate without cause.[58] This is due to the nature of the owner/architect relationship, in that, if the owner were to terminate for convenience, the architect would still be entitled to payment for the work performed.[59] In addition, the B101-2017 has added § 9.7, which also allows for the owner and architect to agree to a specified Termination Fee, as well as a "Licensing Fee" if the owner intends to continue using the architect's Instruments of Service following the termination. On the other hand, the AIA has reasoned on behalf of the owner that if the architect had *a unilateral* right to terminate, this could lead to abuses in that an architect who has been paid for his work could then "walk" from the project even if the owner has not technically breached the agreement.[60]

Termination for cause clauses, under any of the form contracts, permit termination if the other side has materially breached the agreement.[61]

---

57. In some states, there is a statutory requirement that a design professional's contract include a termination provision. *See, e.g.*, CAL. BUS. & PROF. CODE § 5536.22(a)(5) (1995).

58. *See* AIA B101-2017, § 9.5.

59. Under the B141 agreement, the architect who was terminated for convenience and without cause was entitled to "Termination Expenses" that included the architect's anticipated contract profits. (*See* AIA B141-1997, § 1.3.8.7.) This anticipated profits provision has been changed in the B101-2017, such that the recovery of the architect's anticipated profits has been removed from the B101.

60. SABO, *supra* note 35, at 83 n.146, discussing *Gunter Hotel v. Buck*, 775 S.W.2d 689 (Tex. Ct. App. 1989) (termination for convenience by owner not absolute).

61. Both the AIA and EJCDC schemes refer to a "substantial" failure of the design professional to perform.

There are certain issues the design professional should consider when drafting or reviewing termination clauses. First, if the owner's agreement with the design professional contains a termination for convenience clause, then the design professional should include a similar provision in agreements with his consultants. This will avoid the unpleasant situation where the owner has terminated the design professional, but the design professional must still go forward with and pay the consultants because they have not breached their contract(s). Second, despite the concerns of abuse by the design professional discussed above, if the owner will accept it, the design professional should consider including a clause permitting him to terminate for convenience. Most design professionals would not abuse the provision (and some have suggested that the design professional's right to terminate for convenience is not absolute and requires some degree of cause[62]). The termination for convenience provision gives the design professional an "out" if there were valid reasons to terminate even if they do not rise to the level of a substantial nonperformance by the owner. Finally, the design professional should pay close attention to the interplay between ownership of the Instruments of Service used for the project and termination, since such ownership can be an important consideration in the decision (especially by the owner) to terminate. If the design professional transfers ownership of the Instruments of Service to the owner upon termination, the owner might have a greater incentive to terminate; the opposite would be true if ownership of the Instruments of Service stays with or reverts to the design professional.[63]

---

62. *See generally* SABO, *supra* note 35, at 81–84, citing *Herbert Shaffer Assocs. v. First Bank*, 30 Ill. Ct. App. 3d 647, 332 N.E.2d 703 (1975), (construing § 1.3.8.4 of AIA B141-1997 as allowing either owner or architect to send a written termination notice if the other breaches the agreement in a "substantial" manner (an oral disagreement between owner and architect was not a material breach by either party)).

63. The AIA scheme contained in B101-2017, § 7.3, provides that the owner's nonexclusive license to use the Instruments of Service is terminated upon termination of the contract, as well as the above-referenced Licensing Fee if the Owner intends to continue using the architect's Instruments of Service following the termination. *See* Chapter 7 of this book for a much more extensive analysis of ownership of project Instruments of Service, including upon contract termination.

Practice Tip

The parties should not take lightly the decision to terminate, since that can frequently lead to disputes and lawsuits. Most contracts (including the AIA documents) include a notice provision to terminate, which one might construe as a "cooling-off" period so the parties may evaluate and negotiate.[64]

8. Budget Estimates

Section II discussed budget and schedule estimates prior to the design professional entering into a contract, and the resulting liability issues. However, what can the design professional do to protect from claims arising when the project runs over budget and schedule?

The answer lies in the use of proper contract language and provisions to define the services provided by the design professional when such estimates are given, and presumably placing obligations on the owner to establish a budget so that there are no misunderstandings. For example, the AIA B101-2017 (as well as the form consultant agreements under the "C" series) devotes an entire Article to "Cost of the Work."[65] The AIA documents also provide requirements for the project owner to maintain and update a budget.[66]

Specifically, B101-2017, § 5.2, provides that the owner shall establish a project budget, which shall include reasonable contingencies. Moreover, the owner must make certain to update the budget as necessary throughout the project duration, and if the owner significantly increases or decreases the budget, the owner shall notify the architect, and the owner shall then agree with the architect to a corresponding "scope and quality." This provision works in conjunction with B101-2017, Article 6, which has seven sections relating to the project budget and cost of the work. This scheme, in conjunction with B101-2017 §§ 3.2.2 and 3.2.6, requires the architect to prepare a preliminary budget (the "preliminary evaluation of the . . . budget for the Cost of the Work"). Thereafter, after complying with the requirements of § 6.3, the architect is

64. *See* Sweet & Schneier, *supra* note 11, at 213.

65. *See* Article 6 of AIA B101-2017; Article 6 of AIA C401-2017 (regarding consultants).

66. *See* § 5.2 of AIA B101-2017

to submit to the owner an estimate of the Cost of the Work.[67] This estimate is then updated throughout the Design Development and Construction Documents phases. The B101 document includes provisions that address contingencies for design, bidding, and price escalation. The AIA provisions also make it clear that the design professional has no control over the contractor or construction costs, and does not warrant the estimate.[68]

The AIA "C" series documents include provisions parroting those of the "B" series.[69] Other form contracts, such as the AGC and EJCDC documents, include provisions related to budgeting, but they are not as detailed as the AIA documents.

There are reported cases involving disputes arising from budget estimates, some where form contracts were used and others with custom contracts. However, the common theme (not surprisingly) appears to be that there is confusion between the design professional and the client as to what the project budget may be (a "hard" budget or "soft" budget),[70] and a misunderstanding as to the design professional's expertise in and responsibility for accurately predicting construction costs. However, the B101-2007 appears to resolve the former issue (related to the extent of the project budget) by stating that the "Cost of the Work" includes the contractor's general conditions costs, overhead, and profit, and the reasonable value of labor, materials, and equipment; excluded from the Cost of the Work are the architect's compensation and other owner's costs such as land acquisition, financing, and contingencies.[71]

One way to minimize these problems is to use a form agreement (such as the AIA) that all parties are comfortable with and are sufficiently sophisticated to understand (or retain counsel or others to assist with the agreement, including any changes), or otherwise carefully draft the contract to define explicitly the design professional's responsibility and qualifications for estimating services, and limits thereon. Another option is to avoid the problem by simply eliminating the design professional's contractual involvement with construction budgeting and/or estimating and leaving those services to others

---

67. Under B101-1997 § 3.2.5 the architect is to also consider "sustainable design alternatives" as part of his or her budget/Cost of the Work, program, and schedule basic services. The owner may also obtain "more advanced sustainable design services" as a Supplemental Service. (*See* § III.B.5, *supra*.)

68. *See* B101-1997 § 6.2.

69. *Id.*

70. *See generally* SWEET & SCHNEIER, *supra* note 11, § 12.03.

71. *See* B101-1997 § 6.1.

who may be better equipped to provide the services—the contractor, construction manager, and/or a separately retained project estimator.

Finally, the owner may attempt to bind the design professional to cost estimates, including verbal, provided before signing the contract. The best method to eliminate this situation is to include an "integration" clause in the contract, stating that the written contract represents the full and complete contract between the parties and supersedes all prior oral or written agreements.[72]

9. *Schedule Estimates*

Design professionals should generally avoid providing schedule estimates for the design phase. The uncertainties and vagaries of the plan check and entitlement processes—and *the numerous personnel involved,* including code enforcement officers who have discretion to interpret and apply provisions of the building code—caution against assignment of dates for completion of the design.[73] At most, milestones and an estimated time for completion of the various stages of design (i.e., an estimated time for each phase, such as six weeks for schematic design, four weeks for plan check, etc.), can be set out in advance.

Wisely, the AIA Document B101-2017 does provide that the architect is to submit to the owner a schedule for performance of *the architect's services.* This schedule is to include anticipated dates for the commencement of construction and substantial completion.[74] As for the contractor's schedule, the architect is required under the B101 only to prepare a preliminary evaluation of the owner's construction schedule noting any inconsistencies discovered.[75] Ultimately, the theme of the B101 is that the project construction schedule does not rest with the architect, and the effect of changes to the project—including schedule—is multifaceted and can entitle her to additional services.[76]

---

72. *See* AIA B101-2017, § 13.1 ("This Agreement represents the entire and integrated agreement between the Owner and Architect and supersedes all prior negotiations, representations or agreements, either written or oral. . . ."). However, there have been cases where an integration clause has been found to be inapplicable or limited in this instance.

73. Richard T. Conrad & Steven R. Winkel, Design Guide to the 1997 Uniform Building Code, Article 2, § 2A, Relationship of the Designer to the Enforcement Official (1998).

74. B101-1997, § 3.1.3

75. *See* B101-1997, § 3.2.2

76. *See* AIA Document B101-2017, § 4.2.1. The fact that construction scheduling is not a listed possible Supplemental Service in B101 § 4.1 would indicate that the intent

10. Copyright Issues

Chapter 7 of this book contains an in-depth discussion of copyright issues affecting design professionals.

The ownership of the project documents (what the AIA calls the "Instruments of Service"), as well as the design itself (which is also protected by copyright law), is important to the design professional because the work represents his work and livelihood above all else. However, the design professional should also be aware that ownership of the project documents can have enormous implications when a dispute arises between the design professional and client, including termination of the contract. The terms of the contract between the owner and design professional (and between the design professional and its consultants) will affect how the project proceeds upon termination, including how it can be completed, and greatly affect potential resolution of the dispute.

11. Dispute Resolution

Like many professional relationships, some have likened the building construction process to a "honeymoon."[77] The parties start out on their best behavior, not anticipating the difficulties that may lie ahead. However, as with many relationships, problems may develop in construction project, and certainly, design professionals are not immune to these disputes. Unlike the typical marriage, the parties to most construction agreements often include in their contract a "pre-nuptial provision" for resolving disputes, typically known as a "dispute resolution" provision.[78] Such dispute resolution provisions can take many forms; however, they often include a few key elements:

- the "forum" for the resolution of the dispute—(typically either litigation or arbitration);
- the use of nonbinding mediation, which usually occurs prior to arbitration or litigation; and
- the possible allocation of attorneys' fees and other expenses (such as the cost of the arbitration expense) to the prevailing party in the dispute.

---

of the AIA document is keep the architect out of the domain of the project construction scheduling, which should be left to the contractor.

77. *See* Justin Sweet, Sweet on Construction Law § 2.21 (1997).

78. The term currently used in the AIA form contracts for such dispute resolution provisions is "Claims and Disputes." The Associated General Contractors of America (AGC) uses the title "Mediation and Arbitration" for its dispute resolution clauses.

Arbitration and mediation are the typical methods of alternative dispute resolution (ADR). Private ADR providers have been in existence for decades. For instance, the American Arbitration Association (AAA) has been conducting construction arbitrations and other disputes since 1926. However, over the past couple of decades the use of other ADR forums has come to the forefront, most notably mediation. Because of this transformation, many national and local dispute resolution providers have been formed.[79] The AAA now offers mediation services, and resources for advance dispute avoidance techniques, such as its publication titled *The Construction Industry's Guide to Dispute Avoidance and Resolution*.[80]

The construction industry has firmly embraced ADR, especially mediation. The AIA first included mediation as a condition precedent to arbitration of a dispute in the 1997 edition of its form documents, and mediation as a condition precedent continues to this day. This is also true of the AGC and EJCDC form contracts, as the industry has realized the benefit of mediation to work to avoid disputes, prior to the expenditure of time, resources, and expense on litigation or arbitration.

Finally, as for arbitration, the AIA has since the inception of its form contract documents mandated arbitration for dispute resolution. However, with the 2007 revisions to the AIA documents came a significant departure from the tradition of mandated arbitration. Starting in 2007 and continuing, the AIA adopted a "check the box" scheme, whereby the parties could select (by a "check box") in the AIA agreement, arbitration, litigation in court, or some "other" process the parties may desire to utilize.[81] And, notably, if the parties do not select a method by checking one of the boxes on the form, then litigation is the default. However, if arbitration is chosen, then the American Arbitration Association is the default provider, pursuant to a series of somewhat detailed arbitration procedures in the contract.[82]

---

79. Examples of such providers, in addition to the American Arbitration Association (AAA), include the Judicial Arbitration and Mediation Service (JAMS), FORUM (formerly the National Arbitration Forum), and the Alternative Resolution Centers (ARC).

80. *See* the AAA's Web site *at* http://www.adr.org for this and other resources.

81. *See* B101-1997, § 8.2.4.

82. *Id.*

Practice Tip

The design professional contract should include a clause requiring mediation prior to arbitration or litigation, even if this requires modification of an existing (including a form) contract. The authors have found that many disputes, no matter how far apart that parties may seem to be, can be resolved through good, strong mediation efforts at the onset of a dispute, particularly with a mediator experienced in construction matters. In addition, a "condition precedent" mediation provision will often provide some guidance on the selection of the mediator and require a minimum amount of time for the mediation so the mediator has sufficient time to work to achieve a resolution.

Finally, as for the topic of the allocation of litigation expenses, a detailed discussion of all of the considerations surrounding this subject is beyond the scope of this chapter. However, one should carefully consider these clauses, since the attorney's and expert's fees frequently exceed the amount in dispute, and as a result can potentially create unintended consequences such as inequitable negotiation leverage of one party over the other.

12. Insurance

The availability of insurance is an important aspect of the construction industry and how it conducts business. At a bare minimum, every design professional should understand that regardless of working in an incorporated business, he or she can still be held *personally* liable for the consequences of his or her negligent actions or failure to act. This fact alone should compel the design professional to obtain professional liability insurance.[83] Many construction contracts, including the form contracts discussed in this book, contain clauses providing certain insurance requirements for the design professional.

For the design professional, having the proper professional liability insurance (as well as general liability and other necessary coverage) is a must, even if not required by the terms of a contract. The construction process is inherently risky. Claims and lawsuits against the design professional can come from

83. *See* the "Professional Liability" section of the *Practice Management Guide* at the CNA/Victor O. Schinnerer Web site *at* http://www.schinnerer.com.

many directions, including the owner, contractors, and third parties to the construction project.[84]

The AIA form contracts between the owner and architect have in the more recent editions (since the 2007 editions of such agreements) included provisions requiring insurance of the design professional, including "professional liability covering negligent acts, errors and omissions in the performance of professional services."[85] Similarly, § 2.8.6 of the AIA C401-2017 Standard Form of Agreement between Architect and Consultant requires the consultant to maintain professional liability insurance. At the same time, it is notable that the EJCDC E-500 Agreement Between Owner and Engineer for Professional Services does not include a requirement that the engineer procure professional

---

84. While B101-2017 § 10.5 provides that "[n]othing contained in this Agreement shall create a contractual relationship with or a cause of action in favor of a third party against either the Owner or Architect[,]" it is the inherent nature of design that can give rise to a number of such third-party claims, depending on the type of project constructed and the underlying basis of the claim. One significant example that is often cited of this is the lawsuits resulting from the July 17, 1981, collapse of two suspended walkways in the Kansas City Hyatt Regency. As a result of that accident, more than 100 separate lawsuits were pending in the year following the collapse, and 113 persons eventually died from injuries sustained as they fell with the walkways or were crushed underneath; 180 more were injured, many of them maimed for life. A detailed explanation of the design, the construction (containing fatal changes to the initial design), and the ultimate tragedy can be found at Steven S. Ross, *Construction Disasters: Design Failures, Causes and Prevention,* ENGINEERING NEWS RECORD, at 388–406 (McGraw-Hill Book Company 1984). The cause of the collapse was traced to a single change in the design of a support detail apparently made to facilitate the erection of the walkways. All parties denied having approved the change in the walkway's suspension, apparently from various court filings, blaming any and all other project principals for the fatal change. *Id.* at 406. However, the *Kansas City Star* published a steel fabricator's drawing in mid-August, indicating that all of the project principals had known of the design change. *Id.* at 397. The Hyatt Regency case illustrates the continuing liability exposure to third-party claims long after a commercial project is designed and constructed. It also involves another potential area of liability exposure when pre-engineered components are integrated into the architectural and/or structural design of a building, involving various participants in the fabrication of the component, over whom the design professional may have little or no control.

85. B101-2017, -1997 at Article 2, including § 2.5.6. And, over the years, the contract clauses for provision of insurance have become a greater focus for the AIA; for instance, in 2017 the AIA promulgated a separate A101-2017 *Exhibit A, Insurance and Bonds.* This *Exhibit A* document is intended to be used in conjunction with AIA Document A201-2017, General Conditions of the Contract for Construction.

liability insurance. However, even if the design professional enters into a nonindustry form manuscript contract, she should not resist obtaining a professional liability policy, and meeting other insurance requirements that the owner may require, while also consulting with her insurance professional and/or legal counsel if the owner makes what appears to be an unreasonable request to procure insurance.

13. Consequential Damages—Waiver and Related Issues

The 1997 edition of the AIA form documents added a provision where the contracting parties (the owner, architect, or contractor) waived the right against the other contracting party to recover "consequential damages." Most practitioners and commentators consider this a very significant development in the evolution of these form documents, including the secondary impact on construction contracting generally. We will examine the nature of consequential damages, how and why this new development occurred, and why it has had such an impact.

The AIA's consequential damages waiver arose primarily from a New Jersey case where the court found a construction manager liable to a casino owner for an arbitration award of $14.5 million, when its fee was in the range of $600,000.[86] This decision, which in part dealt with whether the arbitrator had made a mistake of law in the award, created such a sufficient concern and uproar that the AIA inserted consequential damages waivers into its 1997 AIA form contracts, with such waiver language continuing to appear in subsequent versions of the AIA forms thereafter.[87]

The impact of this addition to the AIA documents has been widespread for all concerned, with the design professional[88] probably gaining a greater benefit. With respect to the AIA owner/contractor agreements, the contractor obtains more of a benefit. Although a design professional could potentially

---

86. Perini Corp. v. Greate Bay Hotel & Casino, Inc., 129 N.J. 479, 610 A.2d 364 (1992).

87. *See* § 8.1.3 of the B101-2017 for the current architect-owner waiver of consequential damages provision.

88. It is generally considered that contractors gain a greater benefit over owners from waiver of consequential damages provisions, even though contractors give a broad waiver of such claims under the specific definition of consequential damages found in AIA A201-2017, § 15.1.7. This is because of the seemingly broad scope and extent of the waiver of the owner's potential claims and damages, as opposed to amounts that might be more limited for the contractor (and the design professional, as discussed above).

assert consequential damages in a claim (such as lost profits, lost business opportunities, etc.), it is more likely that it will be the owner (or contractor, for that matter) who will be claiming consequential damages. The owner's claims will probably be of a much greater dollar figure (such as the casino owner in *Perini Corp.*[89]). Most construction professionals can envision a plethora of situations where the most substantial damage claim in a construction-related dispute is the consequential damage claim by the owner, which could easily overshadow any claims of repairs for defective construction, or even delays in construction (casinos, malls, hotels, and stadiums are but a few of many examples).[90]

Therefore, as a risk management tool the design professional should include a waiver of consequential damages provision in all of his contracts, including form agreements and personally/manuscript drafted contracts.

14. Limitations of Liability

A Limitation of Liability (LOL) provision is an important risk control mechanism for design professionals. LOL clauses typically arise where a disparity exists between the fees charged by design professional in comparison with the potential risk assumed on a project (based on the project's size, complexity, and other factors). Many design professional firms are small and may not be able to absorb the risks. Other factors that justify an LOL are the pressures of the professional liability insurance market, and the fact that in many jurisdictions the architect's or engineer's signing and stamping of plans can render them personally liable for claims that may be asserted.

The design professional's LOL clauses come in many different forms, but always have the objective of placing a financial limit on the design professional's responsibility to the owner or some other party with whom the design professional has contracted. The limits that are typically used are a limitation up to a specified amount, to the design professional's fee, or to the amount of the insurance proceeds available to the design professional.[91]

---

89. *Supra* note 86.

90. A good discussion of the impact of consequential damages appears in THE CONSTRUCTION CONTRACTS BOOK: HOW TO FIND COMMON GROUND IN NEGOTIATING DESIGN AND CONSTRUCTION CONTRACT CLAUSES, *supra* note 40, at Chapter 6.

91. Most all designer's professional liability insurance policies are written on a "burning limits" basis—that is, the policy limits are reduced by each application of coverage under the policy to defend a claim, including the payment of attorney's fees. Although the subject is beyond the scope of this discussion, if the LOL clause is lim-

Jurisdictions in the country have treated the issue of enforceability of LOL clauses in various ways. Courts typically struggle to balance the rights of parties to enter into contracts on their own terms (i.e., the right to "freedom of contract") versus the possibility that the limitation of liability clause could be considered a "contract of adhesion," where the party providing the limitation is not able to properly assess or negotiate an allocation of the risks involved.[92]

---

ited to coverage remaining under the design professional's insurance policy limits, the careful design professional and his counsel will make certain that the LOL clause reflects this reality—that is, that the limitation is stated as being only to the remaining limits on the policy. *See generally* the design professional practice and risk management resources of Victor Insurance Managers Inc. (fka Victor O. Schinnerer & Company, Inc.), at https://www.victorinsuranceus.com/.

92. A good discussion of limitation of liability clauses with citations to differing state court rulings is contained in SWEET & SCHNEIER, *supra* note 11, § 15.03D. *See also* the compendium of LOL cases at https://www.skellengerbender.com/wp-content/uploads/2018/06/LOL-Bibliography-May-2018.pdf. The difference in approach by the various states to the enforceability of such clauses is illustrated by two cases involving design professionals, cited in SWEET & SCHNEIER. The facts in the cases were similar, but the outcome differed. The New York case of *Ricciardi v. Frank*, 655 N.Y.S.2d 242, 170 Misc. 2d 777 (1996), involved a claim by a consumer against an inspecting engineer who had agreed to perform a house inspection for $375. *Id.* While the New York trial court refused to enforce the LOL clause in the contract at issue that had limited liability to $375 (compared to actual damages in the case that were close to $3,000), the New York Appellate Term enforced the clause on appeal. In *Estey v. MacKenzie Eng'g, Inc.*, 927 P.2d 86 (Ore. 1996), a structural engineer was retained to make a limited, visual review of a house that his client was considering purchasing. The contract limited liability to $200 for any negligence by the engineer, the amount of his fee for the review. The client prevailed in a negligence action against the engineer, proving losses at trial of $190,000 for needed repairs with an estimated cost of $150,000 to be incurred. While the intermediate Oregon court enforced the clause, the Oregon Supreme Court refused to enforce the limitation of liability.

Several factors can be gleaned from Professor Sweet's work that the courts may be considering in deciding whether to enforce LOL's such as relative bargaining strengths, the opportunity for informed consent, type of client (public, private, business, lay), freedom of contract, market realities for desired services, dampening effect on willingness to undertake risky projects, insurance rates, risk compared to compensation, opportunity for counsel, and whether the LOL clause is sought to be applied in a consumer or a commercial context. JUSTIN SWEET & MARC M. SCHNEIER, LEGAL ASPECTS OF ARCHITECTURE, ENGINEERING AND THE CONSTRUCTION PROCESS (7th ed.

15. *Modifications and Changes to the Contract: Changes in Services*

A contract modification is one that the parties agree to by mutual written assent.[93] In contrast is a change to the contract terms, which typically one

2004). It could be said, especially in view of the Oregon and New York cases, that the kind of services sought as well as the structure of the process when entering into a contract can be a factor. In these two cases, the work did not involve design services open to continual input by clients but a predetermined bundle of services to be rendered by the engineers in performing the inspections. Thus, in the context of pre-design, design and pre-construction phase services—where a client would have greater opportunity to participate in, control, or influence the eventual outcome of the professional services bargained for—limitation of liability clauses may be more enforceable. Indeed, as pointed out by Professor Sweet, a number of jurisdictions have enforced LOL clauses. The California appellate court decision of *Markborough v. Superior Court*, 227 Cal. Ct. App. 3d 705 (1991), held that a LOL clause in a preprinted contract was valid, even though it had not been specifically negotiated or initialed. An important consideration for the court was the existence of an opportunity to negotiate, taking the form of a cover letter from the design professional, which gave the client the option to accept, reject, or modify any element of the contract. Another consideration was the relative bargaining power of the parties. *Markborough* also involved design services in which client interaction is inherent, and not inspection or other type of "off the shelf" consumer service bundles.

93. AIA Document B141-1997, Article 1.4, Scope of Services, 1 1.4.1.

party to the agreement makes unilaterally.[94] The AIA B101-2017 form contract deals explicitly with changes in services (as "Additional Services") in § 4.2. This section provides that the parties can change the services in many ways, including by mutual agreement in writing, because of circumstances beyond the control of the design professional, or because of any of the numerous circumstances discussed in § 4.2.1. Many of these situations are ones that might arise during the project construction, but just as easily could involve changes during the design phase. Examples of these project changes include changes in codes, laws, or regulations, or changes in the project size, quality, or budget.

It would appear that the conditions of § 4.2.1 would be easier to apply than a broad determination of "circumstances beyond the Architect's control." On its face, such circumstances would at a minimum seem to include calamities such as fire or other disaster. More tenuous would be project changes to scope or schedule, which might appear to be contractor issues but could also allegedly include design professional involvement. Disputes may arise in this manner. However, at the same time, it would be impossible for an agreement to list each and every possible unforeseen condition or calamity that might require a contract change. Therefore, it is necessary and fair to leave the broad language of the right to change the contract if there are conditions beyond the design professional's control.

The AIA C401-2017 form contract between the architect and consultant also includes an additional services provision and generally refers to the owner-architect contract for the scope of circumstances that could give rise to the need to modify the contract because of a change in services.[95]

It is also notable that the ConsensusDocs 240 Standard Agreement Between Owner and Design Professional has only very general language allowing for a change in scope, stating that the design professional shall be compensated for additional services on a lump sum or cost reimbursable basis as the parties may agree by change order.

---

94. *See* Sweet, *supra* note 77, § 6.11(a). Sweet explains that the owner may typically make changes to the contract for construction by way of a "change order" *See also* Sweet, *supra* note 77, § 6.14. This procedure is unique to the contractor's contract, although it may have impact on the design professional's contract, as discussed in Chapter 4, *infra*.

95. AIA C401-2017, Article 4.

IV. The Design Services Phase: Roles and Responsibilities

A. Contractual Roles and Liabilities

Under the AIA model, there are three distinct design phases: Schematic Design, Design Development, and Construction Documents. Although there are no precise definitions for these phases, there is an understanding across the disciplines in the design professions as to the general meaning of these terms. With advances in computer aided design and drafting and Building Information Modeling or BIM, these various design phases are merely iterations in the process of the development of the design and are not the separate and distinct stages of the development of the design that they once were.

1. Schematic Design

Schematic Design is the stage of design where the architect finalizes and confirms the project size and scope with the owner. If a clearly defined program does not exist before the commencement of this phase, the Schematic Design phase may be long and tedious. Otherwise, this phase involves only the prime design professional, usually the architect, and the owner. The end product is typically the outline of the project, with confirmation of certain fundamentals.

In the case of architects, the Schematic Design may contain the seeds of potential design liability that may surface much later in the other phases of the design or during construction. These liabilities can be divided broadly into two categories: (1) liability arising from the failure of the design to conform to owner's requirements; and (2) liability arising from entitlement issues, violation of private restrictions on the use and improvement of land, and zoning code violations or nonconformance with other applicable standards.

If the Schematic Design fails to conform to the owner's requirements, and the owner does not discover the failure until a later phase of the project (through no fault of his own), the design professional incurs liability to the owner. The owner can assert liability under the legal theories of breach of contract, negligence, negligent misrepresentation, and perhaps others.

The Schematic Design is, of course, a work in progress. Therefore, one cannot necessarily scrutinize it for building code violations. However, there may be aspects of Schematic Design that may be fixed and final and subject to an evaluation for conformance with applicable law. For example, a schematic architectural design must conform to applicable land use and zoning laws, such as height limits and setbacks. It must also comply with any applicable private restrictions such as restrictions as to height, step-backs, view corridors, easements, solar easements, and so on. Failure of the Schematic Design to conform with such laws or private restrictions if not detected early can result in costly revisions to completed design documents or expensive changes during construction and is potentially actionable under the theories of negligence, breach of contract, and perhaps negligence per se (discussed *infra*).

2. Design Development

Design Development is a significant phase in the development of the project, in that it involves the integration of multiple design disciplines. In addition to areas of potential liability highlighted under Schematic Design above, design professionals face potential liability during this phase for failure to coordinate the various design disciplines into a coherent and functional whole. AIA B101-2017, § 3.1.2 provides that the architect shall coordinate his (and by implication his consultants') services with the services provided by the owner and his respective consultants.

Various commentators and publications have discussed coordination of consultants, and the accompanying issues that arise.[96] In short, responsibility for the coordination of consultants is one that the design professional should not take lightly. Therefore, the prime design professional who undertakes this responsibility should make sure that he has the proper contractual protections in place with the owner and consultants as to responsibilities. Coordination is, of course, an ongoing responsibility of all design professionals throughout the project. It is particularly important during Design Development because in this phase, the project can still undergo significant changes in scope and parameters. It is because of such changes that failure to coordinate occurs, usually through communication failure or untimely communication among design professionals.

It is advisable for the prime design professional to have a coordination protocol in place, including a proper clause in the contract to outline the obligations and limitations.[97] Surprisingly, the AIA C-401 2017 form agreement between architect and the architect's consultant lacks any specific provision concerning coordination responsibilities as between the architect and his

---

96. *See* The Architect's Handbook of Professional Practice, *supra* note 1, § 11.2.

97. *See* Sheila Dixon & Richard D. Crowell, *Multiple Prime Contracts*, *in* The Contract Guide: DPIC's Risk Management Handbook for Architects and Engineers 213–16 (DPIC Companies, Inc. 1993). An updated version of DPIC's Contract Guide, The XL Insurance Contract Guide for Design Professionals: A Risk Management Guide for Architects, is currently being written.

consultants but contains mutual indemnification obligations whereby each party indemnifies the other for claims and liabilities arising from that party's services.

3. *Construction Documents*

The theories of liability against the design professional arising from the Construction Documents Phase are the same as those highlighted in the preceding two sections. However, many questions arise in this phase as to whether the conduct of the design professional met the applicable professional standard of care. During this phase, issues arise as to clarity and organization of the documents, adequacy of detailing, the quality and thoroughness of the specifications, completeness of the documents, and constructability.

Although technically not a part of the Construction Documents Phase, the administration of bidding and answering questions of bidders, also referred to in the most recent edition of the AIA documents as the "procurement phase," can be another area fraught with potential liability, primarily arising from miscommunication with bidders. Issues arising from design professional's services in this phase will usually be subject to expert opinion as to whether the conduct of the design professional met the prevailing standard of care in the profession at the time and in the locale of where the professional performed the services.

B. Implied Obligations of the Design Professional during the Design Services Phases

Beyond the liabilities and obligations that may be expressly stated in the design professional's contract, there are also potential implied obligations of which the design professional should be aware. Such implied obligations may begin to materialize during the design services phase but may also be present during the pre-design phase discussed above and other phases of the project discussed elsewhere in this handbook.

The first and foremost implied obligation in any design professional contract is that the design professional will act with professional care, typically known as the "standard of care." The courts normally define the standard of care as that care and skill ordinarily exercised by design professionals practicing under the same circumstances in the same locale and at the same time as the design professional. Thus, in *Paxton v. County of Alameda*,[98] the court stated that an architect "impliedly represents that he possesses, and it is his

---

98. *Paxton*, 259 P.2d at 938.

duty to possess, that degree of learning and skill ordinarily possessed by architects of good standing, practicing in the same locality."[99]

A further implied obligation could be that the design professional will comply with all codes and laws (certainly including building codes) applicable to the design. In fact, AIA B101-2017, § 3.1.5 refers to the architect "responding" to the requirements of governmental entities reviewing the project rather than "review laws, codes and regulations applicable to the Architect's services," which was the language used in the now-discontinued AIA Document B141-1997, which was referenced in the previous edition of this publication.

The courts also imply in every contract a requirement of "good faith and fair dealing." This covenant provides that the parties to the contract will act and work with each other in good faith and not act to frustrate or harm the others' rights and expectations. Design professional agreements are no different, and the design professional and his contracting party must work with one another to accomplish the intended result of the contract.

Finally, it is worth noting that a warranty is one obligation that the courts should not imply in the design professional's contract. Although counsel for claimants often attempt to clothe the design professional with such a warranty obligation, most jurisdictions have refused to imply such a warranty obligation on the design professional, most often based on the fact that the design professional is providing a service rather than a product.[100]

---

99. Of course, many design professional contracts include an express provision that the design professional will act according to the standard of care. *See, e.g.*, AIA B141-1997, 1 1.2.3.2.

100. *See* Gagne v. Bertran, 43 Cal. 2d 481, 275 P.2d 15 (1954); *cf.* Tamarac Dev. Co. v. Delamater, Freund & Assoc., 234 Kan. 618, 675 P.2d 361 (1984).

CHAPTER 4

Design Professional Legal Responsibilities—Construction and Completion Phases

PAUL T. MUNIZ[1]

I. Introduction

This chapter examines the legal responsibilities of design professionals during the construction and completion phases of a construction project. Although the contract primarily defines these responsibilities, principles of tort and statutory law, as well as the actual conduct of the design professional, influence the determination of whether the design professional may be legally responsible for claims asserted against it. Tort and statutory law determinations are also impacted by contract terms.[2] Further, the delivery method context in which the design professional performs its services plays an important role in defining the nature and extent of its legal responsibilities. This chapter primarily reviews the general principles of design professional responsibility based upon

---

1. The author of this second edition wishes to acknowledge and thank David Hatem for his contributions to this chapter as the author of the first edition.

2. *See, e.g.*, Brettel v. Omron Sci. Techs., Inc., 302 F. Supp. 3d 460, 467 (D. Mass. 2018); Parent v. Stone & Webster Eng'g Corp., 556 N.E. 2d 1009 (Mass. 1990); *Note, Architectural Malpractice: A Contract-Based Approach*, 92 HARV. L. REV. 1075 (1979); P. Jackson, *The Role of Contract in Architectural and Engineering Malpractice*, 51 INS. COUNSEL J. 517 (1984).

relatively standard contract terms and conventional roles of the design professional in the design-bid-build delivery method. Of course, there are always variations on these standard contract terms and the design professional's roles which can and do affect the legal duties, responsibilities, and liabilities of the design professional.

II. Construction Phase: Roles and Responsibilities

As previously noted, the contractual terms of engagement typically define the design professional's duties during the construction phase. These contractual terms include scope of service definition, as well as terms pertaining to standard of care, indemnification, and the allocation of risk and responsibility to other project participants (e.g., construction means, methods, and safety responsibility typically are allocated to the contractor).

A. Roles and Responsibilities of Project Participants in Design-Bid-Build

1. *Traditional Roles and Responsibilities*

Traditionally, the owner is responsible for establishing the project program and budget, securing project funding, and procuring and contracting with the major project participants, notably the design professional and the contractor. In the design-bid-build delivery method, the project owner typically engages the design professional to design the permanent components of the project and to serve as the owner's representative during construction. The owner approves the design as the designer is developing it. During the construction phase, the design professional's services primarily focus on providing the owner with confidence that the work, when fully completed, will conform to the requirements of the contract documents.

The owner engages the contractor to construct the project in accordance with the contract documents (which embody the design developed by the design professional and approved by the owner). In addition, the contractor (directly or through others) is responsible for the design and implementation of the construction means, methods, procedures, sequences, and techniques, as well as safety precautions and programs (construction means/methods and safety) employed in the performance of the work.

Most standard agreements—e.g., published by the American Institute of Architects (AIA) and the Engineers Joint Contract Documents Committee (EJCDC)—describe the roles and responsibilities of the owner, the design professional, and the contractor in a manner generally consistent with the traditional roles and responsibilities previously summarized.

2. Relationship of Roles and Responsibilities to Risk Allocation

Logically and appropriately, there should be a correlation between (1) the contractually defined roles and responsibilities of the respective project participants; (2) their ability to control and manage risk variables; and (3) risk allocation among the project participants.[3]

Application of these basic principles supports the widely accepted obligation of the owner to impliedly warrant the project design adequacy—the so-called *Spearin* Doctrine[4]—predicated on the rationale that the owner selects the design professional, generally approves the design, and has the responsibility to fund project costs. The design professional typically is required to perform its design and other services, including professional services during construction, in accordance with the degree of care and skill exercised by other similarly qualified and experienced design professionals performing under similar circumstances and terms of engagement (the professional standard of care). The professional standard of care does not require perfection. The Supreme Judicial Court of Massachusetts has stated:

> As a general rule, `[a]n architect's efficiency in preparing plans and specifications is tested by the rule of ordinary and reasonable skill usually exercised by one of that profession. . . . [I]n the absence of a special agreement he does not imply or guaranty a perfect plan or satisfactory result. . . . `Architects, doctors, engineers, attorneys and others deal in somewhat inexact sciences and are continually called upon to exercise their skilled judgment in order to anticipate and provide for random factors which are incapable of precise measurement. The indeterminable nature of these factors makes it impossible for professional service people to gauge them with complete accuracy in every instance. . . . Because of the inescapable possibility of error which inheres in these services, the law has traditionally required, not perfect results, but rather the exercise of that skill and judgment which can be reasonably expected from similarly situated professionals.[5]

The contractor typically assumes the risk and responsibility for liability, claims, damages, or losses due to construction means/methods and safety,

3. *See, e.g.*, R. J. Smith, *Allocation of Risk—The Case for Manageability*, 13 INTL. CONSTRUCTION L. REV. 549 (1996).

4. United States v. Spearin, 248 U.S. 132, 39 S. Ct. 59, 63 L. Ed. 166 (1918). A contractor was entitled to damages after the government annulled his contract to build a dry dock. The government breached its implied warranty that a defective sewer, which he was required to move, would be adequate if he followed the plans.

5. Klein v. Catalano, 437 N.E. 2d 514, 525 (Mass. 1982).

since those areas generally fall in the province of the contractor's contractual role, qualification, and actual ability to control.

Based on these standard roles and responsibilities and their underlying risk allocation rationale, most standard contracts define the design professional's performance standard in a manner consistent with the professional standard of care. Those same contracts and standard General Conditions of the Construction Contract state that the contractor is exclusively responsible for construction means/methods and safety, and is obligated to indemnify the owner and design professional for claims and damages due to deficiencies in construction means/ methods and safety.[6]

3. *Variations on Traditional Roles and Responsibilities in Design-Bid-Build*

On design-bid-build projects, the respective roles and responsibilities of the design professional and contractor may vary from their traditionally defined roles and responsibilities. For example, while a design professional retained by the owner is normally not responsible for the design of construction means/ methods, or administrative roles during the construction phase pertaining to that area, owners may prefer that design professionals become involved in providing design and other professional services related to construction means/ methods and other aspects of construction execution and methodology. This role transformation stands in contrast to the traditional role of the noninvolvement of the design professional in construction means/methods. Design professionals may become involved in construction means/methods issues in different ways—such as, preparation of design criteria or performance specifications, or preparation of detailed and mandatory construction means/methods design. Each of these different types and degrees of role transformation carries different legal responsibilities and potential liability exposures for the design professional. When this type of role transformation occurs, the design professional is likely to assume some degree (more or less depending upon the scope and contractually defined level of involvement) of risk and legal responsibility for deficiencies in affected construction means/methods.

Conversely, while a contractor is typically not responsible (directly or vicariously) for the design of *permanent* project work (as distinct from design of construction means/methods), the contractor may assume such responsibility by contractually accepting design delegation responsibilities or proposing

---

6. AIA Document A201-2017, 13.18.1.

and becoming responsible for value engineering modifications to that work.[7] In such circumstances, the contractor typically may assume some degree of risk and responsibility for deficiencies in the design.[8]

These variations in roles and responsibilities are becoming more common in the design-bid-build delivery approach since they may afford reasonable options (if appropriately undertaken) to shift to other delivery method approaches, such as design-build. From the perspective of the design professional, there is nothing especially or absolutely problematic about contractual assumption of these nontraditional roles and responsibilities. The key is to understand the potential risk re-allocation and resulting liability.

B. Roles and Responsibilities of the Design Professional during the Construction Phase

1. *Roles and Responsibilities Defined by Contract and Conduct*

Undoubtedly, contracts are the principal source for definition of the nature and extent of the design professional's obligations during the construction phase. Contracts serve a central function in defining the roles and responsibilities for both contract-based and tort claims against the design professional arising out of construction phase services and occurrences. Succeeding sections of this chapter will discuss some of the more important of these contract provisions.

In addition, the design professional's conduct during the construction phase may have a significant impact upon the design professional's responsibility. For example, if the design professional directs the contractor in the field or limits the contractor's discretion in the areas of work performance, construction means/methods, or safety, the design professional may face potential professional liability exposure despite the clear terms of the contract negating any role or responsibility in that area.[9] Thus, the design professional's prospects of achieving summary judgment based on such contract language may be significantly diminished, if not eliminated entirely.

---

7. *See, e.g.*, David. J. Hatem, *Design Delegation: Risk Management/Allocation Considerations for Design Professionals*, 4 The CA/T Professional Liability Reporter No. 1, 7 (Nov. 1998).

8. *See, e.g.*, AIA Document A201-1997, 1 3.2.10, General Conditions of the Contract for Construction.

9. *See, e.g.*, S. Minnesota Beet Sugar Coop. v. Agri Sys., 427 F. Supp. 3d 1026, 1032 (D. Minn. 2019); Affiliated FM Ins. Co. v. LTK Consulting Servs., Inc., 170 Wash. 2d 442, 444, 243 P.3d 521, 523 (2010).

Courts will generally respect clear contract terms defining roles and limiting responsibilities of the design professional. However, if credible evidence exists that the design professional by its conduct contradicted and did not adhere to its own role as contractually defined, a court may disregard or de-emphasize the contract terms as dispositive in determining responsibility, and resort to more generally applicable tort principles to determine liability. Typical factors that a court would consider to determine whether the design professional's actions evinced an intent to expand his responsibilities beyond the contours of the contract with the owner include: "(1) actual supervision and control of the work; (2) retention of the *right* to supervise and control; (3) constant participation in ongoing activities at the construction site; (4) supervision and coordination of the subcontractors; (5) responsibility for taking safety precautions at the job site; (6) authority to issue change orders; (7) the right to stop the work."[10]

2. *Modification of Roles and Responsibilities during the Construction Phase*

There are circumstances where otherwise clearly defined contractual roles and obligations of the design professional and other project participants are contractually modified due to some evolving project requirement or circumstance (often, owner driven) that develops during the construction phase; for example, an owner's request that its design professional become involved in a construction means/methods issues due to concern about claims involving the contractor. Alternately, and for example, public safety or stability concerns related to abutting property could cause owners to closely monitor or even direct the contractor's operations. Similarly, an obstinate contractor taking advantage of a required change to its contract may engage in brinksmanship negotiations causing the owner to turn to its design professional to rescue it by assuming a duty that the contractor refuses. The design professional all too often is willing to step outside its contractual obligations to assist the client. When previously defined roles and responsibilities change during construction, it is important for the design professional to (1) understand the potential risk and responsibility implications of the proposed change in scope of services to make an informed decision whether to assume it; (2) evidence any change by written modification or amendment to the owner-design professional agreement; and (3) make certain that the new or evolving role of the design professional is

---

10. Westerfield v. Arjack Co., 78 Ill. Ct. App. 3d 137 (Ill. Ct. App. Ct. 1979); *see also* Waltman v. Eng'g Plus, Inc., 264 So. 3d 758, 762 (Miss. 2019).

clearly communicated and understood by all affected project participants (e.g., the contractor).[11]

3. *Standard Contract Terms Regarding Design Professional Roles and Responsibilities during the Construction Phase*

The AIA form contracts define the traditional duties of design professionals during the construction phase.

a. Site Visits

AIA Document B201-2017, ¶ 2.6.2.1 defines the architect's role regarding site visits during construction. Paragraph 2.6.2.1, "Evaluations of the Work," states:

> The Architect shall visit the site at intervals appropriate to the stage of construction, or as otherwise required in Section 3.2.3, to become generally familiar with the progress and quality of the portion of the Work completed, and to determine, in general, if the Work observed is being performed in a manner indicating that the Work, when fully completed, will be in accordance with the Contract Documents. However, the Architect shall not be required to make exhaustive or continuous on-site inspections to check the quality or quantity of the Work. On the basis of the site visits the Architect shall keep the Owner reasonably informed about the progress and quality of the portion of the Work completed, and report to the Owner (1) known deviations from the Contract Documents and from the most recent construction schedule submitted by the Contractor, and (2) defects and deficiencies observed in the Work.

Regarding the architect's evaluative role during construction, ¶ 2.6.1.2[12] and ¶ 2.6.2.1 make clear the following:

---

11. *See* Subsurface Conditions: Risk Management for Design and Construction Management Professionals 1 10.3.4, at 364–67 (David Hatem ed., 1998).

12. § 2.6.1.2 The Architect shall advise and consult with the Owner during the Construction Phase Services. The Architect shall have authority to act on behalf of the Owner only to the extent provided in this Agreement. The Architect shall not have control over, charge of, or responsibility for the construction means, methods, techniques, sequences or procedures, or for safety precautions and programs in connection with the Work, nor shall the Architect be responsible for the Contractor's failure to perform the Work in accordance with the requirements of the Contract Documents.

- It is performed as a representative of the Owner.
- The frequency of site visits is defined by intervals appropriate to the stage of Contractor's operations.
- The purpose of the site visits is to evaluate whether the work, when fully completed, will conform to the requirements of the Contract Documents.
- The architect is not responsible for construction means/methods and safety.

Paragraphs 2.6.1.2 and 2.6.2.1 represent a typical contractual definition and accepted industry understanding of the design professional's function in making site visits during construction. It emphasizes the intent that the design professional's role is focused on *permanent* project work that he or she has designed, and generally does not extend to responsibility for observations or evaluations of construction means/methods or safety. In addition, ¶ 2.6.2.1 makes it clear that the architect's evaluative role is not "exhaustive" or "continuous." In this regard, ¶ 2.6.2.1 reinforces other provisions of the contract documents that assign to the contractor primary responsibility for supervision, inspection, and quality of the work.

The responsibility for construction defects must always be viewed in the light of the contractor's plenary obligation to perform the work in accordance with contract documents. Statutes often reiterate this requirement for public construction projects.[13] The courts will look to the terms and conditions of the design professional's and the construction contractor's contracts to define and distinguish the respective duties of these two parties on a construction project. For example, in an appeal of an OSHA finding related to a fatal accident, the Seventh Circuit Court of Appeals overturned OSHA' s determination that a design professional was "engaged in construction."[14] The appeals court ruled that the design professional had not exercised "substantial supervision over the construction" and expressed its concern that in reaching its conclusion OSHA had ignored the contract language defining the design professional's duties.[15]

Notwithstanding this traditional distinction between the responsibilities of the designer and contractor, owners often argue that their design professional is in a position to detect and prevent defects in the constructed project.

---

13. *See, e.g.*, Mass. Gen. Laws ch. 30, § 39I, prohibiting any willful, substantial deviation from contract documents without specific written authorization from the public owner.

14. CH2M Hill, Inc. v. Herman, 192 F.3d 711 (7th Cir. 1999).

15. *Id.* at 722–23.

A seminal case discussing the design professional's potential liability for its site observations as compared to the more extensive clerk-of-the-works type of continuous presence and inspection services is *Watson, Watson, Rutlan/Architects, Inc. v. Montgomery County Board of Education*.[16] The owner declined its contract option for the design professional to provide clerk-of-the-works inspection services, but still attempted to hold it liable for not detecting contractor defects that led to a leaking roof. Noting the importance of the owner/design professional agreement's language, the *Watson* court reviewed the decisions from other jurisdictions. Ultimately, it concluded that the owner had not carried its burden of proof and ruled in favor of the architect, but also held that a design professional has a duty to report known deficiencies to the owner and could not turn a blind eye to contractor failings that might affect the finished constructed project.

The AIA documents also provide that the design professional performs its site visits as a representative of the owner and, thus, for the benefit of the owner. Put another way, the design professional's site visit role must be understood in the context of the contractor's fundamental role to (a) perform the work in accordance with the contract documents and (b) be primarily responsible for construction means/methods and safety. A split of authority exists in the jurisdictions that have considered and decided whether to hold a design professional responsible for worker injuries resulting from unsafe working conditions.[17] The design professional need also be cognizant of any statutory provisions, such as the Illinois Structural Work Act (repealed by the General Assembly in 1995 but lately the object of a groundswell of support for reinstatement), that could heighten its liability potential for worker injuries.

b. Submittal Review

Generally, contractor submittals, such as shop drawings, are contractually required. The submittals serve an important function in validating the contractor's understanding of the design and Contract Document requirements and provide an opportunity for the contractor to communicate in a more detailed executory way its proposed plan for fulfilling the requirements of the contract documents.

---

16. Watson, Watson, Rutland/Architects, Inc., v. Montgomery County Bd. of Educ., 559 So. 2d 168 (1990); *see also* Shaw v. Cherokee Meadows, LP, 431 F. Supp. 3d 1336, 1343 (N.D. Okla. 2019), and LeBlanc v. Logan Hilton Joint Venture, 463 Mass. 316, 328, 974 N.E.2d 34, 44 (2012).

17. *See, e.g.*, Edwards v. Anderson Eng'g, Inc., 284 Kan. 892, 905, 166 P.3d 1047, 1056 (2007).

AIA Document B 201-2017, ¶ 2.6.4.1 defines the architect's role in the submittal process as follows:

> In accordance with the Architect-approved submittal schedule, the Architect shall review and approve or take other appropriate action upon the Contractor's submittals such as Shop Drawings, Product Data and Samples, but only for the limited purpose of checking for conformance with information given and the design concept expressed in the Contract Documents. Review of such submittals is not for the purpose of determining the accuracy and completeness of other information such as dimensions, quantities, and installation or performance of equipment or systems, which are the Contractor's responsibility. The Architect's review shall not constitute approval of safety precautions or, unless otherwise specifically stated by the Architect, of any construction means, methods, techniques, sequences or procedures. The Architect's approval of a specific item shall not indicate approval of an assembly of which the item is a component.

The intent of ¶ 2.6.4.2, like that of virtually all other standard contract terms addressing the design professional's submittal review role, is to define in a concentrated manner that the architect' s review focuses on submittal content relevant to the design requirements of permanent project work in a manner distinct from the contractor's contemplated construction means/methods. The distinction between design of permanent project work and construction means and methods may be blurred in submittal content, and the design professional should be clear to limit the scope of his or her review to the former. The contract should always require that contractors stamp submittals prior to forwarding them to the design professional for review. The contract should similarly prohibit the contractor from commencing any item of work addressed in that submittal until the contractor has satisfactorily addressed the design professional concerns as indicated by the design professional's acceptance or approval of the submittal.

Design professionals face exposure to professional liability or contract claims from project owners if they fail to review in a timely manner a contractor's submittal, resulting in contractor delay claims against the owner. Indeed, contractors may deliberately attempt to overwhelm the design professional's capacity to review submittals by simultaneously unleashing a barrage of submittals, essentially orchestrating the delay. By including construction contract requirements that the contractor submit a schedule of submittals, the design professional can muster the required resources to perform the expected review and combat any delay allegations caused by deviations from that schedule.[18] Generally, it is good practice for the design professional to maintain a log documenting dates of receipt and review return of contractor submittals, and then monitor that log during the project.

c. Construction Means/Methods

As previously noted, design professionals generally do not design or otherwise become involved in construction means/methods, the latter of which typically falls within the expertise and control of the contractor. However, there are special circumstances in which a design professional may, in varying degrees, become involved in the design of construction means/methods; for example, by preparing a very detailed method specification or design that can only be constructed in a sequence that later proves impossible. The extent of design professional responsibility and potential professional liability exposure that attaches to these varying degrees of construction means/methods involvement of the design professional typically depends upon a complex and fact-intensive analysis. For example, in *CH2M Hill, Inc., v. Herman*,[19] the Seventh Circuit Court of Appeals stated, "whether or not the construction standards apply has previously been a fact-specific inquiry that appears to turn on the responsibilities assumed by the firms in question."[20]

The typical AIA contract between the owner and the general contractor acknowledges this special circumstance by providing that "[t]he contractor shall be solely, subject to the terms of Article 4, responsible for and have control over construction means, methods, techniques, sequences and procedures and for coordinating all portions of the work under the contract unless contract documents give other specific instructions concerning these matters[;] and that [t]he contractor shall take all necessary precautions for safety and shall provide

---

18. *See, e.g.*, AIA B201-2017 § 2.6.4.1 The Architect shall review the Contractor's submittal schedule and shall not unreasonably delay or withhold approval. The Architect's action in reviewing submittals shall be taken in accordance with the approved submittal schedule or, in the absence of an approved submittal schedule, with reasonable promptness while allowing sufficient time in the Architect's professional judgment to permit adequate review.

19. CH2M Hill, Inc., v. Herman, 192 F.3d 711 (7th Cir. 1999).

20. *Id.* at 719.

all necessary protection to prevent damage, injury or loss to all persons on the work and other persons who may be affected thereby."[21]

The author recommends that when a design professional becomes involved in the design of construction means/methods, the extent of that involvement and the allocation of risk should be clearly and consistently stated in both the owner-design professional agreement (or any appropriate amendment thereto) and the general conditions of the construction contract, or in the applicable technical provisions of the specifications or notes on the drawings.

d. Safety

It is widely recognized and accepted in the design and construction industry that since the contractor controls the site and has discretion as to the means/methods by which he executes the work, the contractor should be exclusively responsible for construction means/methods and safety. In circumstances where the contractor's control of those means/methods is limited or otherwise curtailed by provisions of the contract documents or directives issued by others during construction, this general rule may be modified.

This general rule supports the logic of contractual indemnification provisions in favor of the owner and design professional for personal injury and/or property damage claims and liabilities arising out of the contractor's construction means/methods and/or failure to implement or monitor adequate safety precautions or programs.

e. Quality Assurance

Quality Assurance refers to the design professional's role in generally monitoring or auditing the contractor's performance, including the latter's quality control, in the performance of permanent project work. As distinct from the design professional's quality assurance role, the contractor is responsible for quality control including supervision and inspection in the performance of its work and that of the trade subcontractors. Quality control generally includes a plan for detailed supervision and inspection of work and materials furnished by the prime contractor, all of its subcontractors, and their respective materials providers. In performing its quality assurance role, the design professional serves as a representative of the owner; performance of that role does not relieve the contractor of its responsibility for performing the work in accordance with the

---

21. *See, e.g.*, AIA Document A102-2007 § 16.1.2 (Standard Form of Agreement Between Owner and Contractor for Cost Plus with GMP), enumerating AIA Document A201-2007 as part of the contract documents.

requirements of the contract documents and for adherence to its own contractual obligations. However, the design professional may face liability from the owner for failing to detect an ineffective contractor quality control program. For example, if a contractor's quality control procedure contains hold points for self-inspection during a particular construction sequence and the design professional witnesses but fails to recognize or report that the contractor is ignoring or only superficially performing the self-inspection, then the design professional could share liability for defects in that constructed item that might have been prevented had the hold point inspection been implemented.

f. Rejection of Work

Typically, the design professional is empowered under the contract documents to reject work performed by the contractor that does not conform to the requirements of the contract documents. AIA Document B 201-2017, § 2.6.2.2 provides that the architect's authority to reject work or any judgmental decision made in good faith by the architect to exercise or not to exercise that authority shall not give rise to a duty or responsibility of the architect to the contractor.

Of course, as in the performance of all construction phase services, the design professional exercises its authority to reject work as a representative of the owner. If the design professional fails to exercise sound judgment in that regard, especially judgment that fails to meet the professional standard of care, the design professional may face liability to the owner. For example, if the design professional accepts the incorporation of certain mechanical equipment into the work that later proves to be defective or incapable of fulfilling stated performance requirements, the design professional will likely be a target of cost recovery by the owner. Although the construction contract undoubtedly assigns responsibility and therefore primary liability to the contractor for this deficiency, if the damages are substantial, the design professional may become embroiled in the dispute.

Wrongfully rejecting contractor work that turns out to be adequate can also lead to potential liability. Contractors sometimes attempt to recover their additional costs from design professionals for rejected substitutions under unfair business practice statutes or under a theory of negligent misrepresentation. In addition, most construction contracts contain a provision for "uncovering the work" that requires the owner to pay the costs of that uncovering if the item of work proves to be acceptable. If these owner-incurred costs are the result of the design professional's malfeasance, then that design professional can expect to face additional liability to the owner.

Similarly, the design professional needs to avoid an overly aggressive or hyper-technical inspection that is incompatible with the intent of that aspect of the work. For example, if the industry standard for determining the acceptability of repairs to minor damage of concrete is to "sound" the patch with a mason's hammer, then requiring the contractor to adopt a more elaborate and expensive approach such as ultrasonic testing must be resisted. Such an "over-inspection" could give rise to successful contractor claims of a "constructive change" for which the owner could seek recovery from the design professional.[22] Moreover, strict compliance with the contract requirements is not always the measure of acceptability of the installed work. Sometimes the doctrine of economic waste will mandate the acceptance of technically noncompliant work.

The limitations on an owner's right to insist on strict compliance with contract provisions were discussed in *Granite Construction Co. v. United States*,[23] which involved the construction of a lock and dam on the Mississippi River for the Corps of Engineers. The contractor in *Granite* was required to comply strictly with the government specifications for materials. When the government learned that Granite had embedded a noncompliant waterstop in portions of the cast-in-place concrete, it ordered Granite to remove and replace the noncompliant material with the approved waterstop, despite the fact that all evidence suggested that the material would function as well as the one specified. The appeals court recognized the government's right to insist on strict compliance, but found that where the cost of replacement is economically wasteful and the work is otherwise adequate, the government should allow the noncompliant material to remain in place. However, the court held that the contractor owed the government a reduction in contract price.

g. Contractor Claims, Payment Issues, and Interpretation of the Contract Documents

In addition to performing services during construction as the owner's representative, the design professional is usually required to perform certain administrative services with respect to investigating, evaluating, and making recommendations concerning contractor claims and disputes. A routine part of the design professional's services typically includes the review, evaluation,

---

22. *See, e.g.*, Southwest Welding & Mfg. v. United States, 413 F.2d 1167 (Ct. Cl. 1969).

23. Granite Construction Co. v. United States, 962 F.2d 998 (1992), *cert. denied*, 506 U.S. 1048 (1993); *see also* DeAtley Const., Inc. v. United States, 75 Fed. Cl. 575, 582 (2007).

and recommendations regarding contractor payment requests. Similarly, the construction contract nearly always assigns the design professional the responsibility for interpretation of the contract documents. In performing these services, the design professional is required to act impartially, in good faith, and diligently.

The design professional should undertake any investigation and evaluation of contractor claims in accordance with the contractually stipulated procedures, and recommendations should be governed by and consistent with the intent and requirements of the contract documents. The design professional's evaluations and recommendations of a contractor's payment request should also be based upon reasonably objective data and observations of the contractor's work performance and the diligent and good faith exercise of sound judgment. The design professional should always make clear in any payment certification that its representations are based on the limited degree of contractually defined site visits of the design professional. The standard AIA general conditions provisions clearly describe the limitations of the Architect's Certificate for Payment.[24] The AIA agreement between owner and architect also reflects those limitations.[25] Claimants may attempt to imply an expanded role of the design professional in such certifications, resulting in liability problems for design professionals.

When the owner is a public entity, the potential liability for inappropriate payment certifications takes on a new dimension in the form of potential liability under a false claims statute as discussed later in this chapter.

The contractual and industrial context in which the design professional performs its role and review of contractor pay applications is a significant consideration in this regard. The contractor is primarily responsible for the adequacy of its work, warranty, and indemnity obligations. In addition, the system of payment withholding and retention evidences an intention to provide protection to the owner and opportunities for recourse against the contractor for defective work or overpayment. However, the design professional faces potential liability from all sides. Architects may also be subject to suit by sureties complaining that their principals were overpaid by virtue of negligently issued certificates.[26]

Obviously, the original intent and specific requirements of the contract documents should substantively guide the design professional's interpretation of those documents. Rendering these interpretations consistent with contract

---

24. AIA Document A201-2017, ¶¶ 9.4.2, 9.5.1.

25. AIA Document B 201-2017, ¶¶ 2.6.3.1, 2.6.3.2.

26. *See* Peerless Ins. Co. v. Cerny & Assoc., Inc., 199 F. Supp. 951 (1961).

protocol and the prescribed time limitations will minimize contractor claims of ineffective contract administration.

Professional liability problems arise when the design professional does not reasonably adhere to the substantive and procedural requirements of the contract documents or exercise impartial and reasonable diligence in the interpretive process. Given the quasi-judicial nature of these construction administration services—especially interpretation of the contract documents and the making of recommendations and/or decisions regarding construction contractor claims—the design professional may be entitled to a qualified immunity defense in connection with claims arising out of the performance of such services.

For example, in fulfilling its assigned arbitral role, the design professional is exercising an authority that has been assigned to him by the construction contract and agreed to by both the owner and the contractor; he is immune from subsequent action by either party as long as he exercises that authority in good faith.[27] If the design professional acts beyond the scope of its contractually assigned role, fails to act in good faith, or uses its arbitral powers to cover its own defective design, that immunity is no longer available.

AIA B101-2017 Section 3.6.2.3 describes two architectural services: interpretations and decisions. Section 3.6.2.4, and A201-2007 Section 4.2.12 provide that the architect will not be liable for interpretations or decisions rendered in good faith. B101-2017 further shields the architect from interpretation-related claims either by the owner or by anyone claiming as an intended beneficiary of the owner-architect contract. AIA A201-2017 would also shield the architect from interpretation-related claims. The contractual immunity protection would apply to interpretations, such as determining what the terms in the specifications meant, or to matters of performance under the contract. For example, did the contractor's work meet the contractual requirements?

In *Craviolini v. Scholer & Fuller Associate Architects*,[28] a contractor attempted to overcome the architect's presumed immunity for its decisions on disputes between the owner and contractor. The contractor claimed that the architect attempted to destroy the contractor's business after it complained

---

27. Lundgren v. Freeman, 307 F.2d 104, 118 (1962) ("We think he [the architect] should be protected when he acts in good faith, however erroneously, and that such protection is enough. If he acts fraudulently, or with willful and malicious intent to injure the contractor, he should be liable."); *see also* RPR & Assocs. v. O'Brien/Atkins Assocs., P.A., 24 F. Supp. 2d 515, 525 (M.D.N.C. 1998).

28. Craviolini v. Scholer & Fuller Assoc. Architects, 89 Ariz. 24, 357 P.2d 611 (1960).

about defects in the plans and specifications, and that the architect wrongfully disallowed material substitutions. The appeals court ruled that the "cloak of immunity" was available to the architect only when performing in its role as arbitrator, deciding a dispute between the owner and contractor.[29] However, the court considered those decisions made by the architect in its role as construction administrator to be fair game for the contractor's claims of misfeasance. The availability of this quasi-judicial immunity is dependent upon the jurisdiction of the dispute.[30] However, to be entitled to such a defense, the design professional must establish that it acted in good faith, impartially, and with reasonable diligence.[31]

h. Termination of the Contractor

The terms of the contract documents and general common law principles define the circumstances, duties, rights, and remedies pertaining to contract termination. The law favors the formation of contracts and disfavors their dissolution. Accordingly, when a design professional is involved in an owner's effort to terminate a construction contractor, the design professional must rigidly adhere to the principles of good faith and fair dealing. Under the AIA agreements, the owner has a contractual obligation to provide an impartial unbiased architect to perform the construction phase administrative duties. The design professional's role, if any, in the process of an owner's termination of a construction contract likely will be defined in the contract documents. It is critical that the design professional carry out those duties in an impartial and unbiased manner, resisting any pressure by the owner to bolster its case

---

29. *Id.* at 614.

30. City of Durham v. Reidsville Eng'g Co., 255 N.C. 98, 120 S.E.2d 564 (1961).

31. *See* AIA Document B201-2017 § 2.6.2.4. Interpretations and decisions of the Architect shall be consistent with the intent of and reasonably inferable from the Contract Documents and shall be in writing or in the form of drawings. When making such interpretations and decisions, the Architect shall endeavor to secure faithful performance by both Owner and Contractor, shall not show partiality to either, and shall not be liable for results of interpretations or decisions rendered in good faith. The Architect's decisions on matters relating to aesthetic effect shall be final if consistent with the intent expressed in the Contract Documents. JUSTIN SWEET & MARC M. SCHNEIER, LEGAL ASPECTS OF ARCHITECTURE, ENGINEERING AND THE CONSTRUCTION PROCESS 283–85 (7th ed.2004).

for termination by overstating the record of alleged contractor transgressions or failings.[32]

First and foremost, the authority and decision to terminate rests with the owner. The terms of the owner/contractor construction contract may require that the design professional certify that sufficient cause exists to support the owner's termination of the contractor. In such circumstances, the design professional should base its certification on a reasonable investigation that is factually based and well documented. While the design professional should not hesitate to state its opinion and recommendations as discussed above, the ultimate decision to terminate must remain with the owner. The ultimate determination or judgment of whether sufficient cause exists to terminate (whether there has been a material breach of contract) is legal in nature, and therefore best left to the owner and its attorneys. The design professional may present subsidiary facts or objective evidence that provides the basis upon which a legal determination or judgment may be exercised by others (typically, the owner's legal counsel).[33] Finally, the owner or its counsel—not the design professional—should communicate with the contractor or its surety regarding termination.

In the case of an owner terminating its contractor based in part upon the design professional's certification, that design professional may find itself subjected to contractor claims of tortious interference with an advantageous business relationship or violation of an unfair business practices statute. The contractor could pursue this type of claim independent of the owner-contractor agreement, possibly eviscerating the design professional's attempt to invoke quasi-judicial immunity. However, an architect or engineer, acting in a professional capacity and without actual malice, has a conditional privilege to "interfere" with the relationships between the owner and the contractor.[34] Only where the design professional induces a breach of contract, not to further its client's best interests but with the intent to harm the other party or to further its personal goals, is the design professional potentially liable for tortious interference.[35]

---

32. *See* Barr Inc. v. Studio One, Inc., 146 F. Supp. 3d 375, 382 (D. Mass. 2015) (contractor terminated by a project owner brought suit against the architect alleging that the architect falsely certified grounds for termination).

33. *See* Sweet & Schneier, *supra* note 31, at 721–22.

34. Santucci Const. Co. v. Baxter & Woodman, Inc., 151 Ill. App. 3d 547, 104 Ill. Dec. 474, 502 N.E.2d 1134 (2d Dist. 1986).

35. Waldinger Corp. v. CRS Group Engineers, Inc.,775 F.2d 781 (7th Cir. 1985).

4. *Commonly Recognized Implied Obligations of the Design Professional in the Performance of Construction Phase Services*

This chapter has appropriately focused on the central role of the contract in defining the obligations of the design professional during the construction phase. However, the case law amply demonstrates that there are certain implied obligations to which the design professional must adhere in the performance of those services.

A review of case decisions reveals the importance of the design professional's exercise of good faith in its evaluations and recommendations regarding contractor performance and payment issues, review of and action upon contractor submittals, resolution of claims and disputes, and interpretation of the contract documents.[36] In this context, proof of good faith generally means that the design professional can objectively demonstrate that it acted in accordance with the procedural and substantive provisions of the contract documents and in accordance with sound professional judgment and industry custom. In addition to good faith, many case decisions have demonstrated the importance of the design professional's diligent and timely performance of its construction administration services.[37]

5. *Areas of Potential Professional Liability Exposure*

The range of professional liability exposures and claims against design professionals arising out of construction phase services may be classified in a number of ways—by the identity of the claimant, the nature of the legal theory supporting the claim (whether predicated on common law or statutory grounds), and the type of damages or injuries alleged.

a. Owner Claims

Professional liability claims asserted by the owner (typically, the design professional's client) against the design professional arising out of construction phase services represent, by far, the highest percentage of such claims. As a general matter, an owner may predicate its claims on the basis that the design professional failed to meet certain specific contractual obligations and/or failed to perform in accordance with the professional standard of care. In most claims, there is substantial overlap between these two theories.

---

36. *See, e.g.*, Bell v. Jones, 523 A.2d 982, 994 (D.C. 1986) (duty is breached when the architect negligently certifies completion of defective or incomplete work).

37. *See, e.g.*, Nelson v. Commonwealth, 235 Va. 228, 368 S.E.2d 239 (1988); French v. Jinright & Ryan, P.C. Architects, LEXIS 19446 (U.S. Dist. 1983).

In professional liability claims arising out of construction phase services, an owner may assert that the design professional failed to satisfy specific contractual terms, e.g., the frequency of site visits, timeliness of shop drawing reviews, responses to Requests for Information (RFIs), quality assurance, and inadequate or inappropriate certification of contractor applications for payment. To prevail, the owner must establish a breach of the specific contract term or requirement *and* that such breach proximately caused the owner to sustain damage. In a substantial number of such claims, the owner's primary recourse for any damage sustained is and should be against the contractor. Specifically, under the standard contract documents the contractor is responsible for defective work (whether or not the design professional observed or otherwise detected the defect).[38] On public projects in some jurisdictions, statutory requirements reinforce this contract provision.[39] When the owner overpays the contractor based upon the design professional's recommendations, the owner's primary (if not exclusive) remedy should be against the contractor. However, in certain circumstances, when the owner's recourse against the contractor is foreclosed due to the passage of time or warranty periods, and/or the financial insolvency of the contractor, the design professional may have more exposure to a professional liability claim from the owner. Overpayment to a contractor based on a design professional's negligently prepared payment certification could also lead to liability to the contractor's surety that is forced to complete a project for an insolvent contractor that had collected more contract funds than it was entitled to.

The owner must present adequate proof that the design professional failed to meet the professional standard of care. Typically, this would require an expert opinion that the design professional failed to meet the professional standard of care.[40] The scope and terms of the design professional's contract with the owner, as well as the relevant facts and circumstances, will determine whether the design professional met the appropriate standard of care. Clearly, the most significant factor in determining the design professional's liability is whether its contract with the owner required a heightened standard of care; in other words, one requiring a better performance than required by the common law. Similarly, any contractual provision that guarantees a certain result or owner satisfaction will expose the design professional to additional liability.

---

38. AIA Document A201-2017, 1 12.2.1; EJCDC Standard General Conditions of the Construction Contract, 1996, 1 6.19, B.

39. Mass. Gen. Laws ch. 30, § 391 (1960).

40. *See, e.g.,* Atlas Tack v. Donabed, 47 Mass Ct. App. Ct. 221, 712 N.E.2d 617 (1999).

Project cost overruns and schedule impacts represent an important area of professional liability exposure common to both owner and contractor claims often asserted against the design professional. The extent to which such claims pose a substantial risk for the design professional depends on a number of factors and considerations; such as the provisions in the owner-design professional agreement regarding responsibility for indirect or consequential damage, and the status of the economic loss doctrine in the particular jurisdiction. In many instances, the underlying causes of a professional liability claim arising out of cost overruns or schedule delays that manifest during construction originate or relate back to the design phase services of the design professional and, as such, may not be strictly viewed within the scope of this chapter. However, the expression of these claims invariably involves some allegation or complaint regarding the design professional's performance of construction phase services (e.g., failure to review shop drawings or respond to RFIs in a timely manner).[41]

The assertion of cost overrun and schedule delay claims by third parties such as general contractors and subcontractors against the design professional are on an upward trend.[42] In many situations, these claims are asserted against the design professional because the third party's opportunity for cost or time equitable adjustment against its contracting partner is foreclosed by virtue of a "no damage for delay" or related provision.[43]

b. Third Party Claims

Depending upon the governing law, there are a variety of third parties (or non-clients) who may assert claims against a design professional arising out of the latter's construction phase services. These claimants include general contractors, subcontractors, construction lenders, surety companies, injured construction workers, state and federal governmental agencies, and others, who may predicate claims based upon common law theories of negligence, third party beneficiary, or violation of state or federal laws. These claimants,

---

41. *See, e.g.*, Nelson v. Commonwealth, 235 Va. 228, 368 S.E.2d 239 (1988).

42. *See, e.g.*, A. Meagher & M. O'Day, *Who Is Going to Pay for My Impact? A Contractor's Ability to Sue Third Parties for Purely Economic Loss*, The Construction Lawyer, American Bar Association, at 27 (Fall 2005); Justin Sweet, *Contractor Postcompletion Claims: Advice to Engineer*, Journal of Professional Issues in Engineering Education and Practice, ASCE, 298 (Oct. 2004).

43. *See* David. J. Hatem, *The Relevance and Potential Impact of Risk Allocation Provisions in Owner-Contractor Agreements on Professional Liability Exposure of Design Professionals*, Design and Construction Management Professional Reporter I (Oct. 2003).

asserting bodily injury, property damage, or purely economic loss, may also seek statutory fines and penalties. Regardless of the legal theory, type of injury or damage, or relief sought, the terms of the design professional's agreement with its client and the applicable provisions of the contract documents often play an important role in conjunction with the facts surrounding the design professional's performance in determining legal responsibility of the design professional for these claims.

c. Contractor/Subcontractor Claims

As noted previously, contractors and subcontractors may assert a variety of claims against the design professional arising out of the latter's performance during the construction phase. A variety of legal theories, including negligence and third party beneficiary, are available as predicate for these claims. In many respects, the assertion of such claims both contradicts and undermines contractual risk allocation embodied in contract documents, as well as the structure of project participant relationships established in those documents.

More specifically, in the traditional design-bid-build method, the design professional serves during the construction phase under an agreement with and as a representative and an agent of the owner. Any performance deficiencies of the design professional should be addressed and remedied in the context of the direct (privity) relationship between the owner and design professional, and in accordance with risk allocation (i.e., standard of care, indemnification) and other relevant provisions of the owner-design professional agreement. Similar principles of risk allocation dictate that cost or time impacts incurred by the contractor or its subcontractors should be addressed and equitably adjusted, as appropriate, between the contractor and owner consistent with their agreements embodied in the contract documents. The allowance of direct claims by contractors and subcontractors against the design professional serves to circumvent and subvert this structure of project contractual relationships and risk allocation.

The relevance of the design professional's status as the owner's representative and agent during construction is an important factor in the context of such third party claims. For example, in observing and evaluating work performance by the contractor for conformance with contract documents requirements, the design professional represents and serves the interests of the owner in providing the latter with greater confidence that the work, when completed, will meet those requirements. As such, there is often a tension and conflict between the owner's interests to obtain the requisite work quality and performance, and the contractor who may be advocating for the acceptance of a lesser standard. To allow a contractor's claim against the design professional in such circumstances would, in most cases, subject the design professional to an unreasonable burden of defending its performance as the owner's agent in attempting to secure contractor performance in accordance with the requirements of the contract documents.[44]

On the other hand, all parties must ultimately acknowledge that design professionals have an obligation to perform their services in accordance with the professional standard of care, which requires reasonable evaluations, judgments, and recommendations by the design professional. If those evaluations are arbitrary or not supported by the requirements of the contract documents, this could lead to a professional liability claim by third parties who sustain damages as a result thereof (assuming the economic loss doctrine does not preclude such claims).

Perhaps the most commonly pled contractor claim against a design professional that is not precluded by the economic loss doctrine is negligent misrepresentation.[45] There the contractor/plaintiff will allege that it relied to its detriment on the design professionals negligently prepared work product. In the case of *Craig v. Everett M. Brooks Co.*,[46] the Massachusetts Supreme Court discussed the requirements for a negligent misrepresentation claim to qualify as an exception to the economic loss doctrine. *Craig* dealt with a claim related to a contractor's reliance on survey stakes erroneously placed by the defendant surveyor—who placed those stakes for the sole benefit of the contractor. *Craig* recognized the right of a plaintiff to sue the surveyor for misrepresentation based upon the *staking* of catch basins and a road. The court did not permit recovery for the negligent design services such as errors in drawings. However, it did permit recovery for improper surveying services in the nature of staking the land.[47] The court took great care to distinguish the claims based upon

---

44. *See* Bernard Johnson, Inc. v. Continental Constructors, Inc., 630 S.W.2d 365 (Tex. Ct. App. 1982).

45. The majority of jurisdictions follow the Second Restatement of Torts, § 552, for the elements of a negligent misrepresentation claim. With various caveats, § 552 provides: "One who, in the course of his business, profession or employment, or in any other transaction in which he has a pecuniary interest, supplies false information for the guidance of others in their business transactions, is subject to liability for pecuniary loss caused to them by their justifiable reliance upon the information, if he fails to exercise reasonable care or competence in obtaining or communicating the information."

46. Craig v. Everett M. Brooks Co., 351 Mass 497 (1967).

47. *Id.* at 501.

"misrepresentations" in the "plans" (which formed *no* basis for recovery) as opposed to the "placing of stakes."[48]

d. Personal Injury Claims

Injured construction workers often assert personal injury claims against the design professional. Standard contract documents provide substantial legal defenses to such claims on the basis that the design professional, as discussed earlier in this chapter, is generally not responsible for construction means/methods or safety. In addition, in many instances the design professional is entitled to contractual indemnification from the contractor and its subcontractors for such claims and is specifically named as an additional insured under general liability insurance policies procured and maintained by the latter.[49] Note, however, that this contractor-supplied general liability insurance will likely exclude coverage for claims of professional malpractice.

Notwithstanding these formidable contract-based defenses which, in many situations, provide the basis for a legally dispositive summary judgment motion in favor of the design professional, the design professional may assume increased liability exposure for construction worker claims by supervising or directing the work, construction means/methods, or safety precautions and programs. Moreover, if a design professional has actual knowledge of a contractor employing an unsafe practice on a worksite, it is incumbent upon the design professional to take some action to correct or mitigate the danger. The most obvious and direct step that a design professional can take is to call the unsafe situation to the attention of the contractor who is in a position to rectify the situation. For the most part, however, injured construction worker claims against the design professional are consistent with basic risk allocation principles embodied in standard contract documents, and should be highly defensible. Additionally, many states provide statutory protection to design professionals from worker injury claims. For example, the Immunity for Third-Party Design Professional statute in Alaska provides:

> (a) A person entitled to compensation under this chapter as a result of injury occurring at the job site of a construction project may not bring a civil action to recover damages for that injury against a design professional or an employee of a design professional who provides professional services for the construction project.

---

48. *Id.* at 499–501.

49. *See, e.g.*, AIA Document A201-2017, 1 3.18.1.

(b) This section does not apply to a person receiving compensation under this chapter who is injured at a job site at which the design professional or employee of the design professional

(1) specifically assumed responsibility for job site safety practices under a contract;

(2) actually exercises control over the premises where the injury occurred; or

(3) prepared design plans or specifications, the plans or specifications contributed to the injury, and the plans or specifications were prepared negligently, recklessly, or with intentional misconduct.

(c) In this section,

(1) "design professional" means a person registered under AS 08.48 as an architect, engineer, or land surveyor;

(2) "professional services" means services provided by a design professional that are within the scope of services for which the design professional is registered.[50]

e. OSHA

The design professional's potential exposure to fines and penalties under the Occupational Safety and Health Administration (OSHA) regulations is dependent upon the degree and level of the design professional's involvement during the construction phase. A design professional intimately involved with a construction contractor's means/methods, and safety precautions or programs should expect heightened scrutiny and potential fines and penalties from OSHA. OSHA assigns regulatory enforcement to its regional offices, each of which has somewhat different interpretations and expectations of design professionals involved in construction. The degree of the design professional's apparent or actual engagement in construction work and its power to control the process and/or substantial supervision of construction work will determine whether OSHA has authority over the design professional's activities.[51] The case law supports the proposition that if the design professional's contractual scope of services and actual conduct do not involve physical construction work, or substantial control or supervision over the contractor's construction means/methods, safety precautions or programs, or work performance, the

---

50. AS 23.30.017 ("Immunity for Third-Party Design Professional").

51. *See, e.g.,* CH2M Hill, Inc., v. Herman, 192 F.3d 711 (1999).

design professional should be able to successfully defend claims predicated upon alleged violations of OSHA and regulations promulgated thereunder.[52]

f. False Claims Act

In the performance of services on publicly funded projects, the design professional may provide express or implied certifications or representations regarding a contractor's entitlement to payment. The third party prosecuting the false claim act claim may be the sovereign or it may be an individual in *a qui tam* action wherein a whistleblower, informer, or otherwise interested person brings the claim on behalf of himself and the sovereign. In general, federal and state[53] false claims legislation provides the government with a remedy for actual and punitive damages against parties who submit or cause to be submitted a false claim for payment.[54] Under a typical false claims act statute, a person is liable if he/she (1) knowingly presents, or causes to be presented, a false or fraudulent claim for payment or approval, or (2) knowingly makes, uses, or causes to be made or used, a false record or statement to obtain payment or approval of a claim by the public entity.[55] Cases interpreting the federal False Claims Act have generally refused to find liability where the certification, "reflects an engineering judgment and recommendation."[56] Nevertheless, aggressive owners have recently attempted to mischaracterize payment certifications in order to invoke the statutes and threaten design professionals with

---

52. *See* Subsurface Conditions: Risk Management for Design and Construction Management Professionals, at 305–12 (David Hatem ed., 1998); Sweet & Schneier, *supra* note 31, at 274–79; Reich v. Simpson, Gumpertz & Heger, Inc., 3 F.3d 1 (U.S. Ct. App. 1993).

53. Thirty-one states, including Arkansas, California, Colorado, Connecticut, Delaware, Florida, Georgia, Hawaii, Illinois, Indiana, Iowa, Louisiana, Maryland, Massachusetts, Michigan, Missouri, Montana, Nevada, New Hampshire, New Jersey, New Mexico, New York, Oklahoma, Rhode Island, Tennessee, Texas, Vermont, and Virginia, as well as the District of Columbia, have enacted false claims statutes similar to the federal statute.

54. The False Claims Act, 31 U.S.C. §§ 3729-3310 (1994); Mass. Gen. Laws ch. 12, § 5B (2000); Cal. Gov't Code § 12650 (1997); 740 Ill. Comp. Stat. Ann. 175/3(a)(2) (2006).

55. *See* The Massachusetts False Claims Act, Mass. Gen. Laws ch. 12, § 5B (2000).

56. Boisjoly v. Morton Thiokol, Inc., 706 F. Supp. 795, 809 (D. Utah 1988).

the associated penalties which, in some cases, include treble damages.[57] Thus, design professionals face potential exposure in connection with certifications, representations, or recommendations that they make concerning contractor payment applications or requests.[58] The federal False Claims Act has been in existence since the Civil War and the law is well developed. Many of the state statutes, however, are more recent, and the courts have not had the opportunity to rule on a large number of construction cases. Based upon claim trends on public construction projects, this will likely be an area of increasing professional liability exposure.[59]

III. Completion and Commissioning Phase: Roles and Responsibilities[60]

As a typical construction project nears completion, a heightened sense of urgency tends to envelope all parties. For the contractor, schedule and budget concerns are approaching the day of reckoning. The owner begins to realize that it will soon take possession of the facility and assume responsibility for operation and maintenance. The design professional is increasingly called upon to exercise its role as unbiased arbiter, making decisions of great consequence to the owner and the contractor.

Moreover, new players often emerge. For example, equipment vendors planning to start up, test, and obtain sign off on their particular contributions to the facility; the start-up group assuring that the various pieces of equipment are properly integrated; and regulatory agencies determining compliance with permits and regulations.

Clearly, a project's completion phase requires the close cooperation of all the parties involved as well as a mutual understanding of each party's responsibility. The design professional is often in a position of orchestrating the actions of the various parties and requiring close adherence to contractual

57. *See, e.g.*, The Massachusetts False Claims Act, Mass. Gen. Laws ch. 12, § 5B (2000).

58. *See, e.g.*, David J. Hatem, *Federal and Massachusetts False Claims Act Exposure for Design and Construction Management Professionals*, The CA/T Professional Liability Reporter 1 (July 2001).

59. *See, e.g.*, Erick M. Kerness, *False Claims Can Bring Real Pain*, Design-Build (Oct. 2004).

60. I am indebted to my partner, David H. Hatem, for his significant contribution to this portion of Chapter 4.

terms, with the flexibility to adapt to unforeseen circumstances. In the midst of this flurry of activity, meticulous documentation of progress, accomplishments, and commitments will help to insulate the design professional from subsequent liability.

The completion phase begins with the contractor's request for a determination of substantial completion and runs through final completion, the warranty period, and the resolution of any contractor/owner claims. The completion phase exposes the design professional to certain unique liabilities that must be recognized and managed. The theories of liability that a project owner or contractor might assert against the design professional are generally the same as discussed earlier in this chapter, namely negligence, negligent misrepresentation, and breach of contract. Other more creative theories include tortious interference with a contractual relationship, defamation, and unfair business practices. Proper planning and preparation with experienced personnel and sufficient resources will allow the design professional to successfully navigate the conclusion of the project.

For a design-bid-build construction project where an owner has opted to employ standard form contract agreements from a family of documents such as AIA or EJCDC, it is less likely that a misalignment or misunderstanding of roles and responsibilities exists. The owner-design professional agreement seldom addresses the specific responsibilities of the design professional during the completion phase of a construction contract. However, the owner-contractor agreement likely contains a detailed listing of the owner's and contractor's expectation of the design professional's role. Accordingly, the design professional needs to understand and plan its participation with that specific role in mind. Problems often arise when the past experiences of one party on prior projects, or based on the course of conduct during the present project, lead to erroneous expectations of the design professional's role and scope of authority. Not only must the design professional closely adhere to the procedure and time constraints provided, but successful project completion also requires that it be in a position to encourage and in some cases enforce both the owner's and the contractor's compliance with their respective obligations.

A. Substantial Completion

In addition to being an important symbolic achievement, "Substantial Completion" is a critical contractual milestone. Often found as a defined term in the construction contract's general conditions, many state statutes and the Federal Acquisition Regulations also choose to define substantial completion for publicly procured construction projects.[61] The design professional needs to understand the interplay between the statutory and contractual provisions on those projects. Generally, substantial completion means that the owner has taken beneficial use of the project.

Substantial completion is closely linked with the common law doctrine of substantial performance, which recognizes that contracts are rarely if ever performed perfectly and attempts to protect the promisor (contractor) when it does not perform exactly as promised. The seminal case describing the doctrine of substantial completion is *Jacobs & Young v. Kent.*[62] A general contractor's plumbing subcontractor installed an adequate piping material that was not the brand called for in the owner's material specifications. When the owner learned of this noncompliance, it directed the contractor to replace the piping with the specified "Reading" pipe, notwithstanding the fact that the house was completed, the pipe was encased in the finished walls, and the owner was occupying the house. Because of the noncompliant pipe, the owner refused to make its final payment to the contractor, giving rise to a lawsuit in which the owner prevailed at trial. On appeal, the trial court's decision was overturned, and Judge Cardozo explained the reversal as follows:

> We must weigh the purpose to be served, the desire to be gratified, the excuse for deviation from the letter, the cruelty of enforced adherence. Then only can we tell whether literal fulfillment is to be implied by law as a condition. This is not to say that the parties are not free by apt and certain words to effectuate a purpose that performance of every term shall be a condition of recovery. That question is not here.[63]

The court found that while the owner was entitled to the difference in value, if any, between the noncompliant pipe and the specified pipe, to require replacement of the pipe from attic to cellar would be economic waste. Thus, the doctrine of substantial performance developed by the courts has been adopted "as an instrument of justice"[64] in order to protect a contractor from the harsh reality that contracts are usually not performed exactly as originally envisioned. The construction industry generally understands that after a contractor has achieved substantial completion on a project, it cannot, under the common

---

61. 48 C.F.R. § 552.270-4(k)(2005).
62. Jacobs & Young v. Kent, 230 N.Y. 239, 129 N.E. 889 (1921).
63. *Id.* at 243.
64. *Id.* at 245.

law, be found to have materially breached a contract for some subsequent act or failure to act.[65] While achieving substantial completion in no way relieves a contractor from the obligation of full performance, it does remove the severe material breach of contract action and its harsh remedies for the failure to fully perform. Most public contracts, however, and many form contracts such as the AIA documents, contain provisions that allow the owner to terminate the contractor either for cause or for convenience. These provisions tend to supplement and enlarge the owner's common law rights to end a contractual relationship whether or not a default has occurred.[66]

Achieving substantial completion on a project often affects several important processes; such as, the achievement of a bonus or the assessment of liquidated damages, commencement of the warranty and callback period, partial release of retention, countdown to final completion, and commencement of the running of statutes of limitations and/or repose.[67] Because of its significance in redefining the rights and responsibilities between the owner and contractor, the owner-contractor agreement generally provides a step-by-step procedure with specific time constraints for ushering a project into substantial completion and final completion.[68]

The design professional plays a key role in the determination and declaration that the contractor has achieved substantial completion. The determination of substantial completion on a particular project can range from a very objective to a very subjective exercise by the design professional. For example, the construction contract may define substantial completion as the issuance of a Certificate of Occupancy. Alternately and more frequently, the determination involves the design professional's substantive and subjective determination of the progress of the work. In either case, the design professional is responsible for making that determination and certifying that substantial completion has occurred.[69] Absent fraud or gross mistake, the owner-contractor construction contract generally states that the design professional's certification is final and binding. The design professional must exercise its duty with respect to this determination in a fair and impartial manner. The design professional must resist any pressure from the owner to delay or defer the declaration of sub-

65. Huguet v. Musso P'ship, 509 So. 2d 91, 92 (La. Ct. App. 1987) ("the law is clear that a building contract may not be dissolved after substantial performance has been performed").

66. *See, e.g.*, AIA Document A201-2017, Article 14.

67. *See, e.g.*, AIA Document A201-2017, ¶¶ 9.8.5, 12.2.2.

68. *See, e.g.*, AIA Document A201-2017, 9.10.

69. *See, e.g.*, AIA Document A201-2017, 9.8.4.

stantial completion based upon the owner's desire to influence the outcome of bonus or liquidated damage obligations, or other improper influence. Likewise, the design professional must resist pressure to certify substantial completion motivated by the owner's desire to obtain a certificate of occupancy as soon as possible even though the certification may not be warranted. The former could expose the design professional to contractor claims of fraud, unfair business practices, or tortious interference, while the latter could expose the design professional to claims by third parties based on deficiencies in the work.[70]

B. Punchlists

In the vernacular of the construction industry, a punchlist is a list of all incomplete or unsatisfactory elements of the constructed project. The punchlist is developed concurrently with the application for and declaration of substantial completion. The process of working off the punchlist items often becomes a ritualized event on the project, leading to a modification of the attitudes and dispositions of key players as the project approaches completion. Either the contractor or the design professional may prepare the punchlist. Its purpose is the documentation of the number, character, and value of incomplete work. A typical scenario begins with the contractor submitting a punchlist to the design professional; the design professional then augments and agrees to that list, and assigns estimated values for correcting or completing the listed items. The design professional then utilizes that list as the basis of subsequent inspections.

From a best practices standpoint, the seemingly simple task of making and keeping a list requires close management and control. A complex project will likely require multiple disciplines of engineers to participate in the development and inspection of numerous punchlist items, and the creation and revision of these punchlists can lead to confusion. Contractors tend to view the punchlist as a goal line and the addition of items to subsequent versions of a punchlist as the design professional's attempt to move that goal line. On public construction projects in at least one state, Mississippi, multiple lists are not allowed, and the owner is limited to two punchlists, one at substantial completion and one just prior to final completion.[71] Communication, coordination, planning, and scheduling help to avoid contractor hardships, yet allow the owner the assurance it needs that its contract is being completed in accordance with the contract. Very few punchlist disputes revolve around objectively

---

70. *See generally* Richard C. Lowe & Elise H. Walthall, *When Architects Withhold Certificates of Substantial Completion and Other Problems*, 19 Construction Lawyer 5 (Oct. 1999).

71. Miss. Code Ann. § 31-7-13(t) (2006).

measurable elements of the project such as missing doors, nonfunctioning lights, or torn carpets. However, disputes can easily arise out of differences in subjectively determined and aesthetically judged elements of the work.[72] The design professional's contractually designated role as sole and indisputable judge and final decision maker on all aesthetic elements during the course of a project carries over to its decisions on punchlist items. Moreover, terms such as "to the satisfaction of the engineer" transfer a broad, but not unfettered, license to the design professional to judge the quality of the work. As mentioned previously in this chapter, the design professional generally enjoys a degree of immunity from owner or contractor claims related to these types of decisions on punchlist items, as long as the design professional renders those decisions in good faith.

As with inspecting and rejecting the work discussed earlier in this chapter, the design professional must be mindful of the appropriateness of its acceptance/rejection criteria for punchlist work. The design professional should avoid over-inspection that could lead to delays and or contractor claims of a constructive change or charges of bad faith.

Toward the end of a project when all parties focus on completion, the design professional needs to maintain its vigilance and resist pressure by the owner or contractor to exceed its authority in accepting or rejecting noncompliant work. On private construction projects, the design professional's agency relationship, supported by its apparent and/or implied authority, will impute all of the design professional acts, approvals, or acceptance to the owner unless explicitly prohibited by contract. Thus, a design professional's oral acceptance of work that the owner subsequently rejects will often result in a dispute between the owner and contractor. If the contractor prevails in that dispute, then the design professional will be exposed to owner claims of negligence for knowingly accepting noncompliant work. Misunderstandings related to apparent authority are less of a concern for the design professional on public construction projects. Federal Acquisition Regulations, reflected in contracts with the United States, provide specific limitations on the authority of the design professional to accept deviations from or make modifications to the contract documents.[73] Similarly, the terms and conditions of state construction contracts typically contain explicit limitations on design professional's

72. *See, e.g.*, Varner Constr. Co. v. Mans, LEXIS 275 (Tenn. Ct. App. 2002).

73. 70 F.A.R. 43.102 (2005) provides that: "(a) Only contracting officers acting within the scope of their authority are empowered to execute contract modifications on behalf of the Government. Other Government personnel shall not . . . (1) Execute contract modifications; (2) Act in such a manner as to cause the contractor to believe that

authority in keeping with that state's procurement regulations.[74] Thus, a design professional's commitment to grant a change order or time extension or to accept noncompliant work is not binding on the public owner where the contract or applicable law provides that only the owner can approve changes in contract time and price. Accordingly, any contractor reliance on the design professional's commitment would be patently unreasonable, and a negligent misrepresentation claim by that contractor should fail.

C. Final Completion

Like the application for and achievement of substantial completion, the owner-contractor agreement generally spells out the steps and procedures to obtain final completion. Most agreements call for the design professional to issue a Certificate of Final Completion or a final Certificate for Payment. For example, AIA Document A201, § 9.10.1 states:

> Upon receipt of the Contractor's Notice that the Work is ready for final inspection and acceptance and upon receipt of a final Application for Payment the Architect will promptly make such inspection. When the Architect finds the Work acceptable under the Contract Documents and the Contract fully performed, the Architect will promptly issue a final Certificate for Payment stating that to the best of the Architect's knowledge, information and belief, and on the basis of the Architect's on-site visits and inspections, the work has been completed in accordance with the terms and conditions of the Contract Documents and that the entire balance found to be due to the Contractor and noted in the final Certificate is due and payable.

Under this very typical certification, the design professional represents to the owner that the contract is complete. This includes not just the physical

---

they have authority to bind the Government; or (3) Direct or encourage the contractor to perform work that should be the subject of a contract modification."

74. Mass. Gen. Laws ch. 30, § 39I (1960) provides: "Every contractor having a contract for the construction, alteration, maintenance, repair or demolition of, or addition to, any public building or public works for the commonwealth, or of any political subdivision thereof, shall perform all the work required by such contract in conformity with the plans and specifications contained therein. *No willful and substantial deviation from said plans and specifications shall be made unless authorized in writing by the awarding authority or by the engineer or architect in charge of the work who is duly authorized by the awarding authority to approve such deviations."* (emphasis added).

aspects of the project, but all of the paperwork, record drawings, photo documentation, maintenance manuals, lien waivers, etc., as required by the contract. This certificate is a document that the owner, lending institutions, the contractor's surety, and regulatory agencies will rely upon and take certain actions; such as releasing bonds. That reliance, particularly by the owner but also by third parties such as the surety in certain cases, exposes the design professional to liability for a negligently issued certification. In one example of improper certification, the court found an architect liable to a contractor's surety because the architect failed to obtain and review evidence that the contractor had paid suppliers and material men as required before releasing retainage. Once the contractor received the retainage, it defaulted and the surety was required to satisfy the outstanding claims.

D. Warranties

In addition to the array of implied warranties, a contractor is usually required to provide certain express warranties. For example, AIA Document A201 requires the contractor to provide three basic warranties: (1) that the material and equipment incorporated into the project are new (unless otherwise allowed) and of good quality; (2) that the work will be free from defects; and (3) that the work will conform to the contract documents.[75] The technical specifications normally contain other special warranties for equipment and other incorporated elements of the project.

Warranty issues between the owner and contractor give rise to design professional liability in several different ways. For example, under the AIA family of documents, the architect is required to obtain special warranties for certain enumerated systems and equipment from the contractor.[76] As discussed earlier, the architect's approval of a Certificate of Final Completion means that the contractor has performed all of the work, including supplying warranties in accordance with the contract documents. The erroneous certification that the contractor supplied the required warranties could result in allegations of negligence or negligent misrepresentation against the design professional if the owner is unable to obtain satisfactory resolution of a construction defect, for example, a leaking roof or underperforming piece of equipment.

---

75. *See, e.g.*, AIA Document A201-2017, 1 3.5.
76. *See, e.g.*, AIA Document A201-2017, 1 4.2.9.

E. Project Close-Out Documentation

Close-out documentation is considered the "dotting of i's and crossing of t's" of the construction project. In addition to special equipment warrantees and lien waivers, the contractor is required to submit maintenance manuals, operating instructions, and as-built or record drawings at project completion. Collecting and reviewing these documents for compliance is a tedious and thankless task. If all goes well with the project, these documents will never be removed from their file folder. However, if a subcontractor or material supplier files a lien or an insurance issue arises, the design professional may find itself exposed to liability to the owner for failing to secure these documents or for accepting defective documents.

F. Support to Owner in Evaluation/Defense of Contractor Claims

Throughout the course of a construction project, the design professional is required to make decisions that affect the economic balance between the owner and contractor. Additionally the owner-contractor agreement often assigns the design professional the role of arbiter of construction claims and disputes between the owner and contractor. In this role, the design professional must exercise its decision-making power in contrast to its responsibility of interpreting the contract in a fair, unbiased manner, based on the facts and circumstances. Clearly, however, the resolution of disputes often results in one embittered party who may seek redress from the design professional for its loss. This problem can be exacerbated when owner or contractor suspects that the design professional's decision is influenced by a desire to cover up for defects in the design documents. Moreover, if the contractor files litigation or arbitration challenging the design professional's decisions, that will likely occur after project completion. At that point the owner will often seek the design professional's assistance as an advocate in its defense of contractor claims at which point the cloak of arbitral immunity is, of course, removed.

CHAPTER 5

Design Professionals and the Design-Build Project

BERNARD (B.J.) NODZON, ANNA COVERT, KEVIN MAJOR[1,2]

I. Introduction

Recently, the design-build delivery system has moved from an alternative method to a mainstream project delivery method and is the fastest growing delivery method in the United States.[3] The design-build method allows for cost efficiency and generally allows for on-schedule project delivery compared to design-bid-build and construction manager at risk.[4] Many states throughout the country have passed design-build legislation, allowing state agencies to enter into design-build contracts with construction professionals.[5]

---

1. The authors of this second edition wish to acknowledge and thank Peter Halls for his contributions to this chapter as the co-author of the first edition.

2. The authors of this second edition wish to acknowledge and thank Nathan Brennaman for his contributions to this chapter as the co-author of the first edition.

3. Design-Build Institute of America, DESIGN-BUILD UTILIZATION COMBINED MARKET STUDY, JUNE 2018, *available at* https://dbia.org/wp-content/uploads/2018/06/Design-Build-Market-Research-FMI-2018.pdf.

4. Design-Build Institute of America, *New Research Shows Design-Build Continues to Deliver Project Most Efficiently* (Nov. 9, 2018), *available at* https://dbia.org/new-research-shows-design-build-continues-to-deliver-project-most-efficiently/.

5. According to the Design-Build Institute of America (DBIA), since 2010 many states continue to expand the reach of new design-build legislation. *See* https://www.dbia.org. New York City enacted the New York City Public Works Investment Act

As the popularity of design-build increases, so will the need for design professionals to be familiar with their role and potential liabilities in the design-build process. This chapter examines the different roles of design professionals in design-build delivery systems.

Library References

C.J.S. *States* § 277.
West's Key No. Digests, States <KEY>360.

II. Differing Roles for Design Professionals in Design-Build Projects

This section introduces the four primary roles design professionals can play in design-build projects: (1) acting as a design-builder, (2) acting as a subcontractor to a design-builder, (3) participating with another company in a joint venture or other business entity as a design-builder, and (4) serving as a bridging consultant.

A. Design-Build Led by the Design Professional

When the design professional is the design-builder, the design professional contracts directly with the owner and is responsible for all aspects of the project, including the scheduling, design, estimating, construction, and project management.[6] Design professionals that act as design-builders often do so by

---

for use by many entities including the New York City Department of Design and Construction, Department of Environmental Protection, Department of Transportation, and others. 2019 NY A.B. 7636-B (NY 2019-20) (enacted). Some of the many states to expand design-build legislation since 2010 include Arkansas, California, Colorado, Illinois, Indiana, Iowa, Minnesota, New Jersey, New York, Pennsylvania, Oklahoma, Virginia, Washington, and West Virginia. Additionally, design-build legislation for use on federal highway projects was passed by the U.S. Congress in 2005. *See* P.L. 109-59, 119 STAT. 1764 (Aug. 10, 2005) § 1503.

6. It should be noted that designer-led design-build teams are somewhat rare. *See* Friedlander, *Designer-Led Design-Build Teams*, CONSTRUCTION BRIEFINGS No. 97-9 (Aug. 1997), which notes:

> In design-build contracting, in which one organization is retained for both design and construction, it is rare for a design professional—the architect or engineer (A/E)—to contract directly with the owner both to design and to construct a project. Except for heavy industrial projects using the "engineer, procure, and construct" design-build method, an area dominated by the largest engineering firms, the lead member of the design-build team usually is the

forming separate but related construction companies that in turn subcontract the design services to the design professional. Alternatively, the design professional contracts as the design-builder and performs the design with its own employees, possibly subcontracting certain engineering services to separate engineering firms.

B. Design Professional as a Subcontractor to Design-Builder

Most commonly, the design professional participates in design-build projects as a subcontractor to the design-builder. The design professional is designing the project as it would on a traditional design-bid-build project, but now the designer answers to the design-builder instead of the owner. Because a design-builder's interests are not identical to those of an owner, some designers report pressure, either real or imagined, to compromise their professional judgment in favor of cheaper construction.

C. Design Professional as a Member of a Joint Venture or Other Business Entity

Another means for design professionals to participate in design-build projects is to participate with another company, often a contractor, in the formation of a joint venture, new corporation, limited liability company, or other legal entity that acts as the design-builder. Under this model, the architect and the contractor are either joint venturers or partners, members, or shareholders of an entirely new contractual or legal entity.[7] The joint venture or newly formed entity holds the design-build contract with the owner and is responsible for both the design and construction of the project. Participating in design-build projects in this manner allows design professionals to share in anticipated profits but also requires the design professional to share the risks. In addition, the design professional might be unable to act as the design-builder itself because bonds may be required and the design professional may not have sufficient bonding capacity. By joint venturing or forming a new legal entity with a contractor possessing the requisite bonding capacity, the design professional

---

contractor or the developer. The situation may be simply a historical accident, or it may have occurred because contractors have greater financial capitalization, are more entrepreneurial, or are perceived as more disciplined about issues of cost and constructability than design professionals. Whatever the reason, the construction community seems to have adopted the assumption that a contractor should lead the design-build team with the A/E as a subcontractor or joint venture partner.

7. *See generally* 2A Bruner & O'Connor Construction Law § 6.37 (Jan. 2020 update).

can meet the bonding requirements and participate in the design-builder's prospective profits and control of the project. Further, if the new legal entity is a corporation, limited liability company, or a limited partnership and is properly founded and maintained, the design professional can shield itself from the liability of the design-builder. In some cases, owners may find it difficult to recover from the contractor and design professional when they form a new entity.[8] They may not have sufficiently capitalized these entities to pay significant damages to the owner, which may shield the contractor and design professional from direct liability.[9] As a result, owners and their lenders often insist that the design firm and the contractor guaranty the liabilities of the new entity.

D. Bridging

Under the bridging approach to design-build projects, the owner hires an architect or engineer as a bridging consultant to develop a program and partially design the project. The level of the bridging design varies by project but generally ranges from a detailed program to schematic design level documents. The owner then uses the bridging consultant's partial design in a competitive bidding or request for proposal process to select the design-builder for the project. After the owner has selected a design-builder, the owner's architect or engineer usually remains involved with the project and might provide services, such as reviewing the design-builder's design, construction work, pay applications, and performing other administrative duties on behalf of the owner.

Library References

C.J.S. *Contracts* §§ 1–2, 4, 9, 12.
West's Key No. Digests, Contracts <KEY>95.

III. General Considerations

No matter what role the design professional plays, certain aspects of the design-build process impose increased risks for design professionals. This section discusses some aspects of design-build projects that generally heighten risks for design professionals. Subsequent sections will examine the liability of design professionals in the varying roles they play in the design-build process.

---

8. *See id.* (discussing the difficulties that may arise in attempting to recover from the design-builder that operates as a separate entity).

9. *Id.*

A. Fast-Track Construction

Design-build projects are typically constructed on a fast-track basis. Under the fast-track construction process, construction starts before the entire design is completed.[10] Essentially, the construction phase and the design phase overlap. The theory is that this overlap will shorten the overall schedule and save time in the end. As one commentator notes, "[t]his phased approach to construction has been used in private construction for years as a means of accelerating construction."[11] To accomplish the fast-track procedure, construction work is often divided into "packages." Once the design of a particular construction package is completed, construction begins while the design of the remaining packages continues. Parties can use fast-track construction on any type of project, but it is particularly suited to design-build projects.

There are some disadvantages to the fast-track process. Completing the overall design for a project before construction begins allows the design professional to discover errors that were not evident earlier. Desirable refinements in the later phases of design can require adjustments to design decisions made earlier in the project. When construction begins before the overall design is completed, there is less opportunity for the discovery and correction of design errors before damage results, and it may be difficult or impossible to make adjustments in constructed work to accommodate later refinements. Owners or even design-builders sometimes view the early design's failure to accommodate these later desired refinements as negligence on the part of the design professional.

Finally, scheduling and coordinating the project is often very difficult because the construction progress schedule must be modified to account for design changes.[12] As one court explained:

> [The Owner's] fast track approach resulted in frequent and significant modifications to both the architectural plans and the progress

10. Loulakis et al., *Design-Build*, Construction Briefings No. 2003-12 (Dec. 2003); *see also* Nash, Jr. & Love, Jr., *Innovations in Federal Government Construction Contracting*, 45 Geo. Wash. L. Rev. 309, 384 (1977).

11. Nash & Love, *supra* note 10, at 384.

12. *See* Marriott Corp. v. Dasta Const. Co., 26 F.3d 1057, 1059 (11th Cir. 1994) (discussing the fast-track construction method and listing some advantages and disadvantages); *see also* Stuart M. Saft, *Construction Contracts—Kinds of Construction Contracts*, Commercial Real Estate Workouts (3d ed.) § 4:14 (updated Sep. 2020) ("Excessive cost is the biggest disadvantage of fast-track construction, because costs could exceed all projections when the contractor announces that many aspects of the project are extras and were not included within the original bid.").

> schedule. These modifications prevented [the contractor] from proceeding in the orderly sequence that was anticipated by the original CPM [Critical Path Method Schedule], thereby causing [the contractor] to incur significant additional costs due to inefficiency and underutilized labor.[13]

In addition, it is more expensive to make design changes after completion of some phases of construction, increasing the amount of damages for which a design professional is liable if negligent design caused the problem. As a result, the fast-track method, often used on design-build projects, can potentially lead to increased design liability for the designer.[14]

B. Less Complete Design

Often the design provided by a design-builder is less complete than one on other types of projects. In the traditional design-bid-build project delivery system, because the entity providing the design does not contract directly with the entity that uses the design to construct the project, there can be a greater need to communicate the design with complete and detailed design documents than on a design-build project. One of the advantages for design-build delivery is that there are cost savings because the design documents do not need to be as complete. However, the less complete the documents, the less documentation there is of the designer's design intent and the greater the risk there is of a dispute in the event there is a problem.

Library References

C.J.S. *Contracts* §§ 545–582, 597–598; C.J.S. *Public Contracts* § 13; C.J.S. *States* § 289.
West's Key No. Digests, Contracts <KEY>95, 236–246; Public Contracts <KEY>316H; States <KEY>360.

---

13. *Marriott Corp.*, 26 F.3d at 1059.

14. *See* O'Connor, *The Rights and Responsibilities of Design Professionals, Part II*, Construction Briefings 2002-5 (May 2002) (stating that the fast-track system along with the increasing popularity of the design-build delivery method has made "the practice of architecture and engineering more dangerous than ever"); *see also* Block, *As the Walls Came Tumbling Down: Architects Expanded Liability under Design-Build Construction Contracting*, 17 J. Marshall L. Rev. 1 (1984); Nichwitz, *The Crumbling Tower of Architectural Immunity: Evolution and Expansion of Liability to Third Parties*, 45 Ohio St. L.J. 217 (1984).

IV. Design-Build Led by Design Professional

A. Reduction of Claims by Practice

Although some aspects of design-build may have greater risks than traditional work, there are some hard data to suggest the opposite, especially in designer-led design-build delivery.[15]

While designers acting as design-builders necessarily take on more responsibility and therefore more risk than when they perform only design services, this does not necessarily mean a consequent increase in claims. There are fundamental advantages to the design-build structure that can reduce claims. First, design professionals who are design-builders may be able to catch and resolve problems early in the process before they cause serious damage. Second, the design professional acting as design-builder has more control over the resolution of the problem and the cost thereof. Third, due to the absence of the traditionally adversarial relationship between the architect and the contractor, design errors are not as frequently exploited by contractors and turned into claims with large markups, although that may still happen at the subcontractor level.

Therefore, due to the inherent structure of the design-build project delivery method, there is less finger-pointing, and many traditional architect-contractor claims and grievances will be resolved without involving the owner.

B. Warranty of Design

Generally, courts do not hold architects and engineers to a standard of perfection but are only required to exercise reasonable care and skill.[16] Professional

---

15. *See* G. William Quatman, Design-Build for the Design Professional, § 21.01 (2001). *See generally* Konchar & Sanvido, *Comparison of U.S. Project Delivery Systems*, 124 J. Constr. Eng. & Mgt. 435 (Nov./Dec. 1998).

16. *See generally* James Acret, *Architect and Engineer Malpractice*, 3 Construction Law Digests § 25:17 (updated Nov. 2005); *see also* Smith v. Walsh Constr. Co. II, LLC, 95 N.E.3d 78, 89 (Ind. Ct. App. 2018), *reh'g denied* (Apr. 18, 2018), *transfer denied sub nom.* Walsh Constr. Co., II, LLC v. Case Found. Co., 110 N.E.3d 1146 (Ind. 2018); Corcoran v. Sanner, 854 P.2d 1376, 1378 (Colo. Ct. App. 1993); Fox v. Stanley J. Howard & Assocs., Inc., 309 N.W.2d 520, 525 (Iowa Ct. App. 1981) (holding architect will be held liable for negligence if it fails to exercise ordinary skill of its profession); Klein v. Catalano, 437 N.E.2d 514, 516 (Mass. 1982) (stating architect impliedly promises to exercise that standard of reasonable care required of members of the profession); Prichard Bros., Inc. v. Grady Co., 436 N.W.2d 460, 463 (Minn. Ct. App. 1989) (standard of reasonable care that applies to conduct of architects is same as that applied

liability insurance for design professionals typically excludes coverage for any liability beyond the reasonable care standard. Consequently, design professionals generally avoid warranting that their design will be free from defects. Design-builders, on the other hand, often provide explicit contractual guaranties to the owner that the design will be free from defects. The most recent American Institute of Architects (AIA) form of design-build contract, AIA Document A141-2014, contains an express contractual guaranty of the design by the design-builder.[17]

Design-builders are willing to provide a warranty that the design is free from defects in part because owners often insist upon it and in part because many courts would imply that liability unless the design-builder clearly disclaims it. Although it may be possible to avoid this implied liability by disclaiming it with a carefully drafted contract clause, those clauses are not always easy to negotiate.

There are two types of implied warranties of design that can apply to design-builders. The first is an implied warranty of fitness for a particular purpose. Under this doctrine, courts read into every design-build contract an obligation by the design-builder that the building will be fit for the owner's intended use.[18] Several courts have found design-builders liable under this theory, despite the lack of any express warranty.[19] For example, in *Robertson Lumber Co. v. Stephens Farmers Cooperative Elevator Co.*,[20] a property owner entered into a design-build contract for the design and construction of a grain storage facility. The storage facility, however, collapsed after the owner began storing grain in it. The court held the contractor liable, stating that the design-build contractor impliedly warranted that the building would be fit for its intended purpose.[21] The court noted that the owner furnished no plans, design, specifications, details, or blueprints and relied upon the experience

---

to lawyers, doctors, engineers, and other professionals engaged in furnishing skilled services for compensation).

17. *See* AIA Document A141-2014, Standard Form of Agreement Between Owner and Design-Builder, § 3.1.12.

18. *See, e.g.*, Robertson Lumber Co. v. Stephens Farmers Coop. Elevator Co., 143 N.W.2d 622, 625–27 (Minn. 1966).

19. *See id. See also* O'Dell v. Custom Builders Corp., 560 S.W.2d 862, 867 (Mo. 1978) (holding design-builder impliedly warrants the building will be fit for its intended purpose); Prier v. Refrigeration Eng'g, Co., 442 P.2d 621 (Wash. 1968) (same).

20. 143 N.W.2d 622 (Minn. 1966).

21. *Id.* at 625.

and skill of the design-build contractor.[22] Under these facts, the court found that the design-builder impliedly warranted that the building would be fit for its intended purpose.

Similarly, in *O'Dell v. Custom Builders Corp.*,[23] the owner sued a design-build contractor for damages after the foundation of its home cracked. A jury determined that the contractor breached its duty to design the project so that it would be fit for the owner's intended use. The Supreme Court of Missouri affirmed, stating that the parties' contract impliedly required the design-build contractor to construct the building fit for its intended use.[24]

Prier v. Refrigeration Engineering Co.[25] reached a similar conclusion. There, the owner hired a contractor to design and install a portion of an ice rink. The contractor's design melted the ice, forcing the rink to close. The owner sued the contractor, and the district court awarded the owner a portion of its damages. The owner appealed, and the Washington Supreme Court reversed, holding that the owner was entitled to greater damages.[26] While the court's decision focused on damages, it stated that a design-builder who provides drawings and specifications for the construction of a building or system impliedly warrants that the system or building will be fit for its intended purpose.

The second type of implied warranty is the implied warranty of the quality of the drawings and specifications. In traditional construction where the design professional prepares drawings and specifications for the owner and the owner, in turn, provides drawings and specifications to the contractor, the courts have held that the owner warrants the accuracy and adequacy of those drawings and specifications. This concept is widely known as the *Spearin* doctrine, stemming from a famous U.S. Supreme Court decision of that name from the early twentieth century.[27] The *Spearin* doctrine holds that when an owner furnishes detailed drawings and specifications to a contractor, the owner impliedly warrants that those documents are accurate and suitable for their intended use. The principle is that a contractor is entitled to rely on the accuracy of the drawings and specifications provided by the owner, and later, if there is a problem caused by an error in the drawings and specifications, the owner, and not the contractor, will be liable for the consequences.

---

22. 143 N.W.2d 622 (Minn. 1966).
23. 560 S.W.2d 862 (Mo. 1978).
24. *Id.* at 867.
25. 442 P.2d 621 (Wash. 1968).
26. *Id.* at 624.
27. *See* United States v. Spearin, 248 U.S. 132 (1918).

Design-build turns this famous doctrine on its head.[28] The owner is not furnishing any design—the design-builder furnishes the drawings and specifications to the owner. Not only does this eliminate the owner's implied warranty, but also courts have held that the design-builder impliedly warrants to the owner that the drawings and specifications are free from defects. Some have aptly dubbed this shift in liability from the owner to the design-builder the "reverse *Spearin* doctrine."

Designer-led design-builders must appreciate the increased risks they face in design-build. Compounding these risks is the fact that the designer's typical professional liability insurance program will not provide coverage for such a warranty of defect-free design, and there is usually no general liability insurance coverage available for the correction of one's own defective workmanship.[29]

However, there are some strategies to help limit this risk. First, design-builders can attempt to disclaim the implied warranties of defect-free design and fitness for intended use and negotiate express warranties that apply only to the construction work and not to the design. Second, one can attempt to buy insurance covering the risk of a claim under a warranty of the design beyond the standard of reasonable care. Finally, for any portion of the design done by others, the designer-led design-builders can try to pass whatever warranties that exist in the prime contract through to the design contracts and design-build subcontracts with a suitable indemnification clause.[30]

C. Strict Liability for the Design-Builder

Manufacturers of defective products are strictly liable to consumers if their defective products pose an unreasonable risk to the user, consumer, or property. This liability applies regardless of the level of care used by the manufacturer. This law has developed over time to allow consumers to recover from manufacturers with whom they do not have a contract, since the product may have proceeded down a chain of wholesalers, distributors, and retailers.

---

28. *See generally* Robert L. Meyers, III, CONSTRUCTION BRIEFINGS NO. 2004-5, *Owner's Design Liability Revisited: Spearin Today* (May 2004).

29. *See generally* Michael G. Welbel, *Insurance Coverage for Design Errors: The Owner's Perspective*, ABA, INSURANCE COVERAGE FOR DEFECTIVE CONSTRUCTION II (June 3–5, 1998) (outlining the types of exclusions commonly found in professional liability policies); Robert M. Chemmers & James A. Knox, *When Designs Don't Work: Professional Liability Coverage for Architects and Engineers*, 15 CONSTRUCTION LAWYER 17, 22 (Aug. 1995);

30. *See* QUATMAN, *supra* note 15, § 21.04.

With the increased use of design-build, there has been speculation in recent years as to whether the courts would apply this strict liability standard to building defects causing injuries on design-build projects. Unlike traditional delivery methods, where the roles and responsibilities are independent and compartmentalized, design-builders arguably provide services more like those of a manufacturer, which creates a product.

Fortunately for design-builders, thus far, the courts have not held design-builders strictly liable in tort for construction defects.

D. Contractor-Type Liability

Designers acting as design-builders will have the same liability as a general contractor—liability far beyond what designers are accustomed to or for which they are insured. Contractors typically guaranty to provide work free of defects and have responsibility for on-site safety, disposal of materials, scheduling multiple subcontractors and suppliers, permitting and licensing typically provided by contractors, and testing and inspections of construction work.[31]

E. Insurance Coverage and Bonding

A design firm's insurance needs will depend on whether it is working as a prime contractor, subcontractor, or joint venturer. While insurance is relatively straightforward for design firms providing design services as a subcontractor to a design-builder, insurance issues arise when the design firm is responsible for both design and construction. In order to adequately mitigate the additional risks of design-build construction, it is important for a design professional to understand the differences between contractor's and architect/engineer's insurance.[32] For example, professional liability insurance might exclude coverage for services beyond normal design services. Acting as a design-builder could jeopardize coverage, and an appropriate endorsement may be necessary. For example, a design firm's insurance may exclude coverage for joint ventures. The designer should implement a careful review of its insurance to adapt to being a design-builder. However, the insurers have been attempting to

---

31. *See generally* Thomas H. Asselin & L. Bruce Stout, *Legal Exposure of the Design/Build Participants: The View of the General Contractor*, 15 CONSTRUCTION LAWYER 8, 8–10 (Aug. 1995).

32. *See* § 12:94. Design-build from performance bond surety's perspective—Surety's assessment of specific design-build risks—Second level of analysis—Insurance gaps, conflicts, and deficiencies in coverage, 2A BRUNER & O'CONNOR CONSTRUCTION LAW, § 12:94 (analyzing insurance coverage options for design professionals on design-build projects).

minimize risks to design-builders by moving toward a single policy package to insure general and professional liability on design-build projects.[33]

Design professionals acting as design-builders must become familiar with bonds. Nearly all public projects require bonding. Additionally, private owners often require bonding. Design professionals new to design-build often have never provided bonds and do not have bonding capacity or an established relationship with a surety. Design professionals should also be aware that typically sureties require personal guaranties and indemnities.

F. Increased ADA Liability

Design professionals that act as design-builders risk greater exposure to claims under the Americans with Disabilities Act (ADA). Section 12182(a) provides:

> No individual shall be discriminated against on the basis of disability in the full and equal enjoyment of the goods, services, facilities, privileges, advantages, or accommodations of any place of public accommodation by any person who owns, leases (or leases to), or operates a place of public accommodation.[34]

Since the legislature enacted the ADA in 1990, there has been substantial litigation over whether the courts can hold architects and contractors directly liable for violations under this federal statute. Today, the courts are split on whether architects, contractors, and design-builders are liable under the ADA. This exposure turns on § 12183(a), which provides

> Except as provided in subsection (b), as applied to public accommodations and commercial facilities, discrimination for purposes of section 12182(a) includes—(1) a failure to *design and construct facilities* for first occupancy . . . that are readily accessible to and usable by individuals with disabilities, except where an entity can demonstrate that it is structurally impracticable to meet the requirements of such subsection in accordance with standards set forth or incorporated by reference in regulations issued under this subchapter.[35]

Design professionals and contractors operating in their traditional roles have argued against liability under the ADA because they do not perform both design *and* construction and therefore do not fall under this statute. Some

---

33. *Id.*
34. 42 U.S.C. § 12182(a) (1990).
35. 42 U.S.C. § 12183(a) (emphasis added) (1990).

courts have embraced this argument, agreeing that this phrase of the statute is clearly "conjunctive."[36]

Design-builders, however, are unable to make this argument. Therefore, courts have found that this "design and construct facilities" language of the statute allows design-builders to be sued under the statute.[37] For instance, in *United States of America v. Days Inn*,[38] the court held that it mattered not whether the phrase "design and construct" was conjunctive or disjunctive because the defendants were involved in both the design and the construction of the facility.[39]

Design-builders can argue that they are not within the scope of the persons responsible for meeting the ADA requirements as defined in the statute, but not all courts accept this argument. Section 12183(a) specifically references, and is limited by, § 12182(a) (quoted above), which obligates only the "person who owns, leases (or leases to), or operates a place of public accommodation" to not discriminate. Since the enactment of the ADA, many builders and architects have argued that they are not liable under the ADA because design-builders do not own, lease, or operate a place of public accommodation.[40] The hallmark case supporting this proposition is *Paralyzed Veterans of America v. Ellerbe Becket*.[41] In that case, the court held that the design professional could not be liable because "the limitation in § 12182 to owners, operators, and lessors also applies to § 12183 and thereby excludes architects from liability under the section."[42]

Other courts, however, have disagreed. For instance, in *Johanson v. Ellerbe Becket*,[43] the court denied the design professional's motion to dismiss because "limiting § 12183 to the parties covered by § 12182 would effectively eliminate § 12182's coverage of commercial facilities. . . . If architects are not

---

36. Paralyzed Veterans of Am. v. Ellerbe Becket, 945 F. Supp. 1, 2 (D.D.C. 1996); *see* Kuchmas v. Towson Univ., CIV. A. RDB 06-3281, 2007 WL 2694186, at *7 (D. Md. Sept. 10, 2007); *but see* Johanson v. Huizenga Holdings, Inc., 963 F. Supp. 1175, 1177–78 (S.D. Fla. 1997).

37. *See, e.g.*, United States v. Days Inn of Am., Inc., 997 F. Supp. 1080, 1084 (C.D. Ill. 1998).

38. *Id.*

39. *Id.*

40. *See Paralyzed Veterans*, 945 F. Supp. at 2; United States v. Days Inn of Am., Inc., 22 F. Supp. 2d 612, 615 (E.D. Ky. 1998).

41. 945 F. Supp. 1 (D.D.C. 1996).

42. *Paralyzed Veterans*, 945 F. Supp. at 2.

43. *Johanson*, 963 F. Supp. 1175 (S.D. Fla. 1997).

liable under the ADA, then it is conceivable that no entity would be liable for construction of a new commercial facility which violates the ADA.'"[44]

Thus, because of the volatility of the law in this area, design professionals should be mindful of the added exposure to liability for violations of the ADA that may arise when operating as a design-builder.

G. Economic Loss Doctrine Eroded

Under a traditional delivery method, an architect contracts with an owner but not with contractors or subcontractors. Consequently, claims against architects by contractors or subcontractors are limited in many states by the economic loss doctrine. Under this doctrine, a contractor or subcontractor can recover only for damages to persons or property and cannot recover purely economic loss without privity of contract. Thus, if the floor of a building collapses due to an architect's negligent design and causes injury to a contractor's workers, the contractor would clearly have a claim against the architect even though the contractor did not have a contract with the architect. However, in jurisdictions that enforce the economic loss doctrine, if a project is delayed due to a design error, a contractor or subcontractor cannot file suit against the architect for the architect's negligence because the contractor and subcontractors do not have a contract with the architect and suffered only economic loss—not bodily injury or property damage.

Design professionals in design-build construction are therefore open to a wider range of claims for purely economic damages in many jurisdictions. Indeed, designer-led design-builders may have contracts with numerous contractors and suppliers. Consequently, because there is privity of contract with these contractors and subcontractors, they can now sue the design professional for economic losses, such as delay damages and lost profits, even in jurisdictions recognizing the economic loss doctrine.

H. Contractor Licensing

Many jurisdictions require contractors to be licensed. A design-builder, because he or she undertakes responsibility for construction, must generally be licensed or a contractor in those jurisdictions. This requirement can easily surprise a design professional and the failure to be in complete compliance can be devastating. Design-build firms may utilize various approaches to obtain licensing to provide design-build services, including providing design

---

44. *Id.* at 1178; *see also* United States v. Ellerbe Becket, 976 F. Supp. 1262, 1267–68 (D. Minn. 1997).

and construction services themselves, subcontracting out the design or construction services, or forming a joint venture consisting of a design firm and a contractor.[45]

Generally, jurisdictions that require a contractor's license will find that merely bidding or submitting an offer to work as a contractor or design-builder is a violation of their licensing laws. The consequences can be severe. Many jurisdictions hold that a contractor without a license has no right to payment for work performed, even under theories of *quantum meruit* or unjust enrichment.[46] California law even provides that an owner can sue and recover payments previously made to the contractor.[47]

Library References

C.J.S. *Architects* §§ 1–4, 6–9, 16–17, 19, 21–25, 32; C.J.S. *Contracts* §§ 429, 432, 438, 456, 453–456; C.J.S. *Damages* §§ 51, 52–62; C.J.S. *Insurance* §§ 64, 970–971; C.J.S. *Negligence* §§ 161–163; C.J.S. *Public Contracts* §§ 10, 27–30, 44, 47, 50; C.J.S. *States* §§ 306–311, 322–327; C.J.S. *Torts* § 23; C.J.S. *United States* §§ 163–167, 172–177, 181–182, 190, 208–226.
West's Key No. Digests, Civil Rights <KEY>1021, 1338; Contracts <KEY>196, 205; Damages <KEY>40; Insurance <KEY>2391(7); Licenses <KEY> 11(1), 39.40; Negligence <KEY>321, 322; Public Contracts <KEY>16, 19, 41; States <KEY>101, 104, 107; United States <KEY>67, 70(29), 70(30), 73(17).

V. Contractor-Led Design-Builder

This section explores the risks, roles, and responsibilities of design professionals in the contractor-led design-build process.

---

45. *See* § 6:42. Predominant characteristics of design-build delivery method—Licensing law restrictions on design-build, 2A Bruner & O'Connor Construction Law, § 6:42 (discussing the main approaches design-builders may use to comply with licensing requirements).

46. *See* § 16:17.Consequences of non-compliance, 2A Bruner & O'Connor Construction Law § 16:17 (Jan. 2020 update).

47. Cal. Bus. & Prof. Code § 7031 (2003); *see also* Eisenberg Vill. of Los Angeles Jewish Home for the Aging v. Suffolk Constr. Co., Inc., 53 Cal. App. 5th 1201 (2020); MW Erectors, Inc. v. Niederhauser Ornamental & Metal Works Co., Inc., 36 Cal. 4th 412, 115 P.3d 41 (Cal. 2005).

A. Different Dynamics

Although the contractor may have an opportunity to comment on the design, when the designer works for an owner, the owner makes the design decisions. The contractor does not control payment to the designer, and the designer communicates directly with the owner. When the designer works for a contractor-led design-builder, the dynamics are different. Some designers find that a contractor-led design-builder is more willing than an owner to challenge the design as being excessive. Now the party that has committed to a price to perform the construction work is the one writing the checks to the designer and is between the designer and the owner in the chain of communication. However, as long as the designer and contractor-led design-builder maintain their professionalism, having the design challenged should result in a better design without compromising safety.

Another result of the different dynamics is that with a direct contractual relationship between the designer and the contractor-led design-builder, issues between the two can often be resolved without involving the owner. This may help explain why designers appear to experience fewer claims on design-build projects.[48] However, an owner may be concerned using a contractor-led design-builder because the designer will not be in privity with the owner.[49]

B. Poison Clauses

Poison clauses are onerous contract clauses that can create devastating results. A designer who is under contract to a design-builder might see a new set of poison clauses compared to those an owner might attempt to impose. This section examines some of the onerous clauses that often appear in contractor-led design-builder's subcontracts.

1. Pay-If-Paid or Pay-When-Paid Clauses in Design-Build Contracts

Contractors will often include "pay-when-paid" or "pay-if-paid" clauses in their subcontracts. These clauses state that the contractor will not pay its subcontracts until the contractor receives payment from the owner. Typically, courts disfavor these clauses and strictly construe them against the contractor.[50] Generally, courts will enforce these clauses only if the provision makes

---

48. *See supra* Section IV.A.

49. Robert F. Cushman & Michael C. Loulakis, Design-Build Contracting Handbook § 1.05 (2d ed. 2020).

50. *See, e.g.*, Digesare Mech., Inc. v. U.W. Marx, Inc., 176 A.D.3d 1449, 1452 (N.Y. App. Div. 2019) (stating pay-if-paid or pay-when-paid clauses are against public pol-

payment contingent upon receipt of payment from the owner.[51] Nevertheless, design professionals should be aware of these clauses and avoid including them in their contracts.

2. *Warranty Clauses*

The law does not require that design professionals perform error-free services. Instead, design professionals are required only to comply with the professional negligence standard, meaning the design professional must perform its work to the minimally acceptable standard of care in the profession under the circumstances. The design-builder, however, will often make express warranties in its design-build contract with the owner, guaranteeing that certain aspects of the project—or even the entire project, including the design—will be error free. As referenced above, the AIA design-build forms, AIA Document A141-2014, include such a warranty. Under these forms, the design-builder expressly warrants that its work will be free of defects. The document defines the term "work" to include both design and construction.[52] This contract provision thus expressly warrants an error-free design—a warranty that is higher than the ordinary standard of negligence the law imposes upon design professionals. When design-builders warrant the design to be error free, they will have a strong incentive to impose the same standard on the designer in the subcontract with the designer.

Design professionals must be aware of any clauses in their contracts with the design-builder that give rise to a higher standard of care because the design professional's insurance policy will typically exclude liability coverage for breaching a higher standard of care.

---

icy); Mrozik Const., Inc. v. Lovering Assocs., Inc., 461 N.W.2d 49, 52 (Minn. Ct. App. 1990) (strictly construing a pay-if-paid clause). *See also* L. Harvey Concrete, Inc. v. Argo Const. & Supply Co., 939 P.2d 811 (Ariz. Ct. App. 1997) (pay-if-paid clauses will be strictly construed); Blakeslee Arpaia Chapman, Inc. v. EI Constructors, Inc., 687 A.2d 506 (Conn. 1997) (same).

51. *See Mrozik*, 461 N.W.2d at 52.

52. *See* AIA Document A141-2014, Exhibit A, Terms and Conditions, § A.1.4.3 (defining work as "the design, construction and related services required to fulfill the Design-Builder's obligations under the Design-Build Documents, whether completed or partially completed and includes all labor, materials, equipment and services provided or to be provided by the Design-Builder. The Work may constitute the whole or a part of the Project.").

3. *Indemnification Clauses*

Many contractors will include onerous indemnification clauses in design-build contracts with design professionals. These clauses sometimes require the designer to indemnify the design-builder for 100 percent of the damages even though the designer's percentage of fault was small as compared to that of the design-builder. The indemnification clause could also require the designer to indemnify the design-builder for any design error. Such an indemnification creates a guaranty of design and goes beyond the negligence standard.

Some clauses require that the design professional indemnify the owner and contractor for claims of payment or liens by subconsultants without first requiring that the contractor make payment to the design professional.[53] Further, many of these indemnity clauses do not make any exceptions for when the owner or contractor provides the initial design. In those cases, the owner and the contractor should indemnify the design professional—not the other way around.[54]

4. *Flow-Down Clauses*

Some design-build subcontracts contain flow-down clauses, which provide that the subcontractor has the same obligations to the design-builder that the design-builder has to the owner. Thus, if the design-builder warrants to the owner that the design will be free from defects, a flow-down clause would require the design professional to make the same warranty to the design-builder. As discussed above, this is beyond the reasonable care standard normally applicable to designers and typically beyond the coverage of professional liability insurance.

Another flow-down obligation relates to scheduling. Typically, designers promise no more than to perform within a reasonable time. The design-builder's contract with the owner, however, will normally provide that time is of the essence and impose delay liability on the design-builder for missing time deadlines. If this obligation is flowed down to the designer, the designer will have more responsibility and liability for delay than the designer might otherwise expect, and delay damages can be devastating. In addition, although the design-builder's contract with the owner will usually adjust deadlines for delays beyond the control of the design-builder, often the design-builder is required to provide written notice within a set period of time in order to

---

53. *See* QUATMAN, *supra* note 15, § 5.05[M], at 68 (reviewing various common indemnity provisions in design-build contracts).

54. *Id.*

receive the extension. Design-builders can also flow this notice requirement down to designers, and designers often will not be accustomed to meeting these requirements.[55]

C. Licensing Issues Illegality of Design-Builder Not Having a Design Professional License

As noted in Chapter 2, it is important to be aware of the licensing laws of the state in which the project is located. Some states make it illegal for a design-builder to enter into a design-build contract unless it is properly licensed as a design professional in that state.[56] Design professionals acting as a subcontractor must confirm that the design-builder is properly licensed because it is often a violation of state licensing laws to assist an unlicensed party in the practice of architecture or engineering. Accordingly, a state could sanction a licensed design professional who subcontracts with an unlicensed contractor in a design-build project for assisting an unlicensed design professional. Further, some states hold that design-build contracts with unlicensed contractors are unenforceable, which means the owner does not need to pay the contractor for its work on the project and may even disgorge amounts already paid to the contractor.[57] A design professional acting as a subcontractor in this situation will find it difficult to collect from a design-builder who cannot receive payment from the owner because of an unenforceable prime contract.[58]

D. Bond Claim Limitations

In some jurisdictions, the contractor's payment bond on a contractor-led design-build project might not protect the design professional. Some states have held that since payment bonds usually cover only "labor, materials, or construction equipment," there is no coverage under the bond for the design professional's architectural services.[59] If the designer is relying upon a pay-

---

55. *See* CUSHMAN & LOULAKIS, *supra* note 49, § 7.08 FLOW-DOWN CLAUSES (discussing three primary problems with the implementation of flow-down clauses).

56. *See, e.g.*, CAL. BUS. & PROF. CODE §§ 5536 (2019), 7065 (1989); FLA. STAT. ch. 471.031 (2004); KY. REV. STAT. § 323.020 (1960).

57. *See, e.g.*, CAL. BUS. & PROF. CODE § 7031 (2016); FLA. STAT. ch. 489.128 (2009); NEV. REV. STAT. 624.320 (1953).

58. *See* CUSHMAN & LOULAKIS, *supra* note 49, § 2.03 STATE-BY-STATE SURVEY OF LICENSING REQUIREMENTS (providing an overview of state-by-state licensing requirements).

59. *See, e.g.*, Fields Hartwick Architects v. Capitol Indemn. Corp., 884 P.2d 198, 199 (Ariz. Ct. App. 1994).

ment bond to protect it in the event of nonpayment, it is important to make certain that the design-builder's payment bond covers the designer's services or that there is equivalent protection under the state's mechanic's lien laws and adequate equity in the property.

Library References

C.J.S. *Architects* §§ 1–3, 6–9, 16, 19, 21–23, 25; C.J.S. *Bonds* § 52; C.J.S. *Contracts* §§ 429–430, 438, 456, 450–451, 453, 604–607, 612, 787; C.J.S. *Damages* §§ 63, 65–66, 128.

West's Key No. Digests, Bonds <KEY>58; Contracts <KEY>95; Damages <KEY>115; Indemnity <KEY>208; Licenses <KEY>238.

VI. Member of a Joint Venture or Other Business Entity

A. Choosing a Business Form

Design professionals have several options in choosing what type of business entity they would like to create when teaming with a construction contractor to perform design-build construction. As discussed below, each business form has its advantages and disadvantages.

1. Joint Ventures

A joint venture is the most common business form chosen by design professionals and contractors who wish to join forces to be the design-builder for a project. A joint venture is a contractual relationship created between two persons or companies (or possibly more, but not usually) to share profits from an enterprise similar in many respects to a partnership. One important difference is that a joint venture is limited in scope and duration. Joint ventures in the design-build context are often between a design firm and a contractor for the design and construction of a particular project. The most important similarity of joint ventures to partnerships is that in the event the joint venture faces liability, the claimant can sue the design professional and contractor jointly or severally, just like partners in a partnership. In other words, in a joint venture, the design firm will be liable to the owner and others for the mistakes and negligence of its joint venture partner. This is advantageous to the owner, as all the joint venturers' assets secure performance.[60] Generally, the designer

---

60. *See* Cushman & Loulakis, *supra* note 49, § 3.02 Choosing the Appropriate Legal Entity.

would be entitled to recover contribution from its joint venture partner for the joint venture partner's share, but this is of no benefit if it has insufficient assets to pay its share.

While the term "joint venture" means a contractual relationship with a sharing of profits, sometimes the term is used loosely to mean creating some type of joint endeavor that the parties have not clearly defined, such as a joint venture, new corporation, or other legal entity owned jointly by the two or more firms. This section deals with the technical meaning of joint venture. In any case, joint ventures can put an architect at risk for construction defects by the contractor partner. As professional liability insurance policies typically exclude coverage for work done as a joint venture or construction work, design professionals might well be uninsured for losses relating to these construction defects. Design-builders can attempt to limit their risk for these construction defect losses by including indemnity agreements or limitation of liability clauses in the joint venture agreements. Design firms should think carefully about managing the risk for construction defect liabilities, either by obtaining insurance to cover that exposure to the limited extent that insurance is available or by making sure they draft their joint venture agreements and construction subcontracts in such a way to protect their interests.

2. *Limited Liability Companies*

Limited liability companies, or LLCs, allow the owner of the LLC to realize both the protection from personal liability offered by a corporation and the tax benefits of a partnership. Not every state has permitted design professionals to practice as LLCs.

LLCs are a good business form for design-build joint endeavors. In addition to the tax benefits and limited personal liability, LLCs also have flexible membership requirements. Corporations and general partnerships can be members of an LLC, making it a desirable alternative to a joint venture arrangement for single project associations.

3. *Partnerships*

States normally define a general partnership as "an association of two or more persons to carry on as co-owners of business for profit."[61] Although it is advisable, partners do not need to enter into a written agreement to form a legal partnership, and there are no formal filing requirements or licensing requirements in most states. If there is no written agreement, the applicable

---

61. 59A Am. Jur. 2d, Partnership § 2 (2019).

partnership laws of the state in which they are doing business often govern the rights of the parties.

Partnerships can be general or limited partnerships. In a general partnership, all the partners are general partners. In a limited partnership, there is at least one general partner, and the other partners are limited partners who do not have control over the limited partnership.

As discussed above in the joint venture section, each general partner (whether in a general partnership or a limited partnership) is jointly and severally liable for the liability of the partnership. Limited partners are more like shareholders in a corporation; their investment is at risk, but they do not have personal liability for the debts and liabilities of the limited partnership.

Partnerships have one significant advantage—they are not required to pay taxes. The law imparts profits and losses to the partners. Individual partners, of course, must declare their income and pay taxes on their personal returns; however, the partnership itself does not pay taxes on the income of the partnership, and unlike general corporations, partnerships can avoid double taxation.

4. *Limited Liability Partnerships*

A limited liability partnership, or LLP, is different from a limited partnership despite the similar name. An LLP is at its root a general partnership, and all the partners are general partners and permitted to exercise control. It is a business entity that retains all the benefits of a partnership for tax purposes but not the joint and several liability typical of a general partnership. Thus, while partners of the LLP are still liable for their own negligence, they are not liable for the negligence or other wrongful acts of their partners, and they are not individually liable to creditors, owners, subcontractors, suppliers, or others for general business debts.

5. *Corporations*

While a corporation is by far the most popular business form for designers and contractors individually, designers and contractors do not often use it when they team to perform design-build work. The legal formalities for the formation and maintenance of a corporation are more burdensome than for the other available options.

The obvious advantage of forming a corporation is that its officers, directors, and shareholders are not personally liable for the acts or debts of the business. In other words, this form shields the personal assets of the owners from the creditors and only the corporate assets are at risk. However, design professionals should note that they cannot shed personal liability for their professional design negligence merely by incorporating as a design-builder. Most state licensing statutes provide that architects and engineers remain individually responsible and liable for professional negligence that they personally commit despite their role as an officer or employee of a corporation. It is also common for states to prohibit corporations from offering professional design services.[62]

B. Insurance and Bonding

The different roles of a design firm and the different legal arrangements for participating in design-build projects have different insurance requirements and restrictions. Design firms need to review their insurance programs carefully to make sure they afford proper coverage.[63]

In particular, there are problems with insurance coverage when a design professional participates in a joint venture or other legal entity as design-builder. A careful review of the insurance program for the design professional, the design-builder, and the design firm's joint venturer or partner is important because there are several potential shortfalls in insurance coverage. For example, most professional liability policies for designers contain an exclusion barring coverage when a design firm participates in a joint venture or other legal entity. Naming the joint venture or separate legal entity as an additional insured under the professional liability policy is not a complete solution because most professional liability policies exclude coverage for claims made by one insured against another. As a result, the design firm would not have coverage for claims made against it by the joint venture or other legal entity that is serving as the design-builder. The joint venture or joint ownership exclusion typically bars claims made against the design firm by any entity in which the design firm has an ownership interest in excess of a set percentage, often ranging from 10 to 50 percent. As a result, the design firm must ensure that there is coverage for the joint venture or other legal entity that is acting as the design-builder *and* that it covers claims made against it by the design-builder.

---

62. *See* § 6:42. Predominant characteristics of design-build delivery method—Design-build contracting in state and local government procurement—Licensing law restrictions on design-build, 2A Bruner & O'Connor Construction Law § 6:42 (analyzing how state licensing laws impact design-build services).

63. *See* § 11:539. Insurance coverage for design-build projects, 2A Bruner & O'Connor Construction Law § 11:539 (outlining potential insurance coverage issues on design-build projects such as limitations on builders' risk coverage).

C. Non-Compete and Exclusivity

When a design professional and a contractor join together to pursue a design-build project, one issue to address is to what extent their cooperation on that project will prevent them from competing against each other on other projects, with or without other joint venturers, or even whether they will work with others on the targeted project. Careful parties will address these issues in the written agreements. Contract provisions might prohibit the two parties that are cooperating from hedging their bets by working with a competing offeror, explicitly allow the parties to compete against each other on other projects, and prevent the parties from hiring away or poaching each other's employees.

D. Teaming Agreements

Teaming refers to parties forming strategic alliances to pursue work on a project or projects. Design professionals and contractors have often found it advantageous to team together to pursue design-build projects. Teaming allows firms with complementary strengths to win contracts that they would lose acting alone. Teaming relationships are often (and should be) memorialized in written contracts between designers and contractors that establish basic rules for the working relationship.

Teaming agreements can range from nonbinding letters of intent to detailed binding contracts and can include other key participants in the prospective work, such as key trade contractors or suppliers.

The teaming agreement should define the project or type of projects it covers and the term for which the agreement will be effective and how the parties can terminate it. It should define the roles of the team members in marketing and preparing proposals and how the costs of doing so will be shared and then should address what their roles will be if they are successful in winning the contract—who will sign the contract, what business entity they will form, how it will be controlled, how profits and losses will be shared, what scope of work each will perform, and how liabilities for failure to perform will be handled. The agreement should specify whether it is binding. This is particularly important because teaming agreements are susceptible to being held unenforceable "agreements to agree."[64] For design professionals, it should address ownership of and copyrights in the design. As discussed previously, it

---

64. *See* Cyberlock Consulting, Inc. v. Info. Experts, Inc., 939 F. Supp. 2d 572, 575 (E.D. Va. 2013), *aff'd*, 549 Fed. Appx. 211 (4th Cir. 2014) (analyzing the enforceability of a teaming agreement); Advance Telecom Process LLC v. DSFederal, Inc., 119 A.3d 175, 186 (Md. Ct. Spec. App. 2015).

may also be advisable to address exclusivity, non-competition, and poaching of the other's employees. Often, the parties will share confidential information, and confidentiality agreements are useful to facilitate the process.

Library References

C.J.S. *Contracts* §§ 326–346; C.J.S. *Corporations* §§ 424, 427; C.J.S. *Insurance* §§ 64, 970–971; C.J.S. *Joint Ventures* §§ 1–2, 4, 10, 15, 18, 58–69.
West's Key No. Digests, Contracts <KEY>95; Corporations and Business Organizations <KEY>101; Indemnity <KEY>208; Insurance <KEY>217; Joint Ventures <KEY>226H; Partnership <KEY>289.

VII. Bridging

Because most design-builders are contractors who subcontract the design component to design professionals, owners do not have a design professional protecting their interests as they would in the traditional delivery method.[65] Moreover, the time and resources required for design-builders to prepare designs sufficient to submit cost proposals eliminate many capable design-builders from the proposal process. To remedy these problems, some owners engage an architect or engineer to prepare preliminary designs that can be used as the basis for issuing requests for proposals from competing design-builders and to assist with a request for proposal and selection process. "Bridging" refers to the engagement and retention of an architect by the owner in this design-build context.[66] The AIA and AGC[67] define bridging as follows:

> Bridging is a hybrid of the traditional design-bid-build process and design-build. An owner selects an A-E to develop a project design through design development (approximately 30% to 50% of the design work), and prepares scope of work documents which form the basis for competitive selection of the project delivery team. The A-E specifies the project's functional and aesthetic requirements but leaves the details of construction technology up to the contractor. Construction technology is specified with the performance specifica-

---

65. Quatman, *supra* note 15, § 6.01.

66. *See* § 6:35. Predominant characteristics of design-build delivery method—Bridging: Sharing design responsibility between owner and design-builder, 2A Bruner & O'Connor Construction Law § 6:35 (discussing benefits and considerations when using a bridging arrangement).

67. The Associated General Contractors of America.

tions. The project delivery team then has single-point responsibility for final design in constructing the project.[68]

The owner commonly continues to retain the bridging consultant to monitor the completion of the design by the design-builder, review construction, and help with the administration of the design-build contract. Public owners most often use bridging.

Bridging allows owners to have an architect or engineer consultant loyal to the owner while retaining the benefits of the design-build delivery method. Bridging also gives an owner more control over the end product. The criteria and plan created by a bridging consultant are more detailed and provide greater definition of what the design-builder is to deliver than the typical design-build project. However, having the greater level of definition can also act to limit the creativity and flexibility of the design-builder, lengthen the design process, and increase costs, diminishing some of the benefits of design-build. For public owners, the greater definition of the project allows for meaningful competitive bidding and a greater ability to fairly compare one design-builder's proposal with others.[69]

While work as a bridging consultant can be a marketing opportunity, design professionals who participate as a bridging consultant typically cannot bid or work on the projects for which they have served as the bridging consultant. Many owners would prevent the bridging consultant from being or working for the design-builder. If the bridging consultant could also propose to be the design-builder, others might feel they are at a disadvantage and not submit a proposal. That would also deny the owner the services of the bridging consultant as an independent and impartial overseer of the design-builder. While the law is not fully settled in every state, several states have laws that prohibit architects and engineers from bidding on the plans they prepare for public construction projects.[70]

Finally, bridging can cause confusion and uncertainty as to the responsibility and liability for the plans and specifications on any given project. For

---

68. AIA/AGC, Recommended Guidelines for Procurement of Design-Build Projects in the Public Sector 5 (Jan. 1995).

69. Some states have statutorily required the use of bridging on public design-build procurement. *See, e.g.*, Fla. Stat. ch. 287.055 (2009).

70. For example, Florida, Oklahoma, and South Carolina have laws that prevent the architect or engineer who performed bridging to perform any work on the same project as the contractor. Fla. Stat. ch. 287.055 (2005); Okla. Stat. tit. 59, § 46.27 (2014).

instance, bridging creates a conflict with regard to who is the architect of record or the engineer of record for the project. Similarly, bridging creates a dilemma, both for the bridging consultant and for the design-build designer, neither of whom can say that all the plans were prepared under their direct supervision and control. Of course, the consequence of this uncertainty is that both the bridging consultant and the design-build designer potentially face liability for errors that were not their own.

Library References

C.J.S. *Counties* §§ 144, 157–160; C.J.S. *Municipal Corporations* §§ 1195, 1207–1222; C.J.S. *Public Contracts* §§ 6, 17, 18, 20, 21, 14–25; C.J.S. *States* §§ 287, 291, 295–305; C.J.S. *United States* §§ 156–161.
West's Key No. Digests, Counties <KEY> 104–121; Municipal Corporations <KEY>268; Public Contracts <KEY>316H; States <KEY>360; United States <KEY>393.

CHAPTER 6

The Design Professional and Tort Liability

TERENCE J. SCANLAN, LINDSEY M. PFLUGRATH, TROY HATFIELD, NICOLE R. SPRINGSTROH

I. Claims against Design Professionals[1]

Tort liability for design professionals typically is generally defined in terms of negligence rather than strict liability.[2]

A. Negligence

A negligence claim against a design professional is composed of four elements: (1) duty to exercise an accepted standard of care, (2) breach of that standard of care, (3) causation, (4) and damages.[3] "The test [for negligence] is whether the ordinary person in the [design professional's] position, knowing what he or she

---

1. With limited exceptions, like the economic loss doctrine, the law discussed in this chapter is well settled and current, despite the relative absence of recent seminal cases.

2. La Rossa v. Sci. Design Co., 402 F.2d 937, 942-43 (3d Cir. 1968) (wrongful death suit against engineering firm alleging that pellets used in manufacturing phthalic anhydride were defective).

3. Wells v. Vancouver, 77 Wash. 2d 800, 803, 467 P.2d 292 (1970); Nicholson v. Turner/Cargile, 107 Ohio Ct. App. 3d 797, 801, 669 N.E.2d 529 (1995); *see also* Brown v. Koulizakis, 331 S.E.2d 440 (Va. 1985); E. Steel Constructors, Inc. v. City of Salem, 209 W. Va. 392, 396–97, 549 S.E.2d 266, 270–71 (2001).

knew or should have known, anticipated that harm of the general nature of that suffered was likely to result."[4]

1. Standard of Care for Design Professionals

A design professional is required to apply the skill and learning, as it exists at the time, possessed by a similarly situated design professional in his or her community performing similar services.[5] A design professional has the duty "to exercise reasonable care, or the ordinary skill of the profession, for the protection of anyone lawfully upon the premises whose injury is reasonably foreseeable as the result of negligent design, plans, orders, or directions."[6]

2. Scope of Design Professional's Duty

In order to satisfy the first prong of the negligence test, a claimant will typically allege that a design professional failed to take some action required by the standard of care. When such a claim is made, the prudent practitioner should review the contract between the design professional and its client to determine the scope of services that the design professional agreed to perform.[7] However, a design professional may assume duties beyond the scope of

---

4. Ins. Co. of N. Am. v. Town of Manchester, 17 F. Supp. 2d 81, 84–85 (D. Conn. 1998); *E. Steel*, 209 W. Va. at 397, 549 S.E.2d at 271.

5. Weston v. New Bethel Missionary Baptist Church, 23 Wn. Ct. App. 747, 752, 598 P.2d 411, 414 (1979); RESTATEMENT (SECOND) OF TORTS § 299A (1965). *See also* Mears Park Holding Corp. v. Morse/Diesel, Inc., 427 N.W.2d 281, 285 (Minn. 1988); Winrick v. Halco, Inc., 827 P.2d 1238 (Kan. 1992); Colbert v. B.F. Carvin Constr. Co., 600 So. 2d 719, 729 (La. 1992); Cain v. Springfield Eng'g Corp., No. LAW 135358, 1996 Va. Cir. LEXIS 616 (Mar. 18, 1996); Adobe Masters v. Downey, 118 N.M. 547, 548, 883 P.2d 133, 134 (1994).

6. *See* Chaney Bldg. Co. v. Tucson, 148 Ariz. 571, 574, 716 P.2d 28, 31 (1986); Lavy v. W&M Constr. Corp., No. X08 CV 010187185S, 2003 Conn. Super. LEXIS 1719 (June 10, 2003); Council of Unit Owners v. Carl M. Freeman Assoc., Inc., Nos. 86C-A8-49, 86C-AU-50, 86C-AU-51, 1990 Del. Super. LEXIS 469 (Dec. 20, 1990); Klein v. Catalano, 386 Mass. 701, 718, 437 N.E.2d 514 (1982); Waldor Pump & Equip. Co. v. Orr-Schelen-Mayeron & Assocs., Inc., 386 N.W.2d 375, 377 (Minn. 1986).

7. *See* Seattle W. Indus., Inc. v. David Mowat Co., 110 Wash. 2d 1, 10, 750 P.2d 245, 249–50 (1988) (the scope of an engineer's common law duty of care extends at least as far as the duties assumed by him in the contract with the owner); Esposito v. Shell Oil Co., No. X01 CV9701591825, 2001 Conn. Super. LEXIS 1476 (May 29, 2001) (court dismissed wrongful death suit against firm that designed car wash because defective features were outside the engineer's scope of work); Wiekhorst Bros. Excavating & Equip. Co. v. Ludewig, 529 N.W.2d 33 (Neb. 1995) (citing Dehnert v. Arrow Sprin-

the contract through its affirmative conduct.[8] Thereafter, the inquiry turns to the design professional's conduct while performing his or her duties.

3. *Necessity of Expert Witness Testimony*

Generally, the plaintiff must establish the design professional's applicable standard of care through expert testimony offered by a design professional who practices within the defendant's locality and area of expertise. For example, in Washington, the "duty of a structural engineer[] [must be set forth] by a structural engineer."[9]

However, if the issues are comprehensible to the average juror, then expert testimony may not be required to establish the standard of care required of the design professional.[10] Nevertheless, it is important to note that even where

---

klers, 705 P.2d 846 (Wyo. 1985)) (design professionals have a duty to give honest advice to homeowner if it is within the scope of their contract with the homeowner).

8. *Seattle W. Indus. Inc.*, 110 Wash. 2d at 10, 750 P.2d 245, 249–50 (rejecting jury instruction stating that engineer's duty was only defined by contract); Jones v. Logansport, 436 N.E.2d 1138 (Ind. 1982) (summary judgment proper because defendant construction administrator had neither a contractual duty to ensure plaintiff's safety nor had it assumed a duty through its affirmative conduct); Magnolia Constr. Co. v. Miss. Gulf S. Eng'rs, Inc., 518 So. 2d 1194 (Miss. 1988) (summary judgment in favor of engineer reversed on appeal because it was not clear what the contract contemplated as far as the scope of the engineer's duties).

9. McKee v. Am. Home Prods., 113 Wash. 2d 701, 706–07, 782 P.2d 1045 (1989) (standard of care for pharmacist must be established by expert testimony from pharmacist familiar with the standard of care in Washington); *see also* AA Mech. v. Superior Court of Arizona, 190 Ariz. 364, 367, 948 P.2d 492 (1997); Doe v. Yale Univ., 252 Conn. 641, 686–87, 748 A.2d 834 (2000); Falzarano v. C.E. Floyd Co., Inc., No. CV176031537, 2019 WL 1938067, at *4 (Conn. Super. Ct. Apr. 4, 2019) (expert testimony is required to determine an architect's duty); City Express, Inc. v. Express Partners, 87 Haw. 466, 468, 959 P.2d 836, 838 (1998) (architect's or engineer's standard of care must be established by expert testimony; failing such expert testimony, a prima facie case of negligence has not been established); *Winrick*, 827 P.2d 1238; Martin v. Sizemore, 78 S.W.3d 249 (Tenn. 2001) (architectural disciplinary board's finding was not supported by substantial evidence, i.e., expert testimony); Palladian Bldg. Co. v. Nortex Found. Designs, Inc., 165 S.W.3d 430, 432 (Tex. 2005); McLaughlin v. Langrock, Sperry & Wool, LLP, No. 2:19-CV-00112, 2020 WL 3118646, at *8 (D. Vt. June 12, 2020); Robert M. Shoenhaus, *Necessity of Expert Testimony to Show Malpractice of Architect*, 3 A.L.R.4th 1023 (1981).

10. *See* Hull v. Enger Constr. Co., 550 P.2d 692 (Wash. Ct. App. 1976), *rev. denied*, No. 44381, 1976 Wash. LEXIS 822 (Nov. 23, 1976); *Colbert*, 600 So. 2d at 729 (if

expert testimony is not required to prove negligence against a design professional, it is often very persuasive to the court in deciding whether a design professional has breached its applicable standard of care.[11]

4. *Causation*

To establish negligence, a plaintiff is required to prove that the design professional's alleged error caused the plaintiff's damage. "Proximate cause" is an act or omission that in a natural and continuous sequence, unbroken by any new, independent causes, produces the injury and without which the injury would not have occurred—that is, the design professional's error caused the damage.[12] For example, an engineering firm is entitled to summary judgment of a negligence claim for want of causation where the engineer's client does not build a drainage system as designed by the engineer, even though design errors may exist, because such errors do not cause the claimant's damage when the design is not utilized.[13]

---

laypersons can infer negligence by applying a common sense standard in the case of physicians, then an architect's negligence may on occasion be established without reference to expert testimony); D & 0 Contractors, Inc. v. Terrebonne Parish Sch. Bd., 545 So. 2d 588, 591 (La. 1989); *Adobe Masters*, 118 N.M. at 549, 883 P.2d 133, 135; Mid-Western Elec. v. DeWild Grant Reckert & Assocs. Co., 500 N.W.2d 250, 255 (S.D. 1993); John's Heating Serv. v. Lamb, 46 P.3d 1024, 1038 (Alaska 2002); *see also* Kraft v. OMCO Bldg., LLC, 2019-Ohio-621, ¶ 6, appeal not allowed, 2019-Ohio-2498, ¶ 6, 156 Ohio St. 3d 1445, 125 N.E.3d 921 (expert testimony is required to establish the standard of care, unless the lack of skill or care of the professional is so apparent as to be within the comprehension of a layperson and requires only common knowledge and experience to understand it).

11. Stults & Assocs. v. Neidhart, Nos. 99 CA 11 and 99 CA 17, 1999 Ohio Ct. App. LEXIS 5400 (Nov. 15, 1999) (defendants refused to pay design professional for services; court held that defendants failed to raise issue of material fact to avoid summary judgment and provided no expert testimony to support conclusory statements in affidavits); Martin v. Garner & Law, No. 03A01-9102-CV-00080, 1991 Tenn. Ct. App. LEXIS 768 (Sept. 13, 1991), *rev. denied*, 1992 Tenn. LEXIS 225 (Mar. 9, 1992) (plaintiff's inclusion of expert affidavit creates issue of material fact to survive summary judgment).

12. Brickman v. Walter Schoel Eng'g Co., 630 So. 2d 424, 425 (Ala. 1993); *see also* Union Pac. R.R. v. Sharp, 330 Ark. 174, 181, 952 S.W.2d 658, 662 (1997); *Weston*, 23 Wash. Ct. App. at 752, 598 P.2d at 414 (architect not liable for failure of rockery when it was undisputed that the wall, as built, substantially deviated from the architect's design).

13. *Brickman*, 630 So. 2d at 425.

Conversely, to recover under a theory of breach of express warranty, the plaintiff must prove the existence of the warranty, the warranty's breach, and "direct and proximate cause [between the breach and] . . . the [ensuing] damage."[14]

B. Strict Liability

Strict liability is typically imposed in cases involving the mass production of goods or a large body of distant consumers for whom it would be unfair to require tracing the article to the original manufacturer.[15] For this reason, professional services cases are distinguished from consumer products cases.[16] Even in those jurisdictions that impose a rule of strict liability for products, a majority of court decisions decline to apply strict liability to the provision of professional services.[17] The rationale for the distinction is stated succinctly in *Gagne v. Bertram*, where it was noted that:[18]

---

14. *Martin*, 1991 Tenn. Ct. App. LEXIS 768 (citing Mitchell v. Pearson Enters., 697 P.2d 240, 247 (Utah 1985)); Interwest Constr. v. Palmer, 923 P.2d 1350, 1357 (Utah 1996); *Cain*, 1996 Va. Cir. LEXIS 616 (plaintiff required to show proximate cause where she alleged design professional was negligent in failing to provide an initial site plan that met city requirements for site approval).

15. *Martin*, 1991 Tenn. Ct. App. LEXIS 768 (citing Mitchell v. Pearson Enters., 697 P.2d 240, 247 (Utah 1985)). *See also* Constance Frisby Frain, *Architect and Engineer Liability*, 35 Washburn L.J. 32, 36 (1995). *See also* K-Mart Corp. v. Midcon Realty Grp., Ltd., 489 F. Supp. 813 (Conn. 1980) (theory of strict liability does not extend so far as to include the claim of a building's user that the architect of the building is liable, as a consequence of his sale of allegedly "defective" designs to the person who constructed the building); Abdul-Warith v. Arthur G. McKee & Co., 488 F. Supp. 306 (Pa. 1980), *aff'd*, 642 F.2d 440 (3d Cir. 1981) (design professionals who provide services and participate in assembly or construction of a product may be held strictly liable, while architects or engineers who provide design or supervisory services but do not participate in the construction of the challenged product will not be subject to strict liability); Laukkanen v. Jewel Tea Co., 222 N.E.2d 584, 589–90 (Ill. 1966) (court denied imposition of strict liability on architects and engineers who designed a concrete pylon that fell during a windstorm and caused harm to retail customer plaintiff); Reber v. Chandler High Sch. Dist. #20, 474 P.2d 852, 854 (Ariz. 1970) (court denied imposition of strict liability on an architect where the contractor's employees sustained injuries due to alleged defects in plans and specifications for a school gymnasium).

16. *La Rossa*, 402 F.2d at 942–93.

17. *Id.*

18. 275 P.2d 15, 20–21 (Cal. 1954).

> [T]he general rule is applicable that those who sell their services for the guidance of others in their economic, financial, and personal affairs are not liable in the absence of negligence or intentional misconduct. . . . Those who hire [experts] are not justified in expecting infallibility, but can expect only reasonable care and competence. They purchase service, not insurance.[19]

In those jurisdictions where a design professional may be subject to strict liability, claims are typically asserted under two different theories of liability: (1) as a products liability claim arising from a defective condition in the structure; or (2) as a breach of warranty claim based on affirmative representations made by the design professional.

Some jurisdictions have expressed a willingness to recognize a narrow exception and allow the imposition of strict liability on companies that design and manufacture homes *en masse*.[20] Mass-produced homes (which are akin to other manufactured goods), however, are easily differentiated from structures built from a unique set of plans and specifications.

C. Gross Negligence

1. Definition

"Gross negligence" is the failure to exercise slight care.[21] Failure to exercise slight care does not mean a total absence of care, but care substantially less than ordinary care.[22] In Virginia slight care is "such care as careless or inattentive persons usually exercise, while gross negligence is carelessness

---

19. *Id.*

20. *See* Schipper v. Levitt & Sons, Inc., 207 A.2d 314, 321–28 (N.J. 1965); Wingfield v. Page, 278 Ark. 276, 281, 644 S.W.2d 940 (1983) (plaintiffs did not seek recovery under strict liability theory, but court expressed support for a broad strict liability policy reaching "the party best able to shoulder it").

21. Driggers v. S. Ry. Co., 169 S.C. 157, 160, 168 S.E. 185, 185 (1933) (widow could not recover for decedent's death if the decedent had been grossly negligent, which it defined as willfulness or wantonness and a lack of slight care for his own protection when he was hit by rail car); Jones v. Atchison Topeka & Santa Fe R.R., 98 Kan. 133, 137, 157 P. 399 (1916) (passenger who fell while trying to jump on a freight train could not hold carrier liable because those who venture on freight trains have no right to ask more than slight care and can hold the carriers for nothing less than gross negligence).

22. Restatement (Second) of Torts § 500 (1965).

manifestly and materially greater than want of common prudence."[23] Gross negligence is "that degree of negligence which shows an utter disregard of prudence amounting to complete neglect of the safety of another."[24] Thus, "gross negligence" differs from ordinary negligence only in the degree of disregard for the standard of care, not in the kind of damages suffered.[25] "If the course of conduct is such that the likelihood of injury to other persons or property is known by the actor to be imminent or 'clear and present', then the negligence is gross, whereas other negligence would be simple negligence."[26]

Gross negligence claims generally arise in cases relating to host-guest statutes, state statutory immunity under involuntary commitment laws, personal injuries incurred in the course of adventure sporting activities, railroad injuries, and damage to personal property. The case law involving design professionals and gross negligence is therefore sparse. Importantly, however, to establish gross negligence, one must offer evidence that the defendant knew, or should have known, facts that would lead a reasonable person to conclude that his or her conduct would lead to an unreasonable risk of harm to others.[27] This requirement of foreseeable risk to persons or the property of others appears to exclude the possibility of a gross negligence claim in cases where the plaintiff

---

23. Wallower v. Martin, 206 Va. 493, 497–98, 144 S.E.2d 289 (1965) (passenger action against driver one and driver two of automobile accident).

24. *Id. But see* City of Middlesboro v. Brown, 63 S.W.3d 179, 181 (Ky. 2001) (gross negligence defined as "something more than the failure to exercise slight care . . . there must be an element either of malice or willfulness or such an utter and wanton disregard of the rights of others as from which it may be assumed the act was malicious or willful").

25. Ross v. Rossi, No. CV 89-010491S, 1990 Conn. Super. LEXIS 40 (June 29, 1990) (claim for gross negligence relating to failure of a septic system); Johns v. Council of the Del. Assn. of Prof'l Eng'rs, No. 03A-07-001 WLW, 2004 Del. Super. LEXIS 257 (July 27, 2004) (engineer grossly negligent in designing on-site wastewater disposal systems because design was "an extreme deviation" from the standard of care); Courtney v. Fl. Transformer, Inc., 549 So. 2d 1061, 1064 (Fla. 1989).

26. White v. Godwin, 124 So. 2d 525, 526 (Fla. 1960).

27. Johnson v. Schafer, 110 Wash. 2d 546, 549–50, 756 P.2d 134 (1988) (quoting Restatement (Second) of Torts § 500 (1965)); Wal-Mart Stores v. Berry, 833 S.W.2d 587, 593 (Tex. Ct. App. 1992) (defendant's conscious indifference to the rights, welfare, and safety of others may be inferred when the evidence demonstrates that a reasonable person would have realized that his conduct created an extreme degree of risk to the safety of others); Eister v. Hahn, 420 N.W.2d 443, 446 (Iowa 1988).

has incurred only economic losses, which encompasses a large percentage of claims against design professionals.[28]

2. Effect on Contractual Limitations of Liability

Most states hold that a person cannot contract against liability for his own gross negligence or intentional conduct. Even in jurisdictions that allow parties to contractually limit or completely exculpate themselves from liability for their own negligence, public policy may prohibit parties from shielding themselves from liability for their own gross negligence.[29]

Following that approach, courts in some jurisdictions have held that contract clauses capping a design professional's liability will not apply to damages caused by that design professional's gross negligence.[30] Logically, this would also apply to any contractual provision limiting the liability of a design professional, i.e., a waiver of consequential damages, indemnity for one's own conduct, etc. However, at least one state, Missouri, allows sophisticated businesses to limit their liability for gross negligence.[31]

D. Breach of Fiduciary Duty

A fiduciary or confidential relationship is characterized by a unique degree of trust and confidence between parties, where one party possesses superior knowledge, skill, or expertise and has a duty to represent the interests of the

---

28. See discussion below regarding the economic loss doctrine.

29. *See* Vodopest v. MacGregor, 128 Wn. 2d 840, 848, 913 P.2d 779, 782 (1996); Royal Ins. Co. of Am. v. Sw. Marine, 194 F.3d 1009, 1016 (9th Cir. 1999); Donlon Bros. v. S. Co., 151 Cal. 763, 767, 91 P. 603, 604 (1907) (a common carrier may limit its liability for ordinary negligence but is prohibited from doing so as to its gross negligence); S. Wine & Spirits of Am., Inc. v. Impact Envtl. Eng'g, PLLC, 104 A.D.3d 613, 614, 962 N.Y.S.2d 118, 119 (N.Y. App. Div. 2013) (limitation of liability against public policy where failure to disclose drywells despite availability of information in public records was grossly negligent); Liberty Furniture v. Sonitrol, 770 P.2d 1086 (1989), *rev. denied*, 777 P.2d 1050 (1989) (contractual limitation of liability clause invalidated by security company's gross negligence in failing to notify building owner that fire alarm had been set off); RESTATEMENT (SECOND) OF TORTS § 195 (1981).

30. *See* Sear-Brown Group v. Jay Builders, Inc., 665 N.Y.S.2d 162 (1997); Factory Ins. Ass'n v. American Dist. Tel. Co., 277 So. 2d 569, 570 (Fla. 1973).

31. *In re* NHB, LLC, 287 B.R. 475, 477 (E.D. Mo. 2002) (sophisticated businesses may legally enter into contracts that limit liability for gross negligence or willful injury arising out of the performance of a contract).

other.[32] Simply placing trust or confidence in another is not sufficient to establish a fiduciary relationship.[33] The superior position of the fiduciary or dominant party affords great opportunity for abuse of the confidence reposed in him or her.[34]

Plaintiffs also allege tort liability against design professionals by claiming that a design professional, by virtue of his or her knowledge, expertise, and skill, owes a fiduciary duty to the plaintiff. Specifically, they allege that this special duty is breached when the design professional fails to apply this knowledge or expertise in a manner consistent with the plaintiff's best interests.

The elements in a cause of action for breach of fiduciary duty are (1) the existence of a fiduciary duty owed by the design professional to the plaintiff, (2) breach of that duty by the design professional, and (3) damages proximately caused by the breach.[35]

Breaches of fiduciary duties have been found where fraud, self-dealing, or conflicts of interest were present, although the absence of these elements does not preclude a finding of that breach.[36]

Some jurisdictions require an express agency relationship to exist between the design professional and plaintiff for a fiduciary duty will be imposed.[37] To

---

32. Winsted Land Dev. v. Design Collaborative, No. CV 960071571, 1999 Conn. Super. LEXIS 2180, 47–48 (Aug. 12, 1999) (design professional firm found liable for breach of fiduciary duty where it filled in wetlands pursuant to contract with developer without obtaining the proper permits).

33. Moon v. Phipps, 67 Wash. 2d 948, 954, 411 P.2d 157, 160–61 (1966) (property owner sued defendant husband and wife to rescind an option to purchase her property, which she alleged was obtained from her by fraud and deceit; court found husband was the property owner's agent, that he breached a fiduciary relationship, and that property owner was entitled to rescind the option agreement); State v. Superior Court, 120 Ariz. 501, 504, 586 P.2d 1313, 1316 (1978).

34. *Moon*, 67 Wash. 2d at 160–61, *citing* Murphy v. Wakelee, 247 Conn. 396, 400, 721 A.2d 1181, 1183 (1998).

35. Senn v. Nw. Underwriters, 74 Wash. Ct. App. 408, 414, 875 P.2d 637, 639 (1994); United States *ex rel.* Hill v. Teledyne, Inc., No. 95-55866, 1996 U.S. Ct. App. LEXIS 30178 (9th Cir. Nov. 18, 1996); Griffin v. Fowler, 260 Ga. Ct. App. 443, 445, 579 S.E.2d 848 (2003) (client contended attorney breached his fiduciary duty, but court dismissed the claim as duplicative of the malpractice claim).

36. *Senn*, 875 P.2d at 639,*citing Murphy*, 247 Conn. at 400, 721 A.2d 1181, 1183 (1998).

37. *See* Mullaney, Wells & Co. v. Savage, 78 Ill. 2d 534, 547, 402 N.E.2d 574, 580 (1980); Moss v. Vadman, 77 Wn. 2d 396, 404, 463 P.2d 159, 164 (1969) (accountant who acted as plaintiff's real estate advisor was not agent and, therefore, owed

establish that a defendant is an agent, the plaintiff must prove that the design professional "controlled the manner of performance."[38] "Fiduciary duties, which often produce the duty to disclose, 'are not inherent in normal arm's length business relationship, and arise only when one undertakes to act primarily for another's benefit.'"[39]

In the absence of a fiduciary relationship, allegations of a breach of fiduciary duty through fraudulent concealment will not stand simply because a cause of action remains undiscovered, but will stand if the defendant affirmatively prevents discovery.[40] "Therefore, the [plaintiffs] are required to prove some affirmative act on [the defendant's] part, that [the defendant] designed such act to prevent the [plaintiffs] from detecting their cause of action, and that they were actually prevented from discovering their cause of action."[41]

Whether a fiduciary duty exists, and the scope of that duty are normally questions of law for the court.[42]

---

no fiduciary duty to plaintiff); BancOklahoma Mortg. Corp. v. Capital Title Co., 194 F.3d 1089, 1108 (10th Cir. 1999) (in order to establish a breach of fiduciary duty to the homeowners, mortgage company would have to show that agency relationship existed between the title companies and the homeowners).

38. Uni-Com N.W., Ltd. v. Argus Publ'g Co., 47 Wash. Ct. App. 787, 796–97, 737 P.2d 304, 309–10 (1987), *rev. denied*, No. 54108-6, 1987 Wash. LEXIS 1387 (May 26, 1987); State v. Superior Court, 120 Ariz. 501, 504, 586 P.2d 1313, 1316 (1978) (insurance adjuster's promises of confidentiality and of providing defense counsel with the fruits of the investigation did not make the insurance adjuster defense counsel's agent); Flores v. Brown, 39 Cal. 2d 622, 628, 248 P.2d 922, 925 (1952) (inference of agency drawn between owner of automobile and driver of automobile because owner retains power over how his automobile should be operated).

39. Cleveland v. City of Lead, 2003 S.D. 54, 218, 663 N.W.2d 212, 217–18 (2003); George Cohen Agency, Inc. v. Donald S. Perlman Agency, Inc., 114 A.D.2d 930, 931, 495 N.Y.S.2d 408, 409–10 (1985) (in the absence of a confidential relationship or fiduciary relationship between two parties to a contract, no duty to disclose exists).

40. Cleveland v. City of Lead, 2003 S.D. 54, 218, 663 N.W.2d 212, 217 (2003), *citing* Purdy v. Fleming, 2002 S.D. 156, P20, 655 N.W.2d 424, 431 (2002) (homeowners sued developer and engineers of shopping mall for fraudulent concealment for removing slope, which allegedly caused damage to the homeowners' houses); *see also* Koenig v. Lambert, 527 N.W.2d 903, 905–06 (S.D. 1995); Conway v. Conway, 487 N.W.2d 21, 23 (S.D. 1992); DeLuna v. Burciaga, 359 Ill. Ct. App. 3d 544, 550, 834 N.E.2d 478, 483 (2005).

41. Gades v. Meyer Modernizing Co., Inc., 865 N.W.2d 155, 160 (S.D. 2015).

42. Fuqua v. Taylor, 683 S.W.2d 735, 737 (Tex. Ct. App. 1984) (geologist owed fellow investors a fiduciary duty as a matter of law); Schneider v. Plymouth State Coll.,

E. Fraud Elements

A claim for fraud typically requires proof of representation of an existing fact, materiality and falsity of the fact, the speaker's knowledge of its falsity, the speaker's intent that the plaintiff act, the plaintiff's ignorance of its falsity, the plaintiff's reliance on the truth of the representation, the plaintiff's right to rely upon it, and damages suffered by the plaintiff.[43] The plaintiff must establish each element of fraud by clear, cogent, and convincing evidence, and failure to prove any component typically defeats a claim.[44] An owner might claim fraud when it believes that the design professional intentionally deceived it by affirmatively misrepresenting or concealing material facts related to the contract or the project. Most jurisdictions agree that fraud vitiates any limitation of liability or exculpatory clause; some have codified that policy.[45]

F. Negligent Misrepresentation

A claim for negligent misrepresentation may be asserted when a person in the course of his or her profession or business fails to exercise reasonable care

---

144 N.H. 458, 462, 744 A.2d 101, 105 (1999) (professor who sexually harassed student and college sued for breach of fiduciary duty; court said whether a duty can be imposed upon an entity for the care and protection of a person is a question of law). *But see* Brickner v. Fed. Deposit Ins. Corp., 747 F.2d 1198, 1201 (8th Cir. 1984) (courts have variously characterized the determination that a party breached his fiduciary duty as a question of fact and a question of law; in the present case, the issue might also be described as a mixed question of fact and law).

43. Stiley v. Block, 925 P.2d 194 (Wash. 1996); Hewlett v. Hewlett, 845 S.W.2d 717 (Mo. Ct. App. 1993) (trial court set aside decree of dissolution based upon fraud); Anderson Dunham, Inc. v. Aiken, 133 So. 2d 527 (Miss. 1961) (dump truck buyers filed actions against seller for fraud and deceit based on the ground that the seller falsely represented to them the maximum capacity of the trailers' axles).

44. Shayne v. Julien, Schlesinger & Finz, P. C., 131 A.D.2d 655, 656–57 (N.Y. Ct. App. Div. 1987).

45. *See* Cal. Civ. Code § 1668 (1872) (codifying public policy against contracts that "exempt anyone from responsibility for his own fraud, or willful injury to the person or property of another, or violation of law"); Mont. Code Ann. § 28-2-702 (prohibiting contracts whose object is to exempt anyone from all responsibility for the person's own fraud, willful injury, or violation of law are unenforceable) (2015); *but see* Great Hans, LLC v. Liberty Bankers Life Ins. Co., 05-17-01144-CV, 2019 WL 1219110 (Tex. App. Mar. 15, 2019) (limitation clause in purchase contract negotiated over several months between sophisticated parties was enforceable despite seller's intentional breach and the unavailability of specific performance because the Texas Supreme Court has never held "that fraud vitiates a limitation of liability clause").

in obtaining or communicating, and thereafter supplies false information for the guidance of others in their business transactions and results in the communicator being held liable for any pecuniary loss caused by others' justifiable reliance on the information.[46]

Claims of negligent misrepresentation against design professionals include allegations that an engineer supplied specifications containing false statements of fact or opinion,[47] that an engineer provided false information in an inspection or geotechnical report,[48] and that an engineer's or architect's representations contained errors as to the cost of a project.[49] Jurisdictions are divided on the issue of whether clients may sue a design professional for negligent misrepresentation.[50]

---

46. Restatement (Second) of Torts § 552 (1977). *See also* Ritter v. Custom Chemicides, 912 S.W.2d 128, 130 (Tenn. 1995) (tort of negligent misrepresentation not limited to professionals and privity of contract not essential to a tort action of negligent misrepresentation based on information negligently supplied for the guidance of others); Sav. Bank of Manchester v. Ralion Fin. Servs., 881 A.2d 1035 (Conn. Ct. App. Ct. 2005) (company not liable for misrepresenting status of lessor to bank because bank failed to prove company made false statements on which bank relied).

47. Burns Philp, Inc. v. Cox, Kliewer & Co., P.C., No. 4-99-CV-90033, 2000 U.S. Dist. LEXIS 21653 (S.D. Iowa Nov. 2, 2000) (plaintiffs sued architecture firm, architects, and employee, claiming they made false misrepresentations regarding a mezzanine they designed for plaintiffs).

48. Green Constr. Co. v. Kansas Power & Light Co., 717 F. Supp. 738, 743 (Kan. 1989) (plaintiff contractor sued engineer for misrepresentation when contractor expended more money excavating due to unexpected water levels in the soil not reported in the geotechnical report); Howell v. Fisher, 272 S.E.2d 19 (N.C. Ct. App. 1980) (geological engineer liable to corporate shareholders for negligent misrepresentation in preparation of soil testing for the purpose of inducing their investment in the corporation).

49. Charles L. Hazelton & Son, Inc. v. Teel, 211 N.E.2d 352 (Mass. 1965) (wharf owners sued contractor for alleged misrepresentation regarding cost of repairing wharf; verdict properly directed for contractor where there was no evidence that he knew his estimate to be false).

50. *See* Air Prods. & Chemicals, Inc. v. Eaton Metal Prods. Co., 2003 WL 21697376 (Pa. 2003) (court refuses to recognize causes of action in negligence and strict liability for purely economic injury); Smiley v. S&J Invs., Inc., 580 S.E.2d 283 (Ga. 2003) (homeowner can pursue negligent misrepresentation claim against inspection company based on errors in inspection report); Marcellus Constr. Co., Inc. v. Village of Broadalbin, 755 N.Y.S.2d 474 (2003) (contractor cannot sue engineer for negligent misrepresentation arising from errors in subsurface site condition report); David Pflumm Paving & Excavation, Inc. v. Foundation Servs., Co., 816 A.2d 1164

Library References

C.J.S. *Architects* §§ 19, 21–23; C.J.S. *Contracts* § 271; C.J.S. *Negligence* §§ 91–97, 162–164, 188, 191–192, 197, 803, 805, 808, 810–811; C.J.S. *Products Liability* §§ 1–2.
West's Key No. Digests, Contracts <KEY>114; Negligence <KEY>273, 321, 322, 370, 1657, 1662; Products Liability <KEY> 1.

II. Issues Affecting the Tort Liability of Design Professionals

Although design professionals can manage their risk with prudent contracting, there are common law and statutory constructs that also define liability.

A. Assumption of a Higher Degree of Care

A design professional can agree to be held to a higher standard of care than would otherwise be imposed upon the design professional under common law when the design professional agrees to contract language that contains subject standards, measuring performance based on "the highest standard of the profession," for example, or requiring achievement of specific criteria.[51]

(Pa. 2003) (excavation subcontractor cannot sue engineering firm or township engineer for negligent misrepresentation for errors in report on subsurface conditions). *But see* Koontz v. Thomas, 511 S.E.2d 407 (S.C. 1999) (client could sue architectural firm for negligent misrepresentation, but alleged misrepresentations relating to anticipated construction costs and project duration insufficient to state a claim); Plantation House & Garden Prods., Inc. v. R-Three Investors, 248 A.D.2d 606, 670 N.Y.S.2d 505 (1998) (warehouse owner could pursue negligent misrepresentation claim against engineers based on representation that concrete floor had been completed and installed in accordance with plans and specifications); Empire W. Cos., Inc. v. Albuquerque Testing Labs., Inc., 800 P.2d 725 (N.M. 1990) (negligent misrepresentation claim against geotechnical firm based on statements in report as to suitability of soil allowed to go to trial; verdict for defense); Buchanan v. Scottsdale Envtl. Constr. & Dev. Co., Inc., 787 P.2d 1081 (Ariz. 1990) (homeowner could proceed to trial on claim of negligent misrepresentation against soils engineer based on alleged misrepresentation as to the suitability of the site for residential construction). *See also* Valhal Corp. v. Sullivan Assocs., 44 F.3d 195 (3rd Cir. 1995) (client alleged negligent misrepresentation based on engineer's failure to disclose height restriction on parcel being purchased by client; court did not discuss issue of whether such a claim could be pursued).

51. Town of Breckenridge v. Golforce, Inc., 851 P.2d 214, 216 (Colo. 1992) (court held expert testimony regarding standard of care required of design professional not

In addition to increased liability, the design professional may not have insurance coverage for this greater exposure under the typical professional liability policy.

B. Warranty Disclaimers

Warranty disclaimers are routine in agreements for the sale of goods. However, design professional contracts, along with other construction-related agreements, are typically considered contracts for services, not goods. Therefore, Uniform Commercial Code (U.C.C.) Article 2 warranty provisions do not apply.[52]

There is no consensus between jurisdictions as to the enforceability of disclaimers of express or implied warranties. As a common risk-shifting mechanism, warranty disclaimers are more likely to be enforced when they appear in construction contracts between commercially sophisticated parties. For example, a court held that the jury is permitted to consider a clause in an engineer's

---

necessary where contract defines the standard of care); Ferentchak v. Vill. of Frankfort, 105 Ill. 2d 474, 483, 475 N.E.2d 822, 826 (1985) (engineer not negligent in failing to set the foundation grade elevations because the professional standard did not obligate him to do so and the contract did not obligate him to a heightened standard of care); Strauss Veal Feeds, Inc. v. Mead & Hunt, Inc., 538 N.E.2d 299, 302 (Ind. 1989) (engineering firm not liable for negligence when building complied with all building and safety codes even though it created a biohazard because engineer complied with applicable industry standards and did not assume independent contractual duty to deal with industrial waste treatment and disposal); R.J. Reagan Co. v. Kent, 654 S.W.2d 532, 533 (Tex. 1983) (where no evidence was produced that architect undertook a contractual obligation regarding proper roof construction methods, architect cannot be held responsible for defective construction); Todd Cty. v. Barlow Projects, Inc., Nos. 04-4218 ADM/RLE and 04-4220 ADM/RLE, 2005 U.S. Dist. LEXIS 8648 (Minn. May 11, 2005) (engineering consultant liable only if he did not exercise the care contemplated by the contract with the client); CH2M Hill Se. v. Pinellas Cty., 698 So. 2d 1238, 1240 (Fla. 1997) (if the professional contracts to perform duties beyond those required by ordinary standards of care, the quality of that performance must comport with the contractual terms).

52. Kirkpatrick v. Introspect Healthcare Corp., 845 P.2d 800 (N.M. 1992) (interior designer's predominantly service-oriented contract not subject to U.C.C. Article 2); Pass v. Shelby Aviation Inc., No. W1999-00018-COA-R9-CV, 2000 Tenn. Ct. App. LEXIS 247 (Apr. 13, 2000) (if a contract is predominantly for the sale of goods, it falls under the U.C.C. and the warranty provisions of Article 2 apply; if a contract is predominantly for services, it falls outside the U.C.C. and the warranty provisions of Article 2 are inapplicable).

contract disclaiming any warranty as to the accuracy of cost estimates.[53] Thus, in transactions between sophisticated entities, warranty disclaimers are presumed to be conscionable and enforceable, unless the plaintiff can establish some type of "unfair surprise in the negotiations."[54] In *American Nursery Products, Inc. v. Indian Wells Orchards*,[55] the court stated that the U.C.C. requirement mandating such disclaimers be "specifically negotiated" would not be imposed in the commercial contracts because to do so "would unnecessarily interfere with the freedom to contract in the commercial context."[56]

However, when contracting with an unsophisticated client (i.e., retail consumer), disclaimers may be challenged. Under the U.C.C., disclaimers in consumer contracts are presumed unconscionable, and it is up to the defendant to prove otherwise.[57] Although the U.C.C. does not apply to service contracts, courts may look to it for guidance in determining the conscionability of such disclaimers in contracts with design professionals.[58]

---

53. Post, Buckley, Schuh & Jernigan, Inc. v. Monroe Cty., 851 So. 2d 908, 909–10 (Fla. 2003); *see also* Berschauer/Phillips Constr. Co. v. Seattle Sch. Dist. No. 1, 881 P.2d 986 (Wash. 1994).

54. M.A. Mortenson Co. v. Timberline Software Corp., 998 P.2d 305 (Wash. 2000) (discussing substantive and procedural unconscionability in commercial sales contract); Hewlett-Packard Co. v. Intergraph Corp., No. C 03-2517 MJJ, 2004 U.S. Dist. LEXIS 17601 (N.D. Cal. Sept. 6, 2003) (where parties are commercial entities, warranty disclaimers are presumptively conscionable and the burden is on the party seeking to invalidate the provision to prove it is unconscionable); Alpha One v. Nynex Info. Res. Co., 2 Mass. L. Rep. 568 (Mass. Super. Ct. 1994) ("unconscionability must be determined on a case-by-case basis . . . giving particular attention to whether, at the time of the execution of the agreement, the contract provision could result in unfair surprise and was oppressive to the allegedly disadvantaged party").

55. 115 Wn. 2d 217, 797 P.2d 477 (Wash. 1990).

56. *Id.* at 224, 797 P.2d at 481–82.

57. U.C.C. § 2-302 (2005).

58. *See* Sprague v. Household Int'l, No. 04-0106-CV-W-NKL, 2005 U.S. Dist. LEXIS 11694 (W.D. Mo. June 15, 2005) (principles underlying the common law concept of unconscionability do not differ from those codified in the U.C.C.); Puget Sound Fin. v. Unisearch, Inc., 146 Wash. 2d 428, 440, 47 P.3d 940, 945–46 (2002) (Washington courts may, by analogy, use U.C.C. sections to interpret service contracts).

C. Contract Modifications

1. Use of a Master Agreement

Complex long-term projects require that particular attention be paid to the original owner-design professional agreement. Ideally, where the parties realize that the project will be performed in parts over time, the seminal contract document will identify itself as *a master* or *controlling* agreement. If it is the parties' intent, the contract should explicitly state that the parties intend for the master contract to provide controlling authority for all subsequent agreements, including an explicit statement that the general terms and conditions will control all subsequent contracts.

2. Amendments and Modifications

Subsequent phases of work should be identified explicitly as an *amendment* or *modification* to the original master agreement and, likewise, should explicitly refer to and incorporate the general terms and conditions contained within the master contract.

3. Scope Creep

Design professionals frequently encounter projects that grow in scope, either by plan, necessity, or circumstance. In some instances, the project is intended to be done in phases for which separate written agreements are executed. In other instances, an initial phase of work is all that was originally contemplated, but subsequent events cause the design professional to perform additional services not anticipated in the contract. Both situations should cause the prudent design professional to seek a contract amendment or addendum, addressing the increase in scope.

It is common for a design firm to be perform work not contemplated by the scope of services in the written contract. This happens when the client asks for additional work, prompted by situations encountered in the field. Unfortunately, many design professionals find themselves performing these add-on services without the benefit of a contract amendment. This may occur because the additional scope seems relatively innocuous and minor in nature, or because the individuals actually performing the extracontractual work are field personnel not involved in the contract process. In any event, providing this type of service without the safety net of a contract addendum or amendment puts the design professional at risk. The out-of-scope work may not be governed by the protections negotiated in the contract. Additionally, the design professional's failure to adhere to the terms of the written contract may call into question the enforceability of other clauses in the contract. Although bothersome and frequently at odds with the immediate nature of many requests for add-on services, it is therefore imperative that all work be subject to a written agreement. Ideally this takes the form of an amendment that explicitly refers to the original contract and its general terms and conditions.

D. Preparation of Plans and Specifications

In adjudicating a claim for defective design, a court considers whether the plans and specifications—the "instruments of service"—were prepared in accordance with the standard of care required of the design professional.[59] Plans and specifications do not have to be perfect to protect the design professional from liability;[60] however, they must conform to the standard of care exercised by other design professionals in the community and/or the standard of care stated in the professional agreement governing the work.[61]

Contractors or subcontractors attributing cost increases or delays due to defective design documents often make claims against design professionals.

---

59. Cady v. E. I. DuPont de Nemours & Co., 437 F. Supp. 1030, 1032 (D.C. Tex. 1977).

60. Ramey Constr. Co. v. Apache Tribe of Mescalero Reservation, 673 F.2d 315, 322 (10th Cir. 1982) (architect's plans and specifications adequate for purposes of bidding and construction, even though they contained more than 100 design errors and omissions, given that there were more than 330 drawings and 500 pages of calculations); *Chaney Building*, 148 Ariz. at 574, 716 P.2d 28 at 31 (architect's work can be inaccurate or imperfect without being an actionable deviation from the standard of care observed by design professionals); *see also* Tulsa Zoo Mgmt., Inc. v. Peckham Guyton Albers & Viets, Inc., No. 17-CV-644-GKF-FHM, 2019 WL 1029544, at *17 (N.D. Okla. Mar. 4, 2019).

61. *Ramey*, 673 F.2d at 322; *Mounds View*, 263 N.W.2d at 424 (undertaking by architect implied he possessed skill and ability sufficient to enable him to perform the required services at least ordinarily and reasonably well, and that he would exercise and apply his skills without neglect; it did not imply or warrant a satisfactory result); St. Joseph Hosp. v. Corbetta Constr. Co., 21 Ill. Ct. App. 3d 925, 942–43, 316 N.E.2d 51 (1974) (architect always held to an implied contract that the work shall be suitable and capable of being used for the purpose for which it is prepared); Seiler v. Levitz Furniture Co. of E. Region, Inc., 367 A.2d 999, 1007–08 (Del. 1976) (while an architect does not guarantee a perfect plan or a satisfactory result, he does by his contract imply that he enjoys ordinary skill and ability in his profession, and that he will exercise these attributes without neglect and with a certain exactness of performance to effectuate work properly done).

Owners also may claim that the project exceeded the quoted cost due to defective plans and specifications.[62] Design professionals may defend against these claims by proving that the contractor failed to follow the plans and specifications, or that the plans and specifications meet the standard of care and other conditions caused the damage.[63]

E. Environmental Liability

Engineers may be held liable as "operators" under the Comprehensive Environmental Response, Compensation and Liability Act (CERCLA).[64] In *Ganton Technologies v. Quadion Corp.*,[65] a third party plaintiff (owner) successfully brought a complaint against a supervisor and a contractor who had been hired to clean up PCB contamination, alleging that they further contaminated the site.[66] The court held that liability for violations of the Act as an operator attaches "if the defendant ha[s] authority to control the cause of the contamination at the time the hazardous substances [are] released into the environment."[67]

The Resource Conservation Recovery Act (RCRA) concerns the handling, transportation, treatment, and disposal of hazardous waste and is

---

62. Dep't of Nat. Res. v. Transamerica Premier Ins. Co., 856 P.2d 766, 772 (Alaska 1993) (project owner may sue design professional in tort for economic losses arising from the professional's malpractice, despite existence of a contractual relationship between the parties); Cluett, Peabody & Co. v. Campbell, Rea, Hayes & Large, 492 F. Supp. 67, 74 (Pa. 1980) (plaintiff lessor of building charged architect with breach of its contractual obligations to design and supervise construction of a warehouse; to exercise the skill in its possession in designing and supervising construction of the warehouse; and negligence in the design, selection of material, supervision of construction, and arranging for adequate repairs to the roof resulting in cost incursions by plaintiff to replace roof).

63. Goette v. Press Bar & Cafe, Inc., 413 N.W.2d 854, 856 (Minn. 1987); *see also* Friederick v. Cty. of Redwood, 153 Minn. 450, 451, 190 N.W. 801, 802 (1922) (contractor is not permitted to vary from plans even if he deems them improper and insufficient and, therefore, cannot be held to guarantee that work performed according to the plans will be free from defects).

64. CERCLA § 107(a)(2), 42 U.S.C.S. § 9607 (2018).

65. 834 F. Supp. 1018, 1022 (N.D. Ill. 1993).

66. *Id.* at 1018.

67. *Id.* at 1021–22 (quoting Kaiser Aluminum v. Catellus Dev., 976 F.2d 1338, 1342 (9th Cir. 1992) (excavator grading a section of land for a proposed housing development who spread some displaced contaminated soil from the property over other parts of the property was held liable under CERCLA)).

another regulatory statute that may impose liability on design professionals.[68] The language of the RCRA provides for injunctive relief, as well as civil fines, penalties, and criminal sanctions for violations of the Act.[69]

Other environmental regulations, such as the Clean Air or Clean Water Acts, also may pose a risk to design professionals.[70] However, there is little case law to indicate how these regulations might affect them.

Library References

C.J.S. *Architects* §§ 16, 19, 21–23; C.J.S. *Contracts* §§ 359, 407–420, 434–435; C.J.S. *Damages* §§ 53–61; C.J.S. *Fraud* §§ 4–8, 10–17, 23–25, 28–31, 34–36, 59–60, 62–63, 67–75, 77–78, 80; C.J.S. *Health and Environment* § 170; C.J.S. *Negligence* §§ 162–164; C.J.S. Torts § 26.
West's Key No. Digests, Contracts <KEY>205.25, 205.35, 236–246; Damages <KEY>35; Environmental Law <KEY>445; Fraud <KEY>2–13, 64; Indemnity <KEY>33(5); Labor and Employment <KEY>2607, 2832, 2856; Negligence <KEY>321, 322.

III. Who Can Sue Design Professionals: Economic Loss Rule

Certain states recognize a legal construct called "the economic loss doctrine." The economic loss doctrine can bar tort claims against design professionals when damages caused by them are purely monetary. This doctrine can provide a defense to actions brought by one in privity of contract with the designer, or by a third party who is a stranger to the contract.

A. Application to Parties in Privity of Contract

Parties in privity with design professionals may bring contract actions to recover economic losses.[71] Generally, it is assumed that a design professional owes a common law duty to its clients to exercise the skill and expertise ordinarily used by members of that profession, and a breach of that duty results in liability for any resulting damages. However, some jurisdictions bar tort

68. 42 U.S.C. § 6972 (1984).

69. *Id.*

70. *See* Clean Water Act, 33 U.S.C.A. §§ 1251–1387 (1972), and Clean Air Act, 42 U.S.C.A. §§ 7401–7671 (1990).

71. *Berschauer/Phillips*, 881 P.2d 986.

claims for purely economic losses between parties in contractual privity.[72] Those jurisdictions generally reason that the contract governs the relationship between the parties, including any remedies for breach of that contract and that any claim for breach therefore sounds in contract, not in tort.

The practical effect of this doctrine is that the law applicable to tort actions will not apply to the owner's claim against the design professional; for example, comparison of negligence, joint and several liability, contribution, and the tort statute of limitations. For an excellent discussion of the economic loss doctrine, see *Calloway v. City of Reno.*[73]

B. Application to Third Parties Not in Privity

Under the economic loss doctrine, a third party not in privity of contract cannot sue a design professional in tort if the only damages sustained are monetary losses.[74] This principle is a major bar to lawsuits brought against design professionals.

"Economic loss" is defined as a "diminution in the value of a particular product caused by the product itself or by the failure of the product to function

---

72. *See* Aas v. Superior Court, 24 Cal. 4th 627, 12 P.3d 1125, 101 Cal. Rptr. 2d 718 (2000); *City Express*, 959 P.2d 836.

73. 993 P.2d 1259 (Nev. 2000).

74. *Berschauer/Phillips*, 881 P.2d 986 (economic loss rule prevented a general contractor from recovering purely economic damages from a structural engineer under any tort theory); Spancrete, Inc. v. Ronald E. Frazier Assocs., 630 So. 2d 1197 (Fla. 1994) (subcontractor suing for economic losses not in contractual privity with architect could not state claim under either tort or contract); Floor Craft Floor Covering, Inc. v. Parma Cmty. Gen. Hosp. Ass'n, 560 N.E.2d 206 (Ohio 1990) (in absence of contractual privity, no cause of action exists to recover economic damages against design professional who drafted plans and specifications); Atherton Condo. Apartment-Owners Ass'n Bd. of Dirs. v. Blume Dev. Co., 115 Wn. 2d 506, 534, 799 P.2d 250, 266 (1990) (no cause of action in tort by a third party seeking economic loss damages for negligent design against an architect); *but see* Beachwalk Villas v. Martin, 406 S.E.2d 372 (S.C. 1991) (architect may be liable to homebuyer for negligence in connection with home construction even when no contractual privity exists between homebuyer and architect); Lofts at Fillmore Condo. Ass'n v. Reliance Commercial Const., Inc., 218 Ariz. 574, 577, 190 P.3d 733, 736 (2008) (disapproving prior decision limiting warranty of habitability exception to privity requirement to only homebuilders who are also vendors).

as represented; in other words, to fail economic expectations."[75] Damages for delay, remediation, repair, and diminution in value are economic losses.[76]

The economic loss doctrine is rooted in products liability law. It provides that certain types of "economic loss" damages are recoverable only in contract, generally between parties in privity. The rule marks the fundamental boundary between contract and tort; the former addresses expectancy interests of the parties, while the latter addresses the duty of all persons to exercise reasonable care. In other words, the rule bars recovery in tort for purely economic losses.

An early, seminal case discussing the doctrine is *Seely v. White Motor Co.*[77] (still widely cited, especially in design and construction cases). There, the court noted:

> The distinction that the law has drawn between tort recovery for physical injuries and warranty recovery for economic loss is not arbitrary and does not rest on the "luck" of one plaintiff in having an accident causing physical injury. The distinction rests, rather, on an understanding of the nature of the responsibility a manufacturer must undertake in distributing his products. . . . A consumer should not be charged at the will of the manufacturer with bearing the risk of physical injury when he buys a product on the market. He can, however, be fairly charged with the risk that the product will not match his economic expectations unless the manufacturer agrees it will.[78]

Therefore, the question becomes whether the aggrieved plaintiff is among "the disappointed users . . . [or] the endangered ones."[79] Generally, recovery may be had in contract for the former, and in tort for the latter. In *East River Steamship Corp. v. Transamerica Delaval, Inc.*,[80] the United States Supreme Court approved the distinction drawn between commercial expectation interests reflected in contractual relationships and traditional concepts of duty and

---

75. Wausau Paper Mills Co. v. Charles T. Main, Inc., 789 F. Supp. 968, 971 (W.D. Wis. 1992).

76. *See* E. River S.S. Corp. v. Transamerica Delaval, Inc., 476 U.S. 858, 870, 106 S. Ct. 2295, 2301–02, 90 L. Ed. 2d 865, 876–77 (1986) (economic losses include lost profits, repair costs, and decreased value).

77. 63 Cal. 2d 9, 45 Cal. Rptr. 17, 403 P.2d 145 (1965), *superseded by statute on other grounds.*

78. 63 Cal. 2d at 18, 45 Cal. Rptr. at 23, 403 P.2d at 151.

79. Russell v. Ford Motor Co., 281 Or. 587, 595, 575 P.2d 1383, 1386 (1978).

80. *Infra* note 84.

foreseeable risk contemplated under tort theory. The Court noted that commercial controversies are particularly well-suited to application of the doctrine, and observed that commercial parties have the ability to negotiate contract terms reflecting the economic expectations of the parties.

Numerous jurisdictions have considered the application of the economic loss rule to the construction/design professional industry. The results are mixed and largely dependent on a given state's choice of standards for evaluating economic loss claims and how that state's respective products liability laws apply.[81]

---

81. *See Aas*, 12 P.3d 1125; A.C. Excavating v. Yacht Club II Homeowners Ass'n, 114 P.3d 862, 865 (Colo. 2005) (court reaffirms adoption of the economic loss rule in Colorado but holds that builders have an independent duty to construct a home without negligence, and tort claims may be brought based on breach of a duty independent of the contract); Richards v. Midland Brick Sales Co., 551 N.W.2d 649 (Iowa 1996) (homeowner claim against contractor for negligent brickwork barred by economic loss doctrine); Koss Constr. v. Caterpillar, Inc., 960 P.2d 255 (Kan. Ct. App. 1998), *rev. denied*, No. 96-78054-AS, 1998 Kan. LEXIS 541 (Sept. 10, 1998) (purchaser of hydraulic roller sued manufacturer for product liability; economic loss rule barred negligence or strict liability claims); Young v. City of Plaquemine, 818 So. 2d 892 (La. 2002) (economic loss doctrine bars claim against architect for defective work in the absence of personal injury); Me. Rubber Int'l v. Envt. Mgmt. Gr., 298 F. Supp. 2d 133 (Me. 2004) (land buyer's claim against engineering firm for negligence and negligent misrepresentation in connection with Phase I ESA barred by economic loss rule). *But see* Forte Bros. v. Nat'l Amusements, Inc., 525 A.2d 1301 (R.I. 1987) (contractor allowed to sue architect/site engineer for negligent performance of oversight duties); Goose Creek Consol. Indep. Sch. Dist. v. Jarrar's Plumbing, Inc., 74 S.W.3d 486 (Tex. 2002) (school district's tort claim against architect and contractor for plumbing defects barred by economic loss rule); *E. Steel*, 209 W. Va. at 392, 549 S.E.2d at 266 (contractor claim against design professional not barred by economic loss rule; design firm may owe duty of care to contractor despite absence of privity of contract); Rowe v. Akin Flanders, Inc., 525 S.E.2d 123 (Ga. Ct. App. 1999) (landowner not barred from suing contractor for negligent construction on the basis of economic loss rule); *Waldor Pump*, 386 N.W.2d 375 (engineer liable to subcontractor for negligence in drafting and interpreting specifications; rejected application of economic loss doctrine); Glacier Tennis Club at the Summit, LLC v. Treweek Constr. Co., 87 P.3d 431 (Mont. 2004) (contractor may recover for economic loss against project engineer or architect when design professional knew or should have known that plaintiff was at risk in relying on information supplied); Tommy L. Griffin Plumbing & Heating v. Jordan, Jones & Goulding, Inc., 463 S.E.2d 85 (S.C. 1995) (contractor allowed to sue design profes-

1. Two Tests

States typically follow two schools of thought as to how the economic loss doctrine is perceived and applied: the "damages-driven test" and the "foreseeable duty test."

a. Damages-Driven Test

This perspective approaches the economic loss doctrine by asking what type of damage is alleged to have occurred and determining whether the claim properly lies in tort or contract. This view more clearly defines the nature of the theory of liability by working backward to determine the source of duty owed—either by contractual assumption or pursuant to a standard of care imposed for the activity. This is the majority approach.[82]

b. Foreseeable Duty Test

Foreseeability analysis begins by inquiring, "what duty was owed by" a design professional or whether "it [is] foreseeable that some third party would necessarily rely upon" the design professional's work. When courts make analysis, the outcome may be a foregone conclusion, as a design professional's services are seemingly *always* relied upon by the client, at a minimum.[83] For example, the Montana Supreme Court recently held that "a third party contractor may recover for purely economic loss against a project engineer or architect when the design professional knew or should have foreseen that the particular plaintiff or an identifiable class of plaintiffs were at risk in relying on the information supplied."[84] Other jurisdictions reaching similar conclusions include

---

sional for economic losses because design professional has duty not to negligently design or supervise project).

82. *See Aas*, 12 P.3d at 1125; *Tommy L. Griffin,* 463 S.E.2d at 85 (economic loss doctrine analysis rests first on what kind of damages were caused, and second on what kind of duty was owed).

83. Jim's Excavating Serv., Inc. v. HKM Associates, 265 Mont. 494, 878 P.2d 248 (1994).

84. *Id.* at 255.

Arizona,[85] Connecticut,[86] Michigan,[87] and Alabama.[88] Some states call this foreseeable duty test "the independent duty doctrine" (discussed ahead).

C. Claims against Individual Design Professionals

Few courts have analyzed whether the economic loss doctrine bars tort claims against an individual design professional in the absence of contractual privity between the claimant and that person. As licensed professionals, design professionals do have individual liability for their work.[89]

Florida statutes explicitly provide for the liability of individual professionals and that they are not shielded by being employees of a corporation.[90] Homeowner claimants were therefore permitted to assert a cause of action against individual engineers for services provided during a pre-purchase inspection of a private home, despite the fact the homeowner signed a contract with the employer of the engineers, not the engineers individually.[91]

---

85. Donnelly Constr. Co. v. Oberg/Hunt/Gilleland, 137 Ariz. 184, 187–88, 677 P.2d 1292, 1296 (Ariz. 1984) (the potential for imposing a duty owed to third parties not in privity will be evaluated on a case-by-case basis, using a reasonable "foreseeability of risk and plaintiff" analysis).

86. *Insurance Co. of N. Am.*, 17 F. Supp. 2d 81; Carolina Cas. v. 60 Gregory Boulevard, No. CV 980169383S, 2000 Conn. Super. LEXIS 739 (Mar. 20, 2000).

87. Bacco Const. Co. v Am. Colloid Co., 384 N.W.2d 427 (Mich. Ct. App. 1986) (contractor allowed to bring negligence action to recover purely economic losses from project engineer; court applied foreseeable risk of harm analysis).

88. Keck v. Dryvit Sys., Inc., 830 So. 2d 1 (Ala. 2002) (where one party assumes a duty to another party in contract and it is foreseeable that injury to a third party could occur as result of breach, the promisor owes a duty to all within foreseeable area of risk).

89. *Contrast* John Rocchio Corp. v. Pare Eng'g Corp., 201 A.3d 316 (R.I. 2019), *with* Gerald M. Moore & Sons, Inc. v. Drewery, 467 S.E.2d 811 (Va. 1996).

90. Moransais v. Heathman, 744 So. 2d 973 (Fla. 1999), *receded from by* Tiara Condo. Ass'n, Inc. v. Marsh & McLennan Companies, Inc., 110 So. 3d 399 (Fla. 2013).

91. *Id. See also* A.C. Excavating v. Yacht Club II Homeowners Ass'n, Inc., 114 P.3d 862 (Colo. 2005) (subcontractors owe homeowners a duty of care, independent of any contractual obligations, to act without negligence in the construction of a home; the economic loss rule has no application where a plaintiff's tort claim is based on an independent duty of care); Skender v. Brunsonbuilt Constr. & Dev. Co., LLC, 122 Nev. 1430, 148 P.3d 710 (2006) (homeowner's tort claim against contractor for negligent construction governed by statute, not ELD); G.A. Resort Condo. Ass'n, Inc. v. Chicago Title Timeshare Land Tr., Inc., 19-CV-01870-RM-GPG, 2020 WL 5815029 (D. Colo. Sept. 14, 2020) (extra-contractual fiduciary duty owed to homeowner's association).

A contrary view was expressed by the Virginia Supreme Court which expressly held that even if negligence by an individual engineer is proven, in the absence of contractual privity, the economic loss doctrine bars recovery from the individual (versus the engineering firm employer) for purely economic losses.

D. Exceptions to Application/Enforcement of the Doctrine

1. Negligent Misrepresentation

While generally recognizing the economic loss doctrine as a bar to purely economic damages claims, some jurisdictions have carved out an exception to this rule when the tort claimed is negligent misrepresentation. Illinois has a well-developed lineage of case law on this issue.

Illinois originally adopted the economic loss rule in *Moorman Manufacturing Co. v. National Tank Co.*,[92] but it also recognized two exceptions—intentional fraud and negligent misrepresentation, but only where the defendant "*is in the business of supplying information* for the guidance of others."[93]

Through subsequent decisions, the Moorman rule and its exceptions have been refined and advanced. In *2314 Lincoln Park West Condominium Assn. v. Mann, Gin, Ebel & Frazier*[94] and *Fireman's Fund Insurance Co. v. SEC Donohue, Inc.*,[95] the courts found that the typical object of engineering and architectural efforts is to produce something tangible (a building or structure) and, in those instances, design professionals are not engaged in the business of "supplying information." Thus, in those instances, the negligent misrepresentation exception does not apply to design professionals.

The Illinois Supreme Court has also determined that the rulings in *2314 Lincoln Park West* and *Fireman's Fund Insurance Co.* are not absolute. In *Tolan & Son, Inc. v. KILL Architects, Inc.*,[96] design professionals prepared plans and specifications and provided consulting services during construction. The plaintiff urged the court to bifurcate the two roles filled by the design professional defendants and find that the consulting services performed during construction fell within the negligent misrepresentation exception recognized in *Moorman.* Although the court declined to do so (noting that the consulting services are ancillary to design services and, therefore, a continuation of

---

92. 435 N.E. 2d 443 (Ill. 1982).
93. *Id.* at 452 (emphasis added).
94. 555 N.E. 2d 346 (Ill. 1990).
95. 679 N.E. 2d 1197 (Ill. 1997).
96. 719 N.E.2d 288 (Ill. Ct. App. 1999).

design), it observed that in a purely evaluative or advisory role, a design professional could well "engage in the business of providing information" and, therefore, fall within the exception. This decision clearly raises implications for design firms that engage in purely construction management services on a particular project. The *Tolan* court explicitly allowed for the possibility that design professionals may be sued for negligent misrepresentation when only economic damages are sought.[97]

The negligent misrepresentation "exception" has been adopted in other jurisdictions as well, sometimes with mixed results.[98] For example, in *Council of the Dorset Condominium Apartments v. Dorset Apartments*,[99] engineers hired to perform a pre-purchase inspection report were sued when the repairs noted in the report, estimated to cost $35,000, ballooned to over $700,000. The court held that engineers (but not architects) fall within the exception to the economic loss rule: "Unlike an architect who prepares plans which are converted into a tangible product—a building—engineers prepare information to

97. *See e.g.*, 21 Kristin Condo. Associaton v. Pioneer Eng'g & Envtl. Servs., LLC, 1-19-1868, 2020 WL 5820296 (Ill. App. Ct. Sept. 30, 2020) (plaintiff adequately stated a cause of action against engineer by alleging facts that could support a finding that engineer negligently misrepresented condition of building).

98. *See* Resell Constr. Managers v. EH Constr., LLC, 134 S.W.3d 575 (Ky. 2004) (contractor claim of negligent misrepresentation against construction manager not barred by economic loss doctrine); Nota Constr. Corp. v. Keyes Assocs., 694 N.E.2d 401 (Mass. 1998) (economic losses resulting from negligent misrepresentation are exception to the doctrine, when claimant reasonably relies upon design professional's work product); Belt-Rite Contractors v. Architectural Studio, No. 74 MAP 2002, 2005 Pa. LEXIS 99 (Jan. 19, 2005) (economic loss doctrine does not bar contractor's negligent misrepresentation claim against architect [not in privity], when contractor reasonably relied upon defective plans and specifications); AmSouth Erectors, LLC v. Skaggs Iron Works, Inc., No. W 2002-01944-COA-R3-CV, 2003 Tenn. Ct. App. LEXIS 551 (Aug. 5, 2003) (subcontractor's claim against construction management firm dismissed, because of failure to prove negligent misrepresentation, an exception to economic loss doctrine); New Hampshire Electrical Cooperative, Inc. v. Elster Solutions, LLC, No. 16-cv-440-PB, 2017 WL 2861667 (D.N.H. July 5, 2017) (holding negligent misrepresentation claims fall within the inducement exception to ELD); Atlantic Geoscience, Inc. v. Phoenix Development and Land Investment, LLC, 341 Ga. App. 81, 799 S.E.2d 242 (2017) (reversing summary judgment for a geotechnical firm because it is an exception to ELD where the case concerns an alleged negligent misrepresentation).

99. CIV.A.90C-10-269, 1992 WL 240444 (1992) (unpublished but cited in subsequent decisions in that jurisdiction).

be used as information."[100] Therefore, in Illinois an engineer, but not an architect, is exposed to a claim for negligent misrepresentation where the damages are economic in nature.

2. Sudden/Calamitous Event

Additionally, where the economic loss doctrine otherwise might apply, some jurisdictions nonetheless permit tort claims when there is an allegation of threat to physical safety. In Washington, an exception to the economic loss rule arises when a plaintiff suffers economic damage caused by a "sudden and dangerous" event as described in *Touchet Valley Grain Growers, Inc. v. Opp & Seibold Construction, Inc.*[101] In *Touchet*, the owner of a grain storage building sued the general contractor and metal fabrication subcontractor after its building collapsed. The Washington Supreme Court allowed the plaintiff to recover economic losses from the defendants under a tort theory of liability based on a "risk of harm" analysis previously adopted by the court in a products liability case.[102] The *Touchet* court held that in cases where the otherwise purely economic harm arises out of a "sudden and dangerous" or "calamitous" event, a plaintiff is allowed to seek damages in tort.[103]

This narrow exception is justified on the theory that "sudden and dangerous" events are more likely to result in bodily injury and calamitous property damage. Accordingly, the availability of a tort remedy, even when the plaintiff has suffered only economic losses, provides an important incentive for design professionals to exercise reasonable care whenever there may be this kind of damage.

Maryland has adopted a similar approach. In *Milton Co. v. Council of Unit Owners of Bentley Place Condominium*,[104] the court found that some of the claimed construction defects "clearly . . . pose a risk of serious physical

---

100. *But see* Fletch's Sandblasting & Painting, Inc. v. Fay, Spofford, & Thorndike LLC, 2:15-CV-76-DBH, 2019 WL 847731 (D. Me. Feb. 21, 2019), *reconsideration denied*, 2:15-CV-76-DBH, 2019 WL 1714436 (D. Me. Apr. 17, 2019) (Maine applies economic loss doctrine to claims of negligence, negligent misrepresentation, and product liability); Blake Constr. Co., Inc. v. Alley, 353 S.E.2d 724 (Va. 1987) (refusing to recognize negligent misrepresentation claim for purely economic loss in construction context).

101. 119 Wash. 2d 334, 831 P.2d 724 (1992).

102. Washington Water Power Co. v. Graybar Elec. Co., 774 P.2d 1199 (Wash. 1989).

103. *Touchet*, 119 Wash. 2d at 352, 831 P.2d at 733.

104. 121 Md. Ct. App. 100, 708 A.2d 1047 (1998).

injury" and, therefore, "a plaintiff may recover in tort for purely economic loss where the defect creates a substantial risk of death or personal injury."[105] Illinois and Arizona also recognize a "sudden and dangerous" exception to the economic loss doctrine.[106]

E. The Independent Duty Doctrine

The independent duty doctrine is an emerging concept within the economic loss doctrine lineage of case law. Like the economic loss doctrine, the independent duty rule is intended to maintain the boundary between tort and contract. In adopting the rule, certain courts express a desire to reach the ultimate question of when the duty of care is subsumed within contractual duties and when it arises independently of the contract, based on the services being performed.[107]

Some jurisdictions use independent duty as a supplement to, or test within, economic loss analysis.[108] For others, it is a limit on the reach of the economic loss rule. For example, Wyoming recognizes a specific independent duty of reasonable care owed by home builders, which precludes application of the economic loss doctrine in claims against home builders.[109] Another court refers to the economic loss and independent duty analyses as separate, distinct barriers to tort claims stemming from contractual relationships.[110]

---

105. *Id.* at 115, 708 A.2d at 1054; *see also* Danforth v. Acorn Structures, Inc., No. 90C-JN-30, 1991 Del. Super. LEXIS 390 (Aug. 27, 1991) (court ruled against homeowner who sued contractor for negligence because damages were purely economic; sudden, calamitous event is an exception to the economic loss doctrine, but no such event occurred in this case).

106. Hecktman v. Pac. Indem. Co., 59 N.E.3d 868 (Ill. App. Ct. 2016); Valley Forge Ins. Co. v. Sam's Plumbing, LLC, 220 Ariz. 512, 207 P.3d 765 (Ariz. Ct. App. 2009).

107. *See* Eastwood v. Horse Harbor Found., Inc., 170 Wn. 2d 380, 394, 241 P.3d 1256, 1264 (2010); Town of Alma v. AZCO Const., Inc., 10 P.3d 1256, 1262 (Colo. 2000).

108. *See* Reighard v. Yates, 285 P.3d 1168 (Utah 2012); Wyle v. Lees, 162 N.H. 406, 33 A.3d 1187 (2011); Nat'l Labor Coll., Inc. v. Hillier Gr. Architecture N.J., Inc., 739 F. Supp. 2d 821 (D. Md. 2010); Koontz v. Thomas, 333 S.C. 702, 511 S.E.2d 407 (1999).

109. *See* Rogers v. Wright, 2016 WY 10, 366 P.3d 1264 (Wyo. 2016).

110. Nat'l Credit Union Admin. Bd. v. Deutsche Bank Nat'l Tr. Co., 14-CV-8919 (SHS), 2019 WL 5190889 (S.D.N.Y. Oct. 15, 2019) (unpublished opinion).

IV. Site Safety

A. Background

Nearly every jurisdiction has some sort of workmen's compensation or industrial insurance statute that grants to the employer immunity from suit for injuries sustained by employees while working on a construction project. These statutes represent a tradeoff of interests: the injured worker or the deceased worker's family receive access to a pool of funds available for a defined amount of compensation following an injury; and the contractor/employer, having paid into the workers' compensation fund, has purchased certainty by being made immune from suit by his injured worker or the deceased worker's family. These statutes typically provide compensation for injured workers without requiring proof of fault or negligence of any kind, and that compensation from the fund is the exclusive remedy of the employee against his employer.

However, in many instances, the recovery from state workers' compensation funds is insufficient compared to the damages that can be obtained in a lawsuit. While an injured worker may not sue his or her own employer for a job site injury, he or she may be authorized statutorily to sue any person not hired by the same employer who is at fault for an injury.[111] This presents a risk to design professionals, as the injured claimant seeks recovery from non-immune parties.[112]

The unintended consequence of workers' compensation laws has been to encourage injured workers to seek recovery from parties not shielded by these statutes. Some courts have recognized that the "proliferation of such suits may conceivably be based upon the desire of the injured workman to find a 'deep pocket' to more adequately compensate for serious injury than may be recovered from the employer or general contractor under the limitations of workers'

---

111. Frazier v. St. Paul Ins. Co., 880 So. 2d 406 (Ala. 2003) (under ALA. CODE § 25-5-14 (1984), a workers' compensation exclusivity-of-remedy provision provided complete immunity to employers and limited immunity to others closely affiliated with the employment relationship from liability, but court did not extend immunity beyond this); Williams v. Int'l Paper Co., 129 Cal. Ct. App. 3d 810, 816 (1982) (third-party tortfeasor not immune from common law tort action; self-insured employer does not fall within definition of "person other than employer").

112. Sonners, Inc. v. Dep't of Labor & Indus., 3 P.3d 756 (Wash. Ct. App. 2000); Jansen v. Aaron Process Equip. Co., 207 F.3d 1001, 1003 (7th Cir. 2000) (employee recovered workers' compensation benefits from employer and subsequently recovered a judgment from manufacturer of the equipment involved in employee's injury).

compensation statutes."[113] In response, a minority of states have extended the immunity of their workers' compensation statutes to design professionals (see ahead).

Typically, claims against design professionals either implicate the design as having created the hazard leading to injury or, more commonly, implicate construction site services provided by the design professional. Most state statutes impose principal responsibility for site safety on the contractor, but in some jurisdictions, burdens are placed on owners, who in turn may seek to shift the task to the design professional. Design professionals should know the law concerning site safety in the jurisdiction where the project will be constructed, especially as to the duties imposed on design professionals. Design professionals must also exercise caution while on site, such that on-site conduct does not lead to an assumption of extra-contractual duties, including site safety.

B. Responsibility of the Contractor and Owner

It is important for the design professional to understand the legal and contractual responsibilities imposed on owners and contractors with regard to site safety, if for no other reason than to ensure the design professional does not abrogate these important assignments of risk via contract or conduct.

Under the workplace safety statutes, many jurisdictions assign a nondelegable duty to the general contractor to ensure the safety of all workers on a job site.[114] A number of jurisdictions also recognize that a general contractor owes a duty to all employees at a work site to comply with, or ensure compliance with, safety regulations.[115] This duty to keep the premises in a safe condition

---

113. Hanna v. Huer, Johns, Neel, Rivers & Webb, 662 P.2d 243, 249 (Kan. 1983).

114. Brennan v. RCP Assocs., 257 A.D.2d 389 (N.Y. Ct. App. Div. 1999) (under McKinney' s N.Y. Lab. Law § 240(1) (1981), a nondelegable duty is imposed upon owners and general contractors to furnish proper safety devices and protection in order to ensure the safety of workers exposed to elevation-related risks during the construction, repair, demolition, painting, and alteration of a building or structure); Nave v. Harlan Jones Drilling, 827 P.2d 1239 (Mont. 1992) (general contractor had contractual duty to provide for the safety of all employees at the work site, which it could not delegate to the subcontractor); Pfenninger v. Hunterdon Cent. Reg'l High Sch., 338 N.J. Super. Ct. App. Div. 572, 581, 770 A.2d 1173, 1179 (1999) (decedent died when the trench he was working in caved in; court held a landowner or general contractor has a nondelegable duty to ensure the safety of the premises upon which work is to be performed).

115. Stute v. P.B.M.C., Inc., 114 Wash. 2d 454, 464, 788 P.2d 545, 550–51 (1990) (it was the general contractor's responsibility to furnish safety equipment or to contrac-

may subject the general contractor to direct liability for negligence in two situations: those arising from a premises defect; and those arising from an activity or instrumentality. This duty is based upon the general contractor's "innate supervisory authority" that constitutes, per se control over the workplace and statutory authority.[116]

Absent some form of control over the subcontractor's method of operation, a general contractor and owner of the construction project are not liable for injuries to the subcontractor's employees.[117] The subcontractor, despite the general contractor's duty for workplace safety, retains concurrent responsibility to meet workplace safety standards in the areas under its control.[118]

Such inquiries are often heavily fact reliant. For example, it may be difficult to determine whether an owner maintains control over the site. If the owner retains "only the right to inspect the construction work to see that the contract specifications are met, while the independent contractor controls how and when the work is to be done, there is probably not sufficient retained control to subject [the owner] to liability."[119]

Merely retaining the power to forbid or stop work from being done in an unsafe manner is not a sufficient degree of retained control to subject the

---

tually require subcontractors to furnish adequate safety equipment relevant to their responsibilities at the job site); Arias v. MHI P'ship, 978 S.W.2d 660, 662 (Tex. Ct. App. 1998) (a general contractor on a construction site, who is in control of the premises, is charged with the same duty as an owner or occupier, who has a duty to use reasonable care to keep the premises under its control in a safe condition).

116. *Stute*, 114 Wash. 2d at 457–60, 788 P.2d at 546–49.

117. Stepanek v. Kober Constr., 191 Mont. 430, 433, 625 P.2d 51, 53 (1981) (contractor found liable to subcontractor's injured employee because contractor exercised control over safety conditions at the work site); *but see* Jones v. Logansport, 436 N.E.2d 1138, 1147 (Ind. 1982) (Indiana recognizes exception to this rule if work being performed is intrinsically dangerous).

118. Gilbert H. Moen Co. v. Island Steel Erectors, Inc., 128 Wash. 2d 745, 757, 912 P.2d 472, 478–79 (1996); Lewis v. N.J. Riebe Enters., 170 Ariz. 384, 388, 825 P.2d 5, 9 (1992) (although general contractor has a general duty to provide a reasonably safe workplace for the employees of subcontractors, the scope of this duty extends only as far as the amount of control the general contractor retains over the work of the subcontractor).

119. Werdehausen v. Union Elec. Co., 801 S.W.2d 358, 364 (Mo. 1990) (if the employer retained only the right to inspect the construction work to see that contract specifications were met, while the independent contractor controlled how and when the work was to be done, there was not sufficient retained control to subject the employer to liability).

owner to liability.[120] "Similarly, if the employer retains only standard 'boilerplate' provisions with respect to safety inspections and requirements, but assumes no affirmative duties with respect to safety and never directs the method of performance, there is [likely] insufficient control" to render the employer liable for injury caused by unsafe performance of the work.[121] Nevertheless, it is extremely important to understand that if the owner assumes an affirmative duty to implement safety precautions, by contract or conduct, the owner is liable for injuries caused to others by unsafe work performance where the owner negligently allows unsafe work to continue.[122]

When sued by an injured worker, a design professional firm should consider whether it can crossclaim against the contractor and subcontractor. Alternatively, it may argue to the jury that the contractor or subcontractor is 100 percent at fault (even if the employer is not a party to the suit—the empty chair defense). However, there are legal obstacles to either option. First, the design firm typically does not have contractual privity with either the contractor or any of the subcontractors. This means that the only legal basis for a crossclaim (in the absence of contractual indemnity) is a tort claim for negligence or a statutory claim for contribution.

Second, in certain jurisdictions, a design professional firm may not be able to assert a claim of contribution or seek an allocation of fault against the injured worker's employer (whether that employer is the contractor or a subcontractor). For example, Washington's Tort Reform Act[123] was amended to exclude any assessment of fault against an employer with immunity under Washington's Industrial Insurance Act.[124] In other words, the design firm may not be able to sue the immune employer or use the empty chair defense at trial.

---

120. *Id.*, *citing* Moloso v. State, 644 P.2d 205, 211 (Alaska 1982); *see also* DeVille v. Shell Oil Co., 366 F.2d 123, 125–26 (9th Cir. 1966).

121. *Werdehausen*, 801 S.W.2d at 364.

122. *Id.*; *see, e.g.*, Jones v. Chevron U.S.A., Inc., 718 P.2d 890, 896 (Wyo. 1986) (because owner of work site retained the right to direct the manner of the independent contractor's performance and assumed affirmative duties with respect to safety, owner owed a duty of reasonable care to the independent contractor's employee, even when the employee was injured doing the very work the contractor was hired to perform); Hammond v. Bechtel Inc., 606 P.2d 1269, 1276 (Alaska 1980) (employers contended that they had no duty to inspect, repair, or maintain the independent contractor's equipment; court held that genuine issues of material fact remained regarding whether the employers were responsible for exercising control over work site and turning over site free of safety hazards).

123. WASH. REV. CODE § 4.22.070(1) (2005).

124. WASH. REV. CODE Title 51.

Thus, the design firm could be held liable for the injured worker's employer's share of fault.[125] In these jurisdictions, the design professional should attempt to obtain a waiver of immunity from the owner, and encourage the owner to procure the same from the contractor, as discussed below.

C. Indemnity for the Design Professional

A design firm may be able to protect itself from the risk of suit by an injured worker by requiring the owner to indemnify it from personal injury lawsuits brought by contractors' or subcontractors' employees. Subject to any anti-indemnity statute (discussed below), such an indemnification clause allows the design professional firm to tender defense of the claim to the owner. An alternative approach is to prepare contract documents requiring the contractor and subcontractors to indemnify the design professional and owner from worker injury claims and to waive workers' compensation immunity to that extent.

In Washington, these waivers are valid and enforceable. In *Gilbert H. Moen Co. v. Island Steel Erectors, Inc.*,[126] a subcontractor's employee sued the general contractor, claiming that the contractor had been negligent in failing to require its subcontractors to comply with safety regulations. The contractor settled with the worker and then sued the subcontractor for indemnification. The court held that an indemnification clause, coupled with an express waiver of workers' compensation immunity, was a valid and permissible method for protecting against subcontractor negligence in managing site safety for its own workers.[127]

However, anti-indemnity statutes may limit the scope of any such protection. These laws prohibit clauses that purport to indemnify a party for injury caused by the indemnitee's own negligence or willful misconduct, or the negligence or willful misconduct of those under the indemnitee's control.[128] Anti-indemnity statutes are the product of the public policy concerns that govern contracts purporting to indemnify parties against their own negligence.[129]

---

125. *Gilbert H. Moen*, 128 Wash. 2d 745, 912 P.2d 472.

126. *Id.* at 760–61, 912 P.2d at 480–81.

127. *Id.*

128. Aetna Cas. & Sur. Co. v. Marion Equip. Co., 894 P.2d 664, 670 (Alaska 1995) (court refused to enforce indemnification provision in lease agreement between construction equipment company and contractor due to anti-indemnity statute). *See also* Elliott v. Illinois Cent. R.R. Co., 219CV02807TLPCGC, 2020 WL 4496518 (W.D. Tenn. Aug. 4, 2020) (a party seeking indemnity is precluded from recovery when there was concurrent negligence among both parties).

129. Union Pac. Res. Co. v. Dolenc, 2004 Wy. 36, 86 P.3d 1287 (2004) (anti-indemnity statute applies only to contracts for work dealing directly with the mining of oil and gas).

"Such contracts may remove or reduce the incentives to protect workers and others from personal injury and the anti-indemnity statute helps to insure that persons responsible for the work are properly motivated to provide safe working conditions."[130]

Under an anti-indemnity statute, a design professional firm cannot seek indemnification from the owner for injuries caused by the design firm's sole negligence. It can seek indemnification for such claims when caused by the concurrent negligence of the owner, contractor or subcontractor, but only to the extent of that party's negligence. However, "concurrent negligence" language must be present in the indemnification clause to be valid and enforceable.[131] For example, the Washington law states:

> A covenant, promise, agreement or understanding in, or in connection with or collateral to, a contract . . . relative to the construction . . . of, any building, . . . purporting to indemnify against liability for damages arising out of bodily injury to persons or damage to property:
>
> (1) Caused by or resulting from the sole negligence of the indemnitee, his agents or employees is against public policy and is void and unenforceable;
>
> (2) Caused by or resulting from the concurrent negligence of (a) the indemnitee or the indemnitee's agents or employees, and (b) the indemnitor or the indemnitor's agents or employees, is valid and enforceable only to the extent of the indemnitor' s negligence and only if the agreement specifically and expressly provides therefor, and may waive the indemnitor's immunity under industrial insurance, Title 51 RCW, only if the agreement specifically and expressly provides therefor and the waiver was mutually negotiated by the parties.[132]

---

130. *Id.*

131. *Gilbert H. Moen*, 128 Wash. 2d 745, 912 P.2d 472; *see also* Vargas v. Inland Washington, LLC, 194 Wn.2d 720, 452 P.3d 1205 (2019).

132. WASH. REV. CODE ANN. § 4.24.115 (West, Westlaw through Ch. 1 of the 2020 Reg. Legis. Sess.); *see also* Hoffman Constr. Co. v. United States Fabrication & Erection, 32 P.3d 346, 359 (Alaska 2001) (indemnity agreements that shift liability from the indemnitee to the indemnitor are valid, subject to the restrictions of ALASKA STAT. ANN. § 45.45.900 (West, Westlaw through 2019 First Reg. Legis. Sess.)); and *see* ARIZ. REV. STAT. ANN. § 34-226 (West, Westlaw through Feb. 3, 2020 of the Second Reg. Legis. Sess.); CAL. CIV. CODE §§ 2782, 2782.5 (West, Westlaw through Ch. 870 of the 2019 Reg. Legis. Sess.); CONN. GEN. STAT. ANN. § 52-572k (West, Westlaw through

Therefore, to determine the validity of and requirements for an indemnification provision, a design professional must examine the applicable state law, including any anti-indemnity statute.

D. Theories of Liability against the Design Professional

Injured workers typically allege one or more of three liability theories against design professionals: negligent design; negligent construction management or supervision; and negligent failure to warn of dangerous site conditions.[133] As discussed above, design professionals are obliged to exercise such reasonable care, technical skill and ability, and diligence as is ordinarily required of design professionals in the course of preparing their plans or performing inspections and supervision during construction for the protection of any person who foreseeably and with reasonable certainty might be injured by their failure to do so.[134]

However, a design professional is not liable for injury caused to a third party if design failures resulting in physical injury are caused when those responsible for construction or supervising the construction deviate from the plans and specifications.[135] This is true even if the owner impliedly warrants the adequacy and sufficiency of the plans.[136]

2019 Jan. Reg. Legis. Sess. and 2019 July Spec. Legis. Sess.); HAW. REV. STAT. ANN. § 431:10-222 (West, Westlaw through 2019 Reg. Legis. Sess.); IDAHO CODE ANN. § 29-114 (West, Westlaw through 2019 First Reg. Legis. Sess.); IND. CODE ANN. § 26-2-5-1 (West, Westlaw through 2020 Second Reg. Legis. Sess.); MICH. COMP. LAWS ANN. § 691.991 (West, Westlaw through P.A.2020, No. 23, of the 2020 Reg. Legis. Sess.); N.M. STAT. ANN. § 56-7-1 (West, Westlaw through First Reg. Legis. Sess.); S.C. CODE ANN. § 32-2-10 (West, Westlaw through 2019 Legis. Sess.); TENN. CODE ANN. § 62-6-123 (West, Westlaw through 2019 First Extraordinary Legis. Sess.); UTAH CODE ANN. § 13-8-1 (West, through Westlaw 2019 Second Spec. Legis. Sess.); VA. CODE ANN. § 11-4.1 (West, Westlaw through 2019 Reg. Legis. Sess.); W. VA. CODE ANN. § 55-8-14 (West, Westlaw through 2019 Second Extraordinary Legis. Sess.).

133. *See* Le May v. USH Props., Inc, 338 So. 2d 1143, 1144–45 (Fla. 1976).

134. *Id.*

135. *Goette*, 413 N.W.2d at 856.

136. *Id.*; *see also* United States v. Spearin, 248 U.S. 132, 136 (1918) (if a contractor is bound to build according to plans and specifications prepared by the owner, the contractor will not be responsible for the consequences of defects in the plans and specifications).

E. The Design Professional's Role on Site

Most jurisdictions refuse to impose liability on design professionals for site safety, unless there has been a clear assumption of the duty to monitor site safety.[137]

General contractors have a nondelegable and specific duty to comply with state safety regulations.[138]

In an early court decision interpreting the duty of design professionals to "supervise" or "inspect" a contractor's work, the Minnesota Supreme Court drew a line between inspection for general conformance with the design intent versus a duty to ensure that plans and specifications are carried out in every

---

137. *Hanna*, 662 P.2d 243 (architect not liable for injury caused by contractor error, where contract established the duty to provide and enforce safe working conditions was with the general contractor); *contrast* Balagna v. Shawnee Cty., 233 Kan. 1068, 668 P.2d 157 (1983) (summary judgment was improper where engineer had actual knowledge of an unsafe condition); Waltman v. Eng'g Plus, Inc., 264 So. 3d 758 (Miss. 2019) (knowledge of dangerous conditions does not satisfy factors showing extra-contractual supervisory duty); *see also* Krieger v. J.E. Greiner Co., 382 A.2d 1069 (Md. 1978); Walters v. Kellam & Foley, 360 N.E.2d 199 (Ind. Ct. App. 1977) (neither general contractor nor architect had a duty to supervise the construction site or insure plaintiff's safety; but mechanical engineer, mechanical contractor, and HVAC manufacturer all had a legal duty to insure the plaintiff's safety while he worked on the construction project); Brown v. Gamble Constr. Co., 537 S.W.2d 685 (Mo. Ct. App. 1976) (worker was killed when he fell through a hole in the roof of a partially constructed structure; court held that architects were under no duty to supervise construction, unless they expressly agreed to do so); Seeney v. Dover Country Club Apartments, Inc., 318 A.2d 619 (Del. Super. Ct. 1974) (because engineering firm did not retain or voluntarily exercise any control over the manner or methods used by the contractor in its work, engineering firm not liable for injuries sustained by worker); *Reber*, 474 P.2d 852 (where workers were injured in a structural collapse, court held that statute did not impose a duty upon an architect to directly control the contractor's methods, but only to assure that the results complied with design specifications); Day v. National United States Radiator Corp., 128 So. 2d 660 (La. 1961) (architect liable for injuries arising from boiler explosion during installation when architect's plan were not defective); Jones v. James Reeves Contractors, 701 So. 2d 774, 784 (Miss. 1997) (architect had no duty to supervise the site and, therefore, was not liable for work site injuries); Hobson v. Waggoner Eng'g, Inc., 878 So. 2d 68, 72 (Miss. Ct. App. 2003), *cert. denied*, 878 So. 2d 66 (2004) (general contractor, not engineer, had duty for supervision of the work and project safety).

138. Kamla v. Space Needle Corp., 52 P.3d 472 (Wash. 2002); Rodriguez v. Sea Crest Constr. Corp., 64 Misc. 3d 1214(A), 116 N.Y.S.3d 871 (N.Y. Sup. Ct. 2019).

detail.[139] In that case, a contractor failed to properly fasten a roof to the building and a claim was brought against the architect for failing to ensure that the contractor followed the plans and specifications. The court rejected the claim, noting that the architect's contractual duty to make periodic site visits to review the quality and progress of the contractor's work (including whether the contractor was performing in accordance with the plans and specifications) did not rise to the level of imposing responsibility to *ensure* that the contractor carried out his work in accordance with the contract documents.[140]

This ruling was cited favorably in *Mayor and City Council of City of Columbus, Mississippi v. Clark-Dietz & Associates-Engineers, Inc.*[141] The court noted that a design professional's general inspection services do not impose a duty to make "continuous and exhaustive" inspections of the contractor's work.

Contract documents should contain a limitation on responsibility assigned to the design professional pursuant to which the design professional can avoid any implication of the assumption of control over or direction of the contractor's means and methods, techniques, sequences, or procedures, including safety precautions or programs. For example, the Engineering Joint Contracts Design Committee (EJCDC) Owner-Engineer Agreement provides:

> [The] engineer shall not, during such visits or as a result of such observations of contractor's work of progress, supervise, direct or have control over contractor(s) work. . . .[142]

The American Institute of Architects (AIA) Owner-Architect Agreement expresses a similar limitation of responsibility:

> The purpose of the engineer's [site] visits . . . will be to enable engineer to better carry out the duties and responsibilities assigned to and undertaken by engineer during the construction phase and . . . to provide the owner a greater degree of confidence that the completed work of contractor(s) will conform *generally* to the contract documents. . . .[143]

---

139. Moundsview Indep. Sch. Dist. No. 621 v. Buetow & Assocs., Inc., 253 N.W.2d 836, 837 (Minn. 1977).

140. *Id.*

141. Mayor of Columbus, Miss. v. Clark-Dietz, 550 F. Supp. 610, 627 (Miss. 1982).

142. EJCDC Document No. 1910-1, Standard Form Agreement between Owner and Engineer for Professional Services, 1 1.6.2.3.

143. AIA Document B151-1997, 1 2.6.5 (emphasis added).

The design professional's role at the site, as defined by the contract, plays an important part in identifying the degree to which a duty for site safety may be imposed. Courts may look to several general factors in determining whether a design professional affirmatively undertook responsibility for site safety (as discussed above, some of these same elements may also affect whether any statutory immunity applies). These factors include actual supervision and control of the work, retention of the right to supervise and control, constant participation in ongoing activities at the construction site, supervision and coordination of subcontractors, assumption of responsibilities for safety practices, authority to issue change orders, and the right to stop the work.[144]

Whether an architect or engineer has assumed site safety responsibilities by contract is an often-litigated issue. Courts have found design professionals liable for site safety when the following types of clauses are contained in the contract:

- Engineering firm contracted to develop and execute safety program and had authority to stop contractor operations in case of noncompliance.[145]
- Engineering firm contracted to ensure overall responsibility to maintain a safe construction area, including responsibility to take "every precaution against injuries to persons."[146]
- Architect assumed all duties to manage construction, to perform all managerial functions and to "protect Owner's interest in safety."[147]

In contrast, the following provisions were relied upon by the courts in finding that the design professional was not liable under the common law or the terms of an immunity statute:

- Contract with owner precluded on-site engineer from "advising on or issue directions as to safety precautions and programs in connection with the work."[148]

---

144. *Waltman*, 264 So. 3d at 762; *Hobson,* 878 So. 2d at 72; *Hanna*, 662 P.2d at 243.

145. Riggins v. Bechtel Power Corp., 722 P.2d 819 (Wash. Ct. App. 1986).

146. Piccirillo v. Beltrone-Turner, 284 A.D.2d 854, 727 N.Y.S.2d 721 (Ct. App. Div. 2001) (construction manager held liable to pedestrian injured in fall at airport).

147. Simon v. Omaha Public Power Dist., 202 N.W.2d 157 (Neb. 1972) (architect liable for injury to worker who fell through opening in floor deck).

148. Williams, Hatfield & Stoner, Inc. v. Malcolm, 687 So. 2d 295 (Fla. Dist. Ct. App. 1997); Black v. Gorman-Rupp, 791 So. 2d 793 (La. Ct. App. 2001).

- Engineering firm agreed only "to assure that the projects are constructed in reasonable conformity with plans, specifications, and contract provisions" without any further reference to safety.[149]
- Under AIA standard contract, architect's ability to reject work did not give rise to any duty to the contractor, subcontractors, or their employees.[150]
- Contract stated that engineer had not been retained to design or review contractor's safety practices or the means and methods of work.[151]
- Architect's contract disclaimed control over, or charge of, construction means and methods or for safety precautions or programs.[152]
- Engineer's contract with the Department of Transportation did not give it responsibility to supervise or control activity resulting in worker's death.[153]

Regardless of the contract language, many courts impose liability on design professionals (based upon common law negligence or an exception to an immunity statute) for on-site injuries when the evidence established that the architect or engineer affirmatively acts in a manner to assume responsibility for worker safety.[154]

---

149. Estate of Reyes v. Parsons Brinckerhoff Constr. Servs., Inc., 784 So. 2d 514 (Fla. 2001).

150. *Hanna*, 662 P.2d at 243.

151. *Hobson*, 878 So. 2d at 68.

152. Dillard v. Shaughnessy, Fickel & Scott Architects, 864 S.W.2d 368 (Mo. Ct. App. 1993).

153. Hernandez v. Yonkers Contracting Co., 306 A.D. 2d 379, 760 N.Y.S.2d 865 (N.Y. Ct. App. Div. 2003).

154. Bauer v. Howard S. Wright Constr. Co., 101 Wash. Ct. App. 1046 (2000), No. 44817-0-I, 2000 Wash. Ct. App. LEXIS 1689 (July 17, 2000) (summary judgment for engineer reversed based on exceptions in immunity statute for exerting actual control over the site and negligent preparation of plans and specifications; engineer hired to perform construction monitoring with authority to stop work if unsafe working conditions observed had in fact previously stopped work for that reason; engineer approved changes in the methods for constructing the temporary retaining wall, including the elimination of safety features originally included in the plans); Jones v. Parsons Transp. Grp., Inc., 2004 WL 1254029 (D. Md. May 20, 2004) (no immunity statute involved; court held that while the engineer was retained to perform inspection services, review the contractor's site safety plans, and assure compliance with safety standards, there was no evidence that the engineer undertook these services for the benefit of the contractor or its workers); *see also* Frank Wagner, *Liability to One Injured in Course*

F. Design Professional Immunity Statutes

Many states have addressed this problem through the enactment of design professional immunity statutes, which exempt design professionals from liability for injuries to third persons at construction sites.[155] Under the typical formulation, a design professional is immune from liability to third persons for such injuries unless the design professional specifically assumes responsibility for safety practices in its contract or "actually exercise[s] control over the portion of the premises where the worker [is] injured."[156]

The New York design professional immunity statute omits the requirement that the architect or engineer assume responsibility by a *written* contract:

> No liability for non-compliance with any provision of [site safety responsibility] shall be imposed on professional engineers . . . architects . . . or landscape architects . . . who do not direct or control the work for activities other than planning and design.[157]

Thus, in New York, absent a written contractual assignment for site safety, the exemption can be waived if a design professional directs or controls the contractor's work. Courts will strictly construe the language of immunity statues.[158] For example, in interpreting its state's immunity statute, the Washington Supreme Court limits the application of the statute to the specific area on a large project where construction is actually occurring and broadly

---

of Construction Based upon Architect's Alleged Failure to Carry Out Supervisory Responsibilities, 59 A.L.R.3d 869 (1974 and supp.).

155. E.g., Conn. Gen. Stat. Ann. § 31-293 (West, Westlaw through 2019 Jan. Reg. Legis. Sess. and 2019 July Spec. Sess.); Fla. Stat. Ann. § 440.09 (West, Westlaw through 2019 First Reg. Legis. Sess.); Ga. Code Ann. § 34-9-11 (West, Westlaw through 2019 Sess. of the General Assemb.); Wash. Rev. Code Ann. § 51.24.035 (West, Westlaw through Ch. 1 of the 2020 Reg. Legis. Sess.); Kan. Stat. Ann. § 44-501 (West, Westlaw through July 1, 2019 of the 2019 Reg. Legis. Sess.).

156. *Bauer*, 2000 Wash. Ct. App. LEXIS 1689 (issue of fact existed as to whether consulting engineer exercised actual control during installation of soil nail wall such that engineer could be held liable for physical injuries sustained when wall collapsed). *See also* Pelletier v. Sordoni/Skanska Constr. Co., 264 Conn. 509, 526, 825 A.2d 72, 83 (2003) (general contractor not liable by operation of immunity statute for injuries to subcontractor's employee struck by fallen beam); Agner v. APAC-Fla., Inc., 821 So. 2d 336, 340 (Fla. 2002) (design professional immune from liability based on design professional immunity statute concerning motorist killed due to road-side construction).

157. N.Y. Lab. Law art. 10, § 241-a (McKinney 2002).

158. *See* Michaels v. CH2M Hill, Inc., 171 Wn.2d 587, 257 P.3d 532 (2011).

construes behavior that could be considered for the "negligent preparation of design plans and specifications."[159] The *Michaels* court held that the relevant statutory language in the immunity statute does not apply to an engineering firm that negligently makes a design change to wastewater processing equipment that is not actually under construction, even though a treatment plant as a whole is being renovated.[160] The *Michaels* court also determined that the statute does not require plans to be in writing and that there is "no appreciable difference" between recommendations pursuant to an on-call contract and the preparation of written plans and specifications.[161]

Similar to Washington, design professional immunity statutes in other jurisdictions also explicitly decline to extend protection to claims for injuries caused by defective plans and specifications.[162]

G. Control over the Work and OSHA Fines

Exercising control over the work also may expose the design professional to regulatory fines. Congress enacted the Occupational Safety and Health Act (OSHA) in 1970 to help reduce employment-related injuries and illness.[163] The Secretary of Labor is vested with the authority to enforce OSHA. Pursuant to that authority, the Secretary has issued general industry standards[164] and industry-specific standards.[165] Under certain circumstances, design professional firms can face civil liability for a contractor's failure to comply with these regulations.[166]

In *CH2M HILL, Inc. v. Herman*,[167] an OSHA citation was issued to the project engineer following a catastrophic work site accident that resulted in three deaths. The engineer's contract provided that it was not responsible for site safety; rather, the contractor bore that duty. Likewise, the engineer did not have the ability to direct the contractor to make corrections, nor did it have stop-work authority; those duties rested with the municipality/owner.

---

159. *Id.* at 539–40.

160. *Id.* at 540–41.

161. *Id.* at 541.

162. *Pelletier*, 264 Conn. at 526, 825 A.2d at 83; *Agner*, 821 So. 2d at 340; Cowart v. Crown Am. Props., 258 Ga. Ct. App. 21, 22, 572 S.E.2d 706, 708–09 (2002).

163. *See* 29 U.S.C. § 651 (1970).

164. *See* 29 C.F.R. Part 1910.

165. The construction standards are set forth in 29 C.F.R. Part 1926. *See also* George v. Myers, 169 Ore. Ct. App. 472, 480, 10 P.3d 265, 270–71 (2000).

166. CH2M HILL, Inc. v. Herman, 192 F.3d 711 (7th Cir. 1999).

167. *Id.*

Notwithstanding these limitations to the engineer's scope of service, the OSHA citation was issued because the engineer responded when a differing site condition arose (detection of methane gas) and, at the owner's direction, provided clarification as to what type of electrical equipment could be used below ground where there was potential that the equipment could ignite the gas. OSHA found that by engaging in this advisory activity, an engineer has "engaged in construction work." However, the court rejected this formulation, instead turning to the effective contract path to find that CH2M HILL' s work did not constitute "engaging in construction work." The court also found that because CH2M HILL had limited authority (approving types of equipment) that was subject to the owner's ultimate approval, it lacked sufficient control to be classified as engaged in providing construction services, rather than merely consulting services.[168] The court noted that OSHA' s own "substantial supervision" test compels this finding.[169] Thus, it was found that the engineer had no authority over site safety or construction means and methods, and it *did not* function in a manner that was "inextricably intertwined with the actual physical labor of construction."[170]

In contrast to the *CH2M HILL* case, *Carvalho v. Toll Bros. & Developers*[171] involved a wrongful death action, rather than OSHA compliance. There, the engineer was tasked with on-site construction observation duties, but had no authority for site safety (this duty rested with the contractor). The engineer was obliged to monitor the progress of construction on a time-sensitive project, which included the proper handling of underground utilities crossing through a portion of the project area where trenching was to occur. The engineer also had to ensure that the contractor protected utility lines crossing the trench. The engineer's contract further provided that the condition of the trench was relevant to determining construction procedures. While the engineer was present and observing, a worker was killed when an unreinforced trench collapsed on him.

In this instance, the engineer knew that the contractor chose not to use a trench box. To do so would have required cutting through two utility pipes, which later would have to be repaired, and thereby slow the work. As a result, the court denied the engineer's motion for summary judgment. The court found that the circumstances of the engineer's responsibility for the rate-of-progress of the work, combined with being present when the choice was made

---

168. *Id.*
169. *Id.*
170. *Id.* (emphasis added).
171. 675 A.2d 209 (N.J. 1996).

not to use a trench box, "demonstrate[d] the interrelationship between safety and progress." The court focused on the foreseeability of the risk, noting that in other areas where utilities were not a factor, the contractor had recognized the potential danger and used a trench box.

> The connection between the engineer's responsibilities over the progress of work and safety measures at the job site is relevant in determining whether it is fair to impose a duty of care addressed to work site safety conditions.[172]

The court found that the engineer owed a duty of care to workers based upon his responsibility for the work progress and his knowledge, despite the lack of any contractual responsibility for safety.

H. Contract Provisions

To ensure that a design professional does not assume responsibility for site safety, the contract should expressly disclaim any obligation or right to control the behavior of others on site. These provisions are important to avoid liability for negligence and may affect the immunity of the design professional in states where such statutes exist.

Claims against design professionals for construction site injuries most commonly involve allegations regarding the design professional's fieldwork or physical presence on the site. Engineers are routinely charged with performing observation services during construction to verify that the contractor is constructing the project according to the plans and specifications. The degree of involvement at the construction site may range from part-time, intermittent observation, to providing a full-time on-site observation, to actual construction management. Each of these on-site services represents an escalating degree of involvement for the design professional at the project and brings with it varying degrees of scrutiny that will be applied when considering whether the design professional bears responsibility for an accident (and, in certain jurisdictions, whether the design professional will benefit from statutory immunity).

A design professional should guard against inconsistent and potentially conflicting contract terms. For example, the engineer/owner agreement may provide for only "periodic inspections" for conformance with the design intent, yet the general conditions of the construction contract also may require the engineer to "ensure" that the project is being completed according to design parameters. In the event of an accident attributed to the contractor's failure

172. *Id.* at 214.

to perform according to the plans and specifications, the engineer may face a claim for failing to catch the error. Relying on a defense of a limited site inspection duty has no guarantee of success. At the time of contracting, a design professional should be alert to potentially conflicting contractual language.

It is also common for there to be a contractual disconnect between the broad expression of the design professional's duties in the master agreement and a severe limitation on those duties in specific task orders that follow. The contractual expression of duties for site services should be consistent and uniform throughout the contract documents.

I. Duty to Keep Own Employees Safe

Site safety obligations must be distinguished from responsibility for the safety of one's own employees. Typically, a design firm owes its employees a non-delegable duty to ensure their physical safety in any location to which those employees are sent to work.[173] However, an employer is generally immune from civil lawsuits by its own employees for unintentional job site injuries under workers' compensation acts.[174] Owners sometimes ask design firms to

---

173. Ala. Code § 25-1-1 (West, Westlaw through Act 2019-540) (employer must make workplace reasonably safe for employees, including use of proper safety devices and adoption of safety methods); Div. of Occupational Safety & Health of the Indus. Comm'n v. Chuck Westenburg Concrete Contractors, Inc., 193 Ariz. 260, 269–70, 972 P.2d 244, 253–54 (1998) (each employer at a construction site is responsible for assuming that its conduct does not create hazards to any employees at the site, is responsible for violations it reasonably could have been expected to prevent or abate, and must make reasonable efforts to detect violations of standards and to exert reasonable efforts to have them abated); D.C. Code Ann. § 32-808 (West, Westlaw through January 29, 2020) (every employer must furnish a reasonably safe place of employment, use safety devices and safeguards, and adopt practices that are reasonably safe and adequate to render such employment and place of employment reasonably safe); Ohio Rev. Code Ann. § 4101.11 (West, Westlaw through File 24 of the 133rd General Assemb. (2019–2020)) (every employer shall furnish employment that is safe for the employees and shall do every other thing reasonably necessary to protect the life, health, safety, and welfare of such employees and frequenters); Wis. Stat. Ann. § 101.11 (West, Westlaw through 2019 Act 69) (every employer must furnish a safe place of employment for employees and shall do every other thing reasonably necessary to protect the life, health, safety, and welfare of such employees).

174. Flanigan v. Dep't. of Labor & Indus., 869 P.2d 14 (Wash. 1994) (employers who intentionally cause worker injuries are not immune); Rieman v. Washington State Dep't of Labor & Indus., 13 Wn. App. 2d 1018 (Industrial Insurance Act immunizes employers from civil tort actions for workplace injuries); Wood v. Safeway, Inc., 121

waive workers' compensation immunity and indemnify them from claims for injuries sustained by the design firm's employees. Again, each state's laws must be reviewed to determine the enforceability of such indemnification.

J. Hazardous Waste Sites

Special federal regulations regulate worker safety on sites defined as hazardous waste sites. Under 29 C.F.R. § 1910.120, any "employer" with workers performing remediation or emergency response work on such a site must maintain a site health and safety plan. It sometimes can be unclear in traditional owner/contractor, owner/engineer relationships who is the "site manager." In addition, contractors often do not have expertise to develop such plans and will ask an engineer to prepare one. Participation in the preparation of a site safety plan may raise questions regarding the engineer's immunity from suit in the event of a worker injury or exposure.

In addition, the regulations require any "employer" who retains contractors or subcontractors to work in hazardous waste operations to inform those entities of any potential safety hazards and to take steps to ensure adequate training of the contractors' and subcontractors' workers. This requirement may extend to the engineering or environmental consultant acting as an owner's representative at one of these sites. The bottom line is, responsibility for site safety at a hazardous waste site can be more complicated and raise different risks than a traditional construction site.

K. The Safety Dilemma

When a field representative observes an unsafe condition at the construction site, the question posed is always, "How to respond?" The dilemma is that, as seen above, some courts find liability based upon the failure to act, yet taking affirmative steps and becoming involved in site safety could be construed as an assumption of that responsibility. There is authority that holds that architects and engineers, as professionals, cannot idly stand by with actual knowledge of an unsafe condition or unsafe practices on the job site without taking steps to advise or warn the owner or the contractor. While courts recognize

---

P.3d 1026 (Nev. 2005) (Nevada Industrial Insurance Act, Nev. Rev. Stat. 616A–616D (1999), provides the exclusive remedy for employees injured on the job; employer is immune from suit by an employee for injuries arising out of and in the course of the employment). *But see* Granite Constr. Co. v. Mendoza, 816 S.W.2d 756 (Tex. Ct. App. 1991) (contractor's refusal to provide orange safety vests and to close off nearest lane of traffic to protect flagger constituted gross negligence, rendering employer immunity statute inapplicable).

that a design professional does not necessarily assume responsibility for implementing workplace safety measures by reporting observed safety violations to the owner or contractor,[175] the professional may incur liability if he or she witnesses an unsafe condition, recognizes it as such, and fails to warn the workers of the danger.[176]

Therefore, it would be advisable that field representatives avoid the appearance of becoming actively involved in safety but respond in a reasonable manner when there is an imminent danger of injury or death. The appropriate steps will vary based upon the circumstances, but they should always be followed with written confirmation that the design professional is not assuming any control or responsibility for safety.

Absent an imminent threat of immediate injury or death, field personnel should be trained to follow a notification protocol consistent with the contract's allocation of responsibility. Thus, the field personnel's first step may be to notify his or her own supervisor, an owner representative, or the contractor's site safety representative. However, it is important for field personnel to understand that any notification to the owner or the contractor should be framed as advisory only and not construed as a direction or a stop-work order. Further steps to be taken include contemporaneous documentation of the situation observed, to whom notification was given, and the manner in which such information was communicated. In the event that the contractor fails to respond, the field personnel should leave the site and notify appropriate parties of this action.

---

175. Jeffords v. BP Products N. Am. Inc., 2:15-CV-55-TLS, 2019 WL 954818 (N.D. Ind. Feb. 27, 2019), *aff'd*, 963 F.3d 658 (7th Cir. 2020); Rafferty v. Century Eng'g, Inc., 2002 WL 480958 (Del. Mar. 22, 2002).

176. *But see* Herczeg v. Hampton Township Mun. Auth., 766 A.2d 866 (Pa. 2001) (court rejects claim that duty arises based solely upon an engineer's actual knowledge of dangerous conditions); Vonasek v. Hirsch & Stevens, Inc., 221 N.W.2d 815 (Wis. 1974) (architect had no duty to warn workers as to obvious hazard); Young v. Hard Rock Constr., L.L.C., 292 So. 3d 178 (La. Ct. App. 2020), *writ denied*, 2020-C-00544, 2020 WL 5652227 (La. Sept. 23, 2020) (Louisiana recognizes no "moral duty" to observe, warn of, report, or correct unsafe conditions where contract states otherwise); *Waltman*, 264 So. 3d 758 (absent showing that engineer had assumed responsibility for supervision or control of work, safety practices, or authority to change or stop work, knowledge of dangerous conditions did not impose duty).

CHAPTER 7

Design Professional Work Product Ownership and Protection

J. BENJAMIN PATRICK

I. Introduction

A design professional is hired to create designs, details, specifications, bid sheets, and any of a hundred other things, depending on the needs of the project. Besides construction observation services, the primary value a design professional brings to a project is the value of his or her creativity and experience. Both are used to create a package which will (in theory) accomplish what the owner wants to achieve within a budget the owner finds acceptable. Because of the work that goes into their creation, the fruits of a design professional's creativity can have significant economic value. Innovative connection details, efficient floor plans, and inviting curbside elevations are all valuable design elements. Design professionals who create these designs are understandably interested in protecting them.

Copyrights, patents, and trade secret laws afford design professionals protection for the designs they create. Each system of laws operates differently, affording different levels of protection and requiring different levels of proof from the design professional in order to qualify for protection. This chapter discusses the various methods through which design professionals can secure protection for their designs. Currently, copyright law affords the best protection for design professionals' designs. Courts have recently seen an explosion in design copyright litigation, so this chapter focuses primarily on copyright law as a means of protecting designs. However, this chapter will also discuss patents and the ways in which patents differ from copyrights. Finally, it will discuss trade secret laws, which can be used to ensure that a design professional's former employees do not use innovative techniques learned during their employment to compete with their employer at a later time.

II. What Types of Works Are Subject to Copyright Protection?

A. Generally

Virtually any work of authorship can be protected by a copyright: architectural plans, novels, plays, songs, sculptures, paintings, computer programs, and many other works.[1] Within the category of architectural works,[2] authors can copyright plans, specifications, elevations, models, built structures, and even individual details. A work must meet only two requirements in order to be copyright protected: it must fall into one of the categories of works that are subject to copyright protection and it must be sufficiently original to trigger copyright protection. Section IV of this chapter discusses the protection that architectural works are afforded. For purposes of this section, it is sufficient to note that architectural works like those described above fall into one of the categories of works subject to copyright protection. Therefore, the only issue that authors of architectural works must consider is whether their works are sufficiently original to trigger copyright protection.

In the context of copyright eligibility, there is a very low threshold for originality. The United States Supreme Court has said that a work is sufficiently original to qualify for copyright protection so long as the work was independently created by its author (as opposed to being copied from another work) and possesses "some minimal degree of creativity."[3] The degree of creativity required is extremely low—even a slight amount of creativity will

1. 17 U.S.C. § 102 (1990) generally describes works that are subject to copyright protection.

2. The Copyright Act uses the phrase "architectural work." Therefore, this chapter will also use that phrase. However, engineering designs are equally protected under the Copyright Act; the use of the word "architectural" is not intended by the Act to be exclusionary.

3. Feist Publ., Inc. v. Rural Tel. Serv. Co., 449 U.S. 340, 345 (1991).

suffice. Thus, the vast majority of works will qualify, no matter how crude, humble, or obvious the work may be.[4]

B. Copyrights Distinguished from Patents

Patent law is a highly detailed area of law with many of its own unique rules and procedures. It is beyond the scope of this chapter to present the reader with even a fundamental understanding of patent law. However, it is important to distinguish between copyrights and patents, and to understand how patents can play a role in the protection of architectural designs. As noted earlier, copyrights are relatively easy to obtain, and almost every author is entitled to copyright protection for his or her creations. In contrast, patents are incredibly difficult to obtain, and many inventions do not qualify for patent protection. This is because the process for obtaining a patent is essentially adversarial: the inventor will need to prove to the U.S. Patent and Trademark Office that the particular invention is unique, original, and not merely an extension of existing technology. However, the heightened burden of obtaining a patent comes with a greater reward: patent holders can prohibit others from using, in any way, the protected invention, as well as any product that impermissibly duplicates the workings of the protected invention. As discussed below, this protection is more extensive than the protection offered by copyrights.

Architectural designs are seldom eligible for patent protection. It is hard to envision a scenario in which an entire architectural plan could receive a patent. However, some elements of architectural designs, particularly technical construction details, can be protected by patents. Designers who have created particularly innovative construction details and wish to obtain the maximum available protection for them should consider obtaining a patent regarding those details.

Library References

C.J.S. *Copyrights and Intellectual Property* §§ 9–19, 92, 101; C.J.S. *Patents* §§ 1–5, 10–12, 15.

West's Key No. Digests, Copyrights and Intellectual Property <KEY>3–17; Patents <KEY>1.

---

4. *Id. See also* Alfred Bell & Co. v. Catalda Fine Arts, 191 F.2d 99, 103 (2d Cir. 1951) ("Originality in this context means little more than a prohibition of actual copying. No matter how artistically poor the author's addition, it is enough if it be his own.").

III. Who Owns the Copyright?

The threshold question in any copyright dispute is determining who owns the copyright. Ownership of architectural plans is now a common question in contract negotiations between architects and owners. Therefore, it is important to understand who usually owns architectural copyrights and how the nature of that ownership can be altered.

A. The Default Rule: Plans Are Owned by the Designer

For all works that are subject to copyright protection, the default rule is that the author of the work owns the copyright.[5] This principle is also reflected in standard industry contracts.[6] While courts in the past have struggled with the question of whether the designer was the author, this question has now been resolved in the designer's favor.

1. The Work Made for Hire Doctrine

In the past, project owners who wanted copyright ownership for architectural plans claimed that right under the work made for hire doctrine. A work made for hire is one that is "prepared by an employee within the scope of his or her employment; or . . . specially ordered or commissioned for use as a contribution to a collective work . . . [or] a supplementary work . . . [or] a compilation . . . if the parties expressly agree in a written instrument signed by them that the work shall be considered a work made for hire."[7] This doctrine means that the employer is the author of any works made for hire and owns all copyrights in that work.

Owners have previously argued that the nature of hiring a designer makes the works produced by that designer in the course of his or her work for the owner a work made for hire. Courts in recent years have rejected that contention for several reasons. First, the doctrine applies only to nine specifically

---

5. 17 U.S.C. § 201(a).

6. AIA A201-1997, § 1.6.1: "unless otherwise indicated the Architect and the Architect's consultants shall be deemed the authors . . . and will retain all common law, statutory and other reserved rights, in addition to the copyrights." EJCDC E-500, 2002, § 6.03(A): "All Documents are instruments of service in respect to this Project, and Engineer shall retain an ownership and property interest therein (including the copyright and the right of reuse at the discretion of the Engineer)."

7. 17 U.S.C. § 101.

enumerated categories of work.[8] Of those categories, the only ones that could be said to apply to architectural plans are collective works, supplementary works, and compilations. In truth, none of these categories is appropriate for architectural works' and courts have recognized this fact. Second, designers are considered independent contractors, not the owner's employees.[9] Owners often provide input to ensure that the finished design will meet their needs and expectations, but the owner typically lacks control over the details of the designer's work. That fact, combined with the general tenor of the relationship, tends to weigh heavily against finding an employment relationship.[10] When the independent nature of the designer's work is considered, courts commonly find that the work does not fall within the scope of the "work made for hire" doctrine.

2. *Co-Authorship*

Owners have also attempted to claim copyright ownership of architectural plans based on a co-authorship theory. Owners have argued that because their input was vital to the finished plans (program requirements, aesthetic comments, redline changes, etc.), they are co-authors of the plans with the designer. In recent years, courts have rejected this notion.[11]

B. Ownership of the Copyright in the Building Itself

As discussed in detail in Section IV.C ahead, an author can secure two distinct copyrights on architectural works: a copyright in the architectural plans and a copyright in the built product (i.e., the building itself). The default rule is that an architect who obtains a copyright on a building's design also typically

---

8. *Id.*

9. Kirk v. Harter, 188 F.3d 1005 (8th Cir. 1999).

10. *See, e.g.*, M.G.B. Homes, Inc. v. Ameron Homes, Inc., 903 F.2d 1486 (11th Cir. 1990); Kirk v. Harter, 188 F.3d 1005 (8th Cir. 1999); Zitz v. Pereira, 119 F. Supp. 2d 133 (E.D.N.Y. 1999), *aff'd*, 225 F.3d 646 (2d Cir. 2000); Bryce & Palazzola Architects and Assocs., Inc. v. A.M.E. Group, 865 F. Supp. 401 (E.D. Mich. 1994); Joseph J. Legat Architects v. U.S. Dev. Corp., 625 F. Supp. 293 (N.D. Ill. 1985).

11. *See, e.g.*, *M.G.B. Homes*, 903 F.2d at 1492–93; *Zitz*, 119 F. Supp. 2d at 143–45, 225 F.3d at 672; *Bryce & Palazzola*, 865 F. Supp. at 404; *Joseph J. Legat Architects*, 625 F. Supp. at 297–98.

receives the copyright protection in the building itself. Courts have recognized architectural firms' copyright protection for buildings they designed.[12]

C. Conveying Copyright Interests

In the absence of an agreement to the contrary, the designer is the author of the plans and the copyright owner of the plans. In recent years, owners have become increasingly interested in owning all or part of the copyright. The transfer of a copyright or an interest therein must be done in writing.[13] Owners typically enter into contract negotiations for exclusive copyright ownership of the plans to be created by the designer. There are several reasons why designers should be reluctant to give owners absolute ownership of the plans, not the least of which is the designer's desire to reuse parts of the design in later work for other clients. There are also several alternatives to exclusive ownership that will satisfy the needs of most owners. These alternatives are discussed below in descending order of preference from the standpoint of the designer.

1. Ownership by the Designer with a Nonexclusive License for the Owner

Owners are increasingly unwilling to allow the designer to retain absolute ownership over the work. While there are a number of reasons for this, and every owner will have unique needs depending on the nature of the project, the needs of most owners can be satisfied by granting them a nonexclusive license to the work. Under this scenario, the designer retains ownership of the work, but passes a license to the owner which allows the owner expanded use of the work itself. A typical contract provision in such an instance would be:

> The Work is an instrument of the Designer's service. The Designer is the author of the Work and retains all common law, statutory, and other reserved rights in the Work, including the copyright. The Designer hereby grants to the Owner a nonexclusive license to reproduce, modify, and make derivative products from the Work. In return, the Owner agrees, to the fullest extent permitted by law, to indem-

---

12. *See, e.g.*, T-Peg, Inc. v. Vt. Timber Works, Inc., 459 F.3d 97, 115 (1st Cir. 2006) (the court recognized an architect's copyright protection in a "timber-framed" house it designed); Builders Mut. Ins. Co. v. Donald A. Gardner Architects, Inc., 856 F. Supp. 2d 773, 777 (D.S.C. 2012) (the court recognized an architectural firm's copyright protection in the structure of a home).

13. 17 U.S.C. § 204. *See also* Staggers v. Real Authentic Sound, 77 F. Supp. 2d 57, 68–69 (D.D.C. 1994).

> nify, defend and hold Designer harmless from any claim, liability or cost (including reasonable attorney's fees and defense costs) arising or allegedly arising out of the use of the Work by the Owner if such use has not been explicitly approved in writing by the Designer.

This provision accomplishes several important goals. First and foremost, the designer still retains all rights to the work, and is recognized as the author of the work. Second, the owner is placated by the license grant which will allow it to modify the work and use the work in the future for other projects. This satisfies the needs of most owners. Third, the license granted to the owner is nonexclusive, which permits the designer to grant others a license to the work if the need arises. Fourth, in the event the owner uses the work without consulting the designer, the owner is obligated to indemnify and defend the designer from any damages resulting from this use. It is not hard to foresee instances in which the owner would improperly modify the work and expose the design professional to a claim of some type. The designer needs to be protected in these circumstances. However, it is important to note that many states have anti-indemnity statutes that apply to contracts for design work and that could affect the designer's ability to obtain full protection from the owner. Designers pursuing projects in those states should ensure that the indemnity provision complies with the applicable anti-indemnification statute.

2. *A Reverse License*

As noted above, the grant of a nonexclusive license should satisfy the needs of most owners. However, if the owner insists that it own the copyright for the work, the designer needs to address several key concerns. First, the designer should not grant the owner the rights to details that appear in the work but also appear in other materials prepared by the designer (e.g., a standard wall section). Second, the designer should retain the right to create designs which are derivative of the work. This avoids conflict between the owner and the designer if a future project created by the designer ends up looking too much like the project. Third, as with the previous provision, the designer needs to be protected from any claims resulting from the owner's future use of the work if the designer is not consulted. Fourth, the designer needs to ensure that it will be paid for its work. Fifth, the designer should explicitly disclaim any warranties of fitness for a particular purpose and merchantability in order to forestall any claim, at a later date, that the designer made any implied warranties regarding the design. These needs can be addressed with contractual language like this:

> The Work is an instrument of the Designer's service. The Designer is the author of the Work, and the Designer hereby assigns to the Owner, without reservation, all of Designer's common law, statutory, and other rights in the Work, including the copyright, upon full payment of all monies due to the Designer under this Contract, including payment for all additional services. In the event a dispute regarding payment arises, this assignment is not effective until after the dispute has been resolved. To the extent that the Work incorporates information and/or designs previously developed by the Designer, the Designer retains all of its rights in such information and/or designs. The Owner, in turn, grants the Designer a nonexclusive license to use the Work in any way, including the creation of derivative products. The Owner agrees, to the fullest extent permitted by law, to indemnify, defend and hold Designer harmless from any claim, liability or cost (including reasonable attorney's fees and defense costs) arising or allegedly arising out of any use of the Work by the Owner if such use has not been explicitly approved in writing by the Designer. Under no circumstances shall this transfer be deemed a sale by the Designer, and the Designer makes no warranties, either express or implied, of merchantability or fitness for any particular purpose.

3. Ownership of the Work by the Owner

While rare, owners occasionally insist upon retaining full ownership of the designs and do not want the designer to have the right to create derivative works. Such insistence is typically seen where the design is new or unique and the owner is attempting to ensure that it stays that way. If the owner has been unwilling to accept either of the two licensing provisions suggested above, something akin to the following ownership provision should be insisted on by the designer:

> The Work is an instrument of the Designer's service. The Designer is the author of the Work, and the Designer hereby assigns to the Owner, without reservation, all common law, statutory, and other reserved rights in the Work, including the copyright, upon full payment of all monies due to the Designer under this Contract, including payment for all additional services. In the event a dispute regarding payment arises, this assignment is not effective until after the dispute has been resolved. To the extent that the Work incorporates information and/or designs previously developed by the Designer, the Designer retains

> all of its rights in such information and/or designs. The Owner agrees, to the fullest extent permitted by law, to indemnify, defend and hold Designer harmless from any claim, liability or cost (including reasonable attorneys fees and defense costs) arising or allegedly arising out of any use of the Work by the Owner if such use has not been explicitly approved in writing by the Designer. Under no circumstances shall this transfer be deemed a sale by the Designer, and the Designer makes no warranties, either express or implied, of merchantability or fitness for any particular purpose.

This provision is identical to the one suggested in Section III.C.2. above, except that the licensing language has been removed. This clause still accomplishes several important goals from the designer's prospective. First, the designer is protected from any liability arising from the use of the work if the designer is not consulted. Second, the owner does not obtain any ownership interest in the designer's standard details incorporated in the work. Third, the transfer is not complete until the designer is paid in full. Fourth, the designer is protected against unwittingly giving any warranties for the design. Because liability arising from warranties is commonly not covered by the insurance carried by designers, this is a significant concern.

4. Conveying Copyright Interests at a Later Date

Ideally, all issues involving ownership of the design should be resolved ahead of time, and that resolution should be embodied in the contract between the designer and the owner. However, sometimes ownership of the design will need to be changed after the design has been created. Most commonly, owners who find that a design sells particularly well may be interested in owning the design in order to prevent others (including the designer) from reusing the design in whole or part. Additionally, one party may want to change the initial ownership agreement sometime after the work is complete (typically, the owner decides it wants either a license or exclusive ownership of the work). All of these things can be accomplished, but several restrictions must be acknowledged.

a. Licenses

A license is merely a grant of permission by the owner of the rights in the work to another entity. The license can grant the licensee any of a number of rights: the right to use the work but not modify it; the right to modify the work but not use the original work; or the right to do whatever the licensee wants with the work. The license can be a simple, one-page document, signed by both parties, with language like that found in Section III.C.2. The license may also explicitly reference the portion of the original contract which makes the designer the owner of the work.

b. Transfer of Ownership

It is not uncommon for owners to develop a unique type of buyer's remorse regarding the work; i.e., if the work is particularly good, the owner wishes it had secured exclusive ownership of the work in the first place. In these instances, the owner will frequently ask the designer to transfer ownership of the work to the owner. The question of whether, in a given situation, a designer ought to agree to do so cannot be answered generically—each situation must be weighed on its own merits. Some designers commonly transfer ownership upon request (although seldom for free); others never do so. However, it can safely be said that there are situations in which the designer will conclude that it is in his or her best interests to strike a deal with the owner and transfer ownership of the work. Once again, such a transfer can be accomplished in a simple, one-page document, with language like that found in Section III.B.3. A transfer must be in writing.[14] As with licenses, it may be advisable for the transfer agreement to explicitly reference that portion of the original contract which made the designer the owner of the work.

c. Transfer of Copyrights

If the work has been formally registered with the U.S. Copyright Office, transfer of the copyright must accompany transfer of the ownership of the design. However, before the designer agrees to such a transfer, one alternative should be suggested. Owners typically want to hold the copyright in the work in order to prevent anyone else from building similar projects. Owners believe (correctly) that many designers have little interest in pursuing copyright infringement lawsuits against other owners, and for this reason, owners want to hold the copyrights so that they can pursue copyright infringement lawsuits themselves. This particular need on the part of the owner can be fully satisfied without a blanket transfer of all copyrights in the work from the designer to the owner. The designer can transfer to the owner the right to pursue copyright infringement actions while still retaining all other copyrights in the work. The key provision of such an agreement would approximate this language:

---

14. 17 U.S.C. § 204.

> The Work is an instrument of the Designer's service. The Designer is the author of the Work, and the Designer hereby assigns to the Owner the right to bring, in the Owner's name, claims alleging infringement of the copyrights in the Work, including claims which may have accrued prior to the date of this Assignment. The Owner shall bear all of the costs, including all attorney's fees, incurred in pursuing any such claims.

Under such an agreement, the designer loses the ability to bring copyright infringement actions itself, but that result is preferable to losing all rights in the work.

D. Common-Law Copyrights and Registered Copyrights

Upon the completion of a work, it is automatically protected by common-law copyright. No formal process or procedure is necessary. However, there are several procedures that authors should follow to protect and extend these common-law copyrights.

1. *Copyright Notice*

A formal copyright notice identifies the author and date of publication, and places the public on notice that the work is copyrighted. The most common formal notice is simply a line which states "Copyright 2006 by John Author." Alternatively, some authors use the copyright symbol: "© 2006 by John Author." Under prior versions of the Copyright Act, an author lost copyright protection if the work was published without a formal copyright notice attached to the work.[15] For works first published on or after March 1, 1989, this is no longer the case.[16] Under the current version of the Copyright Act, it is no longer necessary to include a formal copyright notice. However, inclusion of the formal notice is still the best practice, and the author can gain advantages in copyright infringement lawsuits if a notice was placed on the work.[17]

---

15. *See* H.R. Rep. No. 94-1476 (1976), *reprinted in* 1976 U.S.C.C.A.N. 5659, regarding history of 17 U.S.C. § 401.

16. 17 U.S.C. § 401 currently provides that "a notice of copyright as provided by this section *may* be placed on" copies of the work (emphasis added). This change in the law was part of the Berne Convention amendments to the Copyright Act. *See also* United States Copyright Office Circular 3, *available at* https://www.copyright.gov/circs/circ03.pdf.

17. 17 U.S.C. § 401.

2. *Formal Registration*

The U.S. Copyright Office[18] provides a method for authors to formally register their copyrighted works. Formal registration of a copyright provides two advantages, both related to copyright infringement litigation. First, it provides the author with some proof of the date of creation of the copyrighted work, because the Copyright Office notes the date of receipt of the formal registration. Second, except for limited situations that are not generally applicable to architectural copyrights, an author cannot commence a copyright infringement lawsuit unless the author has first filed a formal registration for the allegedly infringed work.[19]

Library References

C.J.S. *Copyrights and Intellectual Property* §§ 22, 26–35, 39, 71, 86–91, 93, 95–96, 102–103.
West's Key No. Digests, Copyrights and Intellectual Property <KEY>41–41.3, 43–49, 50.1, 50.15, 101.

IV. What Protection Does the Copyright Afford?

The scope and nature of copyright protection for architectural works have undergone significant evolution in the last twenty years. In order to understand the current state of the law, it is necessary to briefly analyze the foundations of copyright law and its evolution.

A. A Brief History of Copyright Protection for Architectural Plans

The right of an author to protect his or her creations is grounded in the Constitution itself, which provides that "Congress shall have Power to . . . promote the Progress of Science and useful Arts, by securing for limited Times to Authors and Inventors the exclusive Right to their respective Writings and Discoveries[.]"[20] Protection for architectural drawings was first extended by the Copyright Act of 1909, which provided copyright protection to "[d]rawings of plastic works of a scientific or technical nature."[21] Architectural plans

---

18. The U.S. Copyright Office's Web site is located at https://www.copyright.gov. The Web site contains a wealth of information and is generally user friendly.

19. 17 U.S.C. § 411.

20. U.S. Const. art. I, § 8.

21. 17 U.S.C. § 5(i) (1909 Act).

were considered technical drawings under the 1909 Copyright Act. The next major evolution of copyright law came with the Copyright Act of 1976. The 1976 Act continued to afford protection to "technical drawings, diagrams, and models."[22] The House of Representatives Report on the 1976 Act recognized that "[a]n architect's plans and drawings would, of course, be protected by copyright[.]"[23]

The Berne Convention Implementation Act of 1988, which was intended to make copyright protection in the United States coextensive with copyright protection in other countries who were signatories of the Berne Convention, amended the 1976 Act by substituting the phrase "diagrams, models, and technical drawings, including architectural plans," for the phrase "technical drawings, diagrams, and models." Thus, for the first time, the Copyright Act explicitly included architectural plans among the writings subject to copyright protection.

B. The Useful Article Exception

The 1976 Act also gave rise to an exception, which to this day poses problems with architectural copyrights. The 1976 Act defined a useful article as an article having an intrinsic utilitarian function that is not merely to portray the appearance of the article or to convey information.[24] Because the intrinsic function of an architectural plan is to convey information (i.e., the manner in which a structure is to be constructed), an architectural plan is not considered a useful article. However, architectural plans do *portray* a useful article: the structure itself. The 1976 Act indicates that the Copyright Act "does not afford, to the owner of a copyright in a work that portrays a useful article . . . any greater or lesser rights with respect to the making, distribution, or display of the useful article so portrayed than those afforded to such works under the law, whether title 17 or the common law or statutes of a State, in effect on December 31, 1977. . . ."[25] Under the law in effect on December 31, 1977, copyrights for works of utility (including architectural plans) protected only against the copying of such works for purposes of explanation, *not* against the copying of such works for purposes of use.[26]

---

22. 17 U.S.C. § 101 (1976 Act).

23. H. Rep., pp. 53–55. H.R. Rep. No. 94-1476, at 55 (1976), *reprinted in* 1976 U.S.C.C.A.N. 5659.

24. 17 U.S.C. § 101 (1976 Act).

25. 17 U.S.C. § 113 (1976 Act).

26. Baker v. Seldon, 101 U.S. 99, 105 (1879).

Thus, the effect of the useful article exception is that an author who owns a copyright in a set of architectural plans can prevent the copying of those plans, but *cannot* prevent someone from building a structure identical to the structure depicted on those plans. Copyright extended only to the *plans themselves,* not to the structure depicted on those plans, even though the design concepts embodied in the plans may never have been known or used before.[27]

A recent court case in West Virginia[28] demonstrated how problematic the useful article exception can be. In that case, the copyright holder (author) demonstrated that an architect and builder were in possession of the author's copyrighted architectural plans and had used those plans to construct a building which, the author contended, infringed on its copyright. The court noted that "[o]ther courts have found that a technical drawings copyright simply does not give the owner the exclusive right to build the structure depicted in the plan, and a copyright owner has no claim against another who builds the structure from an infringing plan."[29] The court concluded that a building "cannot be an infringing copy of a technical drawing."[30]

Useful articles are protected by copyright, but only to the extent they have design elements that are "separable" from their basic, non-copyrightable "utilitarian" aspects (e.g., a chair or picture frame). Over the years, courts have come up with many "separability" standards[31] to determine when design

---

27. Demetriades v. Kaufmann, 680 F. Supp. 658, 664 (S.D.N.Y. 1988).

28. National Medical Care, Inc. v. Espiritu, 284 F. Supp. 2d 424 (S.D. W.Va. 2003).

29. *Id.* at 435.

30. *Id.* at 424. That holding was echoed in *Beckwith Builders, Inc. v. Depietri,* 2006 WL 2645188 (D.N.H. 2006), where the court simply held "a building is not a copy of an architectural plan." Substantially the same result was reached in *Morgan v. Hawthorne Homes,* 2009 WL 1010476 (W.D. Pa. 2009), where the court held that the architect could not recover from the home builder for building homes from the architect's drawings, but *could* recover if he could prove that his plans were copied. This ruling also highlights a practical change to copyright enforcement brought about by advances in technology. In the past, the construction of a building essentially mandated that physical copies of the design drawings be made—as a practical matter, the contractors could not all work off a single set (or even a few sets) of drawings. Thus, although a designer could not sue a contractor for merely building the building depicted on the plans, it is likely that the owner illegally copied the architect's plans, giving rise to a legitimate copyright violation claim. The widespread use of building information modeling (BIM) and cloud-hosted virtual design documents now means that many buildings *are* built without the design documents ever being physically copied.

31. In *Varsity Brands, Inc. v. Star Athletica, L.L.C.,* 799 F.3d 468 (6th Cir. 2015), the Sixth Circuit cited several separability standards, including "(1) The Primary-

elements have sufficiently unique characteristics to warrant copyright protection. In *Star Athletica, L.L.C.* v. *Varsity Brands, Inc.*,[32] the U.S. Supreme Court announced a uniform standard to determine separability.

In *Varsity Brands*, both plaintiff and defendant were cheerleading uniform manufacturers. Varsity Brands alleged copyright infringement against Star Athletica based on the use of stripes, patterns, and chevrons in the design of Star Athletica's cheerleading uniforms. The trial court held that the stripes, patterns, and chevrons were not conceptually separable from the uniform's utilitarian aspects because they served the utilitarian function of identifying the wearer of the uniform as a cheerleader and a member of a particular cheerleading team.[33] Without such elements of the uniform, the court held, the uniforms would not be cheerleading uniforms.[34] In short, because the designs were not separable from the utility of the article, they were not subject to copyright protection.

On appeal, the Sixth Circuit announced and applied a new five-question separability test and reversed the trial court, holding that the design elements of the cheerleading uniforms were separable from the uniform because the design elements were conceptually separable from, and capable of existing independently of, the utilitarian aspects of the uniform.[35]

On further appeal, the Supreme Court created a new separability test and affirmed the Sixth Circuit, holding the design elements of the cheerleading uniforms were subject to copyright protection. The Supreme Court held "an artistic feature of the design of a useful article is eligible for copyright protection if the feature (1) can be perceived as a two or three-dimensional work of art separate from the useful article and (2) would qualify as a protectable pictorial, graphic, or sculptural work either on its own or in some other medium if

---

Subsidiary Approach: A pictorial, graphic, or sculptural feature is conceptually separable if the artistic features of the design are 'primary' to the 'subsidiary utilitarian function.' (2) the Objectively Necessary Approach: A pictorial, graphic or sculptural feature is conceptually separable if the artistic features of the design are not necessary to the performance of the utilitarian function of the article. (3) The Design-Process Approach: a pictorial, graphic, or sculptural feature is separable if the 'design elements can be identified as reflecting the designer's artistic judgment exercised independently of functional influences.'" *Varsity Brands*, 799 F.3d at 484–85.

32. 137 S. Ct. 1002 (2017).

33. *Id.* at 1007–08.

34. *Id.*

35. *Id.* at 1008.

imagined separately from the useful article."[36] This brings clarity to the useful article test, and resolves the multiplicity of different tests that were developed by various federal circuit courts. However, the essence of the Supreme Court's test is not substantially different from many of the predecessor tests; thus, it is unlikely that this development, by itself, will substantially transform the useful article analysis.

C. The Architectural Works Copyright Protection Act

The most recent evolution of copyright law relating to architectural plans was the 1990 Architectural Works Copyright Protection Act (AWCPA). The AWCPA was intended to provide "previously lacking copyright protection to physical architectural works, not drawings of such works," which already enjoyed copyright protection.[37] The author of architectural plans can now hold two separate copyrights: one in the technical drawings; and one in the physical structure.[38] However, the AWCPA applies only to structures built after January 1, 1990.[39]

D. Rights Protected by Copyright

A copyright confers two essential rights for authors of architectural plans: the right to reproduce the plans themselves and the right to prepare derivative works based on the plans.[40]

1. The Right to Reproduce the Plans Themselves

The author of architectural plans can prohibit others from copying those plans. Thus, a copyright infringement can occur simply by making a photocopy of copyrighted plans, even if no further action is taken. For this reason, most industry contracts contain specific provisions enabling various parties (most commonly, the owner and the prime contractor) to make copies of the plans for the purposes of construction. The owner typically is also permitted to make copies of the plans for the structure maintenance purposes once it is built.

---

36. *Id.* at 1011–12.

37. Guillot-Vogt Assocs., Inc. v. Holly & Smith, 848 F. Supp. 682, 686–87 (E.D. La. 1994).

38. *Id.* at 687 (quoting H.R. Rep. No. 101-735, *reprinted in* 1990 U.S.C.C.A.N. 6935, 6950).

39. While no court has yet considered the issue, it seems likely that a building that was substantially completed after January 1, 1990, would be protected, even though construction started in 1989.

40. 17 U.S.C. § 106.

2. *The Right to Prepare Derivative Works Based on the Plans*

From the designer's point of view, perhaps the most important right secured by copyright is the right to prepare derivative works based on the plans. In the field of residential mass-production architecture (which has the most well-developed body of law regarding architectural copyrights), popular architectural plans can have tremendous economic value. Therefore, the authors of those plans have a strong incentive to protect the plans from being knocked off by architects who develop plans derived from the author's original, successful plan.

E. Scope of Protection for Derivative Works

Authors frequently base new works on works they have previously created. When a new design is based on a work the author previously created, copyright protection for the derivative design is limited to those elements that are unique to the derivative design.[41] Thus, elements in the derivative design that are also incorporated in the original design are not protected. The derivative design is afforded protection only for the new elements. The scope of protection for derivative works is lower than for original works. This is logical: derivative works demonstrate less originality and, therefore, are afforded less protection.

F. Scope of Protection for Works Consisting of Generic Features

It has been said that there is nothing new under the sun.[42] This sentiment certainly applies to architecture and engineering, as designers constantly rely on standard, generic, and tried and true designs and design elements, and incorporate those elements into new designs on a daily basis. New and unique designs are few and far between, particularly in residential construction. When concepts such as bathroom, closet, and kitchen layouts are considered, the simple fact is that all functional layouts have been used at some time in the past.

Designs that gather together generic or standard features into a functional plan are eligible for copyright protection as a compilation work. However, because the level of originality expressed in compilation works is limited, the level of copyright protection afforded to these plans is similarly limited. The author can copyright the particular choices he or she made when selecting which standard features to include in the design and can copyright the particular way in which he or she arranged those features within the design.[43] This

---

41. 17 U.S.C. § 103.

42. *Ecclesiastes* 1:9.

43. 17 U.S.C. § 103. *See also* Tufenkian Import/Export Ventures, Inc. v. Einstein Moomjy, Inc., 338 F.3d 127, 136 (2d Cir. 2003); Ale House Mgmt., Inc. v. Raleigh

is often referred to as thin copyright protection. When considering whether a design infringes on a thinly protected design, courts have found that even modest dissimilarities between the two designs will support a finding that no infringement has occurred.[44] Again, this is logical: a design that merely combines standard features in a particular way shows little originality and, therefore, is entitled to little (but not a complete lack of) protection.

G. The Idea/Expression Dichotomy

One of the fundamental principles of the Copyright Act is that no one can copyright an idea. An author may only copyright the particular manner in which the author expressed that idea. Thus, for example, no author could copyright the idea of two young lovers kept apart by feuding families. However, the particular manner in which that idea is expressed in *Romeo and Juliet* and *West Side Story is* copyrightable. This distinction between an idea and the manner in which that idea is expressed is referred to as the idea/expression dichotomy.

The idea/expression dichotomy plays an important role in determining the scope of protection afforded to architectural works. One court astutely observed that elements such as the placement of functional elements, routing of traffic through a home, and generic methods of construction are ideas that cannot be copyrighted.[45] Therefore, no designer could copyright the idea of placing a closet in or adjacent to a bedroom, nor could any designer copyright the idea of a walk-through closet placed between the master bedroom and master bathroom. However, if a designer were to develop a unique layout for that closet, that layout would be copyrightable.

A corollary to the idea/expression dichotomy is that if a particular idea can be expressed in only a limited number of ways, no author can copyright his or her particular expression of that idea, because any such copyright would give the author a partial monopoly on the idea itself. In architectural design, a

---

Ale House, Inc., 205 F.3d 137, 143 (4th Cir. 2000); Domingo Cambeiro Prof. Corp. v. Advent, 2000 WL 262597 (9th Cir. 2000); Howard v. Sterchi, 974 F.2d 1272, 1276 (11th Cir. 1992); John Alden Homes, Inc. v. Kangas, 142 F. Supp. 2d 1338, 1344–45 (M.D. Fla. 2001), *aff'd*, 37 Fed. Appx. 979 (11th Cir. 2001); LaJoie v. Pavcon, Inc., 146 F. Supp. 2d 1240 (M.D. Fla. 2000).

44. *Varsity Brands*, 137 S. Ct. at 1008.

45. Kootenia Homes, Inc. v. Reliable Homes, Inc., 2002 WL 15594 (D. Minn. 2002). *See also* Attia v. Society of New York Hosp., 201 F.3d 50 (2d Cir. 1999); J. R. Lazaro Builders, Inc. v. R.E. Ripberger Builders, Inc., 883 F. Supp. 336, 343 (S.D. Ind. 1995).

powder room provides an excellent example of an idea that can be expressed in only a limited number of ways. Many homes feature a two-fixture powder room on the main level for use by guests during entertaining, while preserving the privacy of the master bath. There are very few ways to express the idea of a two-fixture powder room: placing both fixtures on one wall with the door at the end or on the other wall, or placing the fixtures facing each other with the door in the middle. Certainly, within those two forms of expression, details such as finishes, dimensions, and the swing of the door can vary. However, the expression remains fundamentally the same. If any designer was given a copyright on one of the expressions of a two-fixture powder room, the architectural industry as a whole would suffer immensely, as no other architect could incorporate that particular two-fixture powder room in their design. Copyright law is designed to promote the progress of science and the useful arts, not to stifle innovation.[46] It is for this reason that copyright law will not permit an author to copyright the expression of an idea if it can be expressed only in a limited number of ways.

Library References

C.J.S. *Copyrights and Intellectual Property* §§ 9–10, 16, 19, 40–41, 45, 47, 57, 59, 92, 97.

West's Key No. Digests, Copyrights and Intellectual Property <KEY>4, 6, 12(3), 35, 64.

V. What Is Copyright Infringement?

A copyright is both a source of affirmative rights (the owner has the right to reproduce the work and prepare derivative works based on the work) and negative rights (no one else is permitted to reproduce the work or prepare derivative works based on the work). Copyright infringement occurs when someone other than the author or a license holder reproduces the work, prepares a derivative work based on the work, or prepares a work that is impermissibly similar to the copyrighted work. The precise elements of copyright infringement vary in different federal jurisdictions; however, the core elements remain essentially the same. This discussion will focus on the basic elements common to all jurisdictions. Authors should take care to carefully research the law in their own jurisdiction before commencing (or defending) an infringement action.

---

46. U.S. CONST. art. I, § 8.

Generally, an author must prove three things in order to demonstrate copyright infringement: the author is the owner of a valid copyright in the allegedly infringed work; the defendant had access to the copyrighted work; and the allegedly infringing work is substantially similar to the copyrighted work.

A. Ownership of a Valid Copyright

The first showing an author must make is that he or she is the owner of a valid copyright in the work. This showing has two essential parts: showing that the author is the owner of the copyright and that the copyright is valid. Demonstrating ownership is typically a simple matter—the plaintiff must either show that he or she is the author of the work or the holder of a valid copyright assignment or a license that gives the plaintiff the right to sue for infringement.

The second showing, that the copyright is valid, is frequently a point of contention in copyright infringement lawsuits. Generally, a copyright may be shown to be invalid in two ways: by demonstrating that the copyrighted work is not subject to copyright protection or the copyright registration is fraudulent. For the reasons discussed in Section II (eligibility for copyright protection), defendants seldom convince a court to invalidate a copyright on the basis that the allegedly infringed work is not subject to copyright protection.

Defendants in copyright infringement lawsuits frequently challenge the validity of a copyright by attacking the contents of the copyright registration. Courts will invalidate a registered copyright when the author obtains that registration through the use of a materially misleading registration. Courts have invalidated copyright registrations based on the author's failure to identify prior works from which the registered work was derived[47] and based on the failure to appropriately attribute authorship to the true author of the work.[48] Courts typically consider whether the copyright registration misstated information which, if correctly stated, may have caused the Copyright Office to

---

47. *See, e.g.*, R. Ready Prods., Inc. v. Cantrell, 85 F. Supp. 2d 672, 691–92 (S.D. Tex. 2000); Russ Berrie & Co., Inc. v. Jerry Elsner Co., 482 F. Supp. 980, 988–89 (S.D.N.Y. 1980); Vogue Ring Creations, Inc. v. Hardman, 410 F. Supp. 609 (D.R.I. 1976); International Biotical Corp. v. Associated Mills, Inc., 239 F. Supp. 511 (N.D. Ill. 1964).

48. *See, e.g.*, M.G.B. Homes, Inc. v. Ameron Homes, Inc., 903 F.2d 1486, 1488–93 (11th Cir. 1990); Zitz v. Pereria, 119 F. Supp. 2d 133, 143–45 (E.D.N.Y. 1999), *aff'd*, 225 F.3d 646, 672 (2d Cir. 2000); Fred Riley Home Bldg. Corp. v. Cosgrove, 864 F. Supp. 1034, 1042–45 (D. Kan. 1994).

reject the registration. If so, the resulting copyright is invalid.[49] If the Copyright Office would have accepted the registration had the information been correctly stated, the resulting copyright is valid. Courts will typically invalidate copyright registrations only if the allegedly incorrect information has been deliberately misstated. However, due to the possibility that a copyright may be held invalid due to errors in the registration process, authors should take care in the registration process.

B. Access to the Copyrighted Work by the Alleged Infringer

A person cannot copy something they have never seen. Therefore, in order to prove that the defendant has infringed on a copyrighted work, the author must prove that the defendant saw the work. This element of proof is called access. Because it is often impossible to prove that the defendant actually saw the copyrighted work, courts have held that access is established as long as the defendant had an opportunity to view the copyrighted material.[50] Furthermore, access can be inferred between parties on the construction team. Thus, if the builder had access to the author's copyrighted material, courts will find that the designer employed by that builder also had access.[51] Plaintiffs can also establish access by showing that the defendant interacted with a third party who possessed the copyrighted material.[52]

C. Substantial Similarity between the Copyrighted Work and the Allegedly Infringing Work

The defendant's work infringes on the author's copyrighted work only if it is *substantially similar* to the author's copyrighted work.[53] In the context of

---

49. For a detailed discussion, *see* Foamation, Inc. v. Wedeward Enters., Inc., 947 F. Supp. 1287, 1296 (E.D. Wis. 1996). *See also* MELVELLE B. NIMMER & DAVID NIMMER, NIMMER ON COPYRIGHT § 7.20 (1978).

50. *See, e.g.*, Herzog v. Castle Rock Entm't, 193 F.3d 1241, 1249 (11th Cir. 1999); Moore v. Columbia Pictures Indus., Inc., 972 F.2d 939, 942 (8th Cir. 1992); Robert R. Jones Assoc., Inc. v. Nino Homes, 858 F.2d 274, 277 (6th Cir. 1988).

51. Kamar Int'l, Inc. v. Russ Berrie and Co., 657 F.2d 1059, 1062 (9th Cir. 1981); Arthur Rutenberg Corp. v. Parrino, 664 F. Supp. 479, 481 (M.D. Fla. 1987); MELVELLE B. NIMMER & DAVID NIMMER, NIMMER ON COPYRIGHT § 13.02[A] (1978).

52. *See, e.g.*, Kamar Int'l, Inc. v. Russ Berrie & Co., 657 F.2d 1059, 1062 (9th Cir. 1981) (concluding the defendant had access to copyrighted stuffed animals because it did business with the same toy manufacturing company as the plaintiff).

53. Courts commonly hold that copyright infringement can be proved either by direct evidence of copying or by demonstrating access and substantial similarity. *See,*

copyright infringement, substantial similarity is a term of art. The exact meaning of substantial similarity, and the process for determining whether one work is substantially similar to another, varies from jurisdiction to jurisdiction. Due to variations in that process, there are also substantial differences in whether expert testimony is ordinarily admissible to assist the jury in determining substantial similarity. Both issues are analyzed below.

1. The Extrinsic/Intrinsic Test

The Ninth Circuit's test for evaluating the substantial similarity of two works entails a bifurcated analysis. First, the court performs the "extrinsic test" and objectively considers whether the two works share substantially similar ideas. Second, the jury performs the "intrinsic test" and determines whether an ordinary observer would perceive that the two works express those shared ideas in a substantially similar way. The Fourth[54] and Eighth[55] Circuits also use this test.

a. Extrinsic Analysis Stage

The extrinsic test involves an examination of "specific criteria which can be listed and analyzed."[56] Expert testimony is often admissible to help identify these criteria and inform the court's comparative analysis.[57]

---

e.g., Nelson v. PRN Prod., Inc., 873 F.2d 1141, 1142 (8th Cir. 1989). However, no court has ever been called on to find infringement via direct copying when the resulting work is *not* substantially similar to the copyrighted work. Therefore, the best view of the law is that substantial similarity will be required even if liability is proved through direct copying. Indeed, the notion that a direct copy can be anything *but* substantially similar to the work from which it was copied is, at best, a philosophical abstraction.

54. *See* Towler v. Sayles, 76 F.3d 579 (4th Cir. 1996). The Fourth Circuit has a slight deviation where the second prong of this test, the intrinsic evaluation, is viewed from the perspective of the intended audience (the next test discussed in this chapter). This means that the perspective of the intended audience may sometimes be different from that of an ordinary observer. However, to date, this deviation has only been applied to children's music and computer programs.

55. *See* Rottlund Co. v. Pinnacle Corp., 452 F.3d 726 (8th Cir. 2006).

56. Sid & Marty Krofft Television Prods., Inc. v. McDonald's Corp., 562 F.2d 1157, 1164 (9th Cir. 1977).

57. *See* Plan Pros, Inc. v. Zych, No. 8:08CV125, 2009 U.S. Dist. LEXIS 124671, at *13 (D. Neb. Dec. 22, 2009) ("In evaluating the extrinsic step, expert testimony is often helpful to ascertain whether the works are objectively similar."); *see also* Nelson Design Group, LLC v. Puckett, No. 3:07CV00177 BSM, 2009 U.S. Dist. LEXIS 69343, at *4 (E.D. Ark. July 28, 2009) ("[S]imilarity of ideas is analyzed extrinsically, with

b. Intrinsic Analysis Stage

If the court finds that the two works share copyrightable ideas, the case advances to the fact finder for the intrinsic analysis. This test does not hinge on specific objective criteria. Rather, it asks what "the ordinary reasonable person" perceives about the two works. Expert opinions are not relevant to that inquiry.[58] Thus, litigants generally may not present expert testimony during the intrinsic stage of analysis.[59]

In *Rottlund Co. v. Pinnacle Corp.*,[60] the Eighth Circuit vacated a jury verdict because the district court admitted expert testimony during the intrinsic stage of analysis. There, the plaintiff sued a group of homebuilders and an architectural firm for infringing its copyrighted architectural designs and works.[61] Before trial, the district court performed the extrinsic test, granting partial summary judgment for the plaintiff after finding that the ideas expressed in the defendants' technical drawings were substantially similar to the copyrighted works.[62]

At trial, certain of the defendants presented the testimony of an architectural expert witness. That expert created electronic overlays of the townhomes at issue and "testified regarding the differences of the key elements of the [architectural] plans."[63] He also highlighted disparities in the kitchen designs, gabled entries, and stairways of the two townhomes.[64] Ultimately, the jury found that none of the defendants' drawings or works infringed upon the plaintiff's copyrights.

On appeal, the Eight Circuit reasoned that the "only issue before the jury was whether the expression in [the defendants'] works was substantially

---

the focus being on the objective similarities in the details. . . . Expert opinion and analytical dissection are admissible to prove similarity of ideas.").

58. *Sid & Marty Krofft Television Prods.*, 562 F.2d at 1164.

59. *Cf.* Dr. Seuss Enters., L.P. v. Penguin Books USA, Inc., 109 F.3d 1394, 1398 (9th Cir. 1997) (stating that "analytic dissection" is allowed during the extrinsic test, but not during the intrinsic test); Rottlund Co. v. Pinnacle Corp., No. 01-1980, 2004 U.S. Dist. LEXIS 16723, at *83 (D. Minn. Aug. 20, 2004) ("Substantial similarity is a legal test with two prongs—extrinsic and intrinsic—and the extrinsic prong is the only prong that accepts expert opinion evidence.").

60. 452 F.3d 726 (8th Cir. 2006).

61. *Id.* at 729.

62. *Id.*

63. *Id.* at 730.

64. *Id.* at 729–30.

similar to the expression in [the plaintiff's] works."[65] And because expert opinion is not relevant to that intrinsic analysis, the district court abused its discretion in admitting the expert's testimony.[66] Thus, the court reversed the district court's judgment and ordered a new trial to determine whether the two works contained substantially similar designs.

2. *The Intended Audience Test*

Other federal appellate courts, including the Sixth, Tenth,[67] and D.C. Circuits,[68] use a different bifurcated analysis to determine whether two works are substantially similar. In step one, the court identifies what aspects of a work, if any, are copyrightable.[69] The second step asks whether, from the perspective of the work's intended audience, "the allegedly infringing work is 'substantially similar' to the protectable elements of the [copyrighted] work."[70] This test is also referred to as the "abstract filtration" test.

a. Protectable Elements Stage

The first part of this test is a question of law that requires the court to "filter out" elements of the copyrighted work that are not copyrightable (hence the "filtration" portion of the "abstract filtration" test).[71] Because courts are reluctant to admit expert testimony on questions of law, the Sixth Circuit and D.C. Circuit "apply a more stringent standard [than the Ninth Circuit] regarding when to allow expert testimony on the first part of the test."[72] Nonethe-

65. *Id.* at 731.

66. *Id.* at 731–32.

67. *See* Country Kids 'N City Slicks, Inc. v. Sheen, 77 F.3d 1280 (10th Cir. 1996).

68. The D.C. Circuit only applies this test if both unprotectable and protectable elements are at issue. If only protectable elements are being evaluated, the D.C. Circuit employs the ordinary observer test established by the Second Circuit. *See* Recording Indus. Ass'n of Am., Inc. v. Verizon Internet Servs., 351 F.3d 1229 (D.C. Cir. 2003); Sturdza v. United Arab Emirates, 281 F.3d 1287, 1291 (D.C. Cir. 2002).

69. Kohus v. Mariol, 328 F.3d 848, 855 (6th Cir. 2003); Sturdza v. United Arab Emirates, 281 F.3d 1287, 1295 (D.C. Cir. 2002).

70. *Kohus*, 328 F.3d at 855 (quoting *Sturdza*, 281 F.3d at 1296).

71. *Kohus*, 328 F.3d at 855; Winfield Collection, Ltd. v. Gemmy Indus., Corp., 147 Fed. App'x 547, 554 (6th Cir. 2005) ("In performing the filtering process, the basic guidepost to keep in mind is that copyright only protects an author's original expression; thus, courts must exclude as unprotectible [sic] any elements of the work that are not original.").

72. Murray Hill Publ'ns, Inc. v. Twentieth Century Fox Film Corp., 361 F.3d 312, 318 (6th Cir. 2004).

less, these courts will admit expert testimony so long as it helps to "identify whether there are original design elements present" in the plaintiff's work.[73]

b. Substantial Similarity Stage

During the second prong of the test—the substantial similarity analysis—the Sixth and D.C. Circuits apply a more refined standard than the simple "ordinary observer" standard of the Ninth and Second Circuits. This refined standard asks who is the "ordinary observer" of the copyrighted work? That is, who is the intended audience?[74]

Under this standard, expert testimony is prohibited if the intended audience of a copyrighted work is the lay public.[75] However, if the intended audience is expected to possess some specialized expertise, "the specialist's perception of similarity may be much different from the lay observer's, and it is appropriate in such cases to consider similarity from the specialist's perspective."[76] In other words, litigants may use expert testimony if the trier of fact should consider the substantial similarity determination from the perspective of a specialist. The expert's job in these cases is "to educate the trier of fact" about those elements of a work for which the specialized audience will look.[77]

The admissibility of expert testimony in courts applying this test thus hinges on whether the intended audience for architectural designs is the general public. No court has specifically ruled on that question. However, litigants may be able to introduce expert testimony by arguing that their architectural

---

73. Frank Betz Assocs. v. Signature Homes, No. 3:06-0911, 2010 U.S. Dist. LEXIS 31449, at *9, 11–13 (M.D. Tenn. Mar. 29, 2010) (discussing the admissibility of expert testimony regarding the originality of copyrighted works).

74. *Kohus*, 328 F.3d at 856 (stating that the "ordinary reasonable person" standard of the second step in the substantial similarity analysis "is in need of modification").

75. *Winfield Collection*, 147 Fed. App'x at 554 (holding that, because the parties agreed that the lay public was the intended audience, "expert testimony should not be required").

76. *Kohus*, 328 F.3d at 857.

77. *Id.*; RGIS, LLC v. A.S.T., Inc., No. 2:07-CV-10975, 2008 U.S. Dist. LEXIS 4226, at **6–7 (E.D. Mich. Jan. 22, 2008) ("*Kohus* . . . made clear that when technical material is involved [the] 'ordinary observer' test for substantial similarity is insufficient. . . . Because the judicial officers involved in this case lack [computer programming] competence, it is necessary to have the assistance of a competent computer expert capable of factual analysis interpreting and comparing computer source codes.").

designs are not targeted at the general public: such designs are created to help constructors, engineers, and other specialized audiences create buildings.[78]

It is critical to conceptually distinguish between the designs themselves and the built structure. The intended audience for the built structure is likely to be the general public. But that is a wholly separate copyright from the copyright in the design drawings. And, as discussed earlier, design drawings do not infringe on built structure copyrights. The general public almost never sees the design drawings for a building, and few would argue that the general public (rather than contractors and other designers) are the intended audience for design drawings. Thus, one should be able to convincingly argue that design drawings *are* intended for a specialized audience of construction professionals. If the court accepts this argument, expert testimony should be admissible during the substantial similarity analysis.

3. *The Ordinary Observer Test*

The First,[79] Second,[80] Third,[81] Fifth,[82] Seventh,[83] and Eleventh Circuits[84] use what is commonly referred to as an "ordinary observer" test. A court summarized the "ordinary observer" test for substantial similarity as "where an aver-

---

78. At least one circuit court was willing to consider this argument. In *Sturdza v. United Arab Emirates*, 281 F.3d 1287 (D.C. Cir. 2002), the D.C. Circuit declined to rule on the issue of whether the parties in an architectural design copyright infringement case could present expert testimony during the substantial similarity stage of analysis. The court, however, remanded the case with an invitation for the parties to revisit the issue in a subsequent appeal "with the benefit of full briefing." *Id.* at 1301.

79. *See* T-Peg, Inc. v. Vt. Timber Works, Inc., 459 F.3d 97 (1st Cir. 2006); Concrete Mach. Co. v. Classic Lawn Ornaments, Inc., 843 F.2d 600, 606 (1st Cir. 1988).

80. *See* Arnstein v. Porter, 154 F.2d 464, 472–73 (2nd Cir. 1946). The Second Circuit has developed an additional analysis when the works involve both unprotectable and protectable elements. This variation asks whether, looking at the protectable elements, the overall look and feel of the compared works are substantially similar. *See* Tufenkian Import/Export Ventures, Inc. v. Einstein Moomjy, Inc., 338 F.3d 127 (2nd Cir. 2003); Boisson v. Banian, Ltd., 273 F.3d 262 (2nd Cir. 2001).

81. *See* Ford Motor Co. v. Summit Motor Products, Inc., 930 F.2d 277 (3rd Cir. 1991); Universal Athletic Sales Co. v. Salkeld, 511 F.2d 904 (3rd Cir. 1975).

82. *See* Peel & Co. v. The Rug Mkt., 238 F.3d 391 (5th Cir. 2001).

83. *See* Selle v. Gibb, 741 F.2d 896 (7th Cir. 1984); Scott v. WKJG, Inc., 376 F.2d 467 (7th Cir. 1967); Sanford v. CBS, Inc., 594 F. Supp. 713 (N.D. Ill. 1984).

84. *See* Intervest Constr., Inc. v. Canterbury Estate Homes, Inc., 554 F.3d 914 (11th Cir. 2008); Original Appalachian Artworks v. Toy Loft, Inc., 684 F.2d 821 (11th Cir. 1982).

age lay observer would recognize the alleged copy as having been appropriated from the copyrighted work."[85] Expert testimony is usually admissible if it will assist the trier of fact with deciding whether an infringement occurred. The expert must rely on copyrightable expressions when analyzing the substantial similarity of two works; if an expert relies on uncopyrightable ideas, the report and testimony are excludable.[86]

D. Defenses

There are two primary defenses to a copyright infringement claim: independent creation and fair use.

1. Independent Creation

The most important defense a designer can assert to a copyright infringement claim is to argue that the designer independently created the work accused of infringement. If an architectural design is the result of the designer's own creativity and ingenuity, that design does not infringe on any other design, even if that design is identical to another design.[87] The critical factor in asserting this defense is the defendant designer's ability to prove that he or she, in fact, independently created the design in question. The more alike the two designs are, the more persuasive the plaintiff designer's accusation of copying will be. At a certain point, the plaintiff will be able to convincingly place the two designs next to each other and assert that the level of similarity between the designs means that the defendant designer must have copied the earlier work.

Designers should view the independent creation defense as their best defense against a charge of copyright infringement. Therefore, designers should take affirmative steps to implement interoffice policies designed to place the designer in the best position to assert such a defense. In a typical design process, dozens of alternative designs are considered and either adopted in whole or in part or discarded entirely. All of these designs should be saved, as they will help the designer rebut a charge of copying. The designs that were

---

85. Original Appalachian Artworks, Inc. v. Toy Loft, Inc., 684 F.2d 821, 829 (11th Cir. 1982).

86. Corwin v. Walt Disney World Co., 475 F.3d 1239, 1250–51 (11th Cir. 2007) (affirming the district court's exclusion of four expert reports because they focused on the concepts and ideas behind a building, rather than on the expressions of those concepts and ideas).

87. *See, e.g.*, Repp v. Webber, 132 F.3d 882, 889 (2d Cir. 1997); CMM Cable Rep., Inc. v. Ocean Coast Props., 97 F.3d 1504, 1513, 1525 (1st Cir. 1990); Kootenia Homes, Inc. v. Reliable Homes, Inc., 2002 WL 15594 (D. Minn. 2002).

adopted in whole or in part are particularly critical, because they demonstrate the design process and can be used to help explain certain similarities. For example, a plaintiff designer may assert that the defendant's kitchen layout is so similar to the plaintiff's design that it must have resulted from copying. If the defendant designer can produce his or her earlier concept drawings which show the layout of the kitchen evolving to its final format, the defendant designer will be able to persuasively rebut this charge.

2. *Fair Use*

The fair use defense is seldom applicable in architectural design copyright infringement lawsuits. Therefore, it is not exhaustively analyzed here. The fair use doctrine holds that it is not infringement to use a copyrighted work for purposes such as criticism, comment, news reporting, teaching (including multiple copies for classroom use), scholarship, or research. In determining whether the use of a work in any particular case is a fair use, the court will consider factors such as: (1) the purpose and character of the use, including whether such use is of a commercial nature or is for nonprofit educational purposes; *(2)* the nature of the copyrighted work; (3) the amount and substantiality of the portion used in relation to the copyrighted work as a whole; and (4) the effect of the use upon the potential market for or value of the copyrighted work.[88] When the copyrighted work is used for commercial purposes, the fair use doctrine seldom applies. For this reason alone, the fair use doctrine is of limited use in architectural copyright infringement lawsuits.

3. *Statute of Limitations*

The statute of limitations is very short for copyright infringement. Actions must be commenced within three years after the claim accrued.[89] The statute begins to run when the alleged infringement took place, regardless of whether the author had notice of the accrual of the claim.

E. Damages

If the plaintiff designer prevails, and the defendant is found to have infringed on the plaintiff's copyrighted design, the plaintiff is entitled to damages. There

88. 17 U.S.C. § 107.

89. 17 U.S.C. § 507(b). *See also* Zitz v. Pereira, 119 F. Supp. 2d 133 (E.D.N.Y. 1999), *aff'd*, 225 F.3d 646 (2d Cir. 2000); Wood v. Santa Barbara Chamber of Commerce, 507 F. Supp. 1128 (D. Nev. 1980).

are several methods of calculating damages in copyright infringement lawsuits. The plaintiff must choose between one of the following types of damages.

1. Plaintiff's Actual Damages

The Copyright Act provides that the copyright owner may recover "actual damages suffered . . . as a result of the infringement" but does not explicitly define the components of "actual damages."[90] Actual damages are often a measure of the profits the plaintiff would have made but for the defendant's infringement.[91]

> *Example:* Apartment Builder has worked extensively with Architects A and B and wants to hire one of them to design a new apartment building. Architect B knows that Apartment Builder really liked Architect A's last apartment design. So, Architect B borrows Architect A's design, slightly modifies it, and presents it to Apartment Builder as his proposed design for the new apartment building. Apartment Builder likes the modified design so much, he hires Architect B to design the new apartment building. Apartment Builder would have hired Architect A if not for Architect B's modified design. Architect A, in this instance, will be entitled to recover from Architect B the profits Architect A would have earned designing the apartment building for Apartment Builder, because Architect A would have been awarded the job if not for Architect B's infringement.

Another measure of actual damages is based on the "lost fair market value of the architectural plans."[92] Although there is some variation in how those damages are calculated in different circuits, most courts agree that the "fair market value" of an infringed-upon design equals the amount it would have cost the defendant, as a willing buyer, to rightfully acquire the infringed-upon design from the plaintiff, as a willing seller.[93] Thus, for example, if Architect A charges $4.00 per square foot for designing customized architectural plans,

---

90. 17 U.S.C.A. § 504(b).

91. *See, e.g.*, Johnson v. Jones, 149 F.3d 494 (6th Cir. 1998).

92. Van Brouck & Associates, Inc. v. Darmik, Inc., 329 F. Supp. 2d 924, 937 (E.D. Mich. 2004) (quoting Associated Residential Design v. Molotky, 226 F. Supp. 2d 1251, 1254 (D. Nev. 2002)).

93. *See, e.g.*, *VanBrouck & Associates*, 329 F. Supp. 2d at 929; Eiben v. A. Epstein & Sons International, Inc., 57 F. Supp. 2d 607, 612 (N.D. Ill. 1999); Aitken, Hazen, Hoffman, Miller, P.C. v. Empire Construction Co., 542 F. Supp. 252, 263 (D. Neb. 1982).

and Architect B infringed upon a 2,000-square-foot design, the lost fair market value to Architect A would be up to $8,000.[94]

2. Defendant's Profits Resulting from the Infringement

The plaintiff can also recover any profits earned by the defendant as a direct result of the infringement. Using the preceding example, Architect A would be able to collect all of the profits Architect B earned from designing the new apartment building. A plaintiff may elect to recover the defendant's profits if the plaintiff's profit margin is smaller than the defendant's profit margin, or in cases where the plaintiff cannot prove that it would have received the work but for the infringement. For example, if a one-man architectural firm that operates exclusively in Arizona proves that an architect in Massachusetts has infringed on one of its designs for a single-family custom home by designing a custom home for a client in Massachusetts, that Arizona architect will likely have suffered no actual damages, as it would not have been hired to design the Massachusetts house.

To establish the infringer's profits, the copyright owner must present proof of the infringer's revenue. The burden then shifts to the defendant to prove any deductible expenses and the "elements of profit attributable to factors other than the copyrighted work."[95] The defendant cannot carry its burden of establishing either legitimately deductible expenses or profits attributable to other factors by merely offering proof of its average profit margin.[96] If the defendant fails to provide appropriate proof, the plaintiff may recover the defendant's gross revenue from the infringement.

The purpose of awarding a plaintiff the infringer's profits is to "prevent the infringer from unfairly benefiting from a wrongful act[.]"[97] For that reason, the plaintiff need not prove that it incurred actual damages in order to recover the infringer's profits. Consequently, this measure of damages is especially useful in cases where the plaintiff cannot prove it incurred any actual damages. For example, if an architect who operates exclusively in California proves that an architect in Alabama infringed on one of its designs in Alabama, the California architect may have suffered no actual damages because she would not have been hired to design the Alabama structure. However, the

---

94. *VanBrouck & Associates*, 329 F. Supp. 2d at 928–29.

95. 17 U.S.C.A. § 504(b).

96. Johnson v. Jones, 149 F.3d 494 (6th Cir. 1998).

97. *Van Brouck & Associates*, 329 F. Supp. 2d at 936–37.

plaintiff is not left without a remedy because she will be able to recover the profits earned by the Alabama architect.

Although a plaintiff is entitled to both actual damages and infringer's profits, the plaintiff may not recover twice for the same injury.[98] Thus, the Copyright Act stipulates that a plaintiff can receive only that portion of the infringer's profits that have not been taken into account in computing actual damages.[99] For example, if all of the infringer's sales were counted as sales lost by the copyright owner for purposes of determining actual damages, and the infringer's profit margin is less than the copyright owner's, all of the infringer's profits attributable to the infringement will have already been accounted for in the actual damage award.[100] In such a case, the infringer's profits may not be recovered in addition to actual damages.

3. *Statutory Damages*

The Copyright Act provides for statutory damages in appropriate cases. The court, in its discretion, decides what the appropriate amount of statutory damages is, within the limitations set forth in the Copyright Act. A plaintiff typically seeks statutory damages only when its actual damages (as discussed above) are very small, or where the plaintiff believes it cannot prove it suffered any damages. Using the California architect example above, if the Alabama architect made no profit on the job, there are no infringer's profits to recover. Therefore, the California architect would likely elect to receive statutory damages.

The plaintiff may elect to recover statutory damages rather than other damages at any time before final judgment is rendered.[101] For cases where the court does *not* find the infringement was willful, the court may award a sum at its discretion between $750 and $30,000. Where the plaintiff proves that infringement was committed willfully, however, the court may award up to $150,000 in statutory damages.[102]

A plaintiff is only entitled to statutory damages if the infringement at issue in the action commenced after registration of the copyright.[103] The dual

---

98. *See, e.g.*, Sparaco v. Lawler, Matusky, Skelly Engineers, 313 F. Supp. 2d 247 (S.D.N.Y. 2004).

99. 17 U.S.C.A. § 504(b).

100. Robert R. Jones Associates, Inc. v. Nino Homes, 858 F.2d 274, 281 (6th Cir. 1988).

101. 17 U.S.C.A. § 504(c)(1).

102. 17 U.S.C.A. § 504(c)(2).

103. 17 U.S.C.A. § 412(1).

purpose behind making statutory damages available is to incentivize copyright owners to register promptly and to encourage potential infringers to check the federal register. Thus, statutory damages will be imposed only on infringers who had constructive notice the work was covered by a valid copyright, with constructive notice being presumed upon registration.

In the case of continuing infringement, infringement "commences" for purposes of statutory damages when the first infringing act in a series occurs. In other words, that first act "commences" a single, continuing infringement.[104] Thus, for example, the first steps of infringement on an architectural work, such as tracing floor plans, commence the infringing conduct, not the completion of the finished product.[105] Even if some of the alleged acts of infringement occurred after the copyright was registered, statutory damages will be unavailable if the first act occurred prior to registration.

4. *Injunctive Relief*

In addition to the damages awards discussed above, the plaintiff can (and likely will) seek injunctive relief, a court order compelling the defendants to cease producing the infringing architectural designs and buildings.[106] The plaintiff also can seek an initial injunction, in the form of a temporary restraining order, compelling the defendants to cease producing the infringing architectural designs and buildings during the course of the lawsuit.[107]

5. *Attorneys' Fees and Costs*

Regardless of the measure of damages the plaintiff elects, a plaintiff can recover the reasonable attorneys' fees and costs it incurred pursuing the lawsuit if the plaintiff's copyright was registered before the infringement occurred.[108] However, this provision is mutual. If the defendant wins, the defendant can also request that the court award it the reasonable attorneys' fees and costs

---

104. *See, e.g.*, Johnson v. Jones, 149 F.3d 494 (6th Cir. 1998) (quoting Parfums Givenchy, Inc. v. C & C Beauty Sales, Inc., 832 F. Supp 1378, 1393 (C.D. Cal. 1993)).

105. Cornerstone Home Builders, Inc. v. McAllister, 311 F. Supp. 2d 1351 (M.D. Fla. 2004).

106. 17 U.S.C. § 502.

107. *Id.*

108. 17 U.S.C. § 505. *See also* Johnson v. Jones, 149 F.3d 494, 506 (6th Cir. 1998); Mason v. Montgomery Data, Inc., 967 F.2d 135, 143 (5th Cir. 1992); Cornerstone Home Builders, Inc. v. McAllister, 311 F. Supp. 2d 1351, 1352 (M.D. Fla. 2004).

it incurred defending the lawsuit.[109] The court has the discretion to decide whether or not to award attorneys' fees and costs in all cases and to determine the size of any award.

Library References

C.J.S. *Copyrights and Intellectual Property* §§ 8, 10, 41, 43–46, 48, 57, 61–75, 77–82, 98–100.
West's Key No. Digests, Copyrights and Intellectual Property <KEY>51–53.2, 64, 72–90.

6. What Information Is Protected by Trade Secret Laws?

State trade secret laws can provide protection for certain types of information. Trade secrets are protected under state laws, which vary from state to state. However, a trade secret is commonly defined as information which:

1. is not generally known;
2. derives independent economic value from not being generally known; and
3. is the subject of reasonable efforts to protect its secrecy.

A client database is one example of potential trade secret information. During the course of a client relationship, a designer may discover information like the range of fees the client is willing to pay, the number of projects the client undertakes every year, contract clauses the client is willing to negotiate (or not), and marketing information like names of the client's family, and the client's birthday. All of this information may be bundled into a client database which allows the designer to retain the client's business and maximize profitability on projects for that client. This information is not generally known and part of its value to the designer is that none of the designer's competitors know this information. As long as the designer takes reasonable steps to protect this information from discovery, the information is likely subject to trade secret protection. Password-protecting the database is usually sufficient protection to secure the information's secrecy.

Library References

West's Key No. Digests, Antitrust and Trade Regulation <KEY>413, 421.

---

109. 17 U.S.C. § 505.

VI. Conclusion

Most design firms rent their office space. The office is full of computers, plotters, telephones, and furniture, all of which is commonly leased or financed. The only significant asset most design firms possess is the firm's intellectual property, embodied in the designs the firm develops for their clients. As a design firm grows, it typically builds on its past in a literal fashion by developing new designs based, in whole or in part, on previous successful designs. For this reason, designers need to view intellectual property as a critical part of their business and need to take concrete steps to safeguard that property. The first step is to develop a corporate vision—the designer must determine what should be protected and how it should be protected. The second step involves establishing interoffice policies aimed at protecting the firm's intellectual property. At the same time, the firm can adopt interoffice policies that protect the firm from claims of copyright infringement from other designers. The final step is an ongoing process to follow through on the vision and interoffice policies the firm has established and to regularly audit those policies to see if adjustments are needed. No policy, no matter how well written, is of any value if it is not routinely followed by the employees responsible for executing it. This fact must be kept in mind at the time the policies are developed—policies that are cumbersome, or interfere with key processes, will not be followed, and therefore, are useless.

The purpose of this chapter has been to summarize the law governing protection of designers' intellectual property, particularly copyright law. Designers who want to establish protection for their intellectual property, and who want to protect themselves from claims made by other designers, should give serious consideration to the issues discussed here and begin the process of establishing policies to protect themselves and their designs.[110]

---

110. The author would like to thank Miles Maurino and Vanessa Schlaich, both of whom are associates in Gordon Rees Scully Mansukhani's San Francisco office, for their invaluable assistance in updating this chapter.

CHAPTER 8

Design Professional Risks: Indemnification and Professional Liability Insurance

KAREN ERGER [1]

I. Introduction

Design professionals have complex and challenging roles in construction projects, and these demands can be further complicated by the contractual arrangements between the parties. This chapter describes two of the primary means of managing the risks of construction projects—contractual indemnification clauses and insurance—and their impact on design professionals.

Clauses whereby one party agrees to indemnify another are commonplace in construction contracts. Ideally, these risk-shifting provisions are deployed to assign a particular risk to the party best able to bear such risk.[2] For design

1. The author of this second edition wishes to acknowledge and thank Katherine Davitt Enos for her contributions to this chapter as the author of the first edition. The author is also grateful to Sten Larson for providing additional citations and edits for this chapter. Mr. Larson is a second-year law student at the University of Colorado and a law clerk at the firm of Beltzer Bangert & Gunnell LLP (BBG). Prior to joining BBG, Mr. Larson worked as a mechanical engineer for the U.S. Navy performing maintenance and repairs on fast attack submarines and guided missile destroyers.

2. Gilbane Bldg. Co./TDX Constr. Corp. v. St. Paul Fire & Marine Ins. Co., 97 N.E.3d 711, 717 n.4 (N.Y. 2018)

professionals, however, the reality is often otherwise. Client-drafted professional services agreements frequently include indemnity clauses that shift most or all of the risks of loss to the design professional. This chapter examines the impact of different types of indemnity clauses on design professionals and aims to assist them and their advisors in making informed decisions.

Insurance is another tool for managing design risk. For the design professional, professional liability (PL) insurance coverage is an important risk transfer strategy that also provides risk management support and resources. There is no standard policy form for design professionals' PL policies. Furthermore, PL coverage operates very differently from other liability policies, such as commercial general liability (CGL). This chapter outlines the general working of PL policies as well as their interplay with GCL insurance.

II. Managing the Risks of Contractual Indemnification

One of the simplest ways to manage risk is to transfer it to another party, which can be achieved through indemnification clauses, which are also referred to as hold harmless agreements.[3]

Design professionals can use contractual indemnification clauses proactively as a risk management tool. Too often, however, design professionals experience these clauses as a risk that itself must be managed. Increasingly, project owners and clients demand that their design professionals agree to extremely far-reaching indemnification clauses in professional services agreements.[4] Under some sweeping indemnification clauses, the design professional essentially indemnifies the project owner for any losses suffered in connection with the project, regardless of whether or not the loss is caused by the design professional.

The following sections identify the various forms of indemnification clauses, describe the operation of various state laws upon their enforceability, explain the problems that overreaching indemnification clauses can cause for design professionals (and their clients), and offer some ideas for negotiating a more equitable allocation of risk.

---

3. Bryan A. Garner, *Indemnify A. and Hold Harmless; Save Harmless*, 15 GREEN BAG 2D 17, 23 (2011) (explaining difference between indemnify and hold harmless in various jurisdictions).

4. Jeffrey M. Hummel, *Indemnification Principles and Restrictions on Construction Projects*, CONSTRUCTION BRIEFINGS NO. 2005-8.

A. Classification of Indemnification Clauses

Indemnification clauses are commonly grouped into three categories: broad form, intermediate form, and comparative or limited form.[5] Some courts and attorneys refer to those clauses as Type I, Type II, and Type III, respectively. Although this chapter uses the more descriptive names, the alternative designations are included for reference.

In each of the indemnification provisions, one party (the indemnitor) agrees to compensate the other party (the indemnitee) with respect to certain losses or damages incurred on the project. The difference between the different categories of indemnity is one of scope.

1. Broad Form (Type I) Indemnification

A broad form indemnity provision transfers the entire risk of the loss from one party to another, regardless of the degree of fault of either party.[6] The clause's broad coverage applies to any losses that the indemnitee may suffer, even if those losses are attributable to the indemnitee.

The following is an example of a broad form indemnification clause:

> Design Professional agrees to indemnify and hold harmless Client from all claims, losses, damages, and expenses (including attorneys' fees and other legal expenses) arising out of, caused by, related to, or in any way connected with the Project or Design Professional's services.

Despite what some design professionals believe, broad form indemnification provisions do not *void* PL insurance coverage altogether. Coverage exists for those risks that have been accepted through the contract of insurance between the design professional and the insurer. Generally speaking, the PL policy covers damages caused by the insured design professional's negligence (i.e., its failure to perform its professional services in accordance with the applicable standard of care).[7] Unless the contract between the parties says otherwise, the standard requires the design professional to utilize the reasonable

---

5. James v. Burlington N. Santa Fe Ry. Co., 636 F. Supp. 2d 961, 967–68 (D. Ariz. 2007) (examining differences between the three forms of indemnity).

6. *James*, 636 F. Supp. 2d at 968.

7. Domson, Inc. v. Kadrmas Lee & Jackson, Inc., 918 N.W.2d 396, 405 (S.D. 2018), *reh'g denied* (Oct. 26, 2018).

judgment and skill that another reasonable prudent professional facing the same or similar facts and circumstances would exercise.[8]

The problem with broad form language is that it requires the design professional to assume liability for damages (1) caused by others, (2) not caused by the design professional's negligence, and (3) that would not be the design professional's responsibility, absent the broad form indemnity provision.[9] None of these are covered by the PL policy. For this reason, indemnitor design professionals assume a significant amount of noninsurable risk when they agree to broad form language.

The indemnitee assumes certain risks under broad form indemnification clauses as well. Without PL insurance coverage, it is unlikely that the design professional will be able to fund the indemnity promise; very few design firms hold assets sufficient to do so. Furthermore, neither party benefits from the coverage battle that is near-certain to arise when an overbroad indemnity provision is at issue in a claim or lawsuit.

PL coverage is the primary source of financial security for the client in the event of a claim. The client who extracts a broad form indemnification from its design professional likely wins a pyrrhic victory.

2. *Intermediate Form (Type II) Indemnification*

The intermediate form of indemnification shifts the entire burden of loss onto the indemnitor so long as the indemnitor is partially responsible for the loss.[10] Under this type of indemnity clause, the indemnitor's liability is not proportional to its percentage of fault. Even if the indemnitor's share of the fault is only 1%, it will pay 100% of the damages.[11] The only instance in which the indemnitor would be exempt from the obligation is when the indemnitee is solely (100%) responsible for the loss.

The following is an example of an intermediate form indemnification clause:

---

8. Sch. Bd. of Broward Cty. v. Pierce Goodwin Alexander & Linville, 137 So. 3d 1059, 1065 (Fla. 4th DCA 2014).

9. Robert A. Crist Jr., *Claims/Design Responsibility & Liability; Joint Defense Agreements Between Owners and Design Professionals*, 29 CONSTR. LAWYER 35 Spring 2009.

10. Bracken v. Burchick Const. Co., Inc., 1432 WDA 2012, WL 10790110, at *8 (Pa. Super. 2014).

11. *Id.*

> Design Professional agrees to hold harmless and indemnify Client from any and all liability arising out of Design Professional's performance except for the sole negligence or willful misconduct of Client.

The risk of the intermediate form to the design professional is almost as grave as the risk posed by the broad form indemnification clause. In most cases, it will not be difficult for competent legal counsel to persuade judge or jury that the design professional bore 1% of the fault.

Also note that as with liability for broad form indemnity, PL insurance will cover only the portion of damages attributable to the design professional's negligence, if any. Any further liability must be satisfied with the design professional's own funds, which, as previously noted, may fall short of full compensation.

3. *Comparative (Limited) Form (Type III)*

Under the comparative form of indemnification provision, each party bears only the risk of loss arising out of its own negligence.[12] Comparative form provisions typically state that indemnity is provided, "but only to the extent" caused by the negligent acts of the indemnitor. This apportionment mirrors the indemnification available under common law and is considered the most equitable allocation of risk. Generally, these clauses will fall within the coverage grant of the design professional's PL insurance and best protect the design professional's balance sheet.

Examples of comparative form indemnification clauses can be found in industry standard contract documents. Here is an example from the American Institute of Architects (AIA) B103-2017 ("Standard Form of Agreement Between Owner and Architect for a Complex Project"):

> § 8.1.3 The Architect shall indemnify and hold the Owner and the Owner's officers and employees harmless from and against damages, losses, and judgments arising from claims by third parties, including reasonable attorneys' fees and expenses recoverable under applicable law, but only to the extent they are caused by the negligent acts or omissions of the Architect, its employees and its consultants in the performance of professional services under this Agreement. The Architect's obligation to indemnify and hold the Owner and the Owner's officers and employees harmless does not include a duty to defend. The Architect's duty to indemnify the Owner under this Sec-

---

12. *James*, 636 F. Supp. 2d at 968.

tion 8.1.3 shall be limited to the available proceeds of the insurance coverage required by this Agreement.[13]

Although this form for "complex projects" includes an indemnification clause, note that the AIA Standard Form of Agreement Between Owner and Architect (AIA B101-2017) does not include an indemnification clause. Absent such a clause, the indemnification scheme existing in common law, namely, that each party is responsible for damages that arise from their own negligence, will apply.[14]

The form documents prepared by the Engineers Joint Contract Documents Committee (EJCDC) include a comparative form of indemnity clause in the Standard Form of Agreement Between Owner and Engineer for Professional Services, the E-500 (2020):

> 6.10 A. Indemnification by Engineer: To the fullest extent permitted by Laws and Regulations, Engineer shall indemnify and hold harmless Owner, and Owner's officers, directors, members, partners, agents, and employees, from losses, damages, and judgments (including reasonable consultants' and attorneys' fees and expenses) arising from third-party claims or actions relating to the Project, provided that any such claim, action, loss, damages, or judgment is attributable to bodily injury, sickness, disease, or death, or to injury to or destruction of tangible property (other than the Work itself), including the loss of use resulting therefrom, but only to the extent caused by any negligent act or omission of Engineer or Engineer's officers, directors, members, partners, agents, employees, Subconsultants or Engineer's Subcontractors. This indemnification provision is subject to and limited by the provisions, if any, agreed to by Owner and Engineer in Exhibit I, "Limitations of Liability."

Of course, it is not always possible for design professionals to employ these standard agreements. Clients often resist using the professional society contracts on the theory that they are biased in favor of the design professionals. The drafters of these documents are aware of this perception and strive to

13. Note the final sentence, which limits the architect's liability to the proceeds available under its insurance. This clause protects the architect in the event that its policy limits are exhausted. The penultimate sentence is a disclaimer of any duty for the architect to defend the owner. This will be discussed at Section III.C.1 of this chapter.

14. Underwood v. Fulford, 128 N.E.3d 519, 525 (Ind. Ct. App. 2019).

make the documents balanced so that they will be acceptable to both parties. Nevertheless, many clients will insist on their own bespoke agreements.

However, even when a client-drafted contract is to be used these clauses can serve as examples of what a reasonably insurable indemnification clause looks like. Comparing the owner's proposed indemnification clause with the form agreements is a useful exercise and can help the design professional identify problem areas and prepare to negotiate a more narrowly tailored indemnity clause.

B. Restrictions on Indemnification

To prevent the abuse of indemnification clauses, most states have enacted anti-indemnification statutes that render certain types of liability transfer unenforceable. Some prohibit transfer of any liability for the indemnitee's negligence, others only prohibit transfer of liability for the indemnitee's sole negligence. Many of these are limited to "construction contracts," which may or may not include contracts for professional design services. Some apply only to public sector projects. Others apply only to private sector projects. These statutes not only vary widely between jurisdictions, but also are often quite complex.[15] Qualified legal counsel should review applicable statutes to determine their impact on proposed contractual language.

In recognition of the continued pressure for design professionals to agree to uninsurable indemnity clauses, several states have enacted legislation specifically targeting professional service agreements and that invalidates provisions requiring design professionals to "defend" the client or assume liability for damages not caused by their negligence.[16] Like the more general construction anti-indemnification statutes, these laws vary widely among jurisdictions that have enacted them, and the advice of competent counsel is essential to understanding their impact on any particular contract.

Even in the absence of specific legislation, states differ in their enforcement of indemnification clauses. Some embrace the legal principle of freedom of contract between parties of perceived equal bargaining position and will enforce any indemnity agreement if the intent is clearly and expressly stated.[17] Others struggle with the burdens imposed by the broad or even intermediate form of indemnification and apply rules of interpretation that narrow the scope

---

15. A 50-state survey is beyond the scope of this chapter.
16. *Id.*
17. Holcim (US), Inc. v. Ohio Cas. Ins. Co., 38 So. 3d 722, 728 (Ala. 2009).

of indemnification provisions.[18] Some, when faced with ambiguous indemnification provisions, apply a strict interpretation that results in no indemnification at all.[19]

State laws regarding indemnification vary widely and change frequently. Because of the complexities of anti-indemnification statutes, it is prudent for the design professional to seek legal counsel who understand the applicable state statutes and provisions before entering into a contract for professional services.

Even if applicable law suggests that a particular indemnification clause would not be enforceable, it is a mistake for design professionals to agree to onerous language on that account. The question may never reach a court, and the design professional's agreement to such language may seriously undermine its position when attempting to settle a claim. It is generally a superior strategy to attempt to negotiate more equitable and insurable language and cite the likely unenforceability of the proposed clause as a point in favor of a redrafting.

C. Negotiating Insurable Indemnity Clauses

A design professional's promise to indemnify its client for damages caused by its negligent performance of professional services will fall within the coverage grant of most if not all professional liability policies. The problem for design professionals is that many clients insist on a much broader indemnification, typically requiring the design professional to (1) defend the client, (2) assume liability for damages caused by others, and/or (3) assume liability for its own non-negligent acts. None of these obligations are covered under PL insurance.

The design professional who agrees to this language must consider that these obligations are uninsured business risks and decide if it makes sense to assume such risk under the circumstances. This should be done in consultation with competent legal counsel who can give the design professional a full understanding of the potential hazards of agreeing to the indemnity clause as-is. If the design professional elects to proceed, it must be certain to impose a similar indemnity clause on its subconsultants, if any.

If the design professional deems the risk of uninsured loss too high to bear, it must negotiate with the client for more insurable terms. Some of the design professional's arguments will be based in equity, including the idea that

---

18. Concord & Cumberland Horizontal Prop. Regime v. Concord & Cumberland, LLC, 819 S.E.2d 166, 171 (S.C. Ct. App. 2018), *reh'g denied* (Oct. 18, 2018).

19. Specialized Contracting, Inc. v. St. Paul Fire & Marine Ins. Co., 825 N.W.2d 872, 878 (N.D. 2012).

the design professional should not be the guarantor of other parties' performance, and the notion that project owners should accept some risk incidental to the project, and not attempt to shift it all to the design professional.

Design professionals can also remind their clients that the risks additionally assumed by the design professional will not be covered by PL insurance. Some clients will respond by stating that this is not their problem, but more sophisticated clients are likely aware that most design professionals are not able to fund the loss absent PL coverage.

A successful argument for an insurable indemnity clause will likely depend in part on convincing the project owner or client that preserving PL insurance coverage is in the best interest of the client and the project. To make that argument, it is necessary for the design professional to understand the basics of PL insurance coverage. This is discussed in the following section.

III. Professional Liability Practice Policies

A. No Standard Form

Understanding the scope of design professionals' PL insurance is hampered to some extent by the fact that there is no standard coverage form in use, as there is for CGL and other coverages. As of April 2020, there are at least 45 markets for design professionals' PL coverage in the US market alone, each writing on its own bespoke form or forms.

There are elements common to all design professionals' PL policies, but there can be very significant differences between policies. Further complicating matters is the fact that many Insureds have negotiated highly customized policy terms that alter the coverage afforded by the underlying policy.

Because every design professional PL policy can be different from others in non-trivial ways, it is impossible accurately to summarize what "every" such policy covers. To avoid ceaseless repetition, we will not remind the reader of this fact as we review the "general" features of professional liability insurance, but it should be remembered when reading this chapter. A phrase from the computer consulting world—RTFM or "Read the Freaking Manual" might be adapted to our purposes as RTFP—"Read the Freaking Policy."

B. What Is Covered

Generally, the design professional's PL policy covers damages caused by the Insured's negligent performance of professional services. Many policies refer to this as a "breach of professional duty" or a "wrongful act," and often define this term expressly as negligence. For example:

> **Breach of Professional Duty** means negligence, defined as the failure to meet the professional standard of care legally required or reasonably expected under the circumstances in the rendering or failure to render **Professional Services** by the **Insured**.[20]

Other policies do not expressly reference negligence in the definition, referring instead to the Insured's liability for acts, errors, or omissions in the performance of professional services. For example:

> **Wrongful act** means an act, error or omission that causes liability in the performance of **professional services** for others by the **Insured** or by any person or entity, including joint ventures, for whom the **Insured** is liable.[21]

These definitions cannot be read in a vacuum and must be construed in the context of all other policy terms and exclusions in order to comprehend the true extent of coverage.

C. Who Is Covered

1. Right and Duty to Defend

Typically, the design professional's PL policy gives the insurer the right and duty to defend claims against the Insured:

> The Insurer has the right and duty to defend any **claim** against the **Insured** seeking amounts that are payable under the terms of this Policy, even if any of the allegations of the **claim** are groundless, false, or fraudulent.[22]

When the policy has a large self-insured retention (SIR) rather than a deductible, a slightly different scheme may apply. A self-insured retention is like a deductible, but with a few key differences. When a claim is made on a policy with a deductible, the insurer will pay indemnity and expense costs and seek reimbursement of the deductible from the Insured. On a policy with a SIR, the Insured must satisfy the SIR before the insurer will respond to the loss.

For example:

---

20. Lexington Insurance Company, Architects and Engineers Professional Liability Policy, LX4204 (07/13), IV.D, p. 6.

21. CNA Professional Liability and Pollution Incident Liability Insurance Policy, CNA79034XX (04-2020) at III (Definitions).

22. *Id.* at I.C.1.

> The **Company** shall not be called upon to assume charge of the investigation, defense or settlement of any **Claim** made against the **Insured**, but the **Company**, at its option, shall have the right and shall be given the opportunity to associate, at its own expense, with the **Insured** in the investigation, defense or control of such **Claim** which would involve or appear reasonably likely to involve the **Company**, in which event the **Insured** and the **Company** shall cooperate in the defense or settlement of the **Claim**.
>
> In the absence of such election by the **Company**, the **Insured** shall arrange for and assume the investigation, defense and settlement of such **Claim** provided that the **Insured** shall take no action or agree to any settlement which alone or together with **Claim Expenses** will exceed the Self-Insured Retention without the prior written consent of the **Company**.[23]

This language gives the Insured the ability to direct the defense of claims within its self-insured retention.

2. Who Is an Insured

For covered claims, the PL policy defends and indemnifies the "Insured" as defined by the policy. This definition includes the Named Insured, typically defined as "the persons or entities identified on the Declarations as the Named Insured."[24] The Declarations will list the current name of the insured firm, may include a list of all of the names and entities under which the firm currently and previously has done business, and those for which it desires coverage under the policy. (Sometimes this list is appended to the policy as an endorsement.) It is important to keep this list complete and up to date, as a claim made against an unlisted entity will not be covered under the policy.

Licensed design professionals are subject to suit in their own right.[25] Accordingly, the design professional PL policy will include current and former employees in the definition of "Insured." For example, one carrier's policy includes the following in its definition of "Insured."

> Any person who is, was, or hereafter becomes a partner, principal, officer, director, member, or employee of the Named Insured, but

---

23. Lexington Insurance Company, Architects and Engineers Professional Liability Policy, CMPL209 LX8532 (12/09).

24. CNA Professional Liability and Pollution Incident Liability Insurance Policy, CNA79034XX (04-2020) at III (Definitions).

25. *See* Michaels v. CH2M Hill, Inc., 257 P.3d 532 (Wash. 2011).

only for Professional Services performed in such capacity on behalf of the Named Insured.[26]

Note that an individual qualifies as an Insured only for professional services performed "on behalf of the Named Insured." The moonlighting design professional will not find coverage for their extracurricular design services under the employer's policy.

In addition, any newly acquired subsidiaries are often included in coverage. Some PL policies also cover retired individuals, so long as they are acting within the scope of their duties as a consultant for the firm, as well as spouses and heirs in the event of death.

A careful reading of the definition of "Insured" under the applicable PL policy will prevent many misapprehensions of the nature and extent of PL coverage. Questions and concerns should be addressed with the insurance agent or broker.

a. Coverage Position of Former Employees

If a claim is made against a design professional regarding services performed for a former employer, the design professional must look to the former employer's PL policy for coverage. Because the PL policy has a claims-made trigger, the policy that will apply is the one in force at the time the claim is made, rather than when the alleged negligence occurred. If in the meantime the employer has gone out of business without purchasing a tail or otherwise has "gone bare," the former employee will be out of luck.

b. Client Cannot Be an Additional Insured

In contrast to the CGL policy, where it is common to add the project owner and other parties involved in the construction project as Additional Insureds, this is not an option on the design professional PL policy. This is often a point of contention between design professional and client, particularly if the client is accustomed to contracting with construction contractors who make the client an Additional Insured under their CGL policies as a matter of course.

The primary rationale for the prohibition on adding the client as an Additional Insured under the PL policy is that the policy provides coverage for the Insured's negligent performance of professional services, so it is meaningless to add as Insureds parties that do not perform such services.

---

26. Berkley Insurance Company, Architects, Engineers & Consultants Policy, BDP0417001, IV.P.3, p. 6.

Some clients have design professionals on staff, which presents another problem. If such a client were added to the design firm's PL policy, the coverage could apply to all of the professional activities of the client's in-house staff, whether or not the design professional was involved with their projects. The design firm, of course, will not want to expose its limits to entities and individuals over which it has no control and to projects for which it receives no reward. Furthermore, clients are arguably better served by purchasing their own PL policies with policy limits and coverage terms that suit their specific needs.[27]

Moreover, adding other parties as Additional Insureds on the PL policy would frustrate, rather than further, their desire for additional security, because the policy excludes coverage for claims made by one Insured against another.[28] Here is a typical "Insured vs. Insured" exclusion:

> This insurance does not apply to … [a]ny **Claim** made by any **Insured** against any other **Insured**, whether collusive or not.[29]

Design professionals purchase PL insurance for the express purpose of compensating their client if the client is damaged by the design professional's negligence. Presumably, clients who demand to be added as Additional Insureds to the PL policy desire the additional benefit of a fully funded defense against third party claims. It should be pointed out to such clients that the PL policy will defend its insured design professional against allegations of negligence, which, to the extent that third party claims arise from those allegations, will redound to the client's benefit as well. But the PL policy will not pay to defend the design professional's client.

D. Fundamental Exclusions

Although each carrier's policy form is slightly different, some exclusions are integral to PL coverage and are found in some form in all professional liability policies. While the exact wording of these will vary from policy to policy, a general understanding of these core exclusions is necessary to understand the scope and extent of PL coverage.

---

27. Victor Insurance Managers, Inc. Intro to Professional Liability Insurance (2020).

28. *Id.*

29. Lexington Insurance Company, Architects and Engineers Professional Liability Policy, LX4204 (07/13), III.G, p.5.

I. Liability Assumed by Contract

The exclusion for "liability assumed by contract" is fundamental to the design professional's PL coverage. This is one of the handful of policy terms that is universal to all such policies, although the policy language varies from carrier to carrier. Here is a typical formulation:

> **Liability of Others Assumed by Contract**
>
> [This insurance does not apply to and the **Company** will not pay **Damages** and/or **Defense Expenses** for any **Claim** based upon or arising out of] the liability of others assumed by any **Insured** under any contract or agreement unless such liability arises as a result of a **Breach of Professional Duty** and would have existed absent such contract or agreement.[30]

One important ramification of this exclusion has to do with the standard of care for design professionals. Absent contractual promises to the contrary, the design professional has a duty to employ a "degree of professional care and skill ordinarily employed by others of the same profession in the same general area."[31] The design professional is not obligated to produce a set of perfect plans unless they agree by contract to do so:

> The key question in determining whether an architect has been negligent is not whether error occurred, but whether the architect breached a duty to exercise the degree of competence ordinarily exercised in like circumstances by reputable members of the profession. Absent a special agreement, an architect does not imply or guarantee a perfect plan.[32]

Project owners often propose contract terms that impose a duty of perfect performance on their design professionals. For example, their contracts might require the design professional to meet the "highest standard of care," or produce a "defect-free design." The Liability Assumed by Contract exclusion makes these promises uninsurable, a fact that design professionals regularly raise in contract negotiations with varying degrees of success.

Insurers are not in the business of insuring against events that are certain to occur; you cannot buy fire insurance for a burning building. Perfect plans do not exist; if perfection is the standard, all designs will fall short, no matter how

---

30. *Id.* at III.I., p.5.
31. Hoffman v. Theriot, 249 So. 3d 297, 301 (La. Ct. App. 2018).
32. Smith v. Walsh Constr. Co. II, LLC, 95 N.E.3d 78, 89–90 (Ind. Ct. App. 2018).

assiduously all involved may strive for it. The Liability Assumed by Contract exclusion nails the coverage firmly to the standard of ordinary care, rather than the aspirational goal of perfection.

The coverage problems arising out of broad and intermediate form indemnity clauses[33] have their roots in the Liability Assumed by Contract exclusion. As noted previously in this chapter, indemnity clauses proposed by clients frequently call for the design professional to indemnify them not only for damages caused by professional negligence, but also for damages arising out of non-negligent conduct, or caused wholly or in part by entities other than the design professional or those for whom the design professional is legally liable. For example:

> Design Professional shall indemnify, and hold harmless, Client from any and all claims, demands, suits, actions, proceedings, loss, cost, and damages of every kind and description, including any reasonable attorneys' fees and/or litigation expenses, caused by, arising out of, or contributed to, in whole or in part, by reasons of any act, omission, professional error, fault, mistake, or negligence of the Design Professional, its employees, agents, representatives, or subcontractors, their employees, agents, or representatives in connections with or incidental to the performance of this Agreement.[34]

To the extent that this indemnification clause imposes liability upon the design professional that would otherwise not exist, it is excluded from coverage under the Liability Assumed by Contract exclusion. A contractual promise to indemnify another party for non-negligent design, or for damages caused by parties for whom would not otherwise be legally liable, is not insurable.

The Liability Assumed by Contract exclusion also bars coverage for the design professional's promise to defend another party, *e.g.* "Design Professional shall indemnify, hold harmless, and defend Client. . . ." Absent this promise, the design professional does not owe the client a defense, so this obligation is excluded from coverage. As noted above, it is not possible to add the client (or other parties who are not part of or related to the insured design professional entity) as Additional Insureds to a design professional PL policy. Accordingly, doing so is not a solution to the coverage problem.

In recognition of the continued pressure for design professionals to agree to uninsurable indemnity clauses, several states have enacted legislation

---

33. Discussed *supra* at Section II.A.3 of this chapter.

34. J. Kent Holland, Jr., Contract Guide for Design Professionals at 94 (3d ed., Construction Risk, LLC and Zurich American Insurance Company 2012).

restricting the enforceability of some of these terms, including the defense obligation and the assumption of liability broader than the design professional's percentage of negligence or fault.[35] Many, but not all, of these statutes apply only to public construction contracts.

2. *Express Warranties and Guarantees*

The PL policy exclusion for express warranties and guarantees is a natural outgrowth of the Liability Assumed by Contract exclusion.

Absent contrary contractual provisions, design professionals are held to the standard of ordinary care and are not legally required to warrant or guarantee their services. Although warranties and guarantees likely fall within the Liability Assumed by Contract exclusion, most policies explicitly exclude coverage for them.

Some Express Warranties and Guarantees exclusions have a carve-out for warranties and guarantees of compliance with the professional standard of care. For example:

> **Express Warranties and Guarantees**
>
> [This Policy does not apply to] [t]hat part of any CLAIM(S) based upon or arising out of express warranties and guarantees. This exclusion does not apply to a warranty or guarantee by the INSURED that the INSURED'S PROFESSIONAL SERVICES are in conformity with the standard of care applicable to such PROFESSIONAL SERVICES . . .[36]

Insurers who offer this carve-out likely reason that the standard of care is not elevated by a warranty or guarantee that it will be met, hence the risk is an acceptable one.

3. *Insured vs. Insured*

Professional liability policies generally exclude coverage for indemnity or defense of claims brought by one Insured against another. For example:

---

35. *See* Catherine Bragg, *Statutory Limitations on Design Professional's Indemnity Obligation under Public Contracts*, 20 Under Construction No. 1 (2018).

36. X.L. America, Inc. Professional, Environmental and Network Security Liability Policy—Architects, Consultants, and Engineers, LDD 050 1116 (2016), V.A.11, p.9.

Claims by Insureds

> [The Insurer will not defend or pay under this Policy for any **claim**] brought by the **Insured** or on the **Insured's** behalf against another **Insured** covered by this Policy.[37]

This exclusion is meant to prevent collusive claims but also serves as a disincentive for having multiple project participants covered under the same professional liability policy.[38] As noted previously, PL insurers typically do not permit parties who are not part of or related to the Insured to be added to the policy as Additional Insureds. Even if this were possible, the Insured versus Insured (or "IvI") exclusion would bar coverage for claims made by the Additional Insured against the Insured.

In a similar vein, PL policies typically exclude coverage for claims against the Insured made by entities that are owned, operated, or otherwise closely related to the Insured. For example:

Owned Entity

> [The Insurer will not defend or pay under this Policy for any **claim**] made against the **Insured** by any entity:
>
> 1. which is operated, managed, or controlled by the **Insured**;
> 2. in which the **Insured** has an ownership interest in excess of 49%; or
> 3. which wholly or partly owns, operates, or manages the **Insured**.[39]

Policies vary in defining what qualifies as an owned entity, so design professionals should review their policies as their business evolves in order to assure that they will qualify for coverage when it is needed.

---

37. CNA Professional Liability and Pollution Incident Liability Insurance Policy, CNA79034XX (04-2020) at IV.A (Exclusions).

38. Stephen D. Palley, Timothy E. Delahunt, John S. Sandberg & Patrick J. Wielinski Construction Insurance: A Guide for Attorneys and Other Professionals (ABA 2011), at 204.

39. CNA Professional Liability and Pollution Incident Liability Insurance Policy, CNA79034XX (04-2020) at IV.F (Exclusions).

E. Claims-Made and Reported Coverage Trigger

One of the most distinctive features of professional liability insurance is the claims-made and reported coverage trigger, which differs from the occurrence-based trigger that applies to most other insurance policies, including the Commercial General Liability policy. Under a claims-made and reported policy, the following conditions must be true for coverage to exist:

- The professional service that is the subject of the claim must have taken place on or after the Retroactive Date stated in the policy Declarations. Ideally, this is the first day of the firm's operations, so that all of the professional services performed by the firm will qualify.
- The claim (as defined by the policy) must be first made against the Insured and reported to the insurer (typically in writing) during the same policy period. Some policies allow claims to be reported during a short period of time (60 days is common) after the conclusion of the policy period.[40]

The key factor in determining coverage under a claims-made and reported policy is when the claim is made and reported to the insurer.[41] Assuming those events occur during the same policy period, the date of the complained-of professional service is irrelevant, so long as it occurs on or after the policy Retroactive Date.[42] Contrast the occurrence-based policy, where coverage is triggered when an occurrence or accident causes harm during the policy period, even if the claim is brought many years later.[43]

The following example will illustrate the operation of claims-made and reported policies.

---

40. *See, e.g.*, X.L. America, Inc. Professional, Environmental and Network Security Liability Policy—Architects, Consultants, and Engineers, LDD 050 1116 (2016), I.A (60 days); Lexington Insurance Company, Architects and Engineers Professional Liability Policy, LX4204 (07/13), I.B.4, p.4. (60 days). *But see* Berkley Insurance Company, Architects, Engineers & Consultants Policy, BDP0417001 (Insuring Agreements), p.1 (120 days).

41. *See* Lua v. QBE Ins. Corp., 421 F. Supp. 3d 1082, 1092 (D. Colo. 2019).

42. *See* Catlin Specialty Ins. Co. v. J.J. White, Inc., 309 F. Supp. 3d 345, 356–57 (E.D. Pa. 2018), *opinion clarified*, 387 F. Supp. 3d 583 (E.D. Pa. 2019).

43. *See* Lightening Rod Mut. Ins. Co. v. Southworth, 55 N.E.3d 1174, 1183 (Ohio Ct. App. 2016).

- January 1, 2020: Allgood Engineering (AE) begins operations and purchases a professional liability policy with a retroactive date of January 1, 2020. AE renews the policy annually with limits of $2 million per claim, $2 million in the aggregate.
- August 1, 2021: Engineer Mary Allgood unknowingly makes an erroneous calculation in her design of the structural supports for a large grain bin for Grain Elevator Company.
- September 1, 2022: The constructed project is put into service.
- October 1, 2023: The grain bin collapses, injuring two workers, spoiling thousands of bushels of grain, and preventing the grain elevator from doing business for the remainder of the season.
- February 1, 2024: Grain Elevator Company files suit against Allgood Engineering and Mary Allgood.
- February 5, 2024: The Complaint at Law is served upon Allgood Engineering and Mary Allgood. A written report is made to the PL insurer that same day.

This claim is made against the Insured and reported to the insurer during the 2024 policy period, so that policy applies, despite the fact that the engineer's miscalculation occurred back in 2021.

Let's consider a few alternative scenarios:

- AE failed to renew the policy at the end of the 2021 policy year and "went bare"—that is, failed to purchase renewal coverage. In this case, there is no coverage for the claim made in 2024 because there is no policy in force at the time the claim was made.
- Assume, as above, that AE went bare during what would have been the 2022 policy year but resumed purchasing coverage on January 1, 2023. After a gap in coverage, it is common for insurers to set the retroactive date on the first day of the new policy, rather than backdating the retroactive date to include a period during which the Insured had no professional liability coverage. If, accordingly, the retroactive date of the new policy and subsequent policies is January 1, 2023, there is no coverage because the engineer's calculation error occurred before that date.
- Suppose AE renewed its policy every year, but in 2022 decided to start purchasing lower policy limits and renewed for the 2023 and 2024 policy years with limits of $1 million per claim, $1 million in the aggregate. Despite the fact that the policy limits were $2 mil-

lion/$2 million when the error was made, the limits that apply are the ones in force in 2024, when the claim was made—namely, $1 million/$1 million.

The claims-made and reported policy is a bit like musical chairs—whatever policy "chair" is in force when the claim is made and the "music stops," is the policy upon which the design professional must rely on for coverage. If the chair in question turns out to be rickety, inadequate, or nonexistent, the design professional will lack PL coverage to support it in its hour of need.

I. Perils of Late Reporting

Under claims-made and reported policies, late reporting of claims may have disastrous consequences. Failure to report the claim during the policy period results in the loss of coverage.[44]

Often, late reporting is due to the firm's failure to recognize that a particular situation qualifies as a claim that must be reported under the policy. The definition of a claim differs from policy to policy, and it is critical that the insured familiarize itself with the exact contours of what must be reported to the insurer. Here is a typical definition:

> **Claim** means a demand for money or services, naming the Insured and alleging a **wrongful act**. . . .[45]

A wrongful act, under this policy, is "an act, error or omission, that causes liability in the performance of professional services."[46] Under this definition, a lawsuit or a demand for arbitration qualifies as a claim, but the definition takes in many other situations. For example:

- A "demand for money" might be a phone call from the client demanding that the design professional pay damages allegedly caused by its negligence. (Some policies require a written demand, but in that case, an email would suffice.)
- A "demand for services" would include the client's statement that it is withholding a certain portion of the design professional's fee as compensation for some alleged negligence.

---

44. *See* Gateway Residences at Exch., LLC v. Illinois Union Ins. Co., 917 F.3d 269, 274 (4th Cir. 2019).

45. CNA Professional Liability and Pollution Incident Liability Insurance Policy, CNA79034XX (04-2020) at III (Definitions).

46. *Id.*

It is easy to see how a design professional might dismiss either of these situations respectively as "client complaining" or "an accounts receivable problem" and fail to see that these situations are not just a business problem, but a claim that must be reported lest coverage be forfeited.

Late reporting is especially problematic when the Insured has changed carriers after the claim is made, but before the claim is reported. If the claim is made against the Insured, but not reported to the carrier during Carrier A's policy, and the Insured renews with Carrier B, the Insured will be in a fix. It will not be possible to satisfy the condition that the claim be made and reported in the same policy period, and moreover, any argument to Carrier A for leniency about the late report will fall upon deaf ears since the Insured is no longer a policyholder.

Design professionals can be reluctant to report claims because they fear that doing so will impair their ability to secure favorable renewal terms. This worry should be discussed with the broker and the insurer, but generally speaking, insurers are concerned with the policy "loss ratio"—a comparison of claims dollars paid by the insurer with premium dollars paid by the Insured over a fixed time period—and not with the number of claims reported. Many claims files are closed without a payment by the insurer, and their impact on the loss ratio is nil. On the other hand, failure to timely report claims jeopardizes coverage, so the scales should tip in favor of reporting when there is any doubt.

2. *Benefits of Circumstance Reporting*

There is another potential benefit for the Insured who is vigilant about detecting and reporting claims. Many policies permit the Insured to report a "pre-claim" situation, often termed a "Circumstance" in the policy definitions. For example:

> **Circumstance** means an event reported to the Insurer during the **policy term** from which the **Insured** reasonably expects that a **claim** could be made.[47]

There are two advantages to such reports. The first is that the Insured may receive "pre-claims assistance" in that the insurer will investigate the claim without cost to the Insured:

---

47. CNA Professional Liability and Pollution Incident Liability Insurance Policy, CNA79034XX (04-2020) at III (Definitions).

> **Pre-claims Assistance**. Until the date a claim is made, the Insurer may pay for all costs or expenses it incurs, at the Insurer's sole discretion, as a result of investigating a circumstance that the Insured reports in accordance with the Section of the Policy entitled CONDITIONS, the condition entitled The Insured's Rights and Duties in the Event of a **Circumstance**.[48]

By paying to employ experts in law, insurance, and construction during the early stages of a controversy, the insurer often can prevent a dispute from maturing into lengthy and expensive litigation. Payments under pre-claims assistance provisions are generally not subject to the deductible and are in addition to the Limit of Liability shown on the Declarations Page of the PL policy.

The second significant benefit of reporting a circumstance is that doing so "locks in" the limit, deductible, and policy terms in force at the time the circumstance is reported.

> **The Insured's Rights and Duties in the Event of a Circumstance.** If the **Insured** reports a **circumstance** for which there may be coverage under this Policy. . . . any **claim** or **related claims** that subsequently may be made against the **Insured** arising out of such **circumstance** shall be deemed to have been made on the date the Insurer received written notice of the **circumstance**.[49]

Even if the facts reported as a circumstance take years to ripen into a claim, that claim is deemed made on the date the circumstance is reported. This is true even when the Insured has since changed carriers, purchased lower limits, or ceased purchasing coverage altogether.

If there is any doubt in the Insured's mind regarding whether a situation rises to the level of a reportable circumstance under the applicable policy, the insured should discuss the relevant facts with the broker or insurance agent. There is no adverse underwriting impact associated with circumstance reports, so the Insured should in favor of reporting in order to secure for the insured the many benefits of pre-claims assistance.

---

48. *Id.* at II.B.
49. *Id.* at VI.C.

3. Extended Reporting Periods and "Tail" Coverage

If it is necessary to have a policy in place to report a claim, what happens when a design firm ceases to operate and stops renewing its PL coverage? What if a claim arises after the expiration of the firm's last PL policy?

Firms can extend the period of time for reporting claims beyond the policy expiration date by purchasing "tail" coverage, often in the form of an Extended Reporting Period ("ERP").[50]

Most PL policies afford a short "automatic" ERP (typically 60 days) if the policy is canceled or nonrenewed by either the insurance carrier or the Insured. However, in light of the fact that it can take several years after professional services are rendered for a claim to arise, design professionals who close their doors should strongly consider purchasing an "optional" ERP. This may extend the reporting time for a period of years (typically, one, two, or three years). It is important to understand that an ERP does *not* provide coverage for services rendered after the policy expires; it only extends the period of time for reporting claims that arise out of professional services provided prior to the policy expiration date.

Ideally, the terms upon which the ERP may be purchased will be set forth in the policy. For example:

> **Optional Extended Reporting Period**
>
> In the event of non-renewal or cancellation of this insurance for any reason by the INSURED, or if the Company should cancel this Policy or terminate it by refusing to renew, for reasons other than the INSURED'S non-payment of Premium and/or Deductible amount and/or non-compliance with the terms and conditions of this Policy, the INSURED:
>
> May purchase an Optional Extended Reporting Period of up to three (3) years or as otherwise required by the regulatory guidelines governing this type of insurance. The minimum premium for this Optional Extended Reporting Period will be one hundred percent (100%) of the expiring annual premium for a one year period, one hundred fifty percent (150%) of the expiring annual premium for a

---

50. *See* Gulf Ins. Co. v. TIG Ins. Co., 103 Cal. Rptr. 2d 305, 314 (Cal. Ct. App. 2001).

two (2) year period, and one hundred eighty-five percent of the expiring annual premium for a three (3) year period.[51]

Typically, as here, the cost of the ERP is stated as a percentage of the premium paid by the Insured for the expiring policy. Even when a multi-year ERP is purchased, the Limits of Liability available to pay claims reported to the ERP do not refresh every year. Whatever Limits of Liability remain on the final PL policy purchased by the firm are all that will be available for defense and settlement of all claims reported during the ERP.

Some carriers offer "retired professionals' policies" and other types of post-expiration coverage that may be advantageous to design firms in various stages of their life cycle.

F. Defense Inside the Limits

Professional liability policies are written with two limits of liability. The first, the per claim limit, is the total amount that the insurer will pay for any one claim, and the second, the aggregate limit, is the total amount that the insurer will pay for all claims made during the policy period. These limits may be the same, or, in some cases, the aggregate limit may be higher, depending on the needs of the Insured and the anticipated frequency and severity of claims.

Typically, design professionals' PL policies are written with defense costs *inside the limits.* This means that the legal costs expended to defend an Insured's claim can reduce and possibly exhaust the applicable limits of the policy, regardless of whether any indemnity payment is made. For this reason, PL policies are often called "declining limits" policies. Conversely, under a defense *outside the limits policy*—in which the only indemnity payments are capped by the policy limit—the insurer must spend whatever it takes to defend the claim. Commercial general liability policies, for example, are typically written with defense outside the limits.

One practical ramification of the declining limits feature of PL policies is that the Insured must consider defense costs in its determination of the proper level of PL policy limits. Another is that every dollar spent to defend the claim is a dollar that will be unavailable for settlement of that claim, so judicious decisions must be made about when and whether to invest in defending a claim as opposed to negotiating a timely settlement.

---

51. X.L. America, Inc. Professional, Environmental and Network Security Liability Policy—Architects, Consultants, and Engineers, LDD 050 1116 (2016), VII, p.11.

It should also be borne in mind that each year's policy limits are subject to depletion not just by claims made on current projects, but rather, at least in theory, on every project performed after the firm's retroactive date. Of course, applicable statutes of limitation and repose operate to terminate one's ability to bring suit against the insured firm. It is true that most claims develop within a few years of substantial completion. Still, the backlog of potential claims is worthy of consideration by the insured firm in determining the appropriate level of PL policy limits to purchase.

I. Project-Specific and Client-Specific Policy Endorsements

In response to project owners' concerns about depletion of PL policy limits, some insurance carriers offer endorsements to the practice policy that provide additional excess limits for a particular project (Specific Job Excess, or SJX) or a particular client (Specific Client Excess or SCX). Other insurers endorse the policy such that the additional limit is primary, rather than excess.

These endorsements can be a cost-effective alternative to increasing a design professional's practice policy limits across the board. They can also be a way for smaller firms that do not qualify for higher policy limits to meet requirements on a particular project. They are not an all-purpose solution, however, and have some drawbacks and limitations.

- Although the additional SJX/SCX limits are dedicated to the project, the underlying limits on the practice policy are subject to erosion by claims on the insured design firm's other unrelated projects.
- These solutions are endorsements to the practice policy, which is renewed annually. Accordingly, there is no way to know in advance the total cost of carrying these endorsements for the desired number of years. Carriers will offer an estimate of each year's renewal premium, but these are not binding, and will have no effect if the firm renews with a different carrier. Moreover, there is no guarantee that the SJX or SCX endorsement will be offered at future renewals.
- The project owner will need to verify that each renewal policy during the desired period includes the SJX or SCX endorsement.

IV. Project-Specific Professional Liability Insurance

So far, we have examined the professional liability "practice" policy that a design firm might purchase to cover all of the professional services performed by that firm on or after the policy retroactive date. We now turn our attention to project-specific professional liability ("PSPL") insurance, which provides coverage and dedicated limits for a single project.

The main attraction of PSPL policies for project owners is the alleviation of concerns that the practice policies carried by the various design professionals involved in the project will be depleted by claims on other project and prove inadequate to resolve any claims that might arise. The advantage for the design professional is clear: the PSPL policy provides an additional layer of "insulation" for the limits carried by the design professional on its practice policy. Furthermore, these policies are highly customizable to meet the specific needs of the project and its participants.

The PSPL policy provides coverage for claims made during the policy term (typically the period of design and construction of the project) as well as during a pre-set extended reporting period. The policy premium is a one-time charge, paid at the inception of the policy. This provides certainty about the cost, availability, and duration of coverage.

Typically, the PSPL policy is written to provide coverage to all design professionals involved in the project. This is said to minimize finger-pointing among design team members and their respective insurers when problems arise. It also affords the advantage of a single point of responsibility for claims handling, and a coordinated approach to claim resolution.

The chief disadvantage of PSPL policies is their cost. They are expensive and are therefore primarily appropriate only for very large projects. Project owners also may have concerns about the fact that the PSPL policy provides coverage to the entire design team, rather than the project owner or the design-builder. When claims arise, it will be the duty of the PSPL carrier to defend the design professionals.

Design professionals afforded coverage under a project policy should assure themselves of the extent and quality of that coverage, as it is their first line of defense. They should also verify that their practice policies sit in excess of the project policy to account for situations where its limits may be depleted by claims.

V. OPPI and CPPI

The Owner's Protective Professional Indemnity ("OPPI") is another potential solution to a project owner's concern that its design professional's PL policy limits are insufficient to cover a loss.[52] The owner is the Named Insured on the OPPI policy; no coverage is afforded to the design professional.

An OPPI policy is purchased by and provides first-party coverage to the project owner—not the design team—for losses caused by design negligence in excess of a predetermined primary limit to be met by the design team's annual practice policies, up to the limit provided by the OPPI policy. To the extent that the OPPI coverage is broader than a design firm's underlying practice policy, the OPPI policy can drop down and respond as primary coverage. An OPPI policy also covers the owner for third-party claims made directly against the owner for damages caused by the design team's negligence.

An OPPI policy allows the project owner to protect itself against the potential exhaustion of the design team's policy limits—even if those limits are depleted by claims unrelated to the owner's project—for a premium that may be as little as half the cost of a PSPL policy. OPPI does, however, have some disadvantages:

- OPPI insurance, unlike PSPL, does not offer the advantage of single-point claims handling. Until the underlying limit required by the OPPI policy is met through payment by the design team's practice policies, multiple design firms and their insurers may be involved in a single claim, each with its own view of the claim and approach to resolution until the claim exceeds the limit required on the OPPI policy. This may result in delays not only to claims resolution but to the project itself.
- If the project owner plans to include a limitation of liability provision in its contract with its design firm, this must be disclosed during the underwriting process, so that the OPPI policy can be structured to attach at the limitation amount, rather than exhaustion of the underlying policy limit. Otherwise, the owner risks having a coverage gap (or perhaps no coverage at all, depending on the policy's verbiage).
- OPPI affords no coverage to the design team, either for claims brought by the project owner or for claims brought by third parties. If a project owner indicates to the design team that "project-specific"

52. *First-party design coverage—Owner's protective professional indemnity coverage*, Bruner & O'Connor Construction Law § 11:579.

coverage will be purchased, the design team should verify that PSPL (which provides coverage to the design team) is meant, rather than OPPI (which provides none).

Contractors Protective Professional Indemnity (CPPI) operates similarly and is typically purchased by design-builders who contract with design professionals.

VI. Commercial General Liability Coverage

The focus of this chapter is primarily on the professional liability policy, but it is important to understand the interplay of PL coverage with the design firm's Commercial General Liability (GCL) policy.

The CGL policy is intended to provide coverage primarily for liability arising out of nonprofessional acts (violations of the personal, business, or property interests of private citizens) that result in bodily injury, property damage, or personal and advertising injury. It is designed to cover an Insured's liability arising out of incidents on the Insured's premises or from the nonprofessional aspects of the Insured's practice. In other words, the CGL policy covers nonprofessional negligent acts.

CGL coverage is written on an occurrence basis. As discussed previously, occurrence coverage is triggered when the accident or occurrence giving rise to the claim actually happens. The CGL policy in effect at the time the event or occurrence happened is responsible for the claim even if the claim is not made until years after the policy expires.

General liability coverage typically works on the principle that everything is covered except what is excluded. Therefore, most general liability policies include a significant number of exclusions from coverage, most of which can be insured through other types of policies. The CGL policy's most significant exclusion is coverage for professional liability claims.

The following sections review the three basic coverage areas of a CGL policy and provide some examples of how they might apply in the design professional arena. However, the complexity of general liability insurance coverage warrants consultation with a qualified insurance broker or agent to assess the liabilities associated with operating a design firm.

A. CGL Coverage

There are three basic coverage areas that comprise a CGL policy: (1) bodily injury and property damage (BI/PD); (2) personal and advertising injury; and (3) medical payments coverage.

I. Bodily Injury and Property Damage

Bodily injury/property damage provides coverage for the legal liability of an Insured for bodily injury or property damage to others arising out of nonprofessional negligent acts or for liability arising out of their premises or business operations. The CGL policy defines property damage as "physical injury to tangible property, including all resulting loss of use of that property."

Bodily injury is defined as "bodily injury, sickness or disease sustained by a person, including death resulting from any of these at any time" in Section V.3 of ISO CG 00 01 04 13. Death that results after a period of time from an earlier injury is covered by the policy in effect at the time the injury was sustained. The meaning of bodily injury is open to judicial interpretation. Some courts hold that mental injuries and emotional distress can be considered bodily injuries, even in the absence of physical bodily harm.

The following is an example of a BI/PD incident involving a surveyor working on an airport runway:

> The surveyor left his tripod and prism standing upright on the side of the runway when he left for lunch. A small Falcon 900 airplane came in for landing, and the leading edge of the right wing, which extended over the edge of the runway, clipped the equipment. The surveying equipment created a dent in the wing's leading edge, but there were no injuries. However, the repairs to the plane and other expenses, such as downtime, parts, and labor, totaled more than $114,000.[53]

This claim sets the stage for a coverage tug-of-war between the surveying firm's CGL insurer and PL insurer. The PL policy provides coverage for the firm's professional negligence; the CGL policy provides coverage for the firm's nonprofessional negligence. The CGL insurer may contend that the damage arose out of the surveyor's professional services and, therefore, was expressly excluded and should have been covered by the PL policy. For its part, the PL carrier may take the position that the claim did not arise from the surveyor's professional services, and thus should be covered by the CGL policy.

To avoid being caught in the middle of this coverage battle, the Insured should engage with its insurance broker, who will be experienced in bringing these situations to a reasonable conclusion.

---

53. This claim possibly could have been avoided if the surveyor had not left the tripod unattended on the job site. Any equipment used on a job site should be secured before leaving the site to avoid causing possible bodily injury or property damage.

The BI/PD coverage under the CGL policy also provides coverage for the Insured's liability arising out of (1) operation, maintenance, or use of a premises and (2) liability arising out of business operations. This includes the Insured's legal responsibility for bodily injury or property damage to others on the Insured's premises, as well as liability arising out of the Insured's business operations or work performed by independent contractors on the named Insured's behalf. For example:

> A visitor walks into a design firm's office lobby, slips on the marble flooring after a rainstorm, and breaks her ankle. The injured woman makes a claim against the design firm for her medical expenses resulting from her broken ankle.[54]

The design firm's CGL policy will cover this claim because it arises out of bodily injury on the Insured's premises.

2. *Personal and Advertising Injury*

The personal and advertising injury coverage under the CGL policy protects an Insured against liability arising out of certain offenses such as libel, slander, false arrest, infringing on another's copyright, malicious prosecution, use of another's advertising idea, and wrongful eviction, entry, or invasion of privacy.

Allegations of libel and slander, in particular, may arise in the course of a design professional's practice. Libel is a written statement about someone that is personally injurious to that person. Slander is similar, but the statement is spoken rather than written.[55] Here are some examples:

- Libel: An engineer makes derogatory comments about a construction contractor's performance or quality of work in a letter to the editor of a local newspaper.
- Slander: An architect makes vituperative remarks to a potential client about the reputation or past work of another architect.

Design professionals must be cautious about making comments, written or oral, about other professionals or members of the project team. Truth is a defense to libel and slander, so any statements made should be based on facts or couched as a professional opinion based on the facts presented.

---

54. This example illustrates the importance of maintaining safe building premises, proper warning signs for hazards, and prompt attention to hazardous situations that may increase the likelihood of an accident. It is also important to note that this policy does not provide BI/PD coverage for employee-related injuries. Such claims will likely be covered by workers' compensation insurance.

55. In other words, "Slander is said; libel is read."

As with BI/PD coverage, these claims present a potential conflict between CGL and PL coverage. Once again, the assistance of a broker or insurance agent who understands the business of design is invaluable in untangling the web of contested coverage.

3. Medical Payments

Coverage for medical payments includes payments for injuries sustained by members of the general public caused by an accident that takes place on an Insured's premises or when exposed to the Insured's business operations. Normally, injuries must be reported within one year of the accident.

Medical payments coverage can be triggered without legal action from a third party. This provides for prompt settlement of smaller medical claims without litigation. It is included in the CGL policy and pays for all necessary and reasonable medical, surgical, ambulance, hospital, professional nursing, and funeral expenses for a person injured or killed in an accident arising out of the premises or business operations of the Insured, regardless of negligence or liability.

There is no defense or legal liability coverage as there is with BI/PD liability and personal and advertising liability since coverage is provided on a no-fault basis.

B. Additional Insured Status on the CGL Policy

The CGL policy, unlike the PL policy, permits the Insured to name others as additional Insureds on the policy. This is typically done through standard form ISO endorsements to the policy, which have evolved since they were first issued in 1985.

A detailed review of each iteration of the ISO forms is beyond the scope of this chapter, but design professionals should be aware that revisions to the forms over time have narrowed the scope of coverage afforded to the additional Insured. For that reason, it is common for client-drafted insurance requirements to require older, outdated additional Insured endorsements that would afford broader coverage. Such actions may not be available to the Insured, so it is essential to review these requirements with the broker or insurance agent prior to the execution of the contract.

VII. Evidence of Insurance

Parties to design and construction contracts need to make certain that the other party has purchased the contractually required coverage. This can prevent parties from being unprotected in the event of a loss, and can forestall situations in which one party, regardless of fault, ends up making good a loss that was wholly or partially caused by another uninsured (or underinsured) party. Design professionals who retain subconsultants must monitor their compliance with insurance mandates because the design professionals often ends up holding the bag if their subconsultants are uninsured or underinsured.

Two types of documents are typically used to evidence coverage: binders and certificates of insurance.

A. Binders

An insurance binder is the equivalent of temporary insurance until a formal policy is issued. Once the insurance policy is issued, the binder is no longer in effect. A binder provides an interim or temporary policy, but it does not constitute part of the policy or create rights for the insured, other than its effective date, and remains subject to underwriting review of the risk intended to be covered. The binder can be canceled, but unless and until it is, the Insured continues to be covered and is insured. Binders should include as many express terms and conditions of the intended insurance coverage as can be provided to avoid ambiguity in the event of a loss before issuance of the policy.

B. Certificates of Insurance

Certificates of insurance evidence that an insurance policy is issued, the limits of liability in effect when the certificate is issued, the coverage period, and the type of insurance being addressed. There are standard certificates of insurance that provide limited information to a certificate holder. They do not create coverage, nor do they create any obligations for the insurance company that are not expressed in the policy. Some certificate holders seek to create legal obligations by requesting modifications to the standard certificate language, but most parties refuse to modify the certificates.

Generally speaking, a certificate of insurance does not obligate an insurance company to the individual or organizations to which the certificate is issued. Design professionals, construction managers, and general contractors typically require evidence of insurance from those parties whose actions can give rise to vicarious liability.

It is important to obtain certificates of insurance evidencing both professional liability and general liability coverage because, when either coverage is inadequate or unavailable, attorneys may assert legal theories in a claim that they hope will trigger coverage available under the other policy. Because insurance carriers' defense obligations are broader than their indemnity obligations, a considerable sum of money can be spent before these issues are sorted out. Remember that the defense obligations of an insurance carrier trigger not only deductible obligations but also the cost of defending a claim under a professional liability policy that is within the policy limits. As a consequence, inadequate or nonexistent general liability coverage can erode the limits available under the professional liability policy.

IX. Further Resources

Risk is inherent in professional design practice. Fortunately, excellent resources exist to help design professionals manage it, and they would be well advised to seek them out *before* trouble strikes.

Specialized insurance brokers serve as important partners in managing the risks of professional practice. A broker who understands the business of design and serves many design professionals is best suited to help a design firm determine what coverages are needed, what limits should be purchased, and which carriers can provide the proper mix of stability, financial security, and desirable terms. Such brokers can be extremely valuable sources of industry intelligence, risk management advice and training, contract negotiation and claims management guidance, and can help the design professional access similar resources offered by many PL carriers.

Another essential risk management resource for design firms is the counsel of a lawyer who is knowledgeable not just about the construction business generally, but specifically about the legal and business challenges faced by design firms. A contract that appears acceptable and insurable from the point of view of a construction contractor may be ruinous to a design firm, so its lawyer must appreciate the unique business and insurance matrix in which design professionals operate. Ideally, the design firm will forge this relationship long before a claim arises, because a knowledgeable lawyer can assist with contract review and answer legal questions that arise while running a design practice.

Finally, professional societies that serve design professionals can provide insight into practice issues, supply standard contractual language, give guidance regarding legislative impacts on the design professional, and provide general professional guidance. Perhaps most important, they provide invaluable opportunity for networking with and learning from other design professionals, along with other professionals who work with the design industry.

CHAPTER 9

Considerations for Subconsultant and Subcontract Agreements for Design Professionals and Construction Managers

L. TYRONE HOLT, CARRIE LYNN H. OKIZAKI

I. Introduction

This chapter provides guidance and recommendations for negotiating design professional subcontracts between the lead or prime design professional or construction manager (Prime Contractor) and its consultants and subcontractors. It provides practical guidance to recommended practices and procedures for documenting these subcontractual relationships.[1]

Today's construction projects typically require the services of a team consisting of two or more professionals, including architects, engineers, cost estimators, schedulers, construction managers, and related construction industry personnel, to deliver the full scope of professional services required for planning, design, and contract administration phases of a typical construction

1. The principles in this chapter are applicable to the CM at-risk procurement method rather than the CM agency, in which the CM enters into prime contracts as the agent for the owner.

project, regardless of the nature of the project. The composition of a project design or construction management team may range from a relatively simple two-person group consisting of an individual architect or designer and one structural engineer who work together to produce a simple three-to-five-sheet set of builder's plans for a single-family, stick-built residence to hundreds of architects, engineers, cost estimators, risk managers, construction managers, and specialty consultants who work together to produce thousands of very complex drawings or utilize sophisticated computer-based 3D designs for large commercial, governmental, industrial, or multifamily projects. One of the many characteristics that the single-family residence and large, complex project teams share is that each team will likely need one or more subconsultants or subcontractors[2] in order to complete its design services for the project.

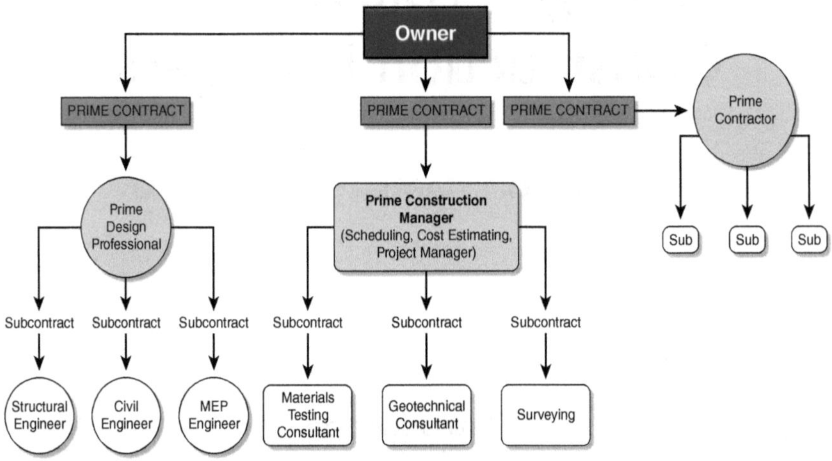

This chart reflects some typical contractual relationships for a construction project, including Prime Contractor/subcontractor roles discussed in this chapter. Construction projects are often made up of a complex web of contracts; each one is a small piece of the whole. Although it is often the negotiation of the prime contract that gets the most attention and care, there are some specific legal and risk allocation considerations that are unique to subconsultant and subcontractor contracts that are explored in this chapter.

2. Design professionals typically refer to their subcontractors as *subconsultants*. Construction or project managers may use the term *subconsultant* or *subcontractor*. In this chapter, the terms *subcontractor* and *subconsultant* will be used interchangeably to refer to the lower-tier subcontractors of the Prime Contractor.

II. The Process of Choosing a Subcontractor

As a part of its efforts to obtain the prime contract for a construction project, the Prime Contractor typically solicits and reviews oral or written fee/scope proposals from a preselected group of potential subcontractors before it begins to negotiate the prime contract with the owner. This is necessary in order for the Prime Contractor to fully develop the scope and price for the services it will provide to the owner.

Depending on the size and complexity of the project, the solicitation of the subcontractor's price and scope for its services for a particular project may be done in a formal request for proposal (RFP) process or by the Prime Contractor simply picking up the telephone to request an estimate from a trusted subcontractor it often uses.

Most public works or governmental projects have some sort of small and disadvantaged business and nondiscrimination policies to which both the Prime Contractor and its subcontractors must adhere. These policies will frequently require the Prime Contractor to solicit subcontractor proposals from businesses with whom it may have little or no prior experience and/or will prompt subcontractors to submit proposals to the Prime Contractor on an unsolicited basis. When working with unfamiliar subcontractors, it is important to perform some added due diligence. This means looking into the reputation of the business, checking references and financials, and ensuring that the subcontractor has the requisite experience.

Potential subcontractors who are interested in working on the project with the Prime Contractor will typically provide specific information that enables the Prime Contractor to evaluate the price, background, experience, and scope of services required for the project. Invariably, this information is submitted in writing and is generally referred to as a subcontractor proposal.

As part of the preparation and submission of the proposals, each prospective subcontractor should become appropriately familiar with the project, the project site, and all material aspects of the services it is proposing before submitting its proposal. There is usually a person (or persons) employed by the Prime Contractor who is the contact person from whom the potential subcontractor can either obtain the pertinent information or learn where such pertinent information can be obtained. After the potential subcontractor obtains basic information about the project, it should carefully review that information and direct any questions that are necessary to properly prepare the proposal for submission to the Prime Contractor in a timely manner. It is the subcontractor's responsibility to diligently review the requirements of the project and be absolutely certain that it is submitting an appropriate and fully responsive proposal. In the event the proposing potential subcontractor has questions or any part of the information obtained lacks clarity, the potential subcontractor should seek all relevant information from the Prime Contractor or other appropriate sources.

Practice Tip

Subcontractors must read, understand, and negotiate the proposed standard terms and conditions for the upstream prime contract and price into its proposal the risk and cost of any terms that the Prime Contractor may agree to on behalf of its subcontractors. Subcontractors should pay close attention to payment, insurance, rework, warranty, indemnity, dispute resolution, and other "flow-down" clauses (discussed later in this chapter). Where possible, the subcontractor should request that the Prime Contractor negotiate certain parts of the prime contract on the subcontractor's behalf.

A Prime Contractor may seek several competing proposals for a project, or it may elect to select a subcontractor with whom it has a long-term and successful relationship. In either case, each potential subcontractor should submit its proposal to the Prime Contractor in writing and in a timely manner for its review, comment, and use in preparing the Prime Contractor's proposal to the owner. The potential subcontractor should submit its price, scope of services, any exclusions from the scope of services, and all other changes to the proposed subcontract agreement in a timely manner. Typically, subcontractor proposals are signed and, as such, constitute the subcontractor's legally binding contractual offer to perform the services, subject to the terms and conditions in the proposal.

The Prime Contractor needs to make sure that it thoroughly reviews not just the subcontractor's scope and fee information but also any other terms, assumptions, or exclusions made by the subcontractor in its proposal. The failure to review and become generally familiar with all of the other terms and conditions submitted by the potential subcontractor is a very common mistake and frequently leads to significant problems for the Prime Contractor, who becomes responsible for the gaps in scope or responsibility not covered by the subcontract agreement.

To minimize the likelihood of these problems occurring, the Prime Contractor should carefully review and fully understand all of the terms, conditions, assumptions, and exclusions of each potential subcontractor's proposal.

It should identify and investigate any items that are inconsistent with its requirements for the prime contract. If any of the potential subcontractors' proposals conflict with the prime contract, the Prime Contractor must address and resolve those conflicts before it relies upon that proposal for its submission to the owner. One should not just look at the scope and fee because other terms and conditions may have equally significant impacts on the project.

Once the Prime Contractor has been selected for the project by the owner and before it signs the prime contract, it should once again carefully review all of the potential subcontractors' proposals and confirm all of the materials, elements, and details of those proposals. It should confirm that the terms and conditions of those proposals are compatible with the final, negotiated terms of the prime contract. Thereafter, once the prime contract is executed, the Prime Contractor should immediately turn its attention to negotiating the precise terms and conditions of its agreements with each of its sub-subcontractors.

Practice Tip

Once it has been awarded the project, and during the final negotiation phase with the owner, the Prime Contractor should review both the prime contract and its prospective subcontracts to make sure that the terms and conditions of each do not conflict and that the Prime Contractor is fully aware of its liabilities and responsibilities to each of the parties.

Upon the completion of the individual draft subcontracts for each potential subcontractor, the customized draft subcontract and a redacted copy of the prime contract should be sent to the subcontractor along with a request for a meeting to discuss the project, the potential subcontractor's proposal, and the draft proposed subcontract agreement. In its transmittal, the Prime Contractor should suggest that the parties and their counsel get together in person to discuss the project and the terms of the subcontract. While it is not necessary that all meetings be in person, it is advisable to hold at least one meeting in person with the subcontractor to discuss and review the subcontract agreement. If the Prime Contractor and the potential subcontractor have not worked together before, the first meeting (or, at the very least, one of the early meetings) should be at the potential subcontractor's office. This is an effective means by which the Prime Contractor can perform informal due diligence on the potential subcontractor's capabilities.

Library References

C.J.S. *Contracts* §§ 57, 59; C.J.S. *Counties* §§ 165–168; C.J.S. *Municipal Corporations* §§ 917–933; C.J.S. *Public Contracts* §§ 6, 14–24; C.J.S. *Schools and School Districts* §§ 409–414, 435, 761; C.J.S. *States* §§ 270, 280–288; C.J.S. *United States* § 113.
West's Key No. Digests, Contracts <KEY>17; Counties <KEY>115; Municipal Corporations <KEY>234; Public Contracts <KEY>5; Schools <KEY>80(2); States <KEY>98; United States <KEY>64.

III. Unique Legal Issues Applicable to the Prime Contractor/Subcontractor Relationship

Before turning to the mechanics of negotiating and drafting a subcontract agreement, it is important to consider legal issues unique to the Prime Contractor/subcontractor relationship. When a dispute arises between the Prime Contractor and the owner or the Prime Contractor and one or more of its subcontractors, it is important to know each party's rights and obligations to the project and to each other. The legal analysis relating to the liability exposure of each of the parties depends on the relationship between and among the design team, the construction team, the owner, and/or the construction manager (CM); the likelihood of a particular jurisdiction to enforce common contractual clauses; the type of project; the type of services that are to be provided; and the applicable law relating to the issues of privity, economic loss, indemnity, and negligence. This section focuses on some of the more common liability issues that arise in Prime Contractor/subcontractor relationships.

In construction projects, the contractual relationships define and govern each of the parties' rights and obligations. In most cases, the Prime Contractor will be vicariously liable for the acts and omissions of its subcontractors. Additionally, the Prime Contractor has certain obligations under its subcontract, most notably payment to the subcontractor, that are dependent on the owner's actions. As a result, many Prime Contractors utilize various risk-shifting or risk-allocating contract clauses that limit their liability to both the owner and the subcontractor. Whether one is representing the Prime Contractor or the subcontractor, it is important to recognize and deal with these contract issues that may arise in the Prime Contractor/subcontractor context.

A. Vicarious Liability, Indemnification, and Contribution

When the Prime Contractor enters into the prime contract and various subcontracts, it is in contractual privity with both the owner and the subcontractors.

As a result, the Prime Contractor is responsible to the owner for the acts and/or omissions of its subcontractors.[3] This, in its simplest terms, is the concept of vicarious liability.

Courts employ several legal theories when holding the Prime Contractor liable for any errors, acts, omissions, or breaches of contract caused by its subcontractors. Using agency law, a court may view the subcontractors as agents of the Prime Contractor, holding the Prime Contractor responsible for the subcontractors' conduct.[4] Additionally, the owner or the employer may have a breach of contract action against the Prime Contractor for errors caused by the subcontractors, depending on the terms of the contract.[5] For example, the contract may provide that the design professional is liable for the work of subcontractors he or she hires. In some jurisdictions, the Prime Contractor may also be liable under tort law, which imposes on the design professional the duty to exercise a reasonable degree of care.[6]

---

3. *See, e.g.*, Scott v. Potomac Ins. Co., 217 Or. 323, 341 P.2d 1083 (1959) (architect held liable for failure of heating system designed by subconsultant engineer); Garver &Garver, P.A. v. Little Rock Sanitary Sewer Comm., 300 Ark. 620, 781 S.W.2d 24 (1989) (engineer held liable for supplier failing to meet specifications); Playskool, Inc. v. Elsa Benson, Inc., 147 Ill. Ct. App. 3d 292, 497 N.E.2d 1199 (1986) (architect held liable for failure of pre-cast concrete floor designed and fabricated by its subconsultants); Eastover Corp. v. Martin Builders, 543 So. 2d 1358 (La. Ct. App. 1989) (architect held liable for its mechanical consultant's failure to detect plumbing defect); R.D. Sepper Co. v. Venetian Iron Works, Inc., No. 89-C4174, 1990 U.S. Dist. LEXIS 17706 (N.D. Ill. Dec. 31, 1990) (architect held liable for its structural engineer consultant's failure to provide adequate specifications).

4. *See, e.g.*, Bayuk v. Edson, 236 Cal. Ct. App. 2d 309, 46 Cal. Rptr. 49 (1965); Hewitt v. NY 70th Street LLC, 126 N.Y.S.3d 11, 13 (App. Div. 2020).

5. *See* Getzchman v. Miller Chem. Co., 232 Neb. 885, 898, 443 N.W.2d 260, 270 (1989) ("If there is an express contract for architectural services, an architect's duties are determined by the contract for the architect's employment."); Kahn v. Terry, 628 So. 2d 390 (Ala. 1993) (quoting *Getzchman*).

6. *See, e.g.*, H. Elton Thompson &Assoc., P.C. v. Williams, 164 Ga. Ct. App. 571, 572, 298 S.E.2d 539, 540 (1982) ("The law imposes upon persons performing . . . engineering[ ]and other professional and skilled services the obligation to exercise a reasonable degree of care, skill and ability, which generally is taken and considered to be such a degree of care and skill as, under similar conditions and like surrounding circumstances, is ordinarily employed by their respective professions.") (citations omitted); Milton J. Womack, Inc. v. House of Representatives, 509 So. 2d 62, 64 (La. Ct. App. 1987) ("The architect's duty is not to provide perfect plans but to exercise the degree of professional care and skill customarily employed by other architects in the

In an attempt to mitigate the liability exposure arising from agency law, some standard contracts describe subcontractors as independent contractors rather than agents of the design professional.[7] Moreover, independent of any contractual language, courts have held that the Prime Contractor is not liable for any acts by its subcontractor if the design subcontractor (1) retained control over the manner and means of the work or (2) was only responsible to the Prime Contractor.[8] Nevertheless, a court may still hold the subcontractor to be an agent of the prime professional depending on the amount of control exercised by the Prime Contractor.

Another method that Prime Contractors use to shift liability to their responsible subcontractors is incorporating into the subcontract the legal concepts of indemnification and contribution. However, note that the statutes governing the application of indemnity and contribution vary from jurisdiction to jurisdiction. Therefore, it is important to determine how applicable statutes will enforce or imply indemnity and contribution principles as they relate to the Prime Contractor/subcontractor relationship. Often, these statutes dictate how such clauses must be drafted. For example, many jurisdictions have statutes that declare provisions that require one party to indemnify another party for the first party's own negligence as void because such broad indemnity provisions are against public policy. Additionally, whether a state has adopted joint and several liability or applies comparative fault principles can also affect the impact of such clauses.

Liability on a particular project may be shifted between a Prime Contractor and its subcontractors or among the subcontractors themselves through the

---

same general area."); Nelson v. Commonwealth, 235 Va. 228, 236, 368 S.E.2d 239, 244 (1988) ("Absent a provision to the contrary, implicit in every contract of employment between an Owner and an architect is the duty of the architect to 'exercise the care of those ordinarily skilled in the business.' . . . This professional standard of care applies to the administration of project construction as well as to project design.") (citations omitted); *see also* Winsted Land Dev. v. Design Collaborative Architects, P.C., No. CV 960071571, 1999 Conn. Super. LEXIS 2180 (Conn. Super. Ct. Aug. 12, 1999); Riggins v. Bechtel Power Corp., 44 Wn. Ct. App. 244, 722 P.2d 819 (Wash. Ct. App. 1986); Laukkanen v. Jewel Tea Co., 222 N.E.2d 584 (Ill. Ct. App. 1966); Donnelly Constr. Co. v. Oberg/Hunt/Gilleland, 677 P.2d 1292 (Ariz. 1984); Vonasek v. Hirsch & Stevens, Inc., 221 N.W.2d 815 (Wis. 1974); Seiler v. Levitz Furniture Co., 367 A.2d 999 (Del. 1976).

7. *See, e.g.*, AIA Doc. C401-2017, Standard Form of Agreement Between Architect and Consultant, at Section 1.4.

8. *See* Schoedinger v. Hess, No. 99AP-1254, 2000 Ohio Ct. App. LEXIS 2409 (Ohio Ct. App. June 8, 2000).

incorporation of an indemnification clause in their contracts. An indemnification clause shifts all or a portion of the liability from one party to another "in a manner that would not have occurred in a predictable manner under common law in the absence of the contract."[9] The scope of a contractual indemnity provision may range from a somewhat narrow obligation of requiring one party to reimburse the other for actual damages paid to a third party following an assessment of damages to the much broader obligation of one party to provide legal counsel for the defense of another party based upon allegations that, if proved, would come within the scope of the indemnity provision.

Some states also recognize equitable indemnification as a part of their common law. Under this principle, if "a passively negligent tortfeasor is required solely through operation of law . . . to pay for damages to a third person which have been primarily caused by the active negligence of another . . . the active tortfeasor will be held to be the indemnifier of the passive tortfeasor."[10] Therefore, with equitable indemnification, one party may be required to indemnify the other as if there was a contractual indemnification clause in place *if* that tortfeasor actively caused the damages paid for by the passive tortfeasor.[11] Although the phrase "equitable indemnity" has been adopted, several states have adopted a hybrid of the concepts of indemnification and contribution.[12]

A second way in which liability may be shifted among multiple subcontractors or between the Prime Contractor and its subcontractor is through

---

9. Robert L. Meyers & Debra A. Perlam, *Risk Allocation through Indemnity Obligations in Construction Contracts*, 40 S.C. L. Rev. 898, 990 (1989); *see, e.g.*, Marino Constr. Co. v. Renner Architects, 214 Wis. 2d 589, 571 N.W.2d 923 (Wis. Ct. App. 1997); Kehoe v. Commonwealth Edison Co., 296 Ill. Ct. App. 3d 584, 694 N.E.2d 1119 (1998).

10. Green Constr. Co. v. Williams Form Engineering Corp., 506 F. Supp. 173, 178 (W.D. Mich. 1980).

11. *See, e.g.*, Woolard v. JLG Indus., Inc., 210 F.3d 1158 (10th Cir. 2000); Medallion Dev., Inc. v. Converse Consultants, 113 Nev. 27, 930 P.2d 115 (1997); District of Columbia v. Murtaugh, 728 A.2d 1237 (D.C. Cir. 1999); Beitzel v. City of Coeur d'Alene, 121 Idaho 709, 827 P.2d 1160 (1992); Winnsboro v. Wiedeman-Singleton, Inc., 307 S.C. 128, 414 S.E.2d 118 (1992); Berschauer/Phillips Constr. Co. v. Seattle Sch. Dist. No. 1, No. 38966-1-I, 1997 Wash. Ct. App. LEXIS 1801 (Wash. Ct. App. Oct. 27, 1997).

12. *See, e.g.*, Benner v. Wichman, 874 P.2d 949 (Alaska 1994) (recognizing right of "equitable apportionment" following state abolition of right to contribution); Far West Fin. Corp. v. D & S Co., 46 Cal. 3d 796, 760 P.2d 399 (Cal. 1988) (concept of comparative equitable indemnity covers whole range of apportionment of liability).

contribution. Contribution is a "[r]ight that gives one of several persons who are liable on a common debt the ability to recover proportionately from each of the others when that one person discharges the debt for the benefit of all."[13] Many states recognize the right to contribution following damages paid for negligent design or construction either under their common law or by statute.[14] Several states recognize a statutory right to contribution, often stemming from comparative negligence principles rather than one grounded in the common law.[15]

B. Exculpatory, Risk Allocation, and Limitation of Liability Clauses

A subcontractor may also seek to limit its liability to the Prime Contractor through the use of a risk allocation or limitation of liability clause. Clauses limiting the liability of a construction professional are frequently found in construction contracts. For example, a structural engineer may limit its liability for performance under the subcontract to the fee earned on the project. These clauses, if clear and unambiguous, will normally be enforced by a court or arbitration panel. However, the laws of each jurisdiction should be reviewed to ensure that such clauses are not void as against public policy or that some unique legal formalities are required to assure their enforceability. A Prime Contractor or subcontractor that is bound by a risk allocation or limitation of liability clause is also well-advised to check with its insurance advisor to make sure that the clause is within the scope of its insurance coverage.

While the courts in some states have never directly addressed the enforceability of limitation of liability clauses contained in professional services contracts, they most likely have, however, considered the enforceability of exculpatory clauses in other contexts. Exculpatory clauses are very similar to those limiting liability; while a limitation of liability places a cap on damages recoverable by the other party to the contract, an exculpatory clause relieves one party of its liability entirely. In some cases, a court will uphold a limitation

---

13. Contribution, Black's Law Dictionary (11th ed. 2019).

14. *See, e.g.*, Hartford Accident & Indem. Co. v. Scarlett Harbor Assoc., 109 Md. Ct. App. 217, 674 A.2d 106 (Md. Ct. Spec. Ct. App. 1996); Standhardt v. Flintkote Co., 84 N.M. 796, 508 P.2d 1283 (1973).

15. *See, e.g.*, Brochner v. Western Ins. Co., 724 P.2d 1293 (Colo. 1986); Mejia v. Quest Diagnostics, Inc., 241 N.J. 360, 371 (2020); Rothberg v. Reichelt, 270 A.D.2d 760, 705 N.Y.S.2d 115 (2000); Clearwater v. L.M. Duncan & Sons, Inc., 466 So. 2d 1116 (Fla. Ct. App. 1985); Good v. Lemcon Dev., Inc., No. 12837, 1992 Ohio Ct. App. LEXIS 847 (Ohio Ct. App. Feb. 24, 1992).

of liability clause where certain exculpatory or indemnity provisions would be unenforceable.[16] In other cases, courts have held limitation of liability clauses void as contrary to that jurisdiction's anti-indemnity statute.[17]

C. Payment Clauses

Timely payment for work performed on a construction project is one of the primary concerns for both Prime Contractors and subcontractors. Therefore, construction contracts frequently include payment provisions that attempt to condition payment on receipt of payment from the upstream party and/or require payment within a certain time frame of the receipt of payment by the upstream party.

Even the largest architect/engineering (A/E) firms and general contractors cannot afford to routinely pay their subcontractors over an extended period without first receiving payment from the owner. Issues arise between the Prime Contractor and its subcontractor when payment from the owner or Prime Contractor's client is late or not forthcoming, or when a dispute arises regarding the services provided by the Prime Contractor that may be unrelated to services provided by all but one of its subcontractors, thereby causing the owner to withhold payment due everyone. These issues are so common they should be addressed as a fundamental provision of the subcontract. In more extreme situations, the owner may become insolvent or otherwise fail to make payment to the Prime Contractor, even though the Prime Contractor and its subcontractors have fulfilled their contractual obligations. Then, the challenge is determining which party can best bear the risk of the owner's nonpayment. Normally, without including risk-shifting provisions in its subcontract agreements, the Prime Contractor will bear the risk of making payments to its subcontractors for work performed despite the owner's nonpayment. However, two commonly used contract clauses may shift some

---

16. *See, e.g.*, Valhal Corp. v. Sullivan Assocs., Inc., 44 F.3d 195 (3rd Cir. 1995) (upholding a limitation of liability provision under Pennsylvania law stating that "[l]imitation of liability clauses are not subject to the same stringent standards applied to exculpatory and indemnity clauses"); Mentis Sciences, Inc. v. Pittsburgh Networks, LLC, No. 2019-548, 2020 WL 5637697, at *4–5 (N.H. Sup. Ct. Sept. 22, 2020); Marbro, Inc. v. Borough of Tinton Falls, 688 A.2d 159 (N.J. Super. 1996) (holding limitation of liability clause between municipality and engineer enforceable); Markborough California, Inc. v. Superior Court, 277 Cal. Rptr. 919 (Ct. App. 1991).

17. *See* City of Dillingham v. CH2M Hill Northwest, Inc., 873 P.2d 1271 (Alaska 1994) (legislative history of Alaska's statute reveals that it was intended to prohibit not only indemnity clauses but also limitation of liability clauses).

or all of this risk to the subcontractor. These are known as the *pay-when-paid* and the *pay-if-paid* clauses.

In general, pay-when-paid clauses are construed merely as timing mechanisms and do not operate to defer payment indefinitely. In other words, these clauses merely provide a general contractor with some reasonable period within which to make payment. The American Institute of Architects (AIA) A401 and the Associated General Contractors (AGC) 650 subcontract forms contain pay-when-paid terms.

From a subcontractor's perspective, these clauses are preferable to pay-if-paid clauses because they do not completely shift the risk of the owner's nonpayment to the subcontractor. With a pay-when-paid clause, as long as the cause for the owner's nonpayment to the general contractor is not related to the subcontractor's work, the general contractor will remain liable to the subcontractor immediately following the expiration of a reasonable time period. The time period is like a grace period for the general contractor, but if the general contractor does not receive payment from the owner through no fault of the subcontractor, the general contractor will still be liable to the subcontractor. An example of a simple pay-when-paid clause is "Final payment to Subcontractor will occur within thirty days of payment to Contractor by owner."

On the other hand, pay-if-paid clauses will preclude a subcontractor from recovering payment from the Prime Contractor if the Prime Contractor is never paid by the owner. In other words, the risk of the owner's nonpayment is shifted to the subcontractor. An example of a pay-if-paid clause follows:

> The Contractor shall be under no obligation to make any payment to the Subcontractor except to the extent that the Contractor has received funds from the owner for the work performed by the Subcontractor. The Subcontractor agrees that payment by the owner is an express condition precedent to contractor's obligation to pay subcontractor. Subcontractor will not be entitled to payment by the Contractor for work performed if, for any reason, including the owner's insolvency or lack of available funds, the owner fails to pay the Contractor in accordance with the General Contract.

When enforced, these clauses forfeit the subcontractor's right to payment under the contract when the Prime Contractor does not receive payment from the owner. However, courts disfavor these provisions and, therefore, require that they be clear and unambiguous. Some states, including New York and California, will not enforce pay-if-paid clauses at all, holding them to be void against public policy.[18] Additionally, North Carolina and Wisconsin have passed statutes voiding such clauses,[19] while other jurisdictions have statutes that do not void pay-if-paid clauses outright but place limits on their enforceability.

Practice Tip

During the negotiation of the contract, make sure that all parties understand the contractually mandated timing for payment, particularly where there is a paid-when-paid or a paid-if-paid clause. The anticipated cycle should include the amount of time it takes (1) for a subcontractor's invoice to be reviewed and approved by the Prime Contractor, (2) for the Prime Contractor to prepare its own invoice that includes the subcontractor's invoice to the owner, (3) for the owner to review and approve the Prime Contractor's invoice including all of its subcontractors, (4) for the owner to pay or reject the invoice, and (5) for payment to be received by the Prime Contractor and paid to the subcontractor. The delay in payment to the subcontractor may cause cash-flow issues for the subcontractor that may impede or delay its services.

D. Insurance Issues

In allocating the risk among multiple parties, proper insurance coverage is essential. Many construction contracts, including the forms published by the Engineers Joint Contract Documents Committee (EJCDC), require that certain parties be listed as "additional insureds" on their Commercial General Liability (CGL) policy. Usually, additional insureds are parties who are upstream from the policyholder. For example, owners have often required general contractors to buy liability insurance that names the owners as additional insureds. In turn, general contractors often require subcontractors to do the same for the general contractor and possibly other upper-tier subcontractors.

Additional insured endorsements allow upstream parties to make a claim directly to the potentially liable party's insurer. For example, if an owner finds

18. Wm. R. Clarke Corp. v. Safeco Ins. Co., 15 Cal. 4th 882, 64 Cal. Rptr. 2d 578, 938 P.2d 372 (1997); Crosno Construction, Inc. v. Travelers Casualty and Surety Company of America, 47 Cal. App. 5th 940, 964 (App. Ct. 2020); West-Fair Elec. Contractors v. Aetna Cas. &Sur. Co., 87 N.Y.2d 148, 638 N.Y.S.2d 394, 661 N.E.2d 967 (1995).

19. *See* N.C. Gen. Stat. § 22C-2 (2020) and Wis. STAT. ANN. § 779.135 (2019).

a construction defect, he or she is most likely to sue the general contractor, even if the defect was caused by one of the general contractor's subcontractors. The endorsement allows the general contractor to make a claim directly on the responsible subcontractor's insurance.

In essence, parties named as additional insureds are entitled to much of the same benefits as the primary insured. Often, these types of arrangements exist even if the additional insured has its own insurance policy. However, usually the policy against which an additional insured claims will be primary and noncontributory, meaning that the limits of that policy must be exhausted before the additional insured's own coverage is triggered. Additionally, the additional insured may be entitled to coverage for damages caused by its own negligence, something that would normally be barred if the additional insured was a third-party claimant against the policyholder. Allowing coverage in such instances acts like a broad form indemnity provision in the contract—that is, forcing one party to indemnify the other for the other's own negligence, which circumvents many states' anti-indemnity laws.

Subcontractors or Prime Contractors who agree to grant additional insured protection to others should be aware of some adverse consequences. These include the risk of exhausting the policyholder's insurance coverage and, for the cost of deductibles and higher premiums incurred, defending the indemnitee's negligence.

Alternatives to additional insured provisions include other available insurance products. For example, owners and contractors protective (OCP) policies, which are separate and distinct from the insured's CGL policy, provide vicarious liability coverage to the policyholder for damages arising from the insured's general supervision of the construction work. Additionally, on large projects, Owner Controlled or Contractor Controlled Insurance Programs (OCIP) or (CCIP) are known as "wrap-up" or "full-wrap" policies where all participants on a project are covered under one policy provided by either the owner or the Prime Contractor.

On the design side, a project professional liability policy (Project Policy) is an alternative insurance product for large projects involving multiple design professionals. Under such a policy, coverage applies to design services provided to the project, rather than an individual firm employed on the project. Rather than having overlapping Project Policies for each design professional employed on the project, where gaps and conflicts in coverage may arise, a Project Policy covers the prime design professional as well as its subcontractors for their collective work on a project. Usually a Project Policy replaces the design professionals' practice policies with regard to services provided for that project, although members of the project design team may have the right to carry their practice policies as excess coverage. To assure that coverage will apply against any potential claims arising out of the project, an extended reporting period should be purchased so that coverage is maintained until the applicable statute of repose has expired.

Practice Tip

Make certain that terms used in the insurance sections of the contracts that are signed are fully understood, and address any related issues. For example, when a contract requires "additional insured" coverage or the parties agree to purchase a Project Policy with a significant deductible, consider drafting a deductible payment agreement to fairly allocate the insurance deductible among the various insureds should a claim arise. For design professionals, one straightforward way in which to divide the payment is to require each consultant to pay the same percentage of the deductible as the total design fees it will receive.

E. Dispute Resolution

If a dispute arises among the parties on a construction project and all efforts to resolve the conflict by informal negotiation fail, there are other more formal dispute resolution methods available to parties who wish to avoid litigation. These dispute resolution procedures, collectively termed Alternative Dispute Resolution or ADR, are usually less costly and more expeditious than litigation, and they are widely used in construction disputes. In fact, some ADR techniques, such as arbitration and mediation, are so popular that calling them "alternative" is somewhat of a misnomer.

ADR procedures are especially popular in the construction industry in light of the fact that several of the standard contracts, including those from the AIA, incorporate optional mediation and/or arbitration clauses.[20] Many states have enacted statutes that regulate ADR procedures, including some version of the Uniform Arbitration Act.[21] There are a few issues that Prime Contractors

---

20. *See, e.g.*, AIA Doc. A101-2017, Section 6.2, and AIA Doc. A201-2017 Sections 15.3 and 15.4.

21. *See, e.g.*, Alaska Stat. § 9.43.010 to § 9.43.180 (2019); Ark. Code § 16-108-201 to § 16-108-233 (2019); Colo. Rev. Stat. § 13-22-201 to § 13-22-507 (2019); Del.

and subcontractors should consider before agreeing to one form of dispute resolution over another.

The first issue is that many construction disputes involve multiple parties and a range of claims. However, parties cannot be forced to mediate or arbitrate a dispute except through an express contractual agreement. Therefore, if ADR is the preferred method of dispute resolution, it is in the best interests of the owner and the Prime Contractors to ensure that all of the subcontract agreements contain similar ADR provisions. Otherwise, a party may be forced to litigate a dispute in two different forums with the risk of differing outcomes.

> *Example:* Assume that an owner sues the A/E for a design error caused by the A/E' s structural engineer. However, the A/E' s prime contract contains an arbitration provision with mandatory mediation, but the A/E's subcontract does not. Rather than being allowed to join the structural engineer as a third party to the arbitration, *passing through* the owner's claim to the structural engineer, the A/E must first defend the arbitration on behalf of its engineer, and then sue the engineer in state court. If the engineer is found at fault in the arbitration, but not in the litigation, the result will leave the A/E in an unfortunate situation.

Practice Tip

The Prime Contractor should review all dispute resolution procedures in both the prime contract and each of its subcontracts to ensure that all parties are required to adhere to the same dispute resolution process. Additionally, if all parties agree to resolve the dispute through arbitration, there should be some language in the contract that allows joinder of all parties and claims in a single proceeding.

Code Ann. § 10-5701 to § 10-5725 (2019); Fla. Stat. ch. 682.01 to § 682.22 (2020); Haw. Rev. Stat. § 658A-1 to § 658A-29 (2019); Idaho Code § 7-901 to § 7-922 (2020); 710 Ill. Comp. Stat. § 5/1 to § 5/23 (2019); Ind. Code § 34-57-2-1 to § 34-57-2-22 (2020); Ky. Rev. Stat. § 417.045 to § 417.240 (2020); Me. Rev. Stat. tit. 14, § 5927 to § 5949 (2020); Md. Code Ann., Cts. & Jud. Proc. § 3-201 to § 3-234 (2020); Mass. Gen. Laws ch. 251, § 1 to § 19 (2020); Minn. Stat. § 572b.01 to § 572b.31 (2020); Mo. Rev. Stat. § 435.350 to § 435.470 (2020); Mont. Code Ann. § 27-5-111 to § 27-5-324 (2019); Neb. Rev. Stat. § 25-2601 to § 25-2622 (2020); N.M. Stat. Ann. § 44-7a-1 to § 44-7a-32 (2020); N.C. Gen. Stat. § 1-569.1 to § 1-569.31 (2020); Tenn. Code Ann. § 29-5-301 to § 29-5-320 (2020); Va. Code Ann. § 8.01-581.01 to § 8.01-581.016; Vt. Stat. Ann. tit. 12, § 5651 to § 5681 (2020).

F. Flow-Down Clauses

Flow-down clauses are contract provisions by which the parties incorporate all or certain terms of the construction or design contract between the owner and the Prime Contractor into that of the lower-tier subcontractor. In other words, the subcontractor agrees to be bound by the obligations and responsibilities that the Prime Contractor has assumed toward the owner. Additionally, a well-crafted flow-down clause may allow the Prime Contractor to reduce its total exposure to its subcontractors by limiting its damages to only those recovered by the Prime Contractor from the owner and "provides a means to pass through to the responsible subcontractors the contractor's damage exposure to the owner."[22]

In addition to increasing the subcontractor's liability to the Prime Contractor, flow-down clauses may severely reduce the subcontractor's ability to recover damages on its contract, especially if the prime contract contains limitations of liability, limitations regarding rights to payment, or other enforceable exculpatory provisions such as no damages for delay or waiver of consequential damages.[23]

Often, it is difficult for subcontractors to remove these clauses from their contracts due to lack of bargaining power with the Prime Contractor. One commentator has suggested that one way to make such clauses more balanced is to insist on a flow-down clause that imposes reciprocal obligations: "For example, if the subcontractor assumes the Prime Contractor's obligations to the owner, then the Prime Contractor should be asked to assume the owner's obligations to the contractor, including the obligation of payment."[24]

However, not all flow-down clauses are necessarily detrimental to the rights of the subcontractor. There are instances where the prime contract actually affords the subcontractor more rights than the subcontract. These added benefits include access to "alternative dispute resolution,[25] payment terms,

22. Andrew Howard, *Flow-Down Clauses*, The Construction Contracts Book: How to Find Common Ground in Negotiating Design and Construction Contract Clauses 9–10 (Daniel S. Brennan et al. eds., 2004).

23. L&B Constr. Co. v. Ragan Enters., Inc., 482 S.E.2d 279, 281–83 (Ga. 1997) (flow-down provision incorporating "no damages for delay" clause from prime contract "remove[d] any conceivable doubt" that subcontractor's recovery was limited to time extension and was prevented from seeking monetary damages resulting from contractor's two-year delay on project).

24. Howard, *supra* note 22, at 9.

25. Turner Constr. Co. v. Midwest Curtainwalls, Inc., 187 Ill. App. 3d 417, 252–53 (App. Ct. 1989) (subcontractor entitled to arbitrate its claims where prime contract contained an arbitration clause but subcontract did not).

notice requirements, completion dates, delay and liquidated damages, indemnity obligations, and conditions of default."[26] To successfully evaluate whether a flow-down provision means added risks or benefits to the subcontractor, the subcontractor must take the time to review and examine the prime contract.

G. Applicability of Economic Loss Rule

While the contract is king on construction projects, tort principles regularly come into play. Most notable is the standard of care required of all design professionals, including consultants. While compliance with the standard of care is often made an express obligation under the contract or subcontract, its genesis is in negligence principles. In other words, if an A/E has breached the standard of care (acted in a way contrary to what a prudent A/E would do in that location under similar circumstances), the A/E has both been negligent and breached its contract. The economic loss rule, as discussed elsewhere in this book, is a judicially created doctrine that provides a party that is prohibited from suing in tort to recover purely economic damages from the breach of a contractual obligation.[27] Under today's modern pleading rules, it is not uncommon for a plaintiff to allege a cause of action against the contractor or design professional for both breach of contract and negligence. However, in the absence of contractual language holding a particular party to a higher standard of care than that imposed by law, the standard of proof for breach of contract will, in most cases, be essentially the same as for negligent violation of a duty.[28] As a result, states in which the courts adhere to the economic loss doctrine will bar such actions in tort.[29]

---

26. HOWARD, *supra* note 22, at 10.

27. Economic loss is defined in the construction context as "the cost to repair or replace defective materials, damage to a structure, diminution in value of a damaged structure not repaired, loss of use or delay in utilizing property for its intended purposes and related lost profits, lost revenue, and costs." 6 BRUNER & O'CONNOR CONSTRUCTION LAW § 19:10 (2005) (citations omitted).

28. *See* Lee County v. Southern Water Contractors, Inc., 298 So. 2d 518 (Fla. Ct. App. 1974).

29. *See, e.g.*, National Steel Erection, Inc. v. J.A. Jones Constr. Co., 899 F. Supp. 268 (N.D. W. Va. 1995); Mentis Sciences, Inc. v. Pittsburgh Networks, LLC, No. 2019-548, 2020 WL 5637697, at *5 (N.H. Sup. Ct. Sept. 22, 2020); World Trade Co. v. Westinghouse Elec. Corp., 256 A.D.2d 263, 682 N.Y.S.2d385, 39 U.C.C. Rep. Serv. 2d 1053 (1st Dept. 1998); Anderson Elec. v. Ledbetter Erection Corp., 115 Ill. 2d 146, 104 Ill. Dec. 689, 503 N.E.2d 246 (1986); DuPage County v. Graham, Anderson, Probst &

With respect to subcontractors, the economic loss doctrine applies where there is no privity of contract. For example, an owner may claim that it was damaged by the negligence of one of the Prime Contractor's subcontractors and attempt to sue that subcontractor directly in tort. This situation also may arise where the general contractor or one of its subcontractors attempts to sue one of the A/E's subconsultants for negligence, or vice versa. Here the question is whether the economic loss doctrine will bar a direct action for damages from negligent conduct against a contractor or subcontractor not in privity with the plaintiff.[30] It may not in states that recognize an "independent duty" between the suing party and the subconsultant.[31]

As the economic loss doctrine is fully discussed in chapter 6, there is no need to reiterate this interesting debate here. However, practitioners should be aware that a number of courts have extended the applicability of the economic loss doctrine to cases where no privity of contract exists between the parties.[32]

White, Inc., 109 Ill. 2d 143, 92 Ill. Dec. 833, 485 N.E.2d 1076 (1985); Doran-Maine, Inc. v. American Eng'g & Testing, Inc., 608 F. Supp. 609 (D. Me. 1985); Berschauer/Phillips Constr. Co. v. Seattle Sch. Dist. No. 1, 124 Wash. 2d 816, 881 P.2d 986, 94 Ed. Law Rep. 610 (1994); American Towers Owners Assn. v. CCI Mech., Inc., 930 P.2d 1182 (Utah 1996); Williams & Sons Erectors v. South Carolina Steel, 983 F.2d 1176 (2d Cir. 1993).

30. Philip L. Bruner et al., *2004 Construction Review*, CONSTRUCTION BRIEFINGS No. 2005-1 (2005).

31. *See, e.g.*, Donatelli v. D.R. Strong Consulting Engineers, Inc., 312 P.3d 620 (Wash. 2013); *See also* S K Peightal Engineers, LTD v. Mid Valley Real Estate Sols. V, LLC, 342 P.3d 868 (Colo. 2015).

32. Miller v. U.S. Steel, 902 F.2d 573 (7th Cir. 1990); Mechanical, Inc. v. Venture Electric Contractors, Inc., 392 Wis. 2d 319, 332 (App. Ct. 2020). *See also* Corporex Dev. &Constr. Mgmt., Inc. v. Shook, Inc., 106 Ohio St. 3d 412, 415, 835 N.E.2d 701, 705 (2005) (project owner could not evade the economic loss rule by suing a subcontractor in negligence; owner had to sue the general contractor for breach of contract and the general contractor could in turn sue the subcontractor); Digicorp, Inc., v. Ameritech Corp., 262 Wis. 2d 32, 662 N.W.2d 652, 666 (Wis. 2003) ("[E]ven in the absence of privity, the economic loss doctrine bars one party in the distributive chain from recovering economic losses in tort from another party in that chain."). Coastal Conduit & Ditching, Inc. v. Noram Energy Corp., 29 S.W.3d 282, 285–90 (Tex. Ct. App. 2000).

Library References

C.J.S. *Agency* §§ 17, 375, 377, 419–421, 423–445; C.J.S. *Contracts* §§ 271, 356, 442–445, 450, 508, 531, 592–593; C.J.S. *Contribution* §§ 5, 9–10, 12–13; C.J.S. *Insurance* §§ 54, 956–957, 970–973; C.J.S. *Negligence* § 58.

West's Key No. Digests, Alternative Dispute Resolution <KEY>112, 442; Contracts <KEY>114, 221(3), 319–321; Contribution <KEY>6; Indemnity <KEY>30(5), 33(5), 34, 67; Insurance <KEY>2359, 2391; Negligence <KEY>463; Principal and Agent <KEY>3(2), 159.

IV. Drafting Subcontract Agreements

This section provides practical drafting tips in addition to a checklist of issues that should be considered in every subcontract. Due to the fact that the Prime Contractor generally takes the lead in drafting the subcontracts, the checklist is geared to the Prime Contractor's perspective. However, listing all of the issues will help subcontractors identify and negotiate important terms that affect their liability, obligations, and responsibilities under their subcontracts.

A. Rule No. 1: Get It in Writing, and Get It Signed!

Every lawyer who practices in this area has heard the typical client lament that "things are not as they used to be." This is usually in reference to the times when everyone in the construction industry knew everyone else and agreements were sealed by a handshake, not a written contract. Those were the days of complete honesty and perfect memories. Those were also the days when it was not unusual for someone to stay with the same company for his or her entire career. Without questioning exactly when those bygone days ended, it is safe to say they have long since passed.

The terms and conditions of every agreement between a Prime Contractor and its subcontractors should be reduced to writing and signed by duly-authorized representatives of each party. Under some circumstances, it may be possible to have enforceable oral subcontracts. However, the statute of frauds, operable in every jurisdiction, will render most verbal construction subcontracts unenforceable. Notwithstanding this fact, unless the terms of the agreement are reduced to writing, disagreements over material and important issues are certain to occur. In general, it is not possible to predict how such disagreements will be resolved. Additionally, in many prime contracts, an obligation is imposed upon the Prime Contractor to pass down or impose certain provisions of the prime contract on the Prime Contractor's subcontractors; this obligation can only be accomplished in a written subcontract. Finally, documenting the terms and conditions of service before any dispute or disagreement arises will often prevent such disputes or disagreements from being unreasonably costly to resolve.

The number of times that a Prime Contractor and its subcontractor will spend weeks or even months negotiating a contract and then never bother executing it is baffling. While courts will usually enforce an unsigned contract if it conforms to the conduct of the parties, it saves both time and money simply to sign the final contract.

B. Rule No. 2: Develop a "Form" Contract for All Subcontracts on the Project

The Prime Contractor should develop or utilize an industry form contract for all of its subcontracts. Even when utilizing an industry contract, the Prime Contractor should review and tailor provisions based upon its specific knowledge of the parties, scope, and risks of the project.

1. Form or Custom Subcontract Agreements

As a starting point for negotiations with all of the subcontractors on the project, the Prime Contractor should prepare a form subcontract agreement. Sometimes this is done well in advance and it may be attached to the Request for Proposal (RFP) or Invitation for Bids (IFB). There are many subcontract forms or templates available in the marketplace today. Among them are subcontract forms from the American Institute of Architects (AIA), the ConsensusDocs, the Engineers Joint Contract Documents Committee (EJCDC), and the Design Build Institute of America (DBIA), to name a few of the most widely known forms.

Many lawyers, Prime Contractors, and subcontractors prefer to use their own, customized subcontract agreements. Others prefer to start with a standard template. In general, the individual conditions of a particular project, coupled with the unique requirements of each contractor's subcontract terms and conditions, will usually require specific language and terms or customization without regard to whether the initial template is a nationally recognized form or individually drafted subcontract agreement. In any event, it is essential to ensure that certain terms and conditions are the same for all subcontractors on the project, that all key subjects are addressed in the final subcontract agreement, and that a properly signed subcontract is in place at the very beginning of the project.

2. *Customizing the Standard or Template-Based Subcontract Agreement*

The next step is to prepare a draft of a customized subcontract for each of the subcontractors on the project using this template. Each individualized draft subcontract should include all relevant information, terms, and conditions, including information from the specific proposals previously submitted by the subcontractor. Once completed, the customized draft subcontract and a redacted copy of the prime contract should be sent to the subcontractor for its review and comment. The fee and reimbursable expenses information of the prime contract should be redacted. Any other confidential or proprietary information should also be redacted from the copy of the prime contract.

Some of the Prime Contractor's consultants may have significant professional responsibilities, and others may have relatively narrow scopes of work with short durations. For example, the structural engineer's scope of work for a project is typically more extensive and involves a greater fee than a subcontractor that is providing drafting or duplication services to the Prime Contractor for the project. To efficiently manage the development of a subcontract for these two different types of subcontractors, it is recommended that the Prime Contractor develop two versions of its subcontract template for the project to support efficient and properly focused contract negotiations with each of these subcontractors.

The Prime Contractor should develop a long-form subcontract template that is comprehensive and detailed for the "major" subcontractors. Major consultants are those whose expertise is typically required to produce the structure, facility, building, development, or project of the type at issue. The professionals who would be considered principal or major consultants vary depending on the type of project, the expertise possessed by the Prime Contractor's staff, and the deal made with the owner.

On the design side, if the Prime Contractor is an architect or engineer, the major consultants will typically be the structural, civil, electrical, mechanical, and plumbing design professionals. The major subconsultants typically consist of licensed or certified professionals who have significant responsibility from the beginning of the design process through the production of final drawings and specifications, which must be stamped, sealed, signed, or certified for submission to the code review authority for approval before a building permit may be authorized for issuance. The principal or major subconsultants typically receive a significant portion of the total fee. Their services constitute significant portions of the total scope of services that are to be provided by the Prime Contractor and/or may include significant potential risk or exposure for the Prime Contractor if they are untimely or deficient.

A more abbreviated short form subcontract agreement should be used for specialty subcontractors[33] with small fees and scopes of work and for limited or shared risk subcontractors.[34] Specialty consultants are subcontractors to

---

33. The evolution of the standard of care that is a minimum performance standard for design professionals has caused some areas of consultancy—that thirty years ago were limited to only high-budget or unique projects—now to become as common and necessary as structural or civil engineering. Some examples include:

- lighting consultants on commercial, office, governmental, or other public facilities;
- security consultants;
- acoustical consultants;
- communications consultants on governmental or headquarters office facilities; and
- elevator or vertical transportation consultants on office complexes, shopping centers, or multimodal transportation hubs.

34. In the modern world of design professional contract negotiation, drafting, evaluation, and review, a third type of subconsultant is frequently encountered. These subconsultants are technically subcontracted to the Prime Contractor but with some significant modification in the normally expected line of authority, reporting relationships, allocation of risk, or responsibility for performance. Unique contractual provisions that modify the normal level of liability of the Prime Contractor typify the agreements between these subconsultants and the Prime Contractors, which have corresponding provisions in the prime design contract. Some examples of these subconsultant disciplines include soils engineering, surveying, environmental, and hazardous materials or explosives removal. A significant characteristic of this grouping is that the discipline or specialty is not insured or insurable under the professional liability insurance of the Prime Contractor. For many years, the use of the project professional liability insurance policy reduced the need for a construction lawyer to have special agreements or provisions for this grouping. However, over the last several years and particularly since 9/11, we have observed project professional liability insurance become less available for certain types of projects, such as condominiums, due to the higher risk. Furthermore, the significant increase in premium costs since 9/11 has

the Prime Contractor retained to provide specialized technical expertise for some particular system or portion of the project. On the design side, examples of specialty consultants include elevator or vertical transportation, interiors, kitchen, acoustical, scheduling, cost estimating, parking, surface transportation, graphic or signage, fire protection, communication, audio/visual, security, curtain wall, shoring, steel connections, and lighting.

Master agreements are sometimes used between a Prime Contractor and a subcontractor who anticipates it will be working together with the Prime Contractor on several projects over the course of several years. Multiple tasks related to a single project or several unrelated projects may be subject to this master agreement. The master agreement contains the commercial terms and conditions that govern all projects involving the Prime Contractor and the subcontractor. Individual projects or tasks are then authorized in purchase orders or other simple scope documents identifying the specific work to be performed for that particular project, the price, and sometimes specific dates that must be met by the subcontractor.

Master agreements can streamline the contracting process. However, there is a danger that no two projects are alike and, therefore, the master agreement should be reviewed prior to commencing each project to determine whether special or supplemental terms and conditions are required to adequately reflect the assigned project and its scope of work. A master agreement can sit in the drawer for years, never reviewed by the contracting parties until a dispute arises. In the interim, laws may have changed, including the way in which the courts interpret or enforce various contract provisions. This means that the master agreement may produce unintended results if not regularly reviewed and updated.

C. Rule No. 3: Identify Key Subcontract Terms and Conditions

Certain issues need to be addressed in every Prime Contractor subcontract in order for it to be legally enforceable and in compliance with the terms of the prime contract. Other issues, subjects, terms, and conditions, based upon the common experience of many people in the construction industry, should always be considered for inclusion in Prime Contractor subcontracts. Good examples of these types of issues are discussed in Section III, above. Finally, there are other issues, subjects, terms, and conditions that may be necessary for a particular subcontract based upon the negotiation of the parties and/or

---

made project policies less attractive even when they are available. Accordingly, contractual risk limitation, sharing, or avoidance will make this grouping more common and special subcontracts more necessary.

the needs of the project. These are usually based on the specific risks to the project and which party is best able to mitigate or carry the financial burden of that risk.

Table 1 lists the terms and conditions that should be evaluated for inclusion in every Prime Contractor subcontract.

Library References

C.J.S. *Contracts* §§ 67, 75.
West's Key No. Digests, Contracts <KEY>31, 35.

V. Subcontract Negotiations

The subcontract negotiations between the Prime Contractor and each of its subcontractors should be conducted with the goal of developing a set of terms and conditions that fairly and accurately reflect the allocation of rights, responsibilities, obligations, and risks between the Prime Contractor and its subcontractors inherent in the project. The negotiations should not be intended to impose unreasonable burdens or liabilities upon either party.

During the process of the negotiations between the Prime Contractor and the owner, the Prime Contractor must be sensitive to the roles of its subcontractors and not agree to unusual or unduly burdensome responsibilities. To avoid this situation, the Prime Contractor should periodically advise its sub-subcontractors of the status of the negotiations.

Practice Tip

A representative of the Prime Contractor and each subcontractor should meet in person to discuss the draft subcontract and discuss their expectations of each other for their working relationship on the project. This provides an opportunity for each party to discuss the particular or unique characteristics and issues associated with the project. It also allows the parties to meet firsthand to address any particularly troublesome or difficult contract issues. After this first meeting, the remaining or unresolved subcontract issues can typically be addressed by exchanges of electronic redlines and clean drafts of the subcontract.

Table 1 is a checklist that the Prime Contractor and subcontractor should consider when negotiating the subcontract agreement.

Table 1 PROVISION CHECKLIST FOR DESIGN PROFESSIONAL/CONSTRUCTION MANAGER SUBCONTRACTS

Type/Subject Matter of Provision	Reason for, or Objective of, Provision(s)	Necessity of Provision	Comments
Names/Identity of the Parties	Full and correct legal names of the parties must be properly reflected at the beginning of the document	Essential	Drafting and reviewing counsel should check with the Secretary of State for the jurisdiction in which the parties are domiciled to make sure that they are in good standing. Use the full legal name, including, if applicable, any fictitious name or "dba." In most jurisdictions, this task can be performed using the Internet.
Name or Title of Document	Name or title of the agreement should be reflected at the top of the first page	Highly desirable	

Type/Subject Matter of Provision	Reason for, or Objective of, Provision(s)	Necessity of Provision	Comments
Project Description	Description of project, including address or location and "name"	Essential	The project description in the subcontract should be identical to the "project description" in the prime contract between the owner and the Prime Contractor. Any differences can create significant problems if there are any claims, disputes, or litigation regarding the Project.

Type/Subject Matter of Provision	Reason for, or Objective of, Provision(s)	Necessity of Provision	Comments
Effective Date of Agreement	Establishes the date on which the contractual relationship terms of the Agreement start to apply to their relationship	Essential	Frequently, the prime contract establishes a date in the past as the date on which the design professionals, construction manager, and their consultants "started" to provide services. As a general rule, the "Effective Date of the Agreement" should be identical to the "Effective Date" in the prime contract between the owner and the Prime Contractor. On a related topic, the parties may want to consider adding a date on which they agree that the statute of limitations begins to run for the purposes of disputes regarding the project.

Type/Subject Matter of Provision	Reason for, or Objective of, Provision(s)	Necessity of Provision	Comments
Incorporation of Applicable Terms of Prime Contract	Requires that applicable provisions of the Prime Agreement that are required to be imposed on the subcontractors be incorporated into their subcontracts	Essential	The prime contract will normally impose on the Prime Contractor an obligation to require that its subcontractors accept and agree to certain terms and conditions of the prime contract.
Notice/Contact/ Designated Representative Information	Identifies the person or persons who are responsible for receiving any official notice or information that is required by the terms of the subcontract agreement	Highly desirable	This provision sets forth the form or forms of notification that may be used for communicating information required or allowed by the subcontract. It also provides the specific contact information, i.e., name, title, address, e-mail, telephone, fax, and other pertinent details for communication between the parties.
Scope of Services	The scope or description of the services that are to be provided; this description should be very detailed and thorough	Essential	

Type/Subject Matter of Provision	Reason for, or Objective of, Provision(s)	Necessity of Provision	Comments
Standard of Performance			
Identification of Subconsultants		Highly desirable	The Prime Contractor's duties and responsibilities under the provisions of the prime contract with the owner will typically include the identification, selection, and management of the services and deliverables required of the Prime Contractor's subcontractors. In many prime design contracts, the Prime Contractor must obtain the owner's approval of its subcontractors.
Schedule, Applicable to Provision of Services or Deliverables, if Any		Highly desirable	Ensure that the subcontractor's anticipated schedule—especially milestone dates—conforms to the prime contract.
Description of Deliverables		Useful	
Budget or Financial Parameters Applicable to Prime Contractor's Services		Highly desirable	

Type/Subject Matter of Provision	Reason for, or Objective of, Provision(s)	Necessity of Provision	Comments
Coordination—Description of Relative Allocation of Duties and Responsibilities	What reporting is required? What type of schedule will be used, and who/how will it be maintained? What regular coordination meetings are required, and how often?	Highly desirable	
Compensation	Amount	Essential	
Terms of Payment	Payment application processes	Highly desirable	
	Pay-when-paid clause/pay-if-paid clause	Highly desirable	In the event that the Owner does not pay Prime Contractor.
Additional Services	Sets forth the terms and conditions on which any out-of-scope or "additional services" may be authorized and the method of determining amount of compensation to be paid		
Insurance	Sets forth the specific insurance types, coverages, and other parameters required of the subcontractor	Highly desirable	

Type/Subject Matter of Provision	Reason for, or Objective of, Provision(s)	Necessity of Provision	Comments
Indemnification	Professional and contractual liability	Highly desirable	
	Intellectual property	Highly desirable	
	Mechanics' lien or claimant liability	Highly desirable	
	Damages incurred by Prime Contractor under the prime agreement due to subcontractor's acts or omissions; the parties should also consider indemnity for exposure to hazardous materials and violation of environmental laws	Highly desirable	This clause is especially important where the prime contract contains liquidated damages. Additionally, such provisions may allow the contractor to "pass through" the owner's claim directly to the subcontractor, thereby incurring minimal expense in the event the owner has a claim based upon the subcontractor's work.
Warranties	Warranties that run from the subcontractor to the Prime Contractor	Highly desirable	It is important to make sure that the warranties in the subcontract and the prime contract are the same.

Type/Subject Matter of Provision	Reason for, or Objective of, Provision(s)	Necessity of Provision	Comments
Dispute Resolution	Consider mediation and arbitration options	Highly desirable	Review dispute resolution procedures in both the prime contract and the subcontract to make sure they conform. Additionally, review and consider joinder issues.
Ownership and Use of Documents	Nonexclusive licenses	Essential	In the event that the owner terminates the Prime Contractor or the Prime Contractor terminates a subcontractor, consider whether the agreement allows an A/E to terminate its license, thereby possibly derailing the project, because the owner or contractor no longer has authority to use the drawings.
	Indemnification for reuse	Useful	
	Termination implications		

Type/Subject Matter of Provision	Reason for, or Objective of, Provision(s)	Necessity of Provision	Comments
Status of Subcontractor	Independent contractor, agency		
Maintenance of Records		Optional	Usually, the records maintenance requirement will conform with the statutes of limitation and repose in the applicable jurisdiction.
Assignment/ Successor		Optional	Usually, the Prime Contractor will not allow assignment of the subcontract by the subcontractor. Otherwise, the Prime Contractor will not have the ability to effectively control subcontractors that it does not know or have a preexisting relationship with.
Authority to Enter into Agreement		Highly desirable	
Integration Clause		Highly desirable	
Counterpart Execution		Useful	

Type/Subject Matter of Provision	Reason for, or Objective of, Provision(s)	Necessity of Provision	Comments
Third-Party Beneficiary		Highly desirable	The question to consider is whether the subcontractor is a third-party beneficiary of the owner/Prime Contractor contract (particularly the payment provisions) or the owner is a third-party beneficiary of the Prime Contractor/subcontractor contract.
Choice of Laws and Forum Selection		Highly desirable	Usually laws of the state in which the project is located will apply.
Signatures		Essential	

VI. Subcontract Issues Unique to International Subcontracting Relationships

Over the last twenty years, many architects, engineers, steel fabricators, and general contractors have used teams of engineers and technicians from other countries as subcontractors on their projects. Detailing and shop drawing for steel fabrication are just a few of the disciplines where personnel from Mexico, the Philippines, India, and other foreign locations continue to provide design or drafting services for projects in the United States.

The principal reason for the creation of these offshore relationships is usually the availability of less expensive services in these foreign locations or a lack of skilled personnel. These foreign personnel often do not hold any U.S. licenses or certifications. Their firms frequently do not possess workers' compensation, commercial general liability, or professional liability insurance. The entity providing the services is typically a lower-tier subcontractor and may not possess the background, experience, and training of comparable domestic personnel.

Before a Prime Contractor engages an offshore subcontractor, it should make sure that there are no formal or informal limitations in the contract that preclude such agreements or relationships. Frequently, governmental, public, or some large private projects limit or prohibit the use of such offshore subcontractors. Accordingly, at the outset, a determination must be made with respect to whether offshore subcontracting is allowed or limited.

If there are no limitations or prohibitions on the use of offshore agreements or personnel, when offshore contracting or subcontracting will be used, the issues listed in Table 2 as well as the factors listed in Table 1 should be discussed and properly addressed.

Table 2 SUPPLEMENTAL CHECKLIST FOR OFFSHORE DESIGN PROFESSIONAL/CONSTRUCTION MANAGER SUBCONTRACTS

Type/Subject Matter of Provision	Reason for, or Objective of, Provision(s)	Necessity of Provision	Comments
Form of Agreement	Will a written agreement be used? Does the written agreement have to comply with any provisions of the prime contract? Who will prepare it, and in what language will it be prepared?	Essential	The costs of preparing such an agreement may erode any savings that were contemplated.

Type/Subject Matter of Provision	Reason for, or Objective of, Provision(s)	Necessity of Provision	Comments
Communications	How will communications be handled (i.e., fax, e-mail, overnight delivery)? What language will be used for the work product and for day-to-day communications? What country's unit of measurements? will be used?	Highly desirable	How will questions and issues associated with understanding the scope of work be addressed?
Delivery Methods	Are there any limitations on the way the offshore subcontractor will obtain its labor or personnel?	Optional	
Payment	When, and in what currency, will payment for services be handled?	Essential	

Type/Subject Matter of Provision	Reason for, or Objective of, Provision(s)	Necessity of Provision	Comments
Insurance	Will the offshore subcontractor carry any insurance? If so, are any requirements with respect to the size, "best rating," or location of the insurance carrier? How will claims, if any, be handled or adjusted?	Essential	Under the concept of vicarious liability, if the subcontractor does not carry insurance or it is not accessible for claims purposes, the next higher-tier subcontractor and the Prime Contractor are effectively providing insurance for it.
Disputes	Jurisdiction: Who has it for purposes of asserting claims? What form of dispute resolution procedure will be used? Where will disputes be heard? What law applies?	Highly desirable	Frequently, arbitration is the only workable dispute resolution procedure.
Deliverables	What are the "deliverables" and where are they to be delivered? Are there any cross-border restrictions of information (i.e., relating to national security such as nuclear power)?		

The use of offshore arrangements or subcontracts may initially appear to be more economical than they are in actual practice. As a result, their use should be very carefully considered.

VII. Conclusion

Every subcontract between a Prime Contractor and its subcontractor must be negotiated based upon the terms and conditions of the prime contract with the owner and include all of the terms and conditions of the subcontractor's service. The pertinent parts of the prime contract should be incorporated by reference into the subcontract, with a redacted copy of the prime contract attached to it. The subcontract and any amendments thereto must always be reduced to writing. Finally, it must be signed by the parties to it and copies must be distributed accordingly.

VIII. Practice Aids

A. Standard Construction Manager and Subcontractor Contract Forms Available

The most widely used standard forms are as follows:

- AIA Contract Documents
- ConsensusDocs Contract Documents
- EJCDC Contract Documents
- DBIA Contract Documents

CHAPTER 10

Damages and Remedies

STEPHEN R. MILLER, STEPHEN A. HESS

I. Introduction

Previous chapters have detailed the various tort and contract rights and obligations that design professionals and construction managers accept in the performance of their work. This chapter outlines the broad spectrum of remedies available to design professionals and construction managers when owners breach their contracts, as well as the remedies available against design professionals and construction managers who find themselves in breach of their own obligations to owners. Additionally, the chapter reviews a number of mechanisms by which parties attempt to limit the damages for which they might be responsible through their contracts.

Before a party can recover damages, it must establish its entitlement to relief by proving a claim against the tortfeasor or the party in breach of the contract. In legal parlance, proving a claim requires establishment of a discrete set of elements, and in the absence of proof of any element of a claim, recovery must be denied. Therefore, the chapter begins with a brief review of what a claimant must establish in order to recover on the types of claims most commonly brought in connection with construction disputes.

Two notes regarding the limitations of this chapter are in order. First, the function of this chapter is to provide an overview of remedies and not an exhaustive discussion of all the nuances of the different aspects of damages that might be recovered. Indeed, even full-length treatises cannot contain exhaustive discussions of all the aspects of construction damages. Second, the principles discussed below are general principles that are common to most jurisdictions. This chapter does not attempt to catalog the differences among the laws of all fifty states and the federal government. Identification of the laws of a particular state requires the services of a construction lawyer well-versed in the laws of a specific jurisdiction.

That much having been said, there is enough in common with respect to the general principles governing remedies and damages to make compact overview possible.

II. Causes of Action

When a party seeks to recover for a loss, it files suit (or an arbitration demand) seeking a remedy for particular acts of malfeasance by the opposing party. There are well-established elements of recovery for different legal theories on which parties to a construction project may rely. When assessing the viability of a potential claim, the first task is to determine those elements a claimant must prove in order to recover and then measure the known facts against those elements. This section details (and comments briefly on) the legal theories most often encountered in construction litigation.

A. Breach of Contract and Related Claims

The bulk of services performed by construction managers are governed by written or oral contracts, and relief for a breach takes the form of a claim for *breach of contract.* However, in some cases, the parties' negotiations may never reach the level of formation of a contract, or the contract may be unenforceable for a variety of reasons. The absence or unenforceability of a contract, however, does not necessarily preclude recovery. The law may still provide a remedy under two different theories. First, under the theory of *promissory estoppel*, a party may be protected to the extent that it reasonably relies on another's promise, even if no contract is formed. Second, a party who provides services without a formal contract may be able to recover under a theory of *unjust enrichment* to preclude the other party from retaining the benefits of those services without some form of payment.

Accordingly, when an attorney pleads claims related to the provision of services on a construction contract, the complaint often includes alternative claims for breach of contract, promissory estoppel, and unjust enrichment. Although related, these claims have different elements and a party may recover on one where the others are unavailing.

I. Breach of Contract

The most common claim in construction litigation is for breach of contract. A breach of contract is nothing more complicated than a party's failure to perform express or implied obligations arising under its agreement with the opposing party. The scope and nature of such express and implied obligations for design professionals and construction managers are set forth in detail in prior chapters.

In order to recover for breach of contract, the claimant is ordinarily required to prove, by a preponderance of the evidence,[1] each of the following elements of the claim for breach of contract:

a. the existence of an enforceable contract;
b. breach of the agreement by the defending party;
c. the claimant's performance of its own obligations (or a lawful excuse for its not having performed); and
d. damages proximately caused by the breach.[2]

Once established, the prevailing party is entitled to compensatory and other damages, the general calculation of which is spelled out in what follows.

As may be gleaned from the chapters setting out the numerous express and implied obligations of design professionals and construction managers, there are many different types of claims that fall under the broad category of breach of contract claims. For example, a breach of warranty claim is a breach of contract claim at heart, where the warranty is simply that portion of the contract at issue. Breaches may be as simple as failing to pay an amount of money when due, or as complicated as providing plans that are not constructible in

---

1. The general standard for all civil actions is *preponderance of the evidence*, which simply means a claimant must establish that it is more likely than not entitled to recover. Henderson v. Copper Ridge Homes, LLC, 273 So. 3d 750 (Miss. 2019). This may be contrasted with the criminal standard under which a defendant may not be convicted unless his or her guilt is established *beyond a reasonable doubt*.

2. *See, e.g.*, EUA Cogenex Corp. v. North Rockland Central Sch. Dist., 124 F. Supp. 2d 861 (S.D.N.Y. 2000); Soos & Associates, Inc. v. Five Guys Enterprises, LLC, 2019 WL 6497377, at *7 (N.D. Ill. 2019). Many courts omit the requirement that the claimant prove its own performance, leaving just three elements. Semac Electric Company, Inc. v. Skanska USA Building, Inc., 195 Conn. App. 695, 705, 2020 WL 611808, at *4 (Conn. App. 2020).

some material respect (thereby, breaching the implied warranty of suitability for construction).

The third element of a breach of contract claim embodies the doctrine of "first material breach," and embodies the principle that a party who is in material breach of a contract is not entitled to the benefit of the other party's return performance. Thus, an owner who has failed to pay a substantial sum due a design professional or construction manager can no longer insist on the return benefit of the contract, and the design professional or construction manager is excused from further performance (and may be entitled to terminate) as long as the owner's material breach remains uncured.

2. *Promissory Estoppel*

Many parties rely on the promises of another party and begin the performance of services or fashion their business relationships with other parties even before those promises are formalized into binding contracts. In many circumstances, the party relying on such a promise is entitled to protection notwithstanding the fact that a binding contract is never perfected. The doctrine of promissory estoppel may be summarized as follows:

> **Promise Reasonably Inducing Action or Forbearance**
>
> (1) A promise which the promisor should reasonably expect to induce action or forbearance on the part of the promisee or a third person and which does induce such action or forbearance is binding if injustice can be avoided only by enforcement of the promise. The remedy granted for breach may be limited as justice requires.[3]

In order to prevail on a claim for promissory estoppel, therefore, a claimant must establish that:

a. the opposing party made a promise;
b. the promise was made intending (or reasonably expecting) to induce action or forbearance on the part of the promise;
c. the promisee reasonably relied on the promise to his or her detriment; and
d. injustice can be avoided only through enforcement of the promise.[4]

---

3. Restatement (Second) of Contracts § 90(1) (1981).

4. Pinnacol Assurance v. Hoff, 375 P.3d 1214, 1221, 2016 CO 53, ¶ 32 (Colo. 2016). *But see* Shawn Ibrahim, Inc. v. Houston-Galveston Area Local Development Corpora-

It is important to note that the doctrine does not create a contract where none existed before, but it has much the same effect: namely, the promisor is prevented (estopped) from denying that he should answer for his failure to perform. By way of illustration, the doctrine of promissory estoppel is sometimes invoked to recover for professional services provided without an enforceable contract. Additionally, promissory estoppel serves as the legal basis under which some contractors attempt to recover from subcontractors who refuse to perform after the contractors win contracts after relying on the subcontractors' bids.

Promissory estoppel differs somewhat from breach of contract in that the measure of damages available for a claim of promissory estoppel may be very different from the damages available for breach of a contract to perform the same promise.

3. Unjust Enrichment

In some circumstances, a party may not be able to recover damages for breach of contract or for promissory estoppel. In such cases, a legal theory on which a party may attempt to seek recovery is unjust enrichment. As its name implies, the theory is designed to ensure that a party is not permitted to retain the benefit of another person's provision of services in circumstances in which it would be unjust to allow the uncompensated retention.

In order to prevail on an unjust enrichment claim, the party seeking relief must generally prove that it:

a. conferred a benefit on another party,
b. without intending to act gratuitously, and
c. the benefit was conferred in circumstances in which it would be unjust to allow the recipient of the benefit to retain the benefit without compensation to the party providing the service.

The most difficult element to apply is the third: what may be "unjust" is left largely to the conscience of the judge, jury, or arbitrator. In addition, it is an important qualification to unjust enrichment that it ordinarily will not apply when there is an express contract that governs the parties' relationship. In other words, a disgruntled party cannot use unjust enrichment as a theory of recovery simply because the contract provides an insufficient remedy.

---

tion, 582 S.W.3d 753, 772 (Tex. App. 2019) (elements are (1) a promise, (2) foreseeability of reliance, and (3) substantial reliance by promise).

B. Tort Claims

Prior chapters set out the various obligations in tort that design professionals and construction managers assume in performing services. As noted therein, tort obligations are obligations imposed by the law apart from any contractual obligations the parties may assume expressly or implicitly. Because they are imposed by the law without regard to the parties' contractual obligations, these duties generally do not require express proof of the existence of a contract as an element of recovery.[5] Instead, a prima facie case for recovery under a tort theory requires that the victim establish:

a. the defendant owed a duty of care to the claimant;
b. the defendant breached that duty of care;
c. the victim suffered damages; and
d. the damages were proximately caused by the defendant's breach of duty.

The question of what duties are owed by a design professional or construction manager to their clients and third parties is addressed in more detail in several prior chapters. For purposes of this discussion, it is sufficient to note the general rule that "one who undertakes to render professional services is under a duty to the person for whom the service is to be performed to exercise such care, skill, and diligence as men in that profession ordinarily exercise under like circumstances."[6]

The failure to exercise reasonable care is typically branded as negligence and may take many forms. As an example, contractors may maintain actions against design professionals to recover their losses under a variety of theories, including negligent supervision or negligent preparation of plans and specifications.[7]

The last element, that of establishing that the damages claimed are *proximately caused* by the asserted negligence, is a judicially imposed limitation that precludes parties from recovering unpredictable damages. More precisely, proximate cause requires not only that the damages were *actually* caused by

---

5. In fact, under the economic loss rule, the existence of a contract may preclude recovery. Bradley Woodcraft, Inc. v. Bodden, 251 N.C. App. 27, 795 S.E.2d 253 (2016).

6. City of Eveleth v. Ruble, 225 N.W.2d 521, 524 (Minn. 1974).

7. Frank D. Wagner, Annotation, *Tort Liability of Project Architect for Economic Damages Suffered by Contractor*, 65 A.L.R.3D 249, § 2[a] (1975); *see also* Matrix v. Malow, 2006 WL 399762 (Mich. Ct. App. 2006) (unpublished opinion); Colonial Sur. Co. v. Lenard Eng'g, Inc., 2004 WL 2943640 (Sup. Ct. Conn. 2004) (unpublished opinion).

the negligence, but also that the damages are a natural and probable consequence of the negligence. For example, some jurisdictions have held that where it is foreseeable that a design professional's actions or inactions may create a risk of harm to a third-party contractor whose responsibility it is to implement the design work of the design professional, a cause of action lies against the design professional, even where no contract exists between the parties.[8]

In outlining the elements of a claim based on the summary above, additional elements may be required for a particular claim as described further in the chapters discussing torts. Thus, for example, when a claim for negligent misrepresentation is brought against a design professional or construction manager, the claimant might not only be required to show a breach of the duty to represent information accurately, but also that the claimant reasonably relied on the misrepresentation at issue.[9]

Library References

C.J.S. *Architects* §§ 33–44; C.J.S. *Conflict of Laws* §§ 35–36, 39, 436, 87, 98; C.J.S. *Contracts* §§ 13, 15–18, 24, 26, 509–512, 600–612, 626, 630, 633–697, 701, 717–719, 726–736, 753, 756–760, 770–771, 777–778, 782–784, 795–804; C.J.S. *Estoppel and Waiver* § 90; C.J.S. *Fraud* §§ 10–17, 23–25, 29–30, 34–35, 59–60, 62–63, 67–75, 77–78, 80; C.J.S. *Implied and Constructive Contracts* § 4; C.J.S. *Negligence* §§ 163–164, 399, 595–596, 598–601, 618–619.

West's Key No. Digests, Contracts <KEY>324–355; Estoppel <KEY>85; Fraud <KEY>8; Implied and Constructive Contracts <KEY>3; Negligence <KEY>322, 1205(4)–1205(10).

III. General Measures of Damages

A measure of damages is simply a statement of how a court will calculate the amount of money a party may recover upon establishing a claim against the defendant. Although there are some differences in particular items of recovery among jurisdictions, the general rules regarding recovery are relatively consistent among jurisdictions.

The measures of damages are different for the various claims outlined above. However, there are some general principles common to all damage claims. First, the claimant bears the burden of proving the existence of damages with a reasonable degree of certainty. This requirement is established not

8. Wagner, *supra* note 7, § 2[a].

9. Presnell Constr. Managers, Inc. v. EH Constr., LLC, 134 S.W.3d 575 (Ky. 2004).

so much by proving the exact amount of damages, but rather by establishing to the satisfaction of the fact-finder (judge, jury, or arbitrator) that the claimant has definitely suffered some damage. Once the fact of damages has been established, courts are less exacting when it comes to quantifying damages. Courts do not require precise quantification, but instead only require a reasonable basis for calculating the damages claimed. Thus, a reasonable basis excludes damages that are merely speculative, as damages may not be recovered where their quantification is left to mere speculation without some basis in the record to support any determination of the amount of such damages.

A. Breach of Contract and Related Claims

1. *Breach of Contract*

Generally, "a party is entitled to have what he contracts for or its equivalent,"[10] which is another way of saying that a party is entitled to the "benefit of his bargain." When a breach by the opposing party deprives the claimant of the benefit of that bargain, a court will endeavor to protect that benefit; in other terms, the goal in most breach of contract matters "is to award a sum that will put the non-breaching party in as good a position as he would have been had the contract been performed."[11] Generally, "rights of the parties with respect to a breach of contract are fixed at the time of breach and . . . damages are measured as of that time."[12]

a. Design Professional and Construction Manager Compensation

A design professional's or construction manager's bargain is typically the compensation to which the design professional or construction manager is entitled under the terms of the contract with the owner. When the owner fails to pay the design professional or construction manager, the measure of damages is typically the difference between the contract compensation and the compensation actually paid. Of course, this measure is appropriate when the owner simply fails to pay. More often, disputes arise because the design professional or construction manager performs services that are arguably outside the scope of the original contract, and the measure of damages then becomes that additional

10. Charlotte v. Skidmore, Owings and Merrill, 407 S.E.2d 571, 580 (N.C. Ct. App. 1991).

11. Hernandez v. Westoak Realty & Inv., Inc., 771 S.W.2d 876, 880 (Mo. Ct. App. 1989).

12. Fairway Builders, Inc. v. Malouf Towers Rental Co., 603 P.2d 513 (Ariz. Ct. App. 1979).

compensation to which the design professional or construction manager is entitled for the extra work. Where the contract provides specified rates for such compensation, the damage calculation is readily performed. Where the contract does not specify how compensation is to be determined, courts will typically award *reasonable* compensation. What is reasonable is simply what a court (or arbitrator) will decide is reasonable after hearing evidence regarding the additional services and the value thereof. In some cases, the design professional or construction manager may also be entitled to recover interest or attorneys' fees permitted in the circumstances discussed below.

b. Owner's Compensation

The owner of a building or project typically contracts to get three elements related to its project. First, it wants the contract to be completed for the contract price. Second, it wants the contract to be completed within the contract time. Third, it wants the project to be of such quality and nature as it has contracted for through the contract documents.

When the project is finished at a greater cost than promised, later than promised, or of lesser quality than promised, the owner may be entitled to recover. The general measure of damages is the same as that recited above: the owner is entitled to recover that amount of money that will put the owner in the same position in which it would have found itself but for the breach.[13] In determining how these damages might be calculated, it is helpful to address the three separate dimensions of performance that the owner expects.

First, the owner is entitled to get the project completed for a specific price. If the contract is for a stipulated sum, this element is easier to measure. The owner is entitled to recover additional expenses when, for example, it must complete work that the contractor leaves unfinished or repair defective work. Similarly, when the contractor's breach forces the owner to spend more on design professional or construction manager fees, the owner is entitled to recover those additional fees so as to protect the benefit of its bargain. Of course, the owner is still required to pay the full contract price. If the owner has paid $9,500,000 of a $10,000,000 contract and then spends another $200,000 completing or repairing work, it is still required to pay the balance of $300,000 to the original contractor. It may not retain the difference as a penalty. Many construction contracts specifically detail the owner's obligation to pay the

13. Semac Electric Company, Inc. v. Skanska USA Building, Inc., 195 Conn. App. 695, 720, 2020 WL 611808, at *11 (Conn. App. 2020).

contractor the balance of the contract price once any damage for completing or repairing work is retained from the contract price.

Second, the owner is entitled to have the project completed on time. When a project is late, the owner may suffer such damages as extended design professional or construction management fees, lost profits or income from the delay in putting the project into service, and additional financing costs associated with the delay. Each of these may be recovered as part of the effort to put the owner in the same position it would have found itself but for the breach.[14]

Third, the owner is entitled to receive a project of the quality promised in the contract documents. When the construction is substandard, two ramifications may arise: the construction may need to be repaired or improved to the quality promised, and the value of the project may be diminished as a consequence of the substandard construction. When construction is substandard, the most common measure of damages to give the owner the benefit of its bargain is the cost of repair.[15]

However, where reasonable repairs may leave the project in a condition in which the fair market value is still diminished below that of the promised construction, the court may award an amount of money representing the diminution in value of the property after repair together with the costs of repair. For example, in *Northern Petrochemical Co. v. Thorsen & Thorshov, Inc.*,[16] an owner brought an action against its architect, structural engineer, and general contractor for the faulty construction and subsequent reconstruction of an industrial building. The Supreme Court of Minnesota held that "[t]he preferred measure of damages in a case such as this is to take either the cost of reconstruction in accordance with the contract, if this is possible without unreasonable economic waste, or the difference in the value of the building as contracted for and the value as actually built, if reconstruction would constitute unreasonable waste."[17]

---

14. As noted above, damages may not be speculative, and thus in some cases lost profits are not available because any award of lost profits would require too much by way of conjecture.

15. State Farm Fire & Casualty Company., et al., Plaintiffs-Appellants, v. Capital Roofing, LLC, et al., 2020-Ohio-642, ¶ 67, 2020 WL 901454, at *15 (Ohio App. 2020).

16. Northern Petrochemical Co. v. Thorsen & Thorshov, Inc., 211 N.W.2d 159, 165 (Minn. 1973).

17. *Id.*

c. Contractor's Compensation

From a general perspective, the contractor's ultimate goal is to protect its profit interest in the contract. When the contract as bid results in a loss to the contractor, of course, the contractor wants to limit its loss. Such a simplistic statement belies the complexity of determining damages from the contractor's perspective for breach by the owner.[18] In more complex cases, it is helpful to characterize the contractor's general expectation interest (that is, the *benefit of the bargain)* as the right to complete the contractual scope of work in accordance with plans and specifications, within the time permitted under the contract, and without interference from the design professional or construction manager. Ultimately, the frustration of any of these expectations affects the contractor's bottom line in a manner that ultimately is measured by reference to the original contract price. However, discussing each of these dimensions is instructive.

First, the contractor is entitled to complete the scope of work within the original plans and specifications. To the extent that the scope of work is expanded by the addition of other tasks not in the original contract, the contractor is entitled to recover its cost and reasonable overhead and profit associated with the additional work. When work is simply added to the contract, the claim is relatively straightforward. More complicated analysis is required when the plans and specifications are deficient in some respect, and the resolution of conflicts or deficiencies arguably adds to the work that the contractor is required to perform. Still, from a conceptual standpoint, a contractor is required to perform (and is entitled to perform) all and only the work set out in the original contract for the contract price.[19]

Second, the contractor is entitled to complete the contract within the time limits set out in the contract, at least to the extent the contractor's original schedule is reasonable. When the contractor's work is delayed as a consequence of problems attributable to others, the contractor will likely lose money through additional expenditures related to the delay. In protecting the benefit of the contractor's bargain, the court will allow recovery of sufficient damages

---

18. When the breach is simply a payment default, damages are easy to calculate. This section presumes that the breach arises from interference by the owner, delay, bad plans and specifications, or other causes resulting in more typical damages described below.

19. This presumes that the contract is a lump sum contract or a cost-plus with a guaranteed maximum price. When the contract price is a cost-plus term, the battle will less often be fought over scope of work and instead focus on the extent to which the contractor's charges for work are reasonable.

to compensate the contractor for those additional expenses related to delay in completion of the work.

Finally, the contractor is entitled to complete the project without unreasonable interference by the owner or those acting on behalf of the owner; conversely, the contractor is entitled to cooperation and assistance from the owner in some respects. Many interference claims are inextricably intertwined with delay claims, but they are analytically distinct. Thus, for example, a contractor is entitled to reasonable access to the property for construction, reasonable response from the owner (or design professional) concerning owner-driven construction choices, reasonable responses to requests for information and submittals, and freedom from actual interference through the owner's, design professional's, or construction manager's unreasonable meddling. For example, when a portion of the property is not available for construction when promised, the contractor may suffer additional mobilization and demobilization costs even though the unavailable portion of the construction is not on the critical path. Of course, if access to the property is necessary to perform critical path work, delay damages may arise as well. Similarly, a contractor may have claims for inefficiency (discussed below) that do not necessarily delay ultimate completion of the contract, but that increase the contractor's cost of performance.

Ultimately, all of these elements of damages address different ways in which the benefit of the contractor's bargain to earn a profit on the project can be frustrated. Although they make computation of damages difficult in some cases, they do not change the general measure of damage that the court will impose for the owner's breach—that is, awarding the contractor that amount of money that will put the contractor in the same financial position in which it would have found itself but for the owner's breach.

A number of these individual elements are discussed in more detail below, as they have their own nuances and rules with which the construction professional should be familiar.

2. *Promissory Estoppel*

The measure of damage for promissory estoppel is somewhat amorphous, as it requires that the court award the promisee an amount of money to protect its reliance on the promise. This *reliance interest is* typically calculated as the amount of money that the promisee lost in reliance on the promise, and in many cases does not include any element of profit for the promisee. In some cases, the reliance interest is very much like the calculation of damages as though a contract had been performed. Thus, for example, if a contractor justifiably relies on a steel erector's bid of $250,000 in bidding for the construction of a warehouse, and the steel erector refuses to perform, thereby forcing the contractor to find a replacement at $300,000, the reliance interest is $50,000—the difference between the bid and the actual cost. This is precisely the measure that would be used for simple breach of the steel erector's contract had it not shown up on the job.[20] However, that is not always the case, and the measure that protects the promisee's reliance should be distinguished from the remedy for breach of contract.

3. Unjust Enrichment

The value of the benefit conferred is the "reasonable value" of what it would have cost the party to obtain it from another person, or the extent to which the party's property has been increased or its other interest advanced.[21] Most courts refer to this remedy as "restitution," as it forces the benefited party to disgorge the value of the benefit, where the value is measured from the perspective of *the enriched party.* Accordingly, unjust enrichment is distinct from both breach of contract and promissory estoppel, which look to the damage to the promisee. Unjust enrichment instead looks to the value conferred on the recipient and is not concerned with adequate compensation of the claiming party as much as it is concerned with making sure the recipient does not benefit unfairly. Thus, for example, if a tenant contracts for the improvement of a building and skips out before paying the bill, the contractor may be able to recover from the owner of the building. However, the measure of damages will not look to the contract price of the improvements, but rather will look to the value of the improvements to the building owner if the contractor can establish entitlement to recovery.

B. Tort Claims

The general measure of compensatory damages for negligence claims is similar to the measure for contract claims: it is that amount of money that will put the injured person in the same position as the injured person would have enjoyed but for the negligence of the defendant. In practical application to construction cases where the alleged negligence is founded on breach of the duty to provide suitable plans and specifications or not to design a project

---

20. Some courts analyze bid defaults under contract principles, others under principles of promissory estoppel.

21. RESTATEMENT (SECOND) OF CONTRACTS § 371 (1981).

negligently, this measure results in calculations similar or identical to those that determine breach of contract damages.

However, there are key differences to the measure of damages anchored on negligence rather than on breach of contract. First, negligence claims very often avoid many contractual limitations or conditions on damages. Second, contract damages are limited to those reasonably foreseen by the parties at the time of their contract as arising from any potential breach. Tort damages, however, are limited by proximate cause, which looks to what a reasonable person would have foreseen as a probable consequence of the commission of the tort at the time it was committed.

Some other tort claims have different measure of damages. For example, the measure of damages for negligent misrepresentation is the difference in value between what the victim would have enjoyed had the facts been as represented and the value of what the victim enjoyed, based upon the actual facts. Although this does not always result in a number that is different from the general calculation, it is a different measure in principle.

The scope of this chapter does not allow a thorough treatment of all the different measures of damage for every conceivable tort related to construction work, but most claims are subsumed within the category of general negligence.

Library References

C.J.S. *Damages* §§ 105–128, 141, 144–153, 163–164; C.J.S. *Parent and Child* § 344.
West's Key No. Digests, Damages <KEY>95–102, 117–126; Implied and Constructive Contracts <KEY> 110–112.

IV. Calculation and Proof of Compensatory Damages

A. General Damages

The general measures of damages are set out above. This section endeavors to summarize some of the most important principles concerning the calculation and proof of damages in construction cases.

The proof of damages that a party is entitled to collect is not a difficult task conceptually; rather, as the saying goes, the "devil is in the details." For example, when the owner contracts for the construction of a hospital for $40,000,000 (inclusive of design and contract administration fees) to be completed in the second year after the contract is let, and the project actually takes four years with substantial elements having been completed by the owner due to the contractor's default at a total cost of $48,000,000, the owner's damages are $8,000,000, plus interest and attorneys' fees when available, plus lost profits or carrying charges (or both). Determining the actual costs is never so simple as this example intimates, however. Similarly, when a contractor agrees to build the hospital for $40,000,000 over two years (with a profit of $3,000,000 built into the budget) but, because of delays by the owner and engineer, it costs the contractor $48,000,000 out of pocket and takes four years, the contractor's damages are $11,000,000 ($48,000,000 in costs plus $3,000,000 in profit, on top of the $40,000,000 contract price), plus home office overhead and consequential damages when recoverable. Of course, merely providing the numbers by way of example skips over the most difficult portion: figuring out what the recoverable costs really are.

B. Direct Costs

I. *In General*

Direct costs are typically those costs that can be identified specifically with and charged in whole or in part to a particular project and a particular cause within the contract. Where the contractor maintains a detailed and sophisticated cost accounting system, it may be possible to extract direct costs related to particular causes from the cost records. For example, if the engineer changes the specification of pumps mid-project, the additional compensation may be as simple as determining the difference in cost between the pumps specified and the pumps actually utilized.

Many claims are not as straightforward. If the substitution of pumps comes at a time when the pumps are on the project's critical path and there is insufficient lead time to order new pumps without delaying the project, the contractor may be entitled to recover not only the additional costs of the pump, but the results of the delay to the work as well. That delay, in turn, may be as simple as a couple of days of idle labor and equipment. More probable is that the calculation of the cost must accommodate the fact that otherwise idle crews or equipment were utilized to accelerate work on different parts of, perhaps diminishing the total delay or at the very least reducing the cost of, other work.

In short, the most accurate calculation of damages will always be to trace the direct consequences of a breach by one party, attribute and document a direct cost to every such consequence, and then award as compensation the sum of those direct costs. On discrete problems in the construction process, a reasonable approximation of direct costs may be had. The accuracy and reliably of direct cost calculations diminish as the ramifications of a particular breach widen.[22]

---

22. Similarly, proof of direct costs diminishes with incompleteness, inaccuracy, or simplicity of the cost accounting system utilized by the contractor.

2. *Price Increases for Labor and Material*

It is not unusual for delay or disruption to a project to result in the performance of work during a later period of time at a higher cost than originally anticipated. The escalation in cost may result from scheduled increases in material costs or wage increases in a collective bargaining agreement. Escalated costs may also occur from unknown or unanticipated events (e.g., a natural disaster that increases construction material costs).

A schedule analysis may be necessary to establish that the uncertainty of the length of delay prevented the contractor from obtaining firm material, labor, or subcontract orders and to establish when such orders would have been placed but for the delay.[23] When changes in prices can be documented (both as to binding commitments for prices at the time work should have been performed and at the time work was actually performed), the difference in such prices may be recovered as part of the calculation of damages.

3. *Idle Equipment and Related Costs*

Where the owner causes delay to a project and a contractor has committed its construction equipment to the project but has been unable to use it, the contractor may be entitled to compensation for costs incurred while the equipment is idle. Equipment costs and delay claims are oftentimes the most significant costs and there is often substantial dispute regarding the rate at which the equipment should be charged.

There are different mechanisms for valuing idle equipment damages. For contractor-owned equipment, the measure is the contractor's actual cost to own the equipment. Ownership costs include the capital cost of the equipment, depreciation, major repairs, storage, taxes, and other direct costs and can be difficult to prove. However, many contracts incorporate equipment schedules for the purpose of establishing equipment costs for change orders, and these schedules can be equally applied to establish damages for idle equipment. When the contractor rents equipment, the cost attributable to idle equipment is easily established by showing an invoice from a third party and payment thereof. If the contractor's record keeping is not sufficiently detailed to determine actual costs, then the contractor may resort to industry-published rates that set forth the average cost of ownership or third-party rental rates.

---

23. Michael Dodd & J. Duncan Findlay, State-by-State Guide to Construction Contracts and Claims § 1.05[c][10] (2005).

4. Home Office Overhead

When a contractor maintains a home office for the management of work over several projects, it expects to recover the cost of that home office through its general overhead and profit on the various jobs it performs. When one job is delayed and precludes the contractor from accepting other work, one effect is that the contractor's home office overhead is spread over fewer jobs, and thereby diminishes the contractor's ability to recover that overhead (in turn, lowering the contractor's overall profitability).

Accordingly, home office overhead is recoverable as an element of delay damages when the owner is responsible for the extended performance of a contract.[24] However, a claimant must establish a prima facie case for recovery of home office overhead, as the general description of the circumstances of home office maintenance are not always accurate. Thus, a contractor must establish that:

a. performance of the contract was delayed due to inexcusable actions or inaction of the owner;
b. the contractor suffered actual damages as a result of the delay;
c. the nature of the delay made it impractical for the contractor to undertake the performance of other work; or
d. the nature of the delay made it impractical to reduce home office overhead costs.[25]

Once established, the claimant must then determine the proper measure of calculating home office overhead damages. As a result of delay to a project, the contractor does not realize direct billings in the same time period as anticipated. Therefore, the home office overhead is unabsorbed or under-absorbed. Unabsorbed overhead occurs when there is no extra work associated with the extended time against which the contractor can bill its overhead. Under-absorbed overhead typically occurs with disruption or partial delay where the contractor is still realizing some direct billings, but the amount of work has been severely reduced.

There are several methods for calculating unabsorbed home office overhead. The most frequently used is the *Eichleay* formula.[26] This formula is

---

24. Altmayer v. Johnson, 79 F.3d 1129 (Fed. Cir. 1996).

25. Mech-Con Corp. v. West, 61 F.3d 883 (Fed. Cir. 1995) (setting out first three elements). Many cases omit the fourth element as an express requirement.

26. *Eichleay Corp*, ASBCA No. 5183, 60-2 B.C.A. (CCH) ¶ 2688, 1960 WL 538 (1960).

designed to calculate the daily home office overhead sustained in order to continue day-to-day operations during an owner-caused delay in a project.[27] In order to determine the amount of unabsorbed home office overhead, the *Eichleay* calculation requires three steps. First, the court must determine the overhead on the delayed contract by multiplying the contractor's total overhead by some ratio between the contractor's billings on the delayed contract and the contractor's total billings for the period of the delayed contract.[28] Next, a daily overhead rate for the delayed contract must be determined by dividing the contract overhead by the total days of contract performance.[29] Finally, the total recoverable overhead must be calculated by multiplying the daily overhead rate for the delayed contract by the total length in days of the delay.[30] Although the *Eichleay* formula is the preeminent method of calculating recoverable home office overhead, courts have developed other formulas that incorporate the same concepts.[31] For example, the *Hudson* formula, which is more prevalent in England and Canada, centers on the percentage of profits and overhead accounted for in the initial bid.[32]

In disputes where contractors have asserted *Eichleay* or similar formulas as a means of home office overhead recovery, owners have asserted a number of defenses that administrative agency decisions have upheld.[33] Among others, the list of defenses and mitigating factors include: (1) failure by the contractor to pursue substitute work;[34] (2) offset of the home office overhead claimed by the contractor for additional compensation paid by the owner during the delay period pursuant to change orders;[35] and (3) negation of the claim due to over-recovery by the contractor in active periods following the delay.[36] Although these and other defenses have prevailed in certain cases, in most situations where a contractor is able to show the existence of the aforementioned

27. John D. Darling, *Delay of Game: One of the Thorniest Issues in Delay and Disruption Litigation Is the Quantification of Actual Damages,* 27 L.A. LAW. 31 (2005).

28. Reginald M. Jones, *Recovering Extended Home Office Overhead: What Is the State of* Eichleay?, 40 PROCUREMENT LAWYER 8 (2004).

29. *Id.*

30. *Id.*

31. Patrick A. McGeehin & Carleton O. Strouss, *Learning from* Eichleay*: Unabsorbed Overhead Claims in State and Local Jurisdictions*, 25 PUB. CONT. L.J. 351, 358 (1996).

32. *Id.* at 359.

33. *Id.*

34. *Id.*

35. *Id.* at 362.

36. *Id.* at 364.

elements, *Eichleay* has become the bench mark means for recovery in owner-caused delay cases.[37]

5. Lost Profits

Lost profits are subsumed within the damage calculations above when the contractor is working under a stipulated sum contract. When the contractor is working under a cost-plus contract, the contractor's lost profit is recoverable as a separate element when establishing the plus portion of the contract entitlement.

Design professionals generally do not seek recovery of lost profits for *additional* work, but instead seek recovery based on the contractual value of their services, which may include a component for profit. On the other hand, when an owner breaches a contract with a design professional by terminating the design professional, for example, the design professional is entitled to recover the value of payments promised less any costs the design professional avoided by not having to perform the work.[38]

Finally, an owner may be entitled to recover its lost profits for delay in completion of a project due to the fault of the general contractor or the design professional or construction manager. The recovery of lost profits for new business has never found much favor in the court inasmuch as lost future profit claims for new businesses involve substantial speculation at times. Indeed, the "new business rule" in many states bars recovery of lost profits for new businesses.[39] The modern trend is not to prohibit the recovery of lost future profits for new businesses outright, but rather to treat the question of such recovery as a matter of evidentiary sufficiency under which the court must assess the extent to which a claim for lost future profits of a new business can survive challenges to the potentially speculative nature of such damage claims.[40] When a business owner can establish with reasonable certainty the fact of its damage, and provide sufficient proof as to what its future profits would have been had the building been completed on time, it may be entitled to recover damages for lost profits.

---

37. *Id.* at 359.

38. Some of the principles, such as the requirement that the design professional mitigate its damages, may alter the calculation in particular circumstances.

39. State-by-State Guide to Construction Contracts and Claims 1.05[C][13], *supra* note 23.

40. ITT Water & Wastewater USA, Inc. v. L D'Agostini & Sons, Inc., 2016 WL 1072632, at *17 (Mich. App. 2016); Drews Co. v. Ledwith-Wolfe Assocs., Inc., 296 S.C. 207, 371 S.E.2d 532 (S.C. 1988).

6. Delay/Disruption Damages

The delay of the completion of a contract increases both the owner's and the contractor's costs. In fact, in many cases damages arising from delay are substantially greater than other damages. By the same token, damages from delay are difficult to quantify, largely because the actual consequences of delay are not always easy to trace, as discussed above. Nonetheless, when a party can establish its additional costs attributable to delay (discussed further below), such costs are generally deemed to be recoverable as part of the overall scheme of compensatory damages. These are generally referred to as *compensable delays.*

There are some delays that excuse a contractor's tardy completion of work but for which the contractor is not entitled to additional compensation. For example, if the project experiences unusually adverse weather, the contractor may be entitled to an extension of contract time without receiving additional compensation, even if the contractor experiences extra costs for idle equipment, etc. These are referred to as *excusable delays* to distinguish them from compensable delays.

7. Loss of Efficiency/Productivity

While *delay* denotes an extension of the time necessary to complete all or part of a project, *inefficiency* and *loss of productivity* generally denote additional expense in the completion of work as a consequence of conditions in the field being different from those the contractor envisioned in accepting the work. Dozens of types of inefficiency have been identified, ranging from the inefficiency that arises from working in adverse weather conditions to inefficiency related to dilution of supervision. Sometimes it is impossible to segregate direct costs from costs incurred as a result of a loss of efficiency. However, the principle for calculating such damages can be stated simply: the actual costs with disruption less what it would have cost without the disruption equals the disruption damages. In practice, determining these two components is more difficult and is met with varying degrees of success. The method for determining damages for loss of efficiency often depends upon the nature of the work and the information available, and is discussed below regarding proof of additional costs.

8. Liquidated Damages

Liquidated damages are contractual instruments used to fix compensatory damages in the event of late completion of a defined scope of work.[41] A

41. William Schwarzkopf & John J. McNamara, Calculating Construction Damages § 13.02, at 257 (2d ed. 2000).

liquidated damage clause sets a specific amount of damages that one party may recover from another as a result of certain breaches of the contract. The provision must represent a reasonable approximation of the damages to be incurred in the event of the stated event. If the provision is merely used to punish a party for delay or the provision is used as an additional incentive to prevent breach or provide additional profit to the nonbreaching party, the liquated damages provision is likely to be held void as an unenforceable penalty.[42]

While contractors often view a liquidated damage clause with trepidation, such clauses may actually be advantageous to a breaching party. Although they relieve the injured party of the obligation to prove actual damage, such clauses may actually provide a significant limitation on the damage otherwise recoverable and provide the party with a known exposure. For instance, on a fast-track casino project, the owner will generally have pro forma projections well supported by historical evidence that can be used to establish large amounts of revenue and profit lost as a result of a late opening. A liquidated damage provision may limit the amount otherwise recoverable by the casino owner.

Liquidated damages are appropriate only if they are a genuine attempt to fix damages—that is, they represent the parties' estimate as to the damages that the injured party would suffer from late completion—and they cannot be a penalty in disguise. Simply referring to the provision as "liquidated damages" does not make it one; rather, the circumstances surrounding the contract and the objective intent of the parties determine the actual nature of the clause.[43] As a general rule, a penalty provision seeks to secure performance, whereas a liquidated damages provision seeks payment in lieu of performance.[44] Case law suggests there is often a fine line between the two concepts, and the distinction hinges primarily on reasonableness and, to a lesser extent, on party intent. A liquidated damages provision deemed unreasonable under the circumstances is void as a penalty; specifically, a provision purporting to award an unreasonably large amount of liquidated damages is void.[45]

Liquidated damages are valid only if actual damages are difficult to ascertain and the proposed sum is reasonable.[46] Liquidated damages are appropriate

---

42. *See, e.g.*, Proulx v. 1400 Pennsylvania Avenue, SE, LLC, 199 A.3d 667, 674 (D.C. App. 2019); U.S. Fidelity & Guar. Co. v. Braspetro Oil Servs. Co., 369 F.3d 34 (2d Cir. 2004) (New York law).

43. United Tunneling Enters., Inc. v. Havens Constr. Co., 35 F. Supp. 2d 789 (D. Kan. 1998).

44. Unified Sch. Dist. No. 315 v. DeWerff, 6 Kan. Ct. App. 77, 79 (1981).

45. Kan. Stat. Ann. § 84-2-718 (2019).

46. *Unified Sch. Dist. No. 31 S*, 6 Kan. Ct. App. at 82.

only where actual damages cannot be demonstrated with reasonable certainty. If damages for breach can be anticipated conclusively, a provision claiming to be liquidated damages is an unreasonable, inappropriate remedy and thus will likely be construed as a penalty.[47]

Under all those factors, a provision is reasonable if (1) the sum resembles the anticipated or actual harm from the breach; (2) there is difficulty proving the amount of loss; and (3) liquidated damages presents the most feasible avenue for adequate relief.[48] In some instances, the court equates "reasonable" with "conscionable," stating that a liquidated damages provision is unreasonable only if it "shocks the conscious" and violates public policy.[49] Regardless of how reasonable the sum for liquidated damages might appear, the provision must be considered a penalty if the drafting party makes no attempt to calculate the amount of actual damages that might be sustained in the event of breach.

The most common liquidated damage clauses concern late completion and are expressed as a specific amount for each specific day that the project completion is late. However, liquidated damage clauses need not be limited merely to delays to project completion.[50]

9. *Interest*

Interest on a claim may be provided by contract or by statute. If provided by contract, the percentage of interest is either specified in the contract or paid to a benchmark, such as one percent above a specified prime rate as published in the *Wall Street Journal.*

If no rate of interest is provided in the contract, most states will have a default rate of interest that will apply. Some jurisdictions also have a Prompt Pay Statute that provides a specified rate of interest. Oftentimes, the interest rate will be the default rate of interest. However, if payment was withheld without just cause or excuse or in bad faith, then an enhanced rate of interest may apply.[51]

Pre-judgment interest on the principal amount is generally recoverable provided that the amount of the principal is liquidated and the date the principal amount became due is known or readily ascertainable. Whether or not it

---

47. Kvassay v. Murray, 15 Kan. Ct. App. 2d 426 (1991).

48. Kan. Stat. Ann. § 84-2-718.

49. TMG Life Ins. Co. v. Ashner, 21 Kan. Ct. App. 2d 234 (1995).

50. State-by-State Guide to Construction Contracts and Claims, *supra* note 23, § 1.02(e), at 13.

51. Mo. REV. STAT. § 34.057(2013).

is liquidated depends upon whether it is undisputed or, although disputed, is capable of determination by mathematical computation.

Post-judgment interest is generally recoverable from the date of the judgment. Post-judgment is interest generally fixed by statute or may be tied to some economic standard, such as the U.S. Treasury rate. In such instances, the applicable rate at the time of the judgment will become the post-judgment rate of interest and will apply throughout collection of the judgment.

10. Attorneys' Fees

Generally, under U.S. law, a prevailing party is not entitled to recover its attorneys' fees from any other party. This system, in which each party is responsible for its own attorneys' fees, is known as the *American Rule.* However, there are several widespread exceptions to the American Rule, and parties may be entitled to recover attorneys' fees when:

a. there is a contractual provision which provides for the recovery of such fees;
b. a statute permits recovery of such fees; or
c. the opposing party has acted either fraudulently or in bad faith in bringing or maintaining the lawsuit.[52]

Under the first exception, many contracts contain a prevailing party attorneys' fees clause under which a party that prevails in litigation, under contract, may be awarded its attorneys' fees. The second exception for statutory attorneys' fees is found most often when a statute is designed not only to protect parties but also when the claim is of a nature that the legislature wants to ensure that claimants are not deterred from potentially meritorious claims because of the relative expense of litigation in light of the size of the typical claim. The third category covers frivolous or groundless suits. Although some parties take comfort in the fact that attorneys' fees may be awarded for the defense against a frivolous or groundless claim in most states, the comfort should be tempered by a realistic understanding that such fee awards are very difficult, as a practical matter, to obtain.

C. Alternative Methods for Calculating Damages

As noted earlier, the most satisfactory and most reliable method for proving damages is to tie particular costs to particular causes. When this method is possible, courts expect proof that is anchored in direct demonstration of the

52. Calculating Construction Damages, *supra* note 41, 10.01, at 213.

resulting costs of another's breach of duty. At the same time, courts recognize that tying individual consequences and costs to particular causes is not always an easy task, and if such demanding proof were required in every case, many parties with meritorious claims would be left without any remedy for want of their ability to prove exact damages through the direct cost method. As a consequence, and with the goal of not denying relief where the fact of damages is certain but the quantification is not susceptible to precise proof, courts have accepted a number of alternatives to proof of direct costs.

1. Total Cost

The simplest but also the most controversial and least accepted method is the total cost method. The total cost method calculates damages as the difference between the total actual costs incurred, including overhead and profit, and the bid amount.[53] While the simplicity of the method appeals to claimants, courts have criticized the method due to the assumption that all cost overruns are the responsibility of the project owner.[54] As such, courts disfavor and, in some cases, reject use of this method to calculate damages.[55]

The courts have been critical of the total cost method because it assumes that the contractor's original bid was reasonable and the work could have been completed for the bid amount absent breach of the contract. It further assumes that all of the cost overruns were caused by the conduct of the breaching party and none of them were caused by the contractor's own problems or inefficiencies. To protect against the inaccuracies and potential inequity inherent in the total cost method, courts have developed four elements that a claimant must establish before proceeding with the total cost method.[56] The claimant seeking damages through the total cost method must prove that:

a. the nature of the particular losses makes it impossible or highly impracticable to determine them with a reasonable degree of accuracy;
b. the contractor's bid or estimate was realistic;
c. the contractor's actual costs were reasonable; and
d. the contractor was not responsible for the cost overrun.[57]

53. *Id.* § 1.03[C], at 14.
54. *Id.*
55. *Id.*
56. *Id.* § 1.03[C], at 15.
57. *Id.*

If the claimant can establish each of the four premises, then the claimant may proceed with the calculation of damages under the total cost method.

2. Modified Total Cost

The modified total cost method was developed to address some of the inherent flaws in the total cost method.[58] Essentially, the modified total cost method reduces the amount calculated under the total cost method by any errors in the bid, costs attributable to the contractor, and costs attributable to parties other than the owner.[59] The resulting damage is presumed to more accurately reflect the damage directly suffered by the claimant.[60]

In a modified total cost, the contractor carefully scrutinizes its bid and takes responsibility for any errors. The contractor also analyzes its own performance on the project and assumes responsibility for any of its own inefficiencies. This is not to say that the contractor must reduce its claim by all inefficiencies that the contractor experienced, as some normal inefficiencies would be assumed in the contractor's bid. The contractor need only assume responsibility for those problems or inefficiencies outside the norm.

3. Measured Mile

In a measured mile approach, the claimant compares the productivity achieved on an unaffected portion of the project with the productivity achieved on an affected portion.[61] Productivity is typically based on hours or dollars per unit of work achieved.[62] It is one of the preferred measures of inefficiency or loss of productivity because it uses actual historical data from the project.[63] It is critical that one prove that the affected and unaffected areas compared represent comparable work, where the only material variable is the disruption caused by the breaching party.[64] In addition, the unaffected work must be large enough to be material and to be representative of the type of work on the project as a

---

58. *Id.* § 1.03[D], at 21.

59. *Id.*

60. *Id.*

61. John D. Darling, *Delay of Game: One of the Thorniest Issues in Delay and Disruption Litigation Is the Quantification of Actual Damages*, 27 L.A. Law. 31, 36 (2005).

62. *Id.*

63. *See id.*

64. *Id.*

whole. If the nonbreaching party cannot prove these criteria, the other party will attack the base line productivity calculations for being faulty.[65]

By its very nature, the measured mile approach requires that some portion of the project be unaffected by the delay or disruption. As a result, this method may not be available where such delay or disruption has continued throughout the project.

4. *Should-Cost Estimates*

If the measured mile approach is not available, an estimate of what the cost should have been without disruption may be a reliable substitute. Where the measured mile approach compares performance on the same project, performance on other projects for substantially similar work may form the basis for reasonably estimating what performance on a particular project should reasonably have cost had there been no disruption.[66]

5. *Industry Standards and Studies*

In certain instances where the measured mile approach and the should-cost estimate may not be available (the entire project was affected and the contractor had not previously performed comparable work), it may be necessary to rely upon industry standards or studies. Such standards and studies have been developed in the industry through the MCAA, Business Round Table, and R.S. Means.

6. *Time-and-Motion Studies*

Where a contractor cannot provide an actual, unaffected performance period for the current job that would allow a measured mile approach or other contemporaneous jobs that would allow a should-cost estimate, the contractor may consider using a time-and-motion study. These studies are generally done by experts, and they attempt to measure the loss in both labor and equipment efficiency by approximating an unaffected sequence and comparing it to an affected sequence.[67]

---

65. *Id.*

66. State-by-State Guide to Construction Contracts and Claims, *supra* note 23, § 1.05[c][6].

67. *Id.* § 1.05[c][8].

7. *Jury Verdict Method*

Where damages cannot be easily determined from a contractor's evidence, a court may allow a jury to consider the evidence and make a reasonable judgment. This is generally expressed by the jury in a lump sum. The court may then still have the option of determining the percentage of damage attributable to the owner's own inefficiency.[68]

The jury verdict method allows the jury to determine the amount of damages suffered based on equitable considerations.[69] The trier of fact is responsible for determining what it considers a fair and reasonable amount as damages.[70] Oftentimes, the total cost method or the modified total cost method is used by a party to establish a basis for the jury or factfinder to make its decision.[71]

D. Consequential Damages

Consequential damages or "special damages" are damages that are caused by a breach of duty, but whose existence or impact is less readily or directly traceable to the breach than compensatory damages.[72] These damages may include lost rents, lost profits other than profits anticipated directly from the work, extended financing costs, loss of business, and loss of bonding capacity.[73] Consequential damages may be recoverable in actions based in contract if reasonably foreseeable. They are generally not recoverable in actions based on unjust enrichment. Consequential damages may be recoverable in tort, depending upon the nature of the tort, where the issue is proximate causation and not reasonable foreseeability.

E. Punitive Damages

Punitive damages are intended to punish a malicious wrongdoer and to deter the wrongdoer and others from behaving in a similar fashion in the future. Punitive damages in the construction industry are rare, and many jurisdictions do not allow the recovery of punitive damages for breach of contract. Because punitive damages are generally not available in breach of contract actions in

---

68. *Id.* § 1.05[c][9].
69. CALCULATING CONSTRUCTION DAMAGES, *supra* note 41, § 1.04[A], at 29.
70. *Id.*
71. *Id.*
72. *Id.* § 1.03, at 9.
73. *Id.* § 1.03, at 9 n.10.

general, in order to recover there must be an independent tort involving outrageous or malicious conduct.[74]

Library References

C.J.S. *Admiralty* § 229; C.J.S. *Costs* § 125; C.J.S. *Damages* §§ 21–33, 38, 425, 53–74, 80–91, 154–162, 175–201, 208–217, 380–382; C.J.S. *Interest and Usury* §§ 12, 13, 60–63, 77–78, 85–87; C.J.S. *Consumer Credit* §§ 34, 37, 41; C.J.S. *Parent and Child* § 344; C.J.S. *Torts* § 26.
West's Key No. Digests, Costs <KEY>194.16; Damages <KEY>15–17, 21–30, 35–46, 66, 74–94, 226; Interest <KEY>29, 31, 38.

V. Defenses to and Mitigation of Damage Claims

A. Economic Waste

While the cost of repair is the basic measure of damage for many breaches of construction contracts, this measure may not be applied where the repair cost is exorbitant, taking into account the nature of the damage, the value of the work at issue, the value of the project in general, and the diminution in value of the product in light of the damage. In other terms, where the cost of repair is manifestly excessive in light of the other elements, a court may not award the cost of repair as the measure of damages.[75] "Where such a case occurs and it is also a case where completion or repair will be inordinately expensive, the policy against economic waste suggests use of the value formula rather than the cost formula."[76] As applied, the value formula consists of the diminution in value of the structure as opposed to the cost actually required to repair the structure.[77]

As an example of economic waste, in the *County of Maricopa v. Walsh Oberg Architects, Inc.*, the county obtained a judgment against its architect for the negligent preparation of plans and specifications for an underground parking garage that was designed to be waterproof but failed to prevent water

---

74. State-by-State Guide to Construction Contracts and Claims, *supra* note 23, § 1.05[f].

75. Sela Roofing and Remodeling, Inc. v. Moot, 2017 WL 3863122, at *3 (Minn. App. 2017); Charlotte v. Skidmore, Owings and Merrill, 407 S.E.2d 571, 581 (N.C. Ct. App. 1991); Restatement (First) of Contracts § 346 cmt. b (prohibiting an award of damages that would result in economic waste, or "cost[s] that would be imprudent and unreasonable").

76. *Id.* (citing D. Dobbs, Handbook of the Law of Remedies 12.21 (1973)).

77. *Id.* at 580.

from dripping onto cars below. The county alleged that it would cost approximately $498,169 to remove landscaping and cover the top of the underground structure with a waterproof membrane. The Arizona Court of Appeals was persuaded by the fact that it cost the county far less to perform an alternate remedy that would protect the vehicles from water damage and prevent further deterioration. As such, the court of appeals recognized that it would be economic waste to award the county more than one-third of a million dollars to merely remove landscaping when an alternate remedy existed.[78]

B. Failure to Mitigate Damages

Even though victimized by the conduct of another party, an injured party has an affirmative obligation to mitigate its damages. That is, the injured party must take reasonable steps to minimize the damages it will suffer. For instance, where a contractor has been prevented from working on one area of the project, the contractor may have an affirmative obligation to make its best effort to continue to work by moving to another unaffected area of the project.

When a party does not undertake reasonable steps to mitigate its damages, it does so at the risk of losing part of its right to recover damages. In particular, a party generally may not recover as part of its damages any money that represents damages that the claiming party could have avoided through more prudent conduct.

C. Betterment

The concept of betterment is widely recognized in the construction industry.[79] As a general principle, when there is a defect in the work or an omission in the plans, the owner should not be placed in a better position than if the error had not occurred. This concept is known as betterment, added value, or added first benefit.[80]

---

78. County of Maricopa v. Walsh and Oberg Architects, Inc., 494 P.2d 44 (Ariz. Ct. App. 1972); *see also* Stovall v. Reliance Ins. Co., 107 P.3d 1219 (Kan. 2005).

79. *See* Jerome V. Bales, Shamus O'Meara & Mark R. Azman, *The "Betterment" or Added Benefit Defense*, 26 CONSTRUCTION LAWYER 14 (2006).

80. "Betterment" created by correction of inadvertent omission from original design for which the owner would have paid is a damage defense frequently asserted by design professionals. *See* Jerome V. Bales, Shamus O'Meara & Mark R. Azman, *The "Betterment" or Added Benefit Defense*, 26 CONSTRUCTION LAWYER 14 (2006); Ben Patrick, *The Added First Benefit Rule*, 24 CONSTRUCTION LAW 26 (Summer 2004); Stewart W. Karge, *Architect Engineer's Damages: The Added First Benefit Theory*,

The courts have generally held that if the design is incomplete, the owner should pay what the omitted component would have cost if it had been included in the original design.[81] Logically, the designer should pay any additional costs to the owner, such as any premium associated with the change order adding the component to the project.

When a design error is not discovered until during or after construction, the owner may be entitled to recover the cost of any retrofitting expense, waste, or an intervening increase in the cost of the labor or materials necessary to correct the error.[82]

Although there are no reported decisions on betterment involving construction managers in an advisor role, the concept should apply to the same extent that a designer could raise the betterment or added value defense.

Contractors are obligated to build a project in accordance with the plans and specifications. However, in some circumstances, contractors and construction managers at-risk may also rely upon the defense of betterment. For example, if the owner must repair or replace defective work, the courts have generally held that it should not recover the cost of any enhancement exceeding the quality evidenced in the contract documents.[83] When the repairs do not involve any enhancement, the owner's damages may still be reduced to the extent of any extended useful life of the building component.[84]

Library References

C.J.S. *Contracts* §§ 377, 565–566, 575–576; C.J.S. *Costs* §§ 125, 127; C.J.S. *Counties* §§ 159, 169; C.J.S. *Damages* §§ 46–52, 165–174; C.J.S. *Mechanics' Liens* § 31; C.J.S. *Municipal Corporations* §§ 944–946; C.J.S. *Principal and Surety* §§ *78, 82,* 120; C.J.S. *Public Contracts* § 28; C.J.S. *Schools and School Districts* §§ 43740, 446–450; C.J.S. *States* §§ 291–294; C.J.S. *United States* §§ 105–106, 127–130, 137, 139–148.

---

9 Construction Lawyer 1 (Nov. 1989). *See also* 6 Philip Bruner & Patrick O'Connor, Bruner & O'Connor Construction Law § 19:26 (2018).

81. *See, e.g.*, Cochrane Eng'g, Inc. v. Willingham Realgrowth Inv. Fund Ltd., 552 So. 2d 228 (Fla. Ct. App. 1989), *rev. denied*, 563 So. 2d 631 (Fla. 1990).

82. *See, e g.*, Grossman v. Sea Air Towers, Ltd., 513 So. 2d 686 (Fla. Ct. App. 1987), *rev. denied*, 520 So. 2d 584 (Fla. 1988).

83. *See, e.g.*, St. Joseph Hosp. v. Corbetta Constr. Co., Inc., 316 N.E.2d 51 (Ill. Ct. App. 1st Dist. 1974).

84. *See, e.g.*, Allied Chem. Corp. v. Van Buren Sch. Dist. No. 42, 575 S.W.2d 445 (Ark. 1979).

West's Key No. Digests, Contracts <KEY>284(1), 308; Costs <KEY>194.32; Counties <KEY> 128, 129; Damages <KEY>58–65; Mechanics' Liens <KEY>36; Municipal Corporations <KEY>253, 254; Principal and Surety <KEY>75, 77; Public Contracts <KEY>22; Schools <KEY>85; States <KEY>107; United States <KEY>67, 73.

VI. Protection for Performance and Payment Rights

A. In General

A party need not rely on its ability to obtain and collect a court judgment to protect its rights to payment for performance of a construction contract. Rather, there are several other protections afforded the parties, as described below.

B. Retention and Limitations Thereon

The first protection that an owner usually has against a contractor's failure to complete work is retention of a part of the contract price until final payment. This nominally ensures that the owner has a source of funds from which it can pay for completion of any work that the contractor does not finish. It also provides some motivation to the contractor not to walk off the job as soon as all but punch list items are done.

At the same time, there are often statutory limits on the amount of money an owner may hold pending completion of work. These statutes specify the amount of money, by percentage, that an owner may withhold from the contractor pending final payment. In general, the percentages are fixed (e.g., five percent or ten percent) and provide that the public owner may continue to retain funds until certain prescribed events, normally substantial completion, in order to ensure performance and payment by the contractor. The statutes alter the amount and timing of the payments that would otherwise be due to a contractor. Such a statute may also govern the relationship between contractors and subcontractors by providing that retention held from subcontractors may not exceed that withheld from the general contractor.

Retention laws are sometimes found within the context of Prompt Pay Statutes. At other times, they enjoy their own statutory scheme. In general, retention laws do not apply to design professionals. Very typically, retention laws are not applicable on private projects but retention may be, and often is, required by private contract.

Both the percentage of permissible retention and the time period for which one may hold retainage vary from jurisdiction to jurisdiction. On large projects, the amount of retainage may be substantial and the length of time in which it may be retained may be long. This can cause a substantial cash flow drain or, at a minimum, a loss of use of funds. As a result, some jurisdictions have allowed a payee to recover interest on its retainage.[85] Whether a person is entitled to interest on retainage varies from jurisdiction to jurisdiction. However, in almost all jurisdictions, retainage will accrue interest at the default statutory rate if not paid by the required date.

Some jurisdictions have addressed the competing interest between an owner's need for security and the contractor's requirements for cash flow by permitting a contractor to substitute a bond in lieu of retainage[86] or by allowing a contractor to pledge collateral, such as marketable securities.[87] An issue may sometimes arise as to whether or not limitations on retainage or entitlement to interest can be waived by contract. Again, as in other instances where an attempt is made by contract to waive statutory protections, such waivers are sometimes found to be void because they violate statute or are found to be unenforceable on public policy grounds.

C. Labor and Material Payment Bonds

Payment bonds, in and of themselves, are merely private contracts that guarantee the payment of certain claimants when specific conditions are met. Generally, these bonds serve to guarantee that materialmen are paid for the materials, equipment, and supplies services they provide.[88] In many cases, these bonds are required by either state or federal law in situations where subcontractors and materialmen cannot avail themselves of the protections of the state's lien statutes.

D. Performance Bonds

Unlike payment bonds, performance bonds are designed to protect owners from a contractor's failure to complete its contractual obligations.[89] Performance bonds are three-party agreements between the owner, also referred to as the *obligee,* the contractor, also referred to as the *principal,* and the surety. Under a performance bond, if a contractor/principal, fails to fulfill its

---

85. *See, e.g.*, OR. REV. STAT. § 701.420(2) (2018).

86. *See, e.g.*, MO. REV. STAT. § 436.312 (2019).

87. *See, e.g.*, OR. REV. STAT. § 279C.560.

88. D. Robert Beaumont, *Assuring Performance in International Construction Contracts,* 19 CONS. LAW. 5, 6 (1999).

89. ROBERT CUSHMAN & JOHN MEYERS, EDS., 2 CONSTRUCTION LAW HANDBOOK 35.01, at 1276 (1999).

obligations under the contract, the surety has an obligation to complete the project. The scope of the surety's obligations depend largely on the terms of the bond itself.[90]

E. Mechanics' Liens

While all states have enacted mechanics' lien laws, these "laws present an extraordinarily varied approach, in substance, and in language, to the issues involved in mechanics' lien legislation. In fact, variation among the states may be greater in this area than in any other statutory area."[91] However, while an individual state's laws must be referenced with regard to any specific question, general observations can be made.

Most states originally enacted mechanics' lien laws to protect construction laborers and contractors.[92] However, in recent years, many states have amended these laws to include the liens of design professionals. Yet, like the underlying lien laws themselves, the states have varied approaches to the protection. For example, Pennsylvania requires that the design professional contract directly with the owner to claim a lien.[93] Additionally, under Pennsylvania law, the design professional's lien is limited to administration services performed under the contract, as opposed to fees associated with preparation of the plans and specifications.[94] Typically, the critical consideration will be whether the services of a design professional or construction manager contributed to the improvement of real property.

F. Miller Act

The Miller Act was enacted to protect persons who supply labor and materials for construction of federal buildings.[95] The Act requires a performance and payment bond be furnished before any contract is awarded for the construction or repair of any U.S. public buildings or public work projects for contracts in excess of $100,000.[96] "The statute limits valid claims under the Act to persons who have a contractual relationship with the prime contractor, called a 'first

---

90. *Id.*

91. Phil Bruner & Patrick J. O' Connor, Bruner & O' Connor On Construction Law, *Payment Process* § 8:124 (2002) (citing Unif. Constr. Lien Act, *Prefatory Note*, *reprinted in* 7 U.L.A., pt. II, at 382).

92. *Id.* § 8:128.

93. *Id.*

94. *Id.*

95. 17 Am. Jur. 2d Contractor's Bonds § 134 (2004).

96. 40 U.S.C. §§ 270a–270f (2005).

tier' claimant, or with a subcontractor, a 'second tier' claimant."[97] Nevertheless, "a person who contracts with an entity holding a management contract for a public facility is also generally considered by the courts to be a Miller Act prime contractor."[98] The Act is highly remedial in nature and is to be construed liberally.[99] Because of this, courts tend to look at the overall relationship between the parties and not to the contract alone when determining if a party is a proper claimant.[100]

Although there is no express statutory requirement for an obligee to give notice to the contractor or surety that it is bringing an action against the performance bond, the bond itself could require notice. Claimants under the payment bond who are not in privity of contract with the contractor typically must give the contractor written notice of the work performed within ninety days from the date of last providing labor and material for which a claim is made.[101]

State statute of limitations governs the time frame for filing a performance bond lawsuit. In contrast, actions on a payment bond must be brought in the district court for the district in which the contract was to be performed within one year of last providing labor or materials.[102]

The Act does not contain a specific provision allowing the prevailing party in an action against a bond to recovery attorneys' fees. Even when state law would allow the recovery of attorneys' fees against a surety, the general rule is that attorneys' fees are not recoverable under a Miller Act bond.[103]

G. State Public Works Claims (Little Miller Acts)

Most states' public works acts limit claims against payment bonds.[104] While a potential claimant must examine the laws of the particular state, many states judicially define a claimant by examining the following factors:

---

97. CONSTRUCTION LAW HANDBOOK, *supra* note 89, § 36.03 [A], at 1318.

98. *Id.* § 36.03 [A], at 1318.

99. F.D. Rich Co. v. United States *ex rel.* Industrial Lumber Co., 417 U.S. 116 (1974).

100. Reagan v. Tri-County Excavating, Inc. 62 F.3d 501 (3rd Cir. 1995); United States *ex rel.* K&M Corp. v. A&M Gregos, Inc., 607 F.2d 44 (3rd Cir. 1979); United States *ex rel.* Greenwald Industrial Products Co. v. Barlows Commercial Constr. Co., 567 F. Supp. 464 (D.D.C. 1983).

101. 40 U.S.C. § 270b.

102. 40 U.S.C. § 270b.

103. F.D. Rich Co. v. United States *ex rel.* Industrial Lumber Co., 417 U.S. 116 (1974); United States *ex rel.* Leno v. Summit Constr. Co., 892 F.2d 788 (9th Cir. 1989).

104. CONSTRUCTION LAW HANDBOOK, *supra* note 89, § 36.03 [B], at 1320.

i. whether an entity constructs a definite or substantial part of the work called for in the prime contract;
ii. whether the work is performed according to the plans and specifications of the prime contract; and
iii. whether the plans and specifications of the prime contract call for a unique product not readily available on the open market.[105]

However, "design professionals and providers of services typically are not eligible as state public works bond claimants unless they perform services for the contractor or a subcontractor."[106]

H. Prompt Payment Statutes

Many jurisdictions have enacted legislation that provides enhanced remedies to contractors and subcontractors in the event that payment does not occur within a specified amount of time. Such legislation is commonly referred to as *prompt pay* legislation. These statutes may be found within the context of public works or lien statutes, or they may have their own legislative framework. Generally, they apply to public contracts, but some jurisdictions have expanded the protection to private contracts as well. The time allowed for payment may vary by jurisdiction. The time period is generally fairly short and rarely exceeds thirty days.

Prompt pay statutes will specify the interest a party may recover on a late payment. In some jurisdictions, an unpaid party may recover interest at a rate in excess of the statutory default rate plus attorneys' fees, if the unpaid party can demonstrate bad faith or a lack of a good faith basis on behalf of the debtor for not paying.[107] An issue sometimes arises concerning whether parties to a construction contract may alter or waive the protections of a prompt pay statute. For instance, if the prompt pay statute requires payment within thirty days, will the parties that specify forty-five days for payment alter the parties' respective rights and obligations? Even more dramatically, may the parties expressly provide that they are waiving the protections of prompt pay statutes and the remedies available thereunder will not apply? While parties are, in general, free to contract, as with other contract clauses that attempt to waive statutorily granted rights, courts sometimes declare such terms void and unenforceable on public policy grounds or because they violate the express

---

105. *Id.* § 36.03 [B], at 1321.

106. *Id.*

107. *See, e. g.*, Mo. Rev. Stat. § 34.057 (2013) (interest at 1½ percent per month if payment was not withheld in good faith).

terms of the statute itself. In general, the courts have been very reticent to find a waiver of prompt pay statute rights since such waivers are often obtained as a result of an unequal bargaining position or inability to negotiate, and the legislative intent is frustrated if waivers are permitted.

Library References

C.J.S. *Architects* §§ 4, 16–17, 19, 21–24, 32; C.J.S. *Contracts* §§ 11, 341, 343, 347, 356, 359, 442–445, 450; C.J.S. *Damages* § 113; C.J.S. *Mechanics' Liens* §§ 252–254; C.J.S. *Negligence* §§ 381–385, 388–393, 398; C.J.S. *Workers' Compensation* §§ 1587–1591, 1656–1662.
West's Key No. Digests, Contracts <KEY>196–199, 205, 221(3); Damages <KEY>118, 122; Indemnity <KEY>33(2), 33(5); Mechanics' Liens <KEY>208; Negligence <KEY>1260; Workers' Compensation <KEY>2084, 2142.25.

VII. Contractual and Other Limitations on Liability

A. Exculpatory Clauses

Exculpatory clauses attempt to limit a party's liability by stating specific activities the design professional is to perform and excluding the specific activities that the design professional is not to perform. These clauses can be extremely helpful in limiting the liability of the design professional.[108] Often, design professionals will include exculpatory language in their contracts with owners in order to eliminate the possibility of third party liability, as, for example, in the American Institute of Architects' *Standard Form of Agreement Between Owner and Architect.* exculpatory clauses are generally enforceable to the extent that they are not the products of oppression, although there are exceptions where the clause seeks to immunize a party from liability for personal injuries.

B. Waivers of Consequential/Incidental Damages

Consequential damages are those damages that indirectly flow from the consequences of an act.[109] Contract clauses that attempt to limit these types of damages are intended to shield design professionals from the sometimes far-reaching risks associated with the design professional's errors.[110] In fact, recog-

---

108. These clauses are not uniformly practiced. *See* James Acret, Architects and Engineers 9.31 (3d ed. 1993).

109. *Id.* § 17.6, at 414.

110. *Id.*

nizing the unpredictability associated with consequential damages, American Institute of Architects (AIA) Document B 141 provides: "[t]he Architect and Owner waive consequential damages for claims, disputes or other matters in question. . . ."[111] As such, the AIA's mutual waiver clause attempts to promote predictability by relieving participants from liability for abnormally large losses because of unanticipated events occurring after formation of the contract.[112] Waivers of consequential damages are generally enforceable.

C. Indemnification Clauses

Clauses that require one party (the "indemnitor") to defend and indemnify another party (the "indemnitee") from claims arising from activities on the project are a common way to shift risk and, hence, the damages for which a party may otherwise be liable. Even though they are almost always included in the same clause, the litigation and defense obligation is distinct from the obligation of indemnity.[113] The obligation to defend requires the indemnitor to either undertake directly the defense of the indemnitee or pay for the cost of defense. The obligation to indemnify requires the indemnitor to either satisfy any perfected claim against the indemnitee or reimburse the indemnitee for costs incurred.

In theory, the fairest way to allocate responsibility is for each party to indemnify the other from damage caused by the indemnitor. That is, each party would bear its share of damages in proportion to its fault. Notwithstanding issues of fundamental fairness, contracts, including industry standard contracts, often allocate risk other than on a comparative fault basis, thereby fundamentally altering the damages and remedies available to parties.

Such risk-shifting clauses are generally enforceable but courts may void them as unconscionable, against public policy or a violation of specific statutes. Therefore, in determining rights and remedies available to a design professional and construction manager, recourse must be made not only to the specific contractual term that may shift normal responsibility, but also to statutes and case law that may void those very indemnity clauses. Indemnity clauses that create exposure that would not otherwise exist absent such a term may have significant risk for design professionals. It may be possible to obtain commercial general liability insurance to cover such contractual liability, but

---

111. Construction Law Handbook, *supra* note 89, § 31.05, at 1158.

112. *Id.*

113. State-by-State Guide to Construction Contracts and Claims, *supra* note 23, § 1.02(b).

it is generally not possible to obtain professional liability insurance because it covers only damages that would have been imposed absent the contract.[114]

Well-drafted indemnification clauses can greatly protect owners and architects and expand the liability of general contractors.[115] For example, an indemnification clause commonly used by owners states that:

> To the fullest extent permitted by law, the contractor shall indemnify, defend, and hold harmless the owner, the architect, and the architect's consultants, and their agents and employees, from and against any and all claims, suits, causes of actions, damages, losses, and expenses, including but not limited to attorneys' fees, arising out of, related to, or resulting from the performance of the general contractor's work in any fashion to the extent that the loss is caused in whole or in part by acts and/or omissions of the general contractor or any person or entity directly or indirectly employed by the general contractor.[116]

D. Disclaimer of Warranties

As described in prior chapters, most construction contracts include express warranties and the law imposes implied warranty for many such contracts. However, most states permit the disclaimer of warranties related to service contracts as long as the disclaimer at issue is conspicuous in the contract in which the disclaimer is contained.

E. Waiver of Lien Rights

All states provide some protection to contractors, subcontractors, suppliers, laborers, and design professionals by providing a claim against the property and/or improvements thereon for amounts unpaid for labor, equipment, materials, or services furnished for the benefit of the real property and/or improvements. Terms are sometimes inserted in contracts requiring a party to waive its lien rights. Given the strong public policy in favor of protecting those who improve real estate, broad form advance waivers of statutory lien rights (prior to payment) are sometimes rendered null and void or unenforceable by the courts on public policy grounds or by a statute specifically prohibiting such waivers.[117]

---

114. *Id.* § 1.02(b), at 10.

115. Calculating Construction Damages, *supra* note 41, 14.02[B], at 282.

116. *Id.*

117. State-by-State Guide to Construction Contracts and Claims, *supra* note 23, 1.02(C), at 12.

F. Limitations of Liability

Oftentimes, a party will attempt to limit its liability by placing a cap on its potential exposure. This may be expressed in a specific dollar amount or a percentage of the design professional's or construction manager's fee. In such instances, the damages are not liquidated; actual damages must still be proven. Such caps do not reduce insurance coverage. They also do not provide indemnification; they merely limit a party's exposure.

Some states find such clauses unenforceable as against public policy or contrary to a specific statute.

G. No Damages for Delay

While owners quite commonly will insert liquidated damage clauses providing specific compensation for contractor-caused delays, they will also frequently include a clause precluding recovery of damages for delay caused by the owner. Such clauses will normally provide that a contractor's sole remedy for delay, regardless of the cause, is for additional time and that no additional compensation will be paid.

No-damages-for-delay clauses are generally enforceable. However, courts will narrowly construe them and scrutinize them under equitable principles. This has resulted in the development of several exceptions regarding the enforceability of no damage for delay clauses. Such clauses are generally not enforceable if the cause of the delay is:

i. the bad faith of the party seeking to enforce the claim;
ii. so long in duration that it amounts to abandonment of the contract;
iii. beyond the contemplation of the parties at the time of contract formation; or
iv. the result of active interference of the parties seeking to enforce the clause.[118]

In addition, these provisions may also be precluded by state statutes.

H. Pay-if-Paid/Pay-When-Paid Clauses

It is not uncommon for construction contracts to contain a clause providing that payment by the owner is a condition precedent to the contractor's obligation to pay its subcontractor. Such terms are generally referred to as *a pay-if-paid*

---

118. John E. Green Plumbing & Heating Co. v. Turner Constr. Co., 500 F. Supp. 910 (E.D. Mich. 1980), *aff'd*, 742 F.2d 965 (7th Cir. 2004).

clause. If enforceable, the contractor does not have to pay the subcontractor, prior to receiving payment from the owner.

Such clauses may be enforceable, but are generally not favored by courts. Therefore, they have been narrowly construed. Many courts have found that unless a pay-if-paid clause expressly and unambiguously states that payment from the owner is *a condition precedent* to payment to the subcontractor by the contractor, then the clause is ambiguous and will be treated as a pay-when-paid clause, requiring the contractor to pay the subcontractor within *a reasonable time,* regardless of whether the contractor has been paid by the owner. Other jurisdictions have struck a middle ground of finding that such clauses may be enforced against a subcontractor unless it can be shown that nonpayment by the owner was caused by some failure of performance on behalf of the contractor for which the subcontractor is not responsible.

The *pay-when-paid* clause is a less harsh limitation on a subcontractor's ability to recover. Under a pay-when-paid clause, there is not an absolute bar to recovery, as may occur with a pay-if-paid clause. Pay-when-paid clauses generally lack clear and unambiguous language establishing that payment by the owner is a risk assumed by the contractor and is a condition precedent to the contractor's obligation to pay the subcontractor. Examples of a pay-when-paid clause would include:

> "The contractor will pay the subcontractor within thirty days of receipt of payment by the contractor from the owner;" or
>
> "The contractor will pay the subcontractor when the contractor receives payment from the owner."

Under such clauses, it is common for the courts to find that the subcontractor need wait only a reasonable time for payment. However, the contractor must ultimately pay the subcontractor regardless of payment from the owner. The courts generally prefer such an interpretation, finding that the contractor was in the best position to determine the financial stability and creditworthiness of the owner with whom it contracted, while the subcontractor looked primarily to the financial capabilities of the contractor.

I. Immunity under Workers' Compensation Laws

All jurisdictions have some form of workers' compensation laws that will protect an employer from claims for bodily injury to, or the property damage of, its employees by providing immunity for such claims to the employer. The immunity exists whether or not the claims arise from site safety or some other cause. The sole remedy against the employer is generally limited to benefits specified by statute (in monopolistic jurisdictions) or the employer's workers' compensation carrier (in non-monopolistic jurisdictions).

In general, an employer will enjoy this immunity if it follows the statutory requirements and its conduct is not intentional, criminal, or reckless. This immunity can be compromised if the employer has agreed to indemnify another party for bodily injury to the employer's own employees. Under workers' compensation laws, claims against parties are not precluded. Therefore, the contractor may face the situation in which it has agreed to defend, indemnify, and hold harmless an owner for all claims arising from the contractor's negligence. When an employee of the contractor is killed on the project as a result of the contractor's negligence, the worker's estate sues the project owner, and the project owner, in turn, sues the contractor, thus allowing a potential *end run* around the statute.

Although most contract rights can be waived, contract provisions that would result in an express or effective waiver of a statutorily granted right or immunity may not be enforceable. This needs to be examined on a state-by-state basis.

J. Immunity from Site Safety Claims

Traditionally, courts have held that design professionals have no legal duty to protect the construction workers from unsafe job site conditions. The courts have reasoned that there is a lack of privity between design professionals and the workers and that the general contractor is in the best position to control the job site and protect the worker. However, this traditional protection has been eroded in recent years in many jurisdictions. Courts have tended to examine the issue based on facts and circumstances and have examined a number of factors in determining whether a legal duty exists. These factors include:

i. retention of any right to supervise and control;
ii. actual supervision and control of the work;
iii. participation in the activities at the construction site;
iv. supervision and coordination of the subcontractors;
v. responsibility for safety practices;
vi. authority to issue change orders; and
vii. knowledge of unsafe conditions.

In response to the erosion of common law protections, some jurisdictions have enacted legislation giving immunity to design professionals from liability for site safety claims with certain well-defined exceptions (e.g., contractual responsibility for site safety, actual control over a portion of the site where the worker was injured, or an injury as a result of the design professional's negligent preparation of plans and specifications).

K. One-Call Statutes and Damage to Underground Structures

Many states have enacted *one-call notification* or utility locate statutes that require contractors to call prior to commencing any excavation. This notice is intended to allow public and private underground utility owners to mark the location of the utilities. The contractor that complies with the statutory requirements is generally immune from responsibility for damage to the utilities.

On the other hand, the failure to comply with such statutes may subject a contractor not only to liability for damages to the utility, but also to consequential damages for interruption of service provided by the utility, as well as civil penalties.

CHAPTER 11

Special Topics in Litigation of Disputes Involving Design Professionals or Construction Managers

ERNEST ISOLA, JESSICA CLOUSE[1]

I. Introduction

Litigation is a large enough topic that an entire Section of the American Bar Association is devoted to litigation, and one of its Committees is dedicated to the topic of construction litigation. Any attempt to summarize all aspects of litigation in a chapter like this would either be so cursory as to be unhelpful or so long as to be impractical. In lieu of providing an overview of the litigation process (there are many perfectly reputable overviews that are available to the professional), this chapter discusses in some detail certain aspects of litigation that are especially important to the litigation of disputes involving design professionals and construction managers.

---

1. The authors of this second edition wish to acknowledge and thank Kenneth Strong for his contributions to this chapter as a co-author of the first edition.

II. Time Limits for Filing Suit

A. Statutes of Limitation and Related Laws

All jurisdictions have statutes of limitations that govern the time period within which a party must file suit after the cause of action accrues. Most jurisdictions utilize the discovery rule under which a cause of action accrues and the deadline to file a suit commences running from the date that the claimant discovered (or reasonably should have discovered) the existence of a cause of action. Where the discovery rule does not apply, the statute commences running at some date that does not depend on the claimant's discovery of the cause of action. For example, the statute of limitations for a breach of contract claim in some states commences at the time of the breach, regardless of whether the claimant knew of the breach at that point.

It is important to be aware of shorter time limitations that may apply either by contract or by code. Virtually all governmental entities are protected by some form of requirement that a claim must be filed against the entity before filing suit. Normally, such statutes provide that a claim cannot be filed until some pre-litigation notice and demand is filed. These statutes further provide that suits be filed against the public entity within a relatively short time, often six months to one year, following accrual of the claim or it is barred.

Many states also empower public entities to prescribe, by written contract, procedures for resolution of claims that are different from those otherwise provided by statute. These procedures may vary or shorten the time to submit claims. In addition, private entities may agree by contract to shorter periods for filing claims, which effectively imposes *a private statute of limitations.* Contracts may also specify that all claims of a particular type are deemed to accrue as of the date of substantial completion. For example, although the AIA owner-architect agreements previously included a "trigger" date of substantial completion as the starting date for the statute of limitations, the AIA abandoned this approach in 2007 in response to owner complaints.[2]

Therefore, it behooves the practitioner to obtain and review all relevant contracts for contractual time limitations on claims to see if such clauses provide a defense or impose a barrier to otherwise viable claims. Where governmental entities are parties or potential parties, strict compliance with contractual or statutory deadlines is essential.

2. *See* AIA Document B141-1997, Section 1.

B. Statutes of Repose

In states that utilize the discovery rule to commence the running of the statute of limitations, there is a danger that a claimant might not discover the cause of action until several years after construction is completed, thereby extending the construction professional's exposure almost indefinitely. For example, if the state utilizes a two-year statute of limitations for claims involving a design professional's negligence, but the owner of a building does not know about the design professional's asserted negligence until fourteen years after a structure is completed, the owner would have the ability to file suit—and the design professional would be exposed to liability—sixteen years after completion of the improvements.

This potential exposure, unlimited by any temporal constraints, presents numerous practical difficulties, and states have enacted *statutes of repose* to avoid these difficulties. A statute of repose limits the time period within which certain types of claims may be brought against parties involved in construction and is keyed to some definite time that is not fixed to anyone's discovery of a claim. Thus, for example, a statute of repose may provide that any claim against a construction professional related to any deficiency in the improvement of property must be brought no more than six years after substantial completion or it will forever be barred. Forty-six jurisdictions have special construction industry statutes of repose that are facially valid.[3]

When a state uses the discovery rule for its statute of limitations and has a coexisting statute of repose, the shorter of the time periods will govern the time before which suit must be filed. Suppose a state uses a two-year statute of limitations in which the period commences running upon discovery of the cause of action and also imposes a six-year statute of repose. If the owner of the building discovers that it has a cause of action against the contractor exactly one year after the building is completed, the owner must file suit by the third anniversary of completion of the improvements. The six-year statute of repose does not come into play because the shorter time period imposed by the statute of limitations applies.

---

3. Kentucky had a statute of repose, but it was declared unconstitutional as conflicting with Kentucky's constitutional grant of open access to courts. Tabler v. Wallace, Ky., 704 S.W.2d 179 (1985), *cert. denied*, 479 U.S. 822 (1986); Perkins v. Northeastern Log Homes, 808 S.W.2d 809 (1991). Kentucky has not stricken its statutes of limitation as unconstitutional. In Ohio, the statutes of repose that were previously held constitutional were invalidated in connection with a general rejection of a tort reform bill that the state supreme court regarded as a usurpation of judicial powers. State *ex rel.* Ohio Academy of Trial Lawyers v. Sheward, 86 Ohio St. 3d 451 (1999).

On the other hand, if the owner discovers the cause of action five years after substantial completion, the statute of limitations would permit filing of a claim until the seventh anniversary of the completion of improvements. However, the statute of repose bars any claim not filed within six years after the completion of the improvements and, thus, would serve as the outside limit for the filing of a claim. In that case, the statute of limitations is of no practical effect, as the shorter statute of repose governs the deadline for filing suit. One consequence of the operation of a statute of repose is that a claimant might actually lose the right to bring a claim before discovering the existence of the cause of action.

Different states take different approaches as to what claims are barred and the time frame in which the statute of repose applies. Tennessee is the shortest at four years,[4] while Indiana's statute is twelve years for design deficiencies.[5] Nine states use a six-year period.[6] Twenty-four states use ten years as the time frame. The average statute of repose is between eight and nine years. Some states split the time frame depending on the nature of the defect. For example, California provides a four-year statute for patent defects[7] and a ten-year statute for latent defects.[8] Other states take a similar bifurcated approach.[9] California's statutes do not apply to claims for personal injuries and most state statutes do not apply to claims by public entities. While most state statutes create a complete bar to claims brought after the time frame set forth in the statute, a few state statutes, such as Kentucky's, create a rebuttable presumption that there was no design defect after five years.[10]

Finally, states vary as to when the statute of repose begins running. Many states use substantial completion of the improvement at issue, but a state may

---

4. Tenn. Code Ann. § 28-3-202 (2020).

5. Burns Ind. Code Ann. § 32-30-1-5 (2020).

6. Colorado, Delaware, Idaho, Massachusetts, Michigan (gross negligence, actions against surveyors), Mississippi, Nevada (patent defects), North Carolina, and Washington.

7. Cal. Civ. Proc. Code § 337.1 (2020).

8. Cal. Civ. Proc. Code § 337.15 (2020).

9. Arkansas (five years for property damage, four years for personal injury), Indiana (twelve years for design defects, ten years for construction defects), Maryland (ten years for protected class, twenty years for others), Michigan (six years for gross negligence and actions against surveyors, ten years for other claims), and Nevada (ten years for willful misconduct or fraudulent concealment, eight years for latent defects, six years for patent defects).

10. Ky. Rev. Stat. § 198B.135 (2020).

use the owner's occupancy of the improvement[11] or the completion of the design to trigger the commencement of the running of the statute of repose.[12]

C. Using Tolling or Standstill Agreements to Defer Litigation

There may be strategic reasons why parties may want to defer litigation beyond the time permitted under an applicable statute of limitations or statute of repose. For example, a contractor may assert a claim for delay and disruption against an owner. In those jurisdictions where it is permitted, the contractor may also sue the architect or the construction manager claiming they are responsible for a portion of its damages. Whether the design professional is sued directly by the contractor or is subject to cross-claim by the owner, the owner and architect or construction manager may want to avoid direct claims against each other during the pendency of the contractor's lawsuit. For example, while they may ultimately have claims against each other, they may want to ensure that the trial does not require them to indict each other's work and, instead, may prefer to present a united defense.

At the same time, the owner and architect recognize that they ultimately may not prevail against the contractor and a victory by the contractor would breathe life back into their claims against each other. However, by the time the contractor's litigation is completed, the statute of limitations or statute of repose may bar those claims.

As a means of avoiding this time problem, the architect and owner can enter into a waiver and tolling agreement under the terms of which the time for either of them to file suit against each other (under a statute of limitations or, where permitted, a statute of repose) will not recommence running immediately. Instead, the time periods will either be "tolled" indefinitely[13] to be commenced upon notice by the other party, or will commence running at a certain later time such as upon entry of a judgment, settlement in the contractor's litigation, or the expiration of a particular product warranty.

Library References

C.J.S. *Employer to Employee Relationship* § 96; C.J.S. *Limitations of Actions* §§ 106, 151–164, 166, 168–169, 171, 182, 188–213, 228–239, 269–270; C.J.S.

---

11. FLA. STAT. ANN. § 95-11(3)(c) (2020).

12. N.J. STAT. ANN. § 2A:14-1.1 (2020).

13. In some jurisdictions, contracts seeking to extend the statute of limitations for an indefinite period of time are unenforceable. T&N PLC v. Fred S. James & Co., 29 F.3d 57 (1994) (based on N.Y. GEN. OBL. LAW § 17-103 (1993)).

Physicians, Surgeons, and Other Health-Care Providers § 129; C.J.S. *RICO* (Racketeer Influenced and Corrupt Organizations) § 21.
West's Key No. Digests, Limitation of Actions <KEY>46, 55, 95, 104.5.
1 Construction Law P 3.11 (2020); 1 Construction Law P 3.03 (2020); 1 Construction Law INDIANA (2020).

III. Certificates of Merit

Design professionals such as architects, engineers, and construction managers provide critical services to construction projects. The role of these consultants typically begins as early as the conceptual design phase and continues through completion of the project. Architects, engineers, and construction managers have always faced significant exposure for breach of contract to their clients. However, in recent years, the number and severity of claims asserted against design professionals and construction managers have increased.

One reason for this increase is that as the barriers of privity and the economic loss doctrine have eroded, consultants are increasingly facing claims from contractors and other third parties. In many jurisdictions, homeowners can sue construction professionals directly for design defects. Moreover, homeowners' associations that govern the common areas of common interest developments have routinely included design professionals in "scattershot" complaints in which all contractors and design professionals that worked on a large residential construction project are named as a matter of course. Developers have also taken advantage of the law to form limited liability companies or have simply gone out of business after project completion. Latent defects may not become apparent until many years after completion of construction. By that point, the professionals may be the only viable entities to sue. An additional reason design professionals may be sued is that professional liability insurance often covers economic damages, whereas a contractor's general liability insurance policy will typically cover property damage or bodily injury arising out of defective construction. Where an owner suffers lost profits due to a delay in completion, it may be easier to recover those damages under an errors and omissions policy as compared to pursuing a contractor's assets.

Although these reasons explain some of the increase in litigation against design professionals, that is not to suggest that these suits are all meritorious. Indeed, over the past two decades, there has been a perception that the number of frivolous suits against licensed professionals—including professionals involved in the construction process—has increased. As a means of trying to curb the number of frivolous suits, a number of states have passed statutes that require an attorney obtain *a certificate of merit* or similar assurance in connection with litigation against a licensed professional.[14] Although initially targeting the medical field to protect against non-meritorious malpractice claims, these protections have been broadened in several states to encompass other professionals, including architects and engineers.

As of 1995, only five jurisdictions had enacted certificate of merit legislation. Over the next twenty-five years, an additional nine states have enacted certificate of merit or review panel statutes that protect architects and engineers, bringing the total to fourteen as of 2020.[15] In addition, several other states have proposed legislation in furtherance of a certificate of merit statute. These states include Missouri, New York, and North Carolina. Although the specific provisions of each statute vary, the underlying purpose of each of these statutes is to protect professionals from meritless lawsuits in the early stages. In some form, they require that before an attorney can pursue a claim for professional negligence against a design professional, there must be some form of consultation with or review by one or more design professionals to determine whether, in their opinion, the claim against the design professional has merit.

Certificate of merit statutes have also been questioned on constitutional grounds. In 2017, the Oklahoma Supreme Court ruled that Oklahoma's certificate of merit statute applying to health care providers is unconstitutional in *John v. Saint Francis Hospital*.[16] There, the plaintiff filed a medical negligence claim against a surgeon, and the surgeon moved to dismiss for failure to attach an affidavit of merit from a qualified expert as required under the statute. The court of appeals held the affidavit requirement was unconstitutional. The Supreme Court affirmed, reasoning that access to the court system is a fundamental right and the statute placed an impermissible barrier on a plaintiff's rights under Article II, Section 6 of the Oklahoma Constitution.[17]

---

14. Not every state uses the same terminology, but these will be referred to as certificates of merit in this discussion for the reader's convenience.

15. These states include Arizona, California, Colorado, Georgia, Hawaii, Kansas, Maryland, Minnesota, Nevada, New Jersey, Oregon, Pennsylvania, South Carolina, and Texas.

16. 405 P.3d 681 (2017).

17. *Id.* at 691.

A. Who Is Covered?

In virtually all jurisdictions that have enacted certificate of merit legislation, the statutes cover licensed professionals who work in the construction field, including licensed architects, professional engineers, and land surveyors. In some jurisdictions, the language is more general—applying to *design professionals*—and may include interior designers. The authors have not located any certificate of merit statutes that explicitly protect construction managers.

B. What Are the Requirements?

While the specific requirements in each jurisdiction are provided by statute and vary from state to state, there are generalizations that can be made. The statutes take one of three forms. Those state statutes that are the least restrictive from a procedural standpoint simply require an attorney affidavit. States following this pattern include California, Colorado, Oregon, and Pennsylvania. Generally, an attorney is required to submit an affidavit to the court either at the same time as the complaint is filed or shortly thereafter. A certificate of merit requires the plaintiff's attorney to consult with a third party design professional prior to filing suit. Generally, the attorney must review the facts of the case, consult a design professional licensed and practicing the same discipline as the defendant, and receive an opinion regarding the professional negligence of the defendant. Only after the consultant's opinion has been given can the attorney file the certificate with the court attesting that there is reasonable and meritorious cause to file the lawsuit.

However, such provisions do not pose much of a deterrence to meritless claims. First, most states do not require that the consultant's opinion be in writing and, therefore, there is no ready way to confirm whether the consultant opined that the professional being sued was negligent.[18] In most jurisdictions, the attorney is not even required to disclose the identity of the consultant in the certificate. Indeed, there is no realistic way to confirm whether the attorney, in fact, consulted with a licensed professional in the same field as the consultant being sued. California provides a mechanism for testing whether the attorney did in fact consult with a licensed professional before filing suit. However,

---

18. Pennsylvania requires that the expert's statement be in writing and has provisions whereby the defendant can request a copy of the written statement if the case is dismissed. Sanctions can also be awarded against the attorney filing the certification if the court finds that the attorney improperly certified that the expert supplied a written statement meeting the code requirements. *See* Pa R.C.P. §§ 1042.3, 1042.9 (2016).

since this mechanism can be invoked only after the conclusion of the litigation, it is worthless for all practical purposes.

Failure to file a certificate typically results in a demurrer or motion to strike. Unlike other states, California does not require dismissal with prejudice for failure to comply with its statute. Instead, a demurrer or motion to strike permits leave to amend, which is routinely and liberally granted to allow the plaintiff to cure the alleged defect. By granting leave to file an amended complaint, the court can give the plaintiff an opportunity to comply fully with the statutory requirements for filing a certificate of merit.

A more stringent variation of the certificate of merit process is followed in Hawaii and Kansas. In those states, the attorney must file a request for a review panel of professionals that issues a nonbinding opinion concerning whether or not the standard of care was met. The cost of the panel either is shared or is the responsibility of the losing party before the panel.

A second approach requires that an expert's affidavit be filed with the initial pleading or shortly thereafter. Arizona, Georgia, Maryland, Nevada, New Jersey, South Carolina, and Texas have statutes that follow this approach. Under Georgia and New Jersey law, the failure to file such an affidavit is grounds for dismissal with prejudice of the complaint.[19]

Nevada is an example of this approach. Nevada requires that an expert report be attached to the attorney affidavit. Under the Nevada statute, the attorney must file an affidavit with the first pleading stating that she reviewed the facts of the case, consulted with an expert knowledgeable in the defendant's discipline, and concluded that the action has merit. In addition, a report prepared by the expert consulted must be submitted that includes the expert's resume, a statement that the expert is experienced in all disciplines in the report, and the conclusions of the expert on the merits of the action. The attorney must also include a copy of each non-privileged document used by the expert in preparing his report, including documents deemed relevant by the expert to the allegations of negligent conduct. Failure to submit either the attorney's affidavit or the expert's report results in dismissal of the action. There is no provision for an extension to file the expert report. However, at the time of filing the attorney affidavit, if the attorney files an additional affidavit stating that she made reasonable efforts to obtain the required non-privileged documents but was unable to obtain them, she will not be required to submit those documents or the expert's conclusion in the report. However, this *escape*

19. Stamps v. Johnson, 535 S.E.2d 1, 2–3 (Ga. 2000); Burt v. West Jersey Health Sys., 339 N.J. Super. 296, 771 A.2d 683 (2001).

valve does require that the expert's report then must be amended to include such documents and information as soon as available.[20]

Statutes like Nevada's provide the design professional an early indication of the precise area in which it is contended his professional services fell below the standard of care and caused the plaintiff's damage. This is particularly beneficial in multiparty cases, such as subdivision defect claims, in which architects ordinarily would have no means of knowing which of the often numerous categories of defects their work is alleged to be deficient. Before suing a design professional, it forces the plaintiff to investigate the claim and at least theoretically provide the expert's details on the claim. In practice, there often is not enough information available at the time a suit is filed to provide the level of detail envisioned in the statute. That is where Minnesota's approach may be more effective.

Minnesota requires an attorney affidavit be served on the defendants with the pleadings. The affidavit must state that the attorney has reviewed the facts with an expert who, based on that review, is of the opinion that the design professional breached the standard of care. This satisfies the desire that attorneys at least consult with an expert about the merits of a claim for professional negligence before filing suit. Minnesota goes on to require that, within 180 days of filing suit, the attorney file a second affidavit identifying the experts who will testify, stating the facts and opinions about which the expert is expected to testify, and summarizing the grounds for each opinion. Failure to file the required affidavits in a timely fashion results in mandatory dismissal with prejudice of the causes of action for professional negligence.[21]

The Minnesota approach allows a party a reasonable time after commencing a suit to investigate and develop the evidence to support a claim for professional negligence. However, it places time limits to prevent frivolous or unsupported claims from being dragged out. Where a court finds an affidavit was not made in good faith, it has the power to issue sanctions including attorneys' fees.

Library References

C.J.S. *Negligence* §§ 750–753, 755–758, 832, 849 .
West's Key No. Digests, Negligence <KEY>1506.

---

20. Nev. Rev. Stat. 40.6884 (2020).
21. Minn. Stat. Ann. § 544.42 (2020).

IV. Management of Litigation through the Use of Special Masters

Complex construction litigation often involves many different parties litigating a multitude of legal and factual issues. For example, a typical construction defect claim may be initiated by homeowners, or homeowners' associations on behalf of an entire development or subdivision, against developers, general contractors, construction managers, and design professionals, which in turn file cross-complaints against subcontractors of every tier, engineers, subconsultants, material suppliers, and other participants in the construction project.

Therefore, construction claims can involve twenty to thirty or more parties litigating literally hundreds of issues. Each party retains counsel and experts to assist in prosecuting and defending against the various design and construction defects alleged, resulting in months of percipient and expert depositions and hundreds of thousands of documents to review, organize, analyze, and prepare for depositions and trial. This process culminates in a jury trial which can span months, sometimes seasons.

Trial judges are typically averse to tying up their courtrooms for five months and subjecting jurors to complex, expert-intensive testimony over the course of a long construction trial. Therefore, judges generally will do everything in their power to avoid sending a complex construction case out to trial. Consequently, mediation and other alternative dispute resolution procedures are generally exhausted before the litigants in a complex construction case are provided a courtroom and trial is commenced.

A growing trend in alternative dispute resolution that has gained popularity in California and other western states is the use of special masters to coordinate discovery and settlement in multiparty construction litigation. Here, the parties to the litigation will generally stipulate or file a motion for the appointment of a special master to oversee pleadings, certain motion work, discovery, investigations, information exchange, and settlement. The special master will be responsible for coordinating most aspects of the case with an eye toward ultimately positioning the case in its most favorable settlement posture.

State laws allowing an order of reference are patterned after Federal Rules of Civil Procedure Rule 53(a), which provides that "a court may appoint a master only to: (A) perform duties consented to by the parties; (B) hold trial proceedings and make or recommend findings of fact on issues to be decided without a jury if the appointment is warranted by (i) some exceptional condition; or (ii) the need to perform an accounting or resolve a difficult computation of damages; or (C) address pretrial and posttrial matters that cannot be effectively and timely addressed by an available district judge or magistrate judge of the district." The process by which an order of reference to a special master is obtained varies from state to state. Most states have promulgated specific procedures that must be followed in order to appoint a special master.

For example, California allows for the appointment of a special master by stipulation of all parties,[22] or either by a motion of a party to the case or on the court's own motion.[23] California courts have the authority to order that a special master act as discovery referee and mediator and that the parties participate in the mediation.[24]

After the parties stipulate in writing to an order of reference to a special master, the fully executed stipulation is then sent to the judge for approval. The approved order of reference is then filed with the appropriate court, and the special master is granted the powers specified in the order of reference. Then, the special master will coordinate most aspects of the litigation through case management orders and will periodically report back to the judge as to the progress of the case. The actions taken by the parties during the special master process are generally afforded full confidentiality, as this allows the parties to conduct objective investigations and evaluate the case without fear of evidentiary fallout later at trial.

Library References

C.J.S. *References* §§ 3, 5–7, 27, 29–31.
West's Key No. Digests, Reference <KEY>3, 24, 27.

V. Use of Experts

In order to establish a claim for professional negligence against an architect, engineer, or construction manager, it is necessary in most cases to offer expert opinion that the professional failed to meet the applicable standard of care. For that reason, the preparation and testimony of retained experts is critical. Three landmark decisions by the U.S. Supreme Court have set the criteria for evaluating the experts offered in litigation and the testimony they propose to give in federal court. Many jurisdictions that model their procedures on the federal rules have adopted these standards.

---

22. Cal. Civ. Proc. Code § 638 (2020).
23. Cal. Civ. Proc. Code § 639 (2020).
24. Lu v. Superior Court, *55* Cal. App. 4th 1264 (1997).

A. The Trial Judge Has a Gatekeeping Obligation Pursuant to *Daubert, Joiner,* and *Kumho Tire*

Prior to three landmark U.S. Supreme Court decisions beginning in 1993, many courts followed the *Frye*[25] test, in which the judge will only admit scientific evidence based on a scientific technique where the technique is generally accepted as reliable by experts in the applicable scientific community. In *Daubert*,[26] the U.S. Supreme Court then held that the trial judge, as the gatekeeper of expert testimony, is to make a preliminary assessment of whether the expert's scientific testimony is based on reasoning or methodology that is reliable and scientifically valid based on a balancing of a number of factors, including (1) whether it can be and has been tested, (2) whether it has been subjected to peer review and publication, (3) its known or potential rate of error, (4) the standards controlling its operation, and (5) the degree of its acceptance in the relevant scientific community. *Kumho Tire*[27] then held that the trial judge's gatekeeping obligation, as described in *Daubert*, applies not only to scientific expert testimony but also to all expert testimony, including that based on technical and other specialized knowledge. In *Joiner*,[28] the Court found that a trial court judge's decision to exclude or to admit scientific evidence could be overturned by an appellate court only if the trial court abused its discretion in admitting or excluding that evidence.

In light of *Daubert*, *Joiner*, and *Kumho Tire*, lawyers who practice construction law have begun to challenge expert testimony with greater frequency. This trio of cases establishes and defines the trial court's gatekeeping function in making preliminary assessments of proposed expert testimony to ensure that the subjects of expert testimony are truly susceptible to such treatment. *Daubert, Joiner,* and *Kumho Tire* do not limit the trial judge's gatekeeping obligation regarding expert testimony to testimony involving scientific evidence. Indeed, the *Daubert* gatekeeping obligation requires the trial judge to make an inquiry into both the relevance and reliability of the expert's testimony to exclude "expertise that is *fausse* and science that is junky."[29]

It is worthwhile to note that the court's gatekeeping function is not "to make ultimate conclusions as to the persuasiveness of the proffered evidence."[30]

---

25. Frye v. United States, 293 F. 1013 (D.C. Cir. 1923).
26. Daubert v. Merrell Dow Pharms., 509 U.S. 579 (1993).
27. Kumho Tire Co. v. Carmichael, 526 U.S. 137 (1999).
28. General Elec. Co. v. Joiner, 522 U.S. 136 (1997).
29. *Kumho Tire*, 526 U.S. at 159.
30. Quiet Tech. DC-8, Inc. v. Hurel-Dubois U.K. Ltd., 326 F.3d 1333, 1341 (11th Cir. 2003).

The sole purpose of a *Daubert* hearing is to determine admissibility through a preliminary assessment of the methodologies underlying the opinion.[31]

An attorney who seeks to rely on an expert's testimony must understand how to lay the groundwork to ensure admission of the testimony. The skillful litigator begins to lay the groundwork on the day he or she retains the scientific or technical expert.

B. *Daubert/Kumho Tire* Extend to Both an Expert's Testimony and the Conclusions Reached by the Expert

Federal Rule of Evidence 702 encapsulates the key rulings from the Supreme Court's trio of cases:

> A witness who is qualified as an expert by knowledge, skill, experience, training, or education may testify in the form of an opinion or otherwise if:
>
> (a) the expert's scientific, technical, or other specialized knowledge will help the trier of fact to understand the evidence or to determine a fact in issue;
>
> (b) the testimony is based on sufficient facts or data;
>
> (c) the testimony is the product of reliable principles and methods; and
>
> (d) the expert has reliably applied the principles and methods to the facts of the case.

The trial court may apply the specific factors of evidentiary reliability set forth in *Daubert* to the testimony of engineers and other experts who are not scientists. While the courts have not specifically stated that *Daubert/Kumho Tire* apply to other technical but not scientific experts like design professionals and construction managers, the *Daubert* and *Kumho Tire* decisions likely encompass such experts because the Court based its opinions on technical or specialized knowledge. Indeed, the federal courts tend to have a more liberal standard compared to the state courts when applying evidentiary rules. There are a number of cases applying *Daubert/Kumho Tire* outside the arena of scientific knowledge, such as expert testimony on damage issues in patent infringement cases as well as to delay damages. Therefore, *Daubert/Kumho Tire* would seem to clearly apply to design professional and construction management experts. While a design professional may be more of a technical expert than a construction management expert, lawyers throughout the country

31. *Kumho Tire*, 526 U.S. at 150.

typically name both design professional experts and construction management experts in construction cases under appropriate situations.

The trial courts will screen such testimony by applying the specific factors of evidentiary reliability set forth in *Daubert* where they are reasonable measures of the reliability of expert testimony. *Kumho Tire* cleared any ambiguity regarding whether the *Daubert* gatekeeping obligation applies to all expert testimony, including testimony involving technical or specialized knowledge. The *Daubert* factors apply to many areas of expertise, including construction scheduling experts who are frequently engineers and typically testify based on their experience, technical, and other specialized knowledge. The *Daubert* gatekeeping obligation ensures that experts and their opinions in construction cases do not go unchecked by the court.

Courts and legislatures in all fifty states have considered whether to adopt the *Daubert* or *Frye* tests for admissibility of expert testimony or some variation of these standards. *Daubert* is by far the majority standard, and the number of jurisdictions that have adopted *Daubert* has continued to grow over the past twenty years. As of 2020, thirty-eight states[32] plus Washington, D.C., have adopted either *Daubert* or a substantially similar[33] test. Eight states[34] continue to rely on *Frye* or some similar variation of that standard, leaving three states[35] using a different test. Since many professional negligence claims against design professionals and construction managers do not raise "scientific" issues, it is also important to note that most jurisdictions that have adopted *Daubert* also follow *Kuhmo Tire*, which extends the *Daubert* test beyond just scientific testimony. Notable states that do not follow this rule are Alabama, Alaska, Connecticut, Montana, New Mexico, Oregon, and West Virginia.

---

32. Alabama; Alaska; Arizona; Arkansas; Colorado; Connecticut; Washington, D.C.; Delaware; Florida; Georgia; Hawaii; Idaho; Indiana; Iowa; Kansas; Kentucky; Louisiana; Maine; Massachusetts; Michigan; Mississippi; Missouri; Montana; Nebraska; New Hampshire; New Mexico; North Carolina; Ohio; Oklahoma; Oregon; Rhode Island; South Carolina; South Dakota; Tennessee; Texas; Utah; Vermont; West Virginia; Wisconsin; and Wyoming.

33. Some jurisdictions listed above have refrained from adopting *Daubert* outright and have instead held that *Daubert* is either "instructive" or "may be considered" among other factors when evaluating admissibility of expert testimony. These states include Colorado, Hawaii, Indiana, Iowa, Maine, and South Carolina.

34. California, Illinois, Maryland, Minnesota, New Jersey, New York, Pennsylvania, and Washington.

35. Nevada (has its own three-prong test), North Dakota (more liberal rule than FRE 702), and Virginia (generally admissible if it will assist the trier of fact).

C. *Daubert/Kumho Tire* Applies in Construction or Closely Related Cases: It Must Be Reasonable for an Expert to Rely on That Which Forms the Basis of His or Her Opinion

A number of courts have used *Kumho Tire* to judge the reliability of engineers who offer testimony on a variety of issues, including causation and standard of care. Several of these cases have involved engineers who provide testimony in construction or closely related cases.

In *Ballard v. Buckley Powder Co.*,[36] the court applied *Kumho Tire* to the testimony of an architectural engineer. Applying *Daubert/Kumho Tire*, the court determined that the engineer's technique was vulnerable to significant sources of unreliability. Specifically, the architectural engineer could not rule out the possibility that ordinary settling or other environmental forces may have caused the damage in question because his inspection occurred ten months after the defendant's blasting activities. The architectural engineer also could not reliably differentiate between damage caused by ordinary settling and damage caused by blasting. Moreover, the engineer's inspection method had never been subjected to peer review and the architectural engineer offered no proof that other members of the engineering field generally accepted his method. Based upon this analysis, the court excluded the expert's testimony because it failed to meet the standards for reliability required by *Daubert/Kumho Tire*.

Similarly, in *Carbotrade, S.P.A. v. Veritas*,[37] the court applied *Kumho Tire* to discredit a naval architect's testimony. The expert's method did not satisfy the court that it could establish, even through calculations, the reduction in hull strength by corrosion and the loading conditions, in terms of bending moment, sustained by a sinking ship. By comparing measurements of the ship's as-built deflection with measurements of its actual deflection before its last voyage, the naval architect in *Carbotrade* calculated that the hull's strength had decreased by about seventeen percent to twenty percent. After applying the *Daubert/Kumho Tire* factors, the court determined that no treatise or scientific literature supported the expert's method of computing corrosion and hull-strength deterioration from compared deflection measurements. The court determined that the method's accuracy had gone untested empirically and questioned the expert's method for his failure to consider the margin of error inherent in his method of measuring deflection. The court also found that two other available computer programs appeared to produce more reliable bending moment val-

---

36. 60 F. Supp. 2d 1180 (D. Kan 1999).
37. 1999 WL 714126 (S.D.N.Y. 1999).

ues than the one on which the expert relied and noted flaws in the charterer's weather expert's data on which the expert based some calculations.

Courts have also applied *Kumho Tire* to experts offering testimony as to an applicable standard of care. These courts stress that experts should look for published industry guidelines or industry regulations to define the proper standard of care. If published guidelines do not exist, then the courts will scrutinize the expert's alternative bases for determining the standard of care under *Daubert/Kumho Tire.*

Kumho Tire has increased the duty of trial judges to scrutinize the reliability of engineer testimony to an unprecedented level. Litigants who fail to offer evidence satisfying the *Daubert/Kumho Tire* standards run a significant risk that the court will exclude their engineer's testimony.

Library References

C.J.S. *Evidence* §§ 636–652,798–799, 808–817, 818, 820–824, 828, 830, 832, 851–853, 856–887, 915–916, 920, 953; C.J.S. *Negligence* §§ 750–753, 755–758, 832, 849, 908, 936.

West's Key No. Digests, Evidence <KEY>538, 555; Negligence <KEY>1506, 1633, 1662.

VI. Discovery, Management, and Use of Evidence in Complex Construction Cases

A. Document Management and Use of Databases

Complex construction litigation often involves large construction projects. Each party to the case, including developers, general contractors, design professionals, subcontractors, material suppliers, etc., can possess extensive project documentation that must be produced to all other parties. These documents must then be organized, reviewed, and analyzed by each party during the course of the litigation. The larger the project, the more documentation that each party must sort through in order to prepare the case for mediation or trial. Eventually, after depositions are completed and all document work is done, a smaller, but still substantial, subset of documents is ultimately introduced into evidence at trial. The process whereby trial counsel begins reviewing hard drives full of electronic information, methodically whittling it down to relevant categories of documents, and ultimately selecting trial exhibits is daunting, to say the least. Fortunately, technology has streamlined the process somewhat and aided the practitioner in managing this seemingly unmanageable sea of information.

The ability to effectively organize voluminous documentation produced during the course of litigation will greatly assist the construction attorney in advocating on behalf of his client. One must take the time at the outset of the litigation to review and organize the documents in a way that subjectively makes sense, because in many cases, a huge number of potentially relevant documents must be reviewed quickly and efficiently before a deposition.

In recent years, construction litigators have come to rely on document databases to assist them in organizing and accessing the voluminous records that are routinely produced in complex construction disputes. Technological advances have made document databases more intuitive and user-friendly, enabling the construction attorney to electronically search through countless documents at any time. A document database is an online platform designed for storing, organizing, and managing documents. Construction attorneys will typically hire an outside e-discovery vendor to input the client's electronic files, scan the client's physical files, and store the files in a retrievable document database. Document productions from other parties in the case can also be stored in the database. The attorney can then access all documents through one user-friendly, secure platform, as opposed to individually reviewing documents stored in various file locations and/or manually leafing through boxes of paper documents. This also allows counsel that are geographically dispersed to effectively review large amounts of data simultaneously.

E-discovery vendors are also offering practitioners advanced features that allow for efficient review of case documents. One of these features is an encoding system. Here, the attorney can select a number of fields, e.g., author, recipient, carbon copies, date sent, type of document, reference subject of the document, and so on. As the attorney is manipulating the documents, she will then be able to run searches and quickly identify documents because of the encoding work performed at the outset. Once the database is created, documents can easily be accessed and retrieved by the attorney. In addition, as the attorney is perusing the database of documents, electronic notes and comments can be kept by the attorney and encoded into the database along with any document or series of documents.

E-discovery databases also provide the ability to create discrete issue tags. These tags can be tailored to both the issues in the case and the objectives of a particular document review project. For instance, if a reviewer is preparing documents to be produced, tags can be created for sorting documents into categories such as privileged, non-responsive, or relevant. Substantive tags can be created to group documents based on the legal theories of the case as well.

Documents can be segregated by category, such as contracts, change orders, requests for information, meeting minutes, correspondence, and so on. Cross-separation of documents by witness may also be helpful.

Depending on the issues raised and the damages claimed, an attorney should utilize some combination of these approaches that intrinsically makes sense within the framework of the claims at issue. For example, in a delay case, it may be helpful to first segregate the documents by task, whether it be critical path, concurrent delay, or so on. Then, within each task, the attorney can separate them by issue, trade, document type, and so on, and this will assist the attorney and expert in analyzing whether a critical path delay took place. However, in a defect case involving a discrete number of issues, it may be helpful to first organize the documents by issue and then by document type within each issue category. Again, the final determination is a subjective one that depends on the peculiar circumstances of the project and the litigation.

E-discovery vendors have developed various tools to both reduce the amount of data for review and/or production and to streamline the review process. One technique that can be used to reduce the amount of overall data is de-duplication. To perform de-duplication, the vendor applies a mathematical algorithm that uses a calculation to assign a unique value to the content of a file. The software then identifies and tracks the duplicates. This tool can be used to extricate all duplicates from a batch set. Some software also can identify "near duplicates," which are files that are similar but not identical. Counsel should be cautious when developing a plan for treating near duplicates and assess whether the near duplicates will contain information that is critical to the case. For example, two copies of an e-mail may be near duplicates wherein the only difference is that a blind copy is listed as a recipient of one but not the other. If the identity of the individuals with knowledge of the information transmitted in the e-mail is a critical issue in the case, counsel would not want to have agreed upon a de-duplication process that omitted the blind copy from production. A common agreement between parties is to allow for near de-duplication within a custodian data set but not across custodian data sets, which would avoid this problem.

Similarly, a helpful tool for reviewing voluminous e-mail productions is e-mail threading. E-mail threading identifies threads, e-mail participants, attachments, and duplicate e-mails and groups them together so that they can be reviewed as one conversation. This tool can be extremely effective in reducing the number of e-mails requiring review and providing the reviewer a more comprehensive perspective of the conversations, which allows for more accurate document tagging.

Another way to streamline the review of a large data set is machine learning. Machine learning utilizes artificial intelligence–powered software to locate the relevant documents for a particular case. To use machine learning, attorneys review a subset of documents and tag them as relevant or non-relevant. Those documents are then loaded into the program, which utilizes algorithms to find other documents that are similarly relevant. This process can be effective in focusing the attorney's review on the documents with the most pertinent information.

Additionally, a more basic tool that can be used when producing large document sets is to apply search terms to locate the documents that are most likely to be relevant to the issues in the case. Counsel may work with opposing counsel to develop a list of agreed-upon search terms for the exchange of documents. These search terms can be run across the universe of the parties' documents and be used to cull only the documents that contain those terms. Counsel may also agree upon the use of the various tools discussed above (de-duplication, e-mail threading, and machine learning) to further reduce the volume of documents exchanged. Depending on the objectives of the various parties (e.g. cost considerations versus the need to uncover certain documents), counsel may be more or less inclined to agree to the use of search terms and such e-discovery tools.

It is important to note that e-discovery tools can be cost prohibitive, so attorneys should solicit price quotes from vendors, undertake a rigorous cost-benefit analysis, and obtain the consent of the client before purchasing and utilizing these litigation tools.

B. Electronic Discovery

Parties to litigation have expansive discovery obligations. They are generally obligated to respond to other parties' discovery requests by producing all information or documentation that is likely to lead to the discovery of admissible evidence. Many states have patterned their rules governing the scope of discovery after the Federal Rules of Civil Procedure Rule 26, which defines the scope of discovery in federal lawsuits and provides that all documents and tangible things that are relevant to a claim or defense of any party must be produced at the outset of the litigation.[38] The standard is not admissibility; it is relevance to the subject matter of the litigation.[39] As a consequence of the

38. FED. R. CIV. P. 26(b)(1) (2020).

39. *See, e.g.*, CAL CODE CIV. PROC. § 2017.010 (2020) ("[A]ny party may obtain discovery regarding any matter, not privileged, that is relevant to the subject matter

liberal rules governing the scope of discovery, it is the most costly and time-consuming aspect of most construction cases.

Federal Rules of Civil Procedure Rule 34 broadly includes the following types of information as responsive to a request for production: "(A) any designated documents or electronically stored information—including writings, drawings, graphs, charts, photographs, sound recordings, images, and other data or data compilations—stored in any medium from which information can be obtained either directly or, if necessary, after translation by the responding party into a reasonably usable form; or (B) any designated tangible things."[40] Advances in technology have drastically changed the way participants in construction projects communicate with each other, and this has materially affected discovery obligations in construction litigation. In the past, one could trace the material communications in a given construction project through the paper documentation generated and stored by the various parties in their project files. If something needed to be documented, a letter would be mailed and/or faxed, and the sender and receiver would each retain copies of the document in their paper files. If litigation ensued, with limited exception, an attorney representing a particular party would sort through the papers in a discrete project file in order to comply with discovery demands made by other parties during the course of litigation.

The rise of electronic media affected the construction industry just as it did the rest of corporate America. Construction participants now communicate and store information electronically by e-mail, through spreadsheets and comprehensive project management software, in scheduling and estimating programs, in AutoCAD and *pdf* files, to name a few. Developers, contractors, design professionals, and construction managers pride themselves on paperless projects, in which all communications are sent electronically, stored on computer hard drives, and backed up on storage devices or to cloud-based services. Individuals often have cellular phones and tablets that are used for taking notes and photographs while on the job. Advances in technology relating to the portable use of computers and the backup and archiving of electronic information have resulted in less printouts of project documents and more reliance upon electronic storage methodologies.

The effect of this trend upon the discovery obligations of parties to construction litigation has been significant, and the concept of electronic discovery continues to evolve. Litigants must pay careful attention to their duties

---

involved in the pending action, . . . if the matter either is itself admissible in evidence or appears reasonably calculated to lead to the discovery of admissible evidence.").

40. Fed R. Civ. P. 34(a)(1).

to preserve, protect, and ultimately produce their electronic files, in order to comply with discovery requests propounded by the other parties to litigation.

A series of decisions arising out of one case in New York defined many of the standards governing electronic discovery and served as a model for other jurisdictions. *Zubulake v. UBS Warburg LLC*[41] involved an employment discrimination claim by Laura Zubulake, an equities trader, against her employer, UBS. In August of 2001, after Zubulake had filed her initial complaint with the Equal Employment Opportunity Commission, UBS's in-house counsel instructed certain key personnel within the company to retain all electronic documentation pertaining to her claims and segregate it from other materials. This request was repeated both verbally and in writing on several occasions over the course of the litigation.[42] As it turned out, a number of key employees deleted relevant electronic data despite the many instructions given, and discovery disputes arose between the parties as a result.[43] The court found that UBS failed to preserve relevant electronic data notwithstanding the early warnings by its counsel.[44] Sanctions were awarded against UBS, and the jury was given instructions that permitted the inference that the electronic data not produced would have been unfavorable to UBS.[45]

Several decisions ensued that have largely defined the scope of electronic discovery obligations. The *Zubulake* decision can be boiled down to the following general rules:

- First, companies should be prepared to produce all information that is relevant to the subject matter of the dispute, even if the information is in electronic form and exists only on backup tapes or media.[46]
- Second, the obligation to preserve electronic information requires reasonable and good faith efforts to retain such information that may be relevant to pending or threatened litigation.[47]

---

41. There are seven published decisions that came out of the *Zubulake v. UBS Warburg, LLC* case, and they are numbered sequentially: *Zubulake I*, 217 F.R.D. 309 (S.D.N.Y. 2003); *Zubulake II*, 230 F.R.D. 290 (S.D.N.Y. 2003); *Zubulake III*, 216 F.R.D. 280 (S.D.N.Y. 2003); *Zubulake IV*, 220 F.R.D. 212 (S.D.N.Y. 2003); *Zubulake V*, 229 F.R.D. 422 (S.D.N.Y. 2004); *Zubulake VI*, 231 F.R.D. 159 (S.D.N.Y. 2005); *Zubulake VII*, 382 F. Supp. 2d 536 (S.D.N.Y. 2005).

42. *Zubulake IV*, 217 F.R.D. at 215; *Zubulake V*, 229 F.R.D. at 423.

43. *Zubulake V*, 229 F.R.D. at 423–24.

44. *Id.* at 436.

45. *Id.* at 437, 439–40.

46. *Zubulake I*, 217 F.R.D. at 317.

47. *Id.*

- Third, the obligation to preserve arises whenever the company "should reasonably know that the evidence may be relevant to anticipated litigation," at which point key players in the company should be ordered to preserve all such information.[48]
- Fourth, both inside and outside counsel are obligated to oversee the retention and production of relevant electronic information and communicate directly with key personnel in control of such information.[49]
- Fifth, courts will engage in a seven-factor balancing test to determine which party or parties should bear the costs of retrieving and producing electronic information that has been stored or is otherwise costly and time-consuming to retrieve,[50] but the company storing/producing the information should be prepared to pay the majority of the costs.[51]

Other courts have followed the *Zubulake* lead and imposed significant sanctions for failure to preserve electronic documents after notice of litigation. In *U.S. v. Philip Morris USA, Inc.*,[52] high-ranking employees of defendant Philip Morris lost or destroyed e-mails and did not follow the company's internal procedures for retaining electronic documentation.[53] The company was sanctioned $2.75 million and precluded from calling those high-ranking

---

48. *Zubulake IV*, 220 F.R.D. at 218; *see also* Knickerbocker v. Corinthian Colleges, 298 F.R.D. 670, 677–78 (W.D. Wash. 2014) (company obligated to suspend retention policy and implement litigation hold to ensure preservation of relevant documents once it knows or reasonably should know the evidence may be relevant to pending or future litigation).

49. *Zubulake V*, 229 F.R.D. at 432–34; *see also* R & R Sails Inc. v. Ins. Co. of State of Pa., 251 F.R.D. 520, 528 (S.D. Cal. 2008) (imposing sanctions against attorney for "failure to search for and timely produce electronically-stored information"); and Treppel v. Biovail Corp., 249 F.R.D. 111, 118 (S.D.N.Y. 2008) ("Counsel must take affirmative steps to monitor compliance so that all sources of discoverable information are identified and searched.").

50. *Zubulake I*, 217 F.R.D. at 322 (the factors are (1) the extent to which the request is specifically tailored to discover the relevant information; (2) the availability of such information from other sources; (3) the total cost of production, compared to the amount in controversy; (4) the total cost of production, compared to the resources available to each party; (5) the relative ability of each party to control costs and its incentive to do so; (6) the importance of the issues at stake in the litigation; and (7) the relative benefits to the parties of obtaining the information).

51. *Zubulake III*, 216 F.R.D. at 289–91.

52. U.S. v. Philip Morris USA, Inc., 327 F. Supp. 2d 21 (D.D.C. 2004).

53. *Id.*

employees to the stand at trial.[54] Additionally, companies that intentionally destroy records can be subject to an adverse inference at trial. Several courts have held that sanctions for failure to preserve evidence require a finding of "intentional destruction indicating a desire to suppress the truth."[55] Other courts have held that the inadvertent, negligent loss of evidence may justify dismissal where the effect of the spoliator's conduct is so prejudicial that it substantially denied the defendant the ability to defend the claim.[56] While other jurisdictions evaluate the failure to produce evidence "along a continuum of fault—ranging from innocence through the degrees of negligence [ordinary vs. gross negligence] to intentional" and determine sanctions accordingly.[57]

In 2015, Federal Rule of Civil Procedure Rule 37(e) was amended to set forth guidelines for remedying situations where electronically stored information should have been preserved through "reasonable" measures and it cannot be restored or replaced through discovery. The rule provides that the court:

- on finding prejudice to another party, may order measures no greater than necessary to cure the prejudice; or
- on finding that the party acted with the intent to deprive another party of the information's use in the litigation, may:
  - presume that the lost information was unfavorable to the party;
  - instruct the jury that it may or must presume the information was unfavorable to the party; or
  - dismiss the action or enter a default judgment.[58]

Since many construction participants have not perfected their policies for electronic document retention, organization, and storage, attorneys and their clients often find it difficult to comply with electronic discovery requests. First, many e-mails and other electronic data are not segregated by project. One can imagine the burden of going through each employee's general inbox, outbox, deleted e-mails, etc. in order to comply with discovery requests and produce

---

54. *Id.*

55. Greyhound Lines, Inc. v. Wade, 485 F.3d 1032, 1035 (8th Cir. 2007); Bashir v. Amtrak, 119 F.3d 929, 931 (11th Cir. 1997) (adverse inference drawn from party's failure to preserve evidence only when bad faith is shown); 103 Investors I, L.P. v. Square D Co., 470 F.3d 985, 989 (10th Cir. 2006) (bad faith finding not required for other sanctions, e.g., dismissing claim, or striking testimony).

56. Silvestri v. General Motors Corp., 271 F.3d 583, 593 (4th Cir. 2001).

57. Adkins v. Wolever, 554 F.3d 650, 652 (6th Cir. 2009) (internal quotes omitted).

58. Fed R. Civ. Proc. 37(e)(1)–(2).

all communications that pertain to the project in litigation. Under *Zubulake,* the majority of the costs associated with sifting through these electronic data will be borne by the party that should have organized it in the first place, and that company risks the imposition of monetary and issue sanctions against it for failing to comply with these rules.

Many companies have simply failed to promulgate or enforce any electronic document policies that would govern the retention, archiving, and disposal of documents after a certain period of time. As explained earlier in this chapter, the statute of repose for bringing claims for latent defects in twenty-four states is ten years, and this can be extended by tolling or through claims for indemnity. Accordingly, a design professional or construction manager in these jurisdictions should not only retain its project files for at least ten years, but also organize and store the electronic files in a way that it is not unduly burdensome to access them at a later date. For example, many companies back up their electronic data by compressing mass amounts of data that have not been identified to any particular project. Later, when litigation is instituted against that company, its representatives and attorney must decompress and sort through an enormous number of undifferentiated files in order to comply with discovery obligations. The failure or inability to do so may result in the sanctions described earlier.

Additionally, project Web sites are often utilized in large construction projects. Here, the construction participants will log onto a Web site and be able to communicate with others and access documentation and project management information electronically. Different individuals typically have different levels of access to the information stored on the Web site. Project Web sites can create interesting discovery and document production issues, especially for construction managers and design professionals with extensive construction administration duties. For example, a construction manager with access to many or all areas in the project Web site may be obligated to produce such information in litigation, and it can be costly and time-consuming to retrieve such information.

C. Demonstrative Evidence

During the course of a trial, attorneys for the parties will attempt to introduce testimony, documentary evidence, and tangible evidence to prove or defend against a given claim. The substantive evidence to be admitted into evidence during a construction trial will consist primarily of project documents, and attorneys must comply with the rules of evidence for that particular jurisdiction in order to successfully introduce the documents into evidence. For example, tangible evidence can consist of construction components that were removed and analyzed during the course of investigating a particular claim. Once the judge admits a document or tangible thing into evidence, the jury may take these items into the jury room when deliberations begin.

Construction trials tend to be very technical and expert oriented. Jurors are susceptible to getting lost in the technical aspects of the case. Therefore, counsel for construction participants should strongly consider using appropriate visual aids to assist the jurors in comprehending the flood of information that passes their way during the course of a complex construction trial. The adage that *a picture tells a thousand words is* very appropriate in trial work, especially in construction trials.

Demonstrative, or illustrative, evidence is therefore commonly relied on by construction attorneys to make a point or explain complicated or technical information to jurors. It can include charts, maps, graphs, slides, models, lists of information, enlarged evidence, video recordings, timelines, computer-generated simulations or animations, or basically anything that provides a visual representation of the evidence. Demonstrative evidence is not actually admitted into evidence. During the course of a trial it may be used by counsel for various purposes, including illustrating or amplifying a point, synthesizing, visually portraying, or explaining admissible testimony or evidence.

Construction litigators typically use demonstrative evidence in opening statements to convey a particular theme to the jury and preview the evidence. Attorneys also routinely rely on demonstrative evidence in closing arguments to synthesize key points and arguments and provide the jury with a summary and visual representation of the oral testimony and voluminous project documentation. Jurors are most attentive to and impressed by computer-generated evidence that is projected onto a large screen, but blown-up poster boards can also be effective on a smaller budget to convey the visual information that jurors may need in order to better understand the issues.

The Federal Rules of Evidence allow attorneys to employ demonstrative evidence as long as certain requirements are met. Under Rule 102, the trial judge has the authority to fashion evidentiary procedures not otherwise covered in the Rules, and demonstrative evidence is one category of information that falls within this discretionary watchdog power.[59] Demonstrative evidence may be excluded if its "probative value is substantially outweighed by the danger of one or more of the following: unfair prejudice, confusing the issues, misleading the jury, undue delay, wasting of time, or needlessly presenting

---

59. FED. R. EVID. 102; United States v. Bibbs, 564 F.2d 1165 (5th Cir. 1977).

cumulative evidence."[60] Most states have similar rules governing the allowance of demonstrative evidence during a trial.

In construction cases, computer-generated simulations and graphs are a very effective way to visually portray the complex issues that were framed by expert testimony during the presentation of evidence. For example, attorneys representing design professionals and construction managers in delay cases should strongly consider offering a computer-generated presentation during closing argument that is projected on a large screen and which synthesizes the mass of confusing and technical information that was presented during the trial. The presentation may contain comparative schedules which outline differences between baseline and as-built schedules, charts depicting the project's critical path and containing information as to how design issues did not negatively impact the critical path, visual aids to assist the jury in understanding home office overhead calculations under the *Eichleay* formula, bar charts characterizing job cost reports, and total cost information, etc.

A litigator may therefore put on a strong case in defense of her design professional or construction manager client, but the points typically need to be illustrated with as many visual aids as possible in order to persuade jurors who simply are not familiar with these types of issues.

As another example, a computer presentation program may be used as demonstrative evidence in a defect claim to underscore the impressive design and resulting structure that is the subject of the litigation. Too often, a defect trial focuses on the negative, i.e., the defects. However, the defects at issue usually constitute a very small percentage of the project; the remainder of the project may have progressed smoothly and without significant problems. If the jury walks into the deliberation room with only the problems and defects in mind, then the plaintiff has prevailed in limiting the jury's frame of reference to only the negative issues.

Where appropriate during closing argument, counsel for a design professional should therefore consider offering the jury a presentation which diverts jurors' attention from the two percent of alleged negligence and illustrates the

---

60. FED. R. EVID. 403; *see, e.g.*, Kehm v. Procter & Gamble Mfg. Co., 724 F.2d 613 (8th Cir. 1983) (trial court has the discretion to admit demonstrations where relevant, as long as they do not create a serious misimpression as to how an event might have occurred); Finchum v. Ford Motor Co., 57 F.3d 526 (7th Cir. 1995) (demonstrations purporting to illustrate that one side's version of the facts is subject to exclusion if there is a substantial risk that the jury, despite instructions, may misuse the evidence as a recreation of a real-life event—that is, where the demonstration is not a close enough approximation of the real-life event).

ninety-eight percent of design professional competence and resulting attractiveness of the finished product. The presentation may contain renderings, photographs depicting aesthetically pleasing design elements, CAD designs, models, computer-simulated views of the project from various vantage points, etc. This will place the defect issues in their proper perspective and help temper jurors' anger if the defects caused the plaintiff to incur significant damages.

Library References

C.J.S. *Discovery* §§ 105–106, 130–132, 135–136; C.J.S. *Evidence* §§ 1056–1059, 1080–1082, 1098, 1177–1191, 1193–1197, 1199, 1200–1236, 1241–1257, 1259, 1276–1278, 1373.
West's Key No. Digests, Evidence <KEY> 194,195, 350–359; Pretrial Procedure <KEY>331, 352, 371.
3 Federal Trial Guide § 65.21 (2019); 2 Federal Trial Guide § 23.20 (2019).
Rutter Group Prac. Guide Fed. Civ. Proc. Before Trial (Nat Ed.) Ch. 11(I)-
1 MB Practice Guide: CA E-Discovery and Evidence 9.32 (2020).

VII. Using Joint Defense Agreements to Avoid Finger-Pointing and Manage the Dispute

A complex construction project is a collaborative process. When problems arise, it is often unclear who is at fault. The natural reaction for litigants in construction dispute may be to point the finger at the other project participants trying to shift the blame. When this occurs, an owner may be able to sit back and watch the members of the design team undercut each other and, from a practical viewpoint, establish the owner's claims that deficiencies in the design and construction administration resulted in defects or increased project costs.

Rather than accepting that litigation will be fought on such terms, parties who are naturally aligned with respect to particular defense strategies may engage in a joint defense agreement, under the terms of which the aligned parties cooperate in presenting common defenses, even if they reserve the right to pursue claims against each other at some later point. The parties with common interests may include separate design professionals, who are defending against claims related to asserted deficiencies in plans and specifications, or they may include an owner and its design professionals in fighting delay claims by a contractor.

The benefits of establishing a joint defense arrangement may be particularly significant in a complex case. These advantages go beyond the presentation of a united front, or a mechanism by which codefendants pool resources to address a common legal threat. A joint defense agreement can provide an effective framework for evaluating alternative theories and developing a mutual strategy. The joint arrangement can expedite the discovery and sharing of information at a time before parties have committed to positions in written discovery or deposition. The information can also be shared at significantly less cost than formal discovery. Indeed, this sharing of information and resources is the strength of a joint defense arrangement. A properly conceived and executed formal joint defense structure can establish an effective litigation framework for the rest of the dispute, including an equitable structure for apportioning litigation costs for expert witnesses, court reporters, and graphic consultants to implement a shared theory of the case. It may even allow them to share counsel in limited circumstances.

There are risks associated with a joint defense agreement. These risks can be broken into three areas: (1) a concern regarding disclosure of confidential attorney-client communications and attorney work product to potentially adverse parties and future adverse use of such information; (2) the potential for waiver of these privileges through disclosures; and (3) the uncertainty as to how any remaining disputes will be resolved.

With respect to the primary concern of a joint defense agreement, the parties must be careful to structure their relationship to ensure that they do not waive the benefit of the attorney-client privilege. Generally speaking, discussions between attorneys and clients are protected from disclosure to outsiders—most importantly, these communications cannot be discovered by the opposing party. However, the client must treat these communications as confidential in order to maintain the benefit of the privilege. If a client discloses the communication to an outsider (or an outsider is present), the privilege may be lost. If an architect and her attorney meet with the owner and its attorney to discuss defending claims against a contractor, all of their discussions fall outside the attorney-client privilege and may be discovered by the contractor in the absence of a joint defense agreement.

A joint defense agreement provides protection against this problem. The joint defense privilege or *common interest rule* is viewed by most jurisdictions as an *extension* of the attorney-client privilege and attorney-work-product doctrine.[61] It is designed to protect communications between individual defendants and their attorneys who, in concert with other defendants, are acting as "part of

61. United States v. Stepney, 246 F. Supp. 2d 1069 (N.D. Cal. 2003).

an on-going and joint effort to set up a common defense strategy."[62] The privilege embodies the fact that the disclosures to third parties were intended to be insulated from exposure beyond the confines of the group by demonstrating that the disclosures would not have been made but for the sake of securing or supplying the legal representation.

The joint defense privilege is not equal to the attorney-client privilege but is an exception to it. In fact, the rationale behind the attorney-client privilege and attorneywork-product doctrine seemingly runs counter to the purpose of the joint defense arrangement, whose purpose is to divulge confidential attorney-client information to other attorneys representing potentially adverse parties. Case authority recognizes that just as the attorney-client privilege is required to promote the free flowing exchange of information between attorney and client in order to improve the quality of the representation, the joint defense privilege encourages attorneys and their clients to communicate to third parties in recognition of their common interests, which will likely result in a more effective and efficient representation of each client.

Case authority recognizes a variety of approaches to the exchange of confidential information among codefendants. For example, there is specific case authority in some jurisdictions establishing *a per se* joint defense privilege,[63] whereas other jurisdictions acknowledge the rationale for protecting confidential information but refuse to recognize an explicit independent privilege. Those jurisdictions view the joint defense privilege as being an exception to or extension of the attorney-client privilege and attorney-work-product doctrine, with limitations on their application to specific factual scenarios.[64] The

---

62. United States v. Bay State Ambulance & Hosp. Rental Serv., 874 F.2d 20, 28 (1st Cir. 1989). *See also* United States v. Moss, 9 F.3d 543, 550 (6th Cir. 1993); *In re* Imperial Corp. of Am., 167 F.R.D. 447, 455 (S.D. Cal. 1995); *In re* Megan-Racine Ass'n, 189 B.R. 562, 570 n.4 (Bankr. N.D.N.Y. 1995) ("Most commentators and courts view it as an extension of the attorney-client privilege or work-product doctrine.").

63. Metro Wastewater Reclamation Dist. v. Continental Cas. Co., 142 F.R.D. 471, 478 (D. Colo. 1992) ("widely accepted by courts throughout the United States"); *see also* People v. Pennachio, 637 N.Y.S.2d 633, 634 (Sup. Ct., Kings County 1995) (stating that the privilege exists in Arkansas, Florida, Hawaii, Louisiana, Minnesota, Nevada, Oregon, South Dakota, Texas, Virginia, and Wisconsin); State v. Maxwell, 691 P.2d 1316 (Kan. Ct. App. 1984) (holding privilege exists in Kansas).

64. Raytheon Co. v. Superior Court, 208 Cal. App. 3d 683, 689 (stating that "there is no 'joint defense privilege' as such in California").

privilege is not recognized in the Federal Rules of Evidence[65] although many jurisdictions have codified the common law attorney-client privilege.[66]

Even in jurisdictions where there is no *per se* joint defense privilege, the case authority follows the same basic analysis to determine whether the confidentiality of communications among and between codefendants has been waived. California courts have used such a waiver analysis since the legislature has limited the court's ability to expand evidentiary privileges. Instead, the parties claiming confidentiality based on the common interest doctrine must show first that the confidential information is protected under traditional attorney-client or work product privileges and then establish that disclosing the information beyond the attorney-client relationship does not result in a waiver because the communication is reasonably necessary to further the interests of the litigant.[67]

Consistent with the other privileges, the burden of establishing the joint defense privilege is on the party asserting it.[68] To assert the joint defense privilege, one must first establish the existence of an attorney-client privilege applying to the communications among attorneys and their clients for the common defense. If the attorney-client or attorney work product umbrellas do not protect the underlying communication, there is no privileged status under which the joint defense protection will apply.[69]

The party seeking to establish the privilege must show that the communications were confidential and made in the course of a joint defense effort.[70]

---

65. Fed. R. Evid. 501.

66. United States v. Moss, 9 F.3d 543, 550 (6th Cir. 1993); United States v. Schwimmer, 892 F.2d 237, 244 (2d Cir. 1989), *cert. denied*, 502 U.S. 810 (1991).

67. Oxy Resources California LLC v. Superior Court, 115 Cal. App. 4th 874 (2004).

68. United States v. Moss, 9 F.3d 543, 550 (6th Cir. 1993); United States v. Schwimmer, 892 F.2d 237, 244 (2d Cir. 1989), *cert. denied*, 502 U.S. 810 (1991).

69. Metro Wastewater Reclamation Dist. v. Continental Cas. Co., 142 F.R.D. 471 (D. Colo. 1992); Sackman v. Liggett Group, Inc., 167 F.R.D. 6, 19 (E.D.N.Y. 1996); *In re* Megan-Racine Ass'n, 189 B.R. 562, 571 (Bankr. N.D.N.Y. 1995); *see also* United States v. McPartlin, 595 F.2d 1321 (7th Cir.), *cert. denied*, 444 U.S. 833, 100 S. Ct. 65, 62 L. Ed. 2d 43 (1979); Hunydee v. United States, 355 F.2d 183 (9th Cir. 1965); Continental Oil Co. v. United States, 330 F.2d 347 (9th Cir. 1964); In the Matter of Grand Jury Subpoena, 406 F. Supp. 381 (S.D.N.Y. 1975).

70. United States v. Bay State Ambulance and Hosp. Rental Serv., 874 F.2d 20, 28 (1st Cir. 1989); *In re* Megan-Racine Ass'n, 189 B.R. 562, 571 (Bankr. N.D.N.Y. 1995) ("The joint defense privilege is only applicable where the party asserting it can demonstrate an agreement between the parties privy to the communication that such communication will be kept confidential.").

This effort can be defined as the parties' protection of common interests which need not be identical but may be aligned on some issues and adverse on others.[71] However, communications about matters of conflicting interest or those that do not further the common interests of the codefendants are not deemed protected by the privilege.[72] The privilege will not attach where the parties' interests are adverse and the information is provided with the expectation that the relationship is not confidential.[73]

Of course, the fact that a joint defense agreement will permit the parties to avoid disclosure of attorney-client communications and their joint work product does not mean that a joint defense is always appropriate. Instead, the parties must first determine whether a joint defense is more beneficial than the potential harm that arises from the mutual disclosure of the joint parties' litigation strategies and evidence. This decision must be based on several factors. Before entering into the joint defense agreement, an attorney should ask:

1. What is your current evaluation of the potential exposure of your client?
2. What is the status of discovery?
3. Have all necessary parties been joined?
4. What is the relative exposure of other defendants and their ability to respond to an adverse judgment?
5. What is the estimated expense of litigation?
6. Are there viable joint defense theories that will limit the collective exposure of the participants?

Once the determination is made to pursue a joint defense, the parties can undertake the task of crafting their relationship through an appropriate agreement.

A. Practical Considerations for a Joint Defense

There are a number of practical and strategic issues that must be addressed, with respect to both the pending action and how the parties to the joint defense agreement will ultimately allocate any adverse judgment or settlement.

---

71. United States v. McPartlin, 595 F.2d 1321, 1335–36 (7th Cir.), *cert. denied*, 444 U.S. 833 (1979); *In re* Megan-Racine Ass'n, 189 B.R. 562, 572 (Bankr. N.D.N.Y. 1995); Visual Scene Inc. v. Pilkington Bros., 508 So. 2d 437, 440 (Fla. Dist. Ct. App. 1987).

72. People v. Pennachio, 637 N.Y.S.2d 633, 634 (Sup. Ct., Kings County 1995).

73. Eisenberg v. Gagnon, 766 F.2d 770, 788, *cert. denied*, 474 U.S. 946 (1985).

The first question determines who will participate in the joint defense arrangement. The nature of the claims and the contractual relationships between the defendants will often control whether the agreement can or should include all of the named defendants or a subset thereof. For example, if the case is one of clear liability on the part of the defendants but the damages are highly suspect, all defendants may be able to admit liability to the plaintiff and then defend the case jointly on the damage issues.

Alternatively, if the dispute involves conflicting theories of liability, such as whether the damages were the result of a faulty design or poor construction, the design team might decide to adopt a joint defense which does not include the contractors. It is not necessary that all of the participants in the joint defense have identical positions. Rather, they only need to have a sufficient commonality of interests to warrant sharing resources and information to achieve a mutually advantageous result.

One possible advantage of a joint defense agreement is that it may permit substantial cost savings through the sharing of experts or even counsel. Without a joint defense agreement, discussions with the joint experts may not be privileged. The agreement will also facilitate the collaboration between individually retained experts, since the communications would fall within the joint defense privilege.

Where the terms of the joint defense agreement ensure a unity of interests at least through trial, the parties may even consider agreeing to representation by one law firm to minimize defense costs. However, without express waivers the law firm would not be able to represent any of the individual parties in the event that lingering disputes between the parties to the agreement must be resolved through subsequent alternative dispute resolution (ADR).

The joint defense agreement contemplates that none of the participants will do anything to prejudice the interests of the other parties to the agreement or to help the plaintiff. Ideally, the parties to the joint defense arrangement will agree at the time of forming the arrangement to share responsibility in equal percentages or on some other agreed allocation. Unfortunately, it is a rare case where this is possible. In most circumstances, the parties view their respective liability differently. Without having certainty as to the exposure, the parties leave for a later determination the ultimate allocation of any judgment or settlement.

In most circumstances, the participants will have agreed not to direct formal discovery towards each other and may agree not to cross-examine the other participants' witnesses during deposition. However, there may be significant strategic and cost impacts from this agreement depending on how the participants intend to allocate an adverse judgment or settlement. For instance, information that is both relevant and necessary to a dispute over allocation of an adverse judgment may not be adequately developed or refuted in the case with plaintiff. This can and will have a potentially serious impact if third party witnesses are not available in the allocation proceeding. Those third party witnesses may also be uncooperative if they have already been deposed in the initial dispute and do not want to be deposed a second time by many of the same parties.

One of the more contentious issues in drafting a joint defense agreement is whether parties can or should be permitted to settle separately with the plaintiff(s).[74]

It is fundamental to most joint defense agreements that none of the participants may settle separately. This is particularly true in jurisdictions where there are barriers to pursuing indemnity claims against settling parties. Otherwise, a participant whose relative liability was not exposed by the other participants could escape with a relatively small share of responsibility. In most agreements, the parties must either settle as a group or try the case as a group. This can be a particularly difficult issue where one of the participants has low limits and/or a wasting insurance policy.

An alternative arrangement may permit the parties to settle separately with the plaintiff but still require them to participate in a subsequent method to resolve the allocation issue. Any settlements are aggregated with any judgment and reallocated through an ADR process. A risk of this approach is that the non-settling parties may perceive they have little to lose by attending trial since any unexpected verdict will be subject to reallocation through the subsequent process. Alternatively, a participant may agree to an unreasonably large separate settlement early to save itself litigation costs, knowing that much of the settlement will be reallocated to other participants.

The cleanest way to avoid disputes and maximize the utility of a joint defense is to include in the joint defense agreement a term allocating specific percentages of responsibility for an adverse judgment or settlement to each participant. If the parties can agree up-front to share responsibility in equal percentages or on some other agreed allocation, most potential areas of disagreement disappear. All parties will have an equal interest in minimizing the

---

74. Settlement strategy is just one of the ethical pitfalls that counsel representing multiple parties under a joint defense agreement need to consider. These ethical issues are discussed in detail in Bruce King & Carol Patterson, *Representation of Multiple Parties in the Construction Arena: Ethical Issues*, 25 CONSTRUCTION LAWYER 5 (Fall 2005).

judgment or settlement and will have certainty as to their financial contribution. Of course, it is important to consider the other participants' financial resources since any agreement reallocating a verdict effectively makes the participants joint tortfeasors. This scheme may not make sense where some of the participants have limited insurance or other assets to satisfy an adverse judgment. In most cases, the parties to a joint defense agreement will decide to resolve any allocation issues through ADR. This allows the participants to preselect the means and method for dispute resolution and to structure the process in a way that makes economic sense. The parties can agree on an expedited process involving only written position papers, a multistep ADR involving mediation and/or a mini-trial, or use traditional binding arbitration under rules similar to the American Arbitration Association's Construction Industry Rules.

B. The Necessity of a Writing

The potential for conflict and dispute over the scope and obligations of a joint defense means that any joint defense agreement should be in writing. Moreover, while an oral joint defense agreement may be respected for purposes of fending off unwanted inquiries into the parties' attorney-client communications and work product, reliance on an oral agreement is haphazard and raises evidentiary concerns that can be avoided easily. As one court explained, "Obviously, a written agreement is the most effective method of establishing the existence of a joint defense agreement, although an oral agreement whose existence, terms and scope are proved by the party asserting it, may be enforceable as well."[75]

In the most pragmatic terms, a joint defense agreement can be crafted in far less time than a brief responding to an opponent's motion to compel discovery of attorney-client communications shared with another party.

Library References

C.J.S. *Contracts* § 86; C.J.S. *Witnesses* §§ 309, 330–361, 364–371, 381, 417, 419, 426.
West's Key No. Digests, Contracts <KEY>32; Common interest doctrine; joint clients or joint defense <KEY>122.

75. Minebea Co., Ltd. v. Papst, 228 F.R.D. 13, 16 (D.D.C. 2005).

INDEX

B

E

G

H

I

J

N

O

S